# The Population of Virginia
*Past, Present, and Future*

# The Population of Virginia

*Past, Present, and Future*

*William J. Serow*

University Press of Virginia
Charlottesville

The publication of this study has been assisted by the Tayloe Murphy Institute of the Colgate Darden Graduate School of Business Administration of the University of Virginia.


THE UNIVERSITY PRESS OF VIRGINIA
Copyright © 1978 by the Rector and Visitors
of the University of Virginia


*First published 1978*

Library of Congress Cataloging in Publication Data
Serow, William J
  The population of Virginia.

  1. Virginia—Population. I. Title.
HB3525.V8S44   312'.09755   77-10340
ISBN 0-8139-0659-8


Printed in the United States of America

# Foreword

The study of population change can be a fascinating one, in part because for extended periods of time and for wide geographic areas there can be a certain inevitability of change, a momentum built in by the existing age structure. Even when there are what might be considered drastic shifts in some of the forces that will ultimately lead to change, the population of an area is usually so great, relative to the natural increase (births minus deaths), that it can be years before the full effect of such forces is felt.

This means that for large areas, such as the United States, and even individual states, it is possible to forecast with relatively small errors a number of subsets of the population. For example, we know now about how many children will be reaching school age in each of the next five years in the United States; they have already been born. We also know that even though there may be a further decline in the birth rate (births per 1,000 women of childbearing age), the total number of births in the United States will rise over the next few years; that was largely predetermined in the period fifteen to thirty years ago when the women who will be in the primary childbearing ages were born.

At the same time, migration can result in significant population change over relatively short periods of time. In the early history of this country, migration played an important role in increasing the population of the nation as a whole and of various regions. Today, migration has diminished in significance for the country as a whole; between 1960 and 1970, net migration accounted for only 13 percent of the population growth of the United States. However, for regions and states and their political subdivisions, migration continues as an important element in population change, and with declining fertility will be even more important in the future. In Virginia between 1960 and 1970 net in-migration accounted for half of the growth of Planning District 8 in northern Virginia, while net out-migration was sufficiently large in five other planning districts to result in a net loss of population.

This book describes historical changes in the population of Virginia and examines some of the changes that may lie ahead. It represents a continuation of work begun over thirty years ago by a predecessor of the Tayloe Murphy Institute.

In 1944 the Population Study of the Virginia State Plannning Board published Sara Gilliam's significant work, *Virginia's People: A Study of the Growth and Distribution of the Population of Virginia from 1607 to 1943*. It was significant in that it represented the first thorough study of population changes in Virginia over such an extensive period of time. In the same year, the Population Study was moved to the University of Virginia and became the Bureau of Population and Economic Research, under the direction of Lorin A. Thompson. As a part of that organization, Thompson, Gilliam, and a third colleague, John Littlepage Lancaster, continued their study of population change in Virginia. Their efforts led to, among other things, the development of methodologies for estimating small area populations and to the publication of annual estimates of the population of Virginia counties and cities.

William J. Serow joined the staff of the Bureau in 1970, soon after the decennial census of that year had been conducted. He began almost immediately to plan the series of studies that would lead to this volume. Each of these studies was to analyze a special set of 1970 Census data as it became available, and to describe the changes that had occurred since the previous census. The intent was to publish each study separately initially so as to disseminate the analyses as soon as possible. At the same time, an effort was to be made to combine these studies, with such revisions as necessary, into a more comprehensive study of population change in Virginia, in effect bringing Gilliam's previous work up-to-date. That is the principal purpose of this volume.

In January 1972 Serow and Michael A. Spar, a research assistant, published *A Demographic Profile*, the first volume of Virginia's Population: A Decade of Change. Subsequent monographs in that series were prepared by Serow, Spar, and Julia H. Martin, who has since joined the staff of Tayloe Murphy Institute as a research associate. The titles were *Net Migration for State Planning Districts,*

*Socioeconomic Characteristics,* and *The Status of Women.* These later volumes were published by the Tayloe Murphy Institute, which was merged with the Bureau of Population and Economic Research in the summer of 1972.

While this book incorporates some of the information previously published in that series, it includes much more. Specifically, it extends those studies by considering historical data (pre-1950), drawing heavily on Gilliam's work, and by discussing how the future population may differ from the present and what the implications of these differences could be. We hope this book will prove valuable as a reference work for those interested in studying Virginia's past; we think it can also be valuable as a point of departure for those looking to the future.

CHARLES O. MEIBURG
*Executive Director*
*Tayloe Murphy Institute*

# Acknowledgments

Many past and present members of the TMI staff have made contributions of one sort or another to this book. The contributions of Dr. Michael A. Spar (presently with the Urban Studies Center of the University of Louisville) and Elsa V. Cooke are acknowledged by listing their joint authorship of several chapters. Clerical assistance was provided at various times by Linda Spar, Nancy Gordon, Virginia Hill, and Barbara Crowder. All graphics were prepared by Barry Jackson. A special note of thanks is due Dr. Charles O. Meiburg, Executive Director of the Tayloe Murphy Institute, for his unfailing support of this research. Finally, the quality of the manuscript has been enhanced by the comments of Robert J. Griffis and Daniel G. Jones of the Economic Research Section of the Virginia Department of Planning and Budget.

WILLIAM J. SEROW

# Contents

# Figures

# Tables

PART I   The Past (1607–1950)

# Chapter 1

# Overview of Demographic Change

In historical writing, there often arises the problem of speaking with certainty. Documentation is frequently difficult, data are usually incomplete. The history of Virginia, reaching back as it does to 1607, offers ample opportunity for missteps. The history of Virginia's population, being specific in subject, escapes many of these problems. Moreover, an area, generally being aware of its growth, will keep fairly good record of its progress. Consequently, the reports of Virginia's population have been kept rather completely through the years.

The problem of accuracy remains. Earliest figures are often estimated, so that absolute specificity is impossible. From 1790 official Census Bureau counts are used; before that date, information stems from other sources. For Virginia's modern history, from 1860 to 1950, the data are usually complete. In 1860 Dickenson and Bland counties had not been created; their populations have been estimated by using population counts of later censuses. Thus the specific figures utilized here may be considered essentially correct.

The causes of population change in Virginia are not elusive; they clearly derived from the historical circumstances of the state and the nation. The history and character of Virginia have been shaped by its various forms of economy. The colony's foundations were laid in an economic venture. For years the colony and state prospered in the agriculture of small farms and plantations, having developed tobacco as its main crop. After the Civil War a transition was made slowly to industry, a movement given impetus by the two world wars.

Virginia's population has changed with its degrees and forms of prosperity (see Table 1.1). Rapid expansion occurred in the first fifty years, because tobacco created a prosperous environment. The crop and the labor to produce it were in great demand. The population of Virginia swelled as indentured servants and, to

Table 1.1.  Population of Virginia, 1610-1950

| Year | Population | Percent Increase |
|------|-----------|------------------|
| 1610 | 210 | --- |
| 1620 | 2,400 | 1,42.9 |
| 1630 | 3,000 | 25.0 |
| 1640 | 7,647 | 154.9 |
| 1650 | 17,000 | 122.3 |
| 1660 | 33,000 | 94.1 |
| 1670 | 40,000 | 21.2 |
| 1680 | 49,000 | 22.5 |
| 1690 | 58,000 | 18.4 |
| 1700 | 72,000 | 24.1 |
| 1710 | 87,000 | 20.8 |
| 1720 | 116,000 | 33.3 |
| 1730 | 153,000 | 31.9 |
| 1740 | 200,000 | 30.7 |
| 1750 | 275,000 | 37.5 |
| 1760 | 346,000 | 25.8 |
| 1770 | 450,000 | 30.1 |
| 1780 | 520,000 | 15.6 |
| 1790 | 691,737 | 33.0 |
| 1800 | 807,557 | 16.7 |
| 1810 | 877,683 | 8.7 |
| 1820 | 938,261 | 6.9 |
| 1830 | 1,044,054 | 11.3 |
| 1840 | 1,025,227 | -1.8 |
| 1850 | 1,119,348 | 9.2 |
| 1860 | 1,219,630 | 9.0 |
| 1870 | 1,338,058 | 9.7 |
| 1880 | 1,512,565 | 13.0 |
| 1890 | 1,655,980 | 9.5 |
| 1900 | 1,854,184 | 12.0 |
| 1910 | 2,061,612 | 11.2 |
| 1920 | 2,309,187 | 12.0 |
| 1930 | 2,421,851 | 4.9 |
| 1940 | 2,677,773 | 10.6 |
| 1950 | 3,318,680 | 23.9 |

Sources:  The data from 1610 through 1780 are primarily from Sara K. Gilliam,
Virginia's People:  A Study of the Growth and Distribution of the Population
of Virginia from 1607 to 1943 (Richmond:  Virginia State Planning Board, 1944).
The data from 1790 through 1950 are the results of the decennial census of
population.  Adjustments are made for all years 1790 to 1860 to reflect the
subsequent loss of those counties which now comprise West Virginia.

a lesser extent, slaves were brought to work the land. Adding
to optimism and growth, "land suitable for raising tobacco was
still cheap and plentiful."[1]

Population increase, very rapid until 1660, slowed thereafter
because of depressions in the tobacco market, land scarcity,

[1] Sara K. Gilliam, *Virginia's People: A Study of the Growth and Distribution of the
Population of Virginia from 1607 to 1943* (Richmond: Virginia State Planning Board, 1944),
p. 11.

and the expense of labor. Slaves were imported in greater numbers, and indentured laborers less, tending "not only to lower wages but to depress the social standing of the laborer."[2] The plantation system was firmly established, an economic fact that discouraged development of industrial activities and urban centers. This system also created a stratified society, closing opportunity to many poorer residents. The subsequent decline of prosperity affected many Virginians, who chose, as an alternative to subsistence farming, out-migration, which for decades to come proved a dominant trend in Virginia's population. It has been such a prevailing component of change that Virginia has been known as a "feeder" of population to other areas.[3] Only in the 1930s and 1940s was this trend reversed: in the first decade 29,016 more persons came to Virginia than left, and in the second 206,197 more came. Table 1.2 traces migration from 1880. Most out-migrants were lured by expanding urban areas and industry elsewhere.

Table 1.2.  Net gain or loss from migration by decades, 1880–1950

| Decade | Number | Percent |
|--------|--------|---------|
| 1880–1890 | −82,795 | −5.5 |
| 1890–1900 | −96,348 | −5.8 |
| 1900–1910 | −74,153 | −4.0 |
| 1910–1920 | −27,696 | −1.3 |
| 1920–1930 | −223,967 | −9.7 |
| 1930–1940 | 29,016 | 1.2 |
| 1940–1950 | 206,197 | 7.7 |

The 1880–1930 estimates are derived from Gilliam (see Table 1.1).

Despite the constant loss of residents to greener pastures, Virginia's population increased steadily and a fairly high rate of growth was maintained during the eighteenth century. By the end of the century, all of Virginia was open to settlement. The Tidewater, being the most thoroughly settled area, grew mainly by natural increase and slave importation. To the Piedmont and the Shenandoah Valley came migrants leaving the Tidewater and other colonies. During the eighteenth century Scotch-Irish

[2] Ibid.
[3] Ibid., p. 14.

and Germans from Pennsylvania and Europe and Swiss and
Germans from the Carolinas settled the valley region. A number
of slaves were brought to the Piedmont plantations, and some to
the valley.

From 1610 to 1790, the date of the first official census, Virginia's
population grew about 3,300 percent. From 1790 to 1950 the state
grew 379.8 percent. The increase between 1940 and 1950
(23.9 percent) is striking, especially since the average increase
during the previous fifteen decades was less than 10 percent. From
1900 to 1950 the state grew 79 percent, averaging 12.5 percent
each decade (see Table 1.1).

In the colony's early years large percentage increases of population were common. There was such great demand for labor
that immigrants flocked to Virginia's shores and thence to the
tobacco fields. Population increased over 1,000 percent between
1610 and 1620; between 1620 and 1640, 331.5 percent. From
1660 until 1790 each decade's growth averaged only 24.3 percent. In 1790 the state had increased by one-third from 1780.
This was the largest percentage growth Virginia experienced
after 1720.

In the 1790 census, Virginia was the largest state. By 1950 it ranked
fifteenth among the forty-eight states. Of the original thirteen
states, Virginia ranked seventh in population in 1950.

Virginia's growth in 1930–50 is characteristic of patterns in the
other southern states. The South Atlantic area is one of the nation's
fastest growing regions. Comprised of Delaware, Maryland, the
District of Columbia, Virginia, West Virginia, North Carolina,
South Carolina, Georgia, and Florida, it grew 18.8 percent between
1940 and 1950. This increase was exceeded only by the fast-
enlarging West, where the Mountain states grew 22.3 percent
and the Pacific states by 48.8 percent. Virginia's growth was
attributed in 1943 to three factors: expansion of war industries
in Hampton Roads, overflow of government activities from
Washington, and the civilian growth concomitant with the
growth of the military. At that time the opinion was expressed
that the pattern would continue: "It is reasonable to assume that
while a number of persons will leave the state at the close of the
war, a substantial portion will remain."[4] From the evidence of

4 Ibid., p. 18.

the 1950 census and those of subsequent decades, Virginia's growth, in great part a result of in-migration, will continue for some time to come.

## Rural-Urban Population

In the 1790 census only 1.8 percent of Virginia's people lived in places qualifying as urban under modern definitions.[5] In 1790 four places were considered urban: Alexandria, Norfolk, Petersburg, and Richmond. The urban population increased each decade by more than 10 percent. In 1920, the first census year when half of the United States was urban, 29.2 percent of Virginia's people were. Virginia in 1940 was 35 percent urban. By 1950, when the state's population had grown by almost a quarter in a decade, and with a new urban definition which counted fringe areas, Virginia's population was 47 percent urban. Under the old defi-

Table 1.3.  Rural-urban composition, 1790-1950 (percent)

| Year | Urban | Rural |
|------|-------|-------|
| 1790 | 1.8 | 98.2 |
| 1800 | 2.6 | 97.4 |
| 1810 | 3.6 | 96.4 |
| 1820 | 3.8 | 96.2 |
| 1830 | 4.8 | 95.2 |
| 1840 | 6.9 | 93.1 |
| 1850 | 8.0 | 92.0 |
| 1860 | 9.5 | 90.5 |
| 1870 | 11.9 | 88.1 |
| 1880 | 12.5 | 87.5 |
| 1890 | 17.1 | 82.9 |
| 1900 | 18.3 | 81.7 |
| 1910 | 23.1 | 76.9 |
| 1920 | 29.2 | 70.8 |
| 1930 | 32.4 | 67.6 |
| 1940 | 35.3 | 64.7 |
| 1950* | 47.0 | 53.0 |

*These figures are obtained from a new urban definition, more inclusive than that of previous decades, instituted in the 1950 census.

[5] Until 1950 a place of 2,500 inhabitants or more incorporated as a city, borough, or village, and in special areas classified as urban under special rules, was considered urban. A new definition was adopted in 1950 adding to the previous definition a consideration of densely settled urban fringe around cities of 50,000 or more and unincorporated places of 2,500 or more outside any urban fringe.

nition, the state would have been 40 percent urban. Table 1.3 outlines urban change.

From 1850 to 1950 Virginia's urban population increased 1,648.5 percent. This is an impressive growth but not large when compared with those of North Carolina and Georgia, states with urban expansions similar to Virginia's. North Carolina's urban population in the hundred years grew 6,381.1 percent; Georgia's urban growth rate was 3,899.2 percent. South Carolina's cities grew about 1,500 percent. All states along the Eastern Seaboard had impressive urban growth rates (see Table 1.4).

Table 1.4.  Growth of urban population in Eastern Seaboard states, 1850-1950

| State | Percent Increase, 1850-1950 | Percent Urban, 1950 |
|-------|-----------------------------|---------------------|
| New Hampshire | 464.7 | 57.5 |
| Massachusetts | 685.8 | 84.4 |
| Connecticut | 2,527.5 | 77.6 |
| Rhode Island | 712.8 | 84.3 |
| New York | 1,352.1 | 85.5 |
| Pennsylvania | 1,259.2 | 70.5 |
| New Jersey | 4,756.7 | 86.6 |
| Delaware | 1,324.4 | 62.6 |
| Maryland | 759.3 | 69.0 |
| Virginia | 1,648.5 | 47.0 |
| North Carolina | 6,381.1 | 33.7 |
| South Carolina | 1,486.1 | 36.7 |
| Georgia | 3,899.2 | 45.3 |
| Florida | ---* | 65.5 |

*No urban population in 1850.

The rural population increased less in constancy and amount. In 1790, 98.2 percent of the population was rural; in 1950, 53 percent. Chief among the causes of rural lag was out-migration resulting from the pull of industry in cities. A simultaneous occurrence was improvement in agricultural technology, which diminished the amount of manpower necessary on the farms. Most of the rural growth was due, therefore, to natural increase; rural areas have a consistently higher birth rate than cities.

Population Change by Planning Districts

The differing rates of urban and rural growth demonstrate the lack of uniformity in the state's population change. Further explanation of the change is provided by examination of Virginia's planning districts. Widely ranging rates of growth occurred among the twenty-two districts in periods between 1860, 1900, and 1950. Growth was highest, of course, in the urban areas, although in certain instances rural expansion was remarkably large. In most cases, however, growth was fairly small in rural districts and a decline occurred in some.

Several changes in municipal organization since 1950 should be noted. The cities of Norton, Galax, Covington, Salem, Lexington, Fairfax, Bedford, South Boston, Emporia, Chesapeake, Franklin, and Virginia Beach have been incorporated since then. Elizabeth City County consolidated with Hampton; Warwick County incorporated and then merged with Newport News; Norfolk County and the city of South Norfolk merged to form Chesapeake; and Princess Anne County consolidated with Virginia Beach. These are changes through 1970 only. Data given here for 1950, when considered by planning districts, regard these localities by their present structures and names. Table 1.5 and Figure 1.1 illustrate regional growth.

Leading all districts in dimensions of expansion was the Peninsula, where population increased over 800 percent between 1860 and 1950. The Peninsula (Planning District 21) includes five localities (the cities of Hampton, Newport News, and Williamsburg and James City and York counties). In this area are several military bases, the state's largest private employer (the Newport News Shipbuilding Company), and Colonial Williamsburg. These establishments provide jobs for thousands in the Peninsula and in the Tidewater area and return a great deal of revenue to the localities.

Cities and counties on the south side of Hampton Roads grew substantially, benefiting from the large port facilities in Norfolk and Portsmouth and from several military installations. This district includes the cities of Norfolk, Portsmouth, Virginia Beach, Chesapeake, Suffolk, and Franklin and Isle of Wight and

Table 1.5.  Growth of Virginia by planning district, 1860-1950  (percent)

| Planning District | 1860-1900 | 1900-1950 | 1860-1950 |
|---|---|---|---|
| 1. Lenowisco | 128.9 | 93.1 | 341.8 |
| 2. Cumberland Plateau | 169.5 | 126.8 | 511.2 |
| 3. Mount Rogers | 95.9 | 43.2 | 180.6 |
| 4. New River Valley | 102.8 | 61.5 | 227.4 |
| 5. Fifth | 151.4 | 141.7 | 507.6 |
| 6. Central Shenandoah | 42.2 | 39.3 | 98.0 |
| 7. Lord Fairfax | 32.7 | 29.4 | 71.8 |
| 8. Northern Virginia | 32.4 | 378.1 | 533.1 |
| 9. Rappahannock-Rapidan | 10.9 | -10.9 | -1.1 |
| 10. Thomas Jefferson | 15.4 | 10.4 | 27.4 |
| 11. Central Virginia | 35.4 | 35.3 | 83.1 |
| 12. West Piedmont | 68.4 | 53.1 | 157.7 |
| 13. Southside | 33.4 | 16.0 | 54.8 |
| 14. Piedmont | 5.7 | -1.4 | 4.2 |
| 15. Richmond Regional | 46.0 | 99.0 | 190.7 |
| 16. RADCO | -7.3 | 19.8 | 11.1 |
| 17. Northern Neck | 26.3 | -0.4 | 25.8 |
| 18. Middle Peninsula | 9.5 | -21.2 | -15.9 |
| 19. Crater | 22.8 | 66.4 | 104.3 |
| 20. Southeastern Virginia | 129.8 | 183.8 | 552.2 |
| 21. Peninsula | 212.8 | 193.8 | 818.9 |
| 22. Accomack-Northampton | 75.4 | 10.3 | 93.6 |

Southampton counties. In 1950 the population was over six times that of 1860.

Northern Virginia grew a great deal in this period, as it has since. In 1950 population in Planning District 8 was six and a third times greater than it was in 1860. Growth from 1900 to 1950 was 378.1 percent. Mostly the area is a suburb of Washington, D.C., affected by the overflow of government activities there. The cities of Alexandria, Fairfax, and Falls Church and Arlington, Fairfax, Loudoun and Prince William counties are members of this district.

The area around Richmond had not expanded greatly by 1950, although the city itself was the state's largest, with over 230,000 residents. Although the population of the total planning district

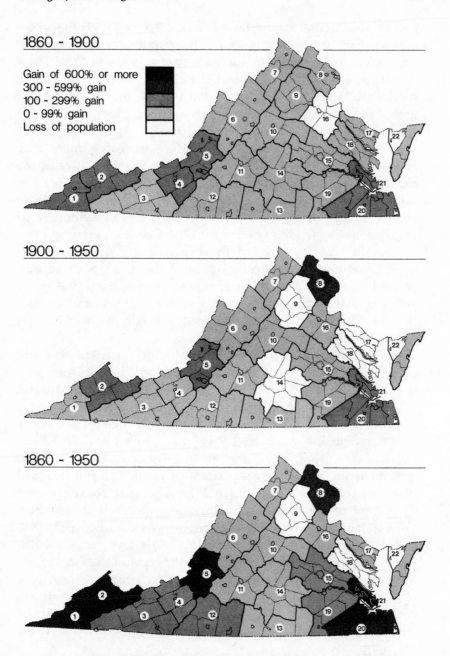

Fig. 1.1.   Population growth by planning district, 1860–1950

(no. 15) almost tripled, the growth rate (290.7) was smaller than those other urban areas experienced. The population of four rural counties in the district actually fell between 1860 and 1950. These were Charles City (-16.6 percent); Goochland (-16.2 percent); New Kent (-32.1 percent); and Powhatan (-33.8 percent). Richmond grew 366.8 percent; its surrounding counties (Henrico, Chesterfield, and Hanover), 27.4 percent together.

Roanoke and its environs (District 5) increased more than 500 percent in the 1860-1950 period. The municipalities of the district do not center around Roanoke geographically. It includes four counties (Roanoke, Craig, Botetourt, and Alleghany) and three cities (Salem, Covington, and Clifton Forge). Only Clifton Forge and Roanoke were incorporated by 1950. Roanoke, growing 415.5 percent in ninety years, led the expansion of this region. All other areas grew 369 percent. Much of the area's advance may be attributed to the addition of much railroad track mileage to accommodate rapid expansion in coal mining. Roanoke quickly became a center of railroad activity, especially as headquarters of the Norfolk and Western company.

Two very rural districts in Southwest Virginia experienced growth of 341 and 511 percent in the 1860-1950 period. The large increases, uncommon in such remote areas, resulted from the development of a large coal mining industry. In Planning Districts 1 and 2 (Lenowisco and Cumberland Plateau), seven counties are under consideration: Lee, Scott, and Wise in District 1 and Buchanan, Dickenson, Russell, and Tazewell in District 2. These counties accounted for almost three-quarters of all mined and quarried materials collected in Virginia in 1929. They also contained over 95 percent of the state's coal mines. Statistics indicate that coal mining increased at a rapid pace in Virginia. Between 1880 and 1890 production grew from 43 to 784 tons, and in 1900, 2,394 tons were produced. Mining continued to increase steadily thereafter.[6] Migration to the coal mines by people seeking jobs obviously accounted for much of the increase in these areas.

Other predominantly rural districts grew at a more moderate rate. The population of some declined. Districts 3 and 4, both in the

[6] U.S. Bureau of the Census, *Statistical Abstract of the United States* (Washington, D.C.: U.S. Government Printing Office, various years).

Southwest, grew 180 and 277 percent, respectively. These districts certainly felt some of the benefits of mining expansion. A slight decline occurred in District 9 (Culpeper, Fauquier, Madison, Orange, and Rappahannock); a large loss, 16 percent, in District 18 (Essex, Gloucester, King and Queen, King William, Mathews, and Middlesex). Since 1900 District 9 has lost 9 percent of its population; District 18 (Middle Peninsula), 20 percent. These districts, offering little other than traditional employment, were the hardest hit by urbanization.

## Variations by Race

The proportions of blacks in Virginia's population declined greatly between 1790 and 1950 (see Table 1.6). In 1790 blacks composed 43.4 percent of the population; in 1950, 22.2 percent. Explanations of such a decline are evident when changes in Virginia's economy are considered.

Variations by race before 1860 may be explained by trends in agriculture and in slavery. A depressed tobacco market in Virginia lasted for most of the first half of the nineteenth century, in contrast to the prospering cotton industry in the Deep South.[7] The tobacco difficulties are attributed to farmed-out soil, unscientifically managed for decades. The result of this depression was a surplus of slaves in Virginia; in contrast, many acreas of new land were opened by westward expansion, and technological developments such as the cotton gin greatly increased productive capacity. Slaves were thus in demand in the new southern states. Virginia planters made large profits from the sale of slaves to the Deep South. A side result of this market was the stabilization of growth in the black population, relieving "the growing apprehension on the part of the planters that they would soon be hopelessly outnumbered by the blacks."[8]

Virginia's black population declined rapidly after the Civil War. The state's economy was of course severely depressed during the

[7] Virginius Dabney, *Virginia, the New Dominion* (Garden City, N.Y.: Doubleday, 1977, pp. 228–29.
[8] Ibid., p. 229.

Table 1.6.  Population of Virginia by race, 1790-1950   (percent)

| Year | White | Nonwhite |
|------|-------|----------|
| 1790 | 56.6 | 43.4 |
| 1800 | 55.4 | 44.6 |
| 1810 | 52.9 | 47.1 |
| 1820 | 52.2 | 47.8 |
| 1830 | 52.1 | 47.9 |
| 1840 | 52.1 | 47.9 |
| 1850 | 53.1 | 45.0 |
| 1860 | 55.0 | 43.3 |
| 1870 | 56.7 | 43.2 |
| 1880 | 56.8 | 41.8 |
| 1890 | 61.6 | 38.4 |
| 1900 | 64.3 | 35.7 |
| 1910 | 67.4 | 32.6 |
| 1920 | 70.1 | 29.9 |
| 1930 | 73.1 | 26.9 |
| 1940 | 75.3 | 24.7 |
| 1950 | 77.8 | 22.2 |

Reconstruction period. Many of the freed slaves went north looking for jobs and a new life. Many also moved to the cities. In 1860, 43.3 percent of Virginia's population was black; by 1900, 35.7 percent. The proportion decreased further by 1940, to 24.5 percent, and had reached 22.2 percent in 1950. It is estimated that 368,231 blacks moved from Virginia between 1880 and 1950, averaging over 50,000 each decade.[9]

[9] Gilliam, p. 117.

Black population in every region of Virginia declined between 1860 and 1950. The largest decline (30.1 percent) occurred in District 10, which includes Charlottesville, Albemarle, Fluvanna, Greene, Louisa, and Nelson. Other Piedmont districts experienced similar large losses of black population. For several reasons, demand for farm labor fell: depleted land being taken from cultivation; extensive poverty after the Civil War; and advanced technology. Whatever the reasons, blacks (and whites also) left the farms by the thousands, and their proportion of population decreased accordingly. Table 1.7 illustrates proportions of blacks by planning districts.

## Population by Age Distribution

Virginia's population aged considerably between 1860 and 1950, when the median age rose from 18.5 to 27.3 years. Chief among the causes of this aging were increased life expectancy and lower birth rates.[10] The median age rose from 18.5 years in 1860 to 20.3 in 1900; the greatest rise, then, occurred in this century. Almost 54 percent of the 1860 population was under 20 years of age; in 1900, 49.4 percent; in 1950, 37.1 percent.

The aging was logically accompanied by increased percentages of older age groups. The great part of this process occurred in the ages of 20–44 years and 45–64 years; the percentage of population 65 years and older increased only 3.3 percent, compared with respective growth of 6.9 and 6.1 percent in the former groups. Thus the working and reproductive ages made considerable gain over the more dependent sectors. Table 1.8 and Figure 1.2 demonstrate the changing age ratios of Virginia's population from 1860 to 1950.

Virginia's white population in each period was older than the black segment. The median age of whites in 1860 was 19.2 years; in 1900, 21.2; and in 1950, 27.8. For blacks, the 1860 median was 17.5 years; in 1900, 19.1; and 1950, 25.3. In most cases the

---

[10] See ibid., 42. The national birth rate per 1,000 population fell from 55.0 in 1820 to 24.4 in 1950; see Irene B. and Conrad Taeuber, *People of the United States in the Twentieth Century* (Washington, D.C.: Bureau of the Census, U.S. Government Printing Office, 1971), p. 357.

Table 1.7.   Percent age of nonwhites in Virginia planning districts, 1860, 1900, and 1950

| Planning District | 1860 | 1900 | 1950 |
|---|---|---|---|
| 1. Lenowisco | 4.9 | 5.4 | 2.5 |
| 2. Cumberland Plateau | 11.7 | 7.4 | 2.9 |
| 3. Mount Rogers | 12.9 | 8.0 | 3.3 |
| 4. New River Valley | 17.5 | 14.2 | 5.0 |
| 5. Fifth | 24.9 | 23.8 | 12.5 |
| 6. Central Shenandoah | 19.6 | 14.8 | 6.1 |
| 7. Lord Fairfax | 21.2 | 11.0 | 5.5 |
| 8. Northern Virginia | 29.6 | 28.6 | 8.9 |
| 9. Rappahannock-Rapidan | 53.0 | 37.8 | 25.5 |
| 10. Thomas Jefferson | 53.9 | 39.5 | 23.8 |
| 11. Central Virginia | 46.9 | 38.6 | 22.8 |
| 12. West Piedmont | 39.4 | 30.0 | 25.6 |
| 13. Southside Virginia | 62.8 | 56.5 | 48.9 |
| 14. Piedmont | 66.7 | 59.5 | 44.9 |
| 15. Richmond Regional | 48.7 | 43.2 | 28.6 |
| 16. RADCO | 55.5 | 42.3 | 26.5 |
| 17. Northern Neck | 54.8 | 48.0 | 41.1 |
| 18. Middle Peninsula | 61.5 | 53.0 | 39.7 |
| 19. Crater | 60.8 | 59.3 | 45.1 |
| 20. Southeastern Virginia | 43.9 | 52.0 | 31.9 |
| 21. Peninsula | 54.3 | 46.1 | 30.4 |
| 22. Eastern Shore | 48.3 | 42.0 | 40.7 |

median age of females was higher than that of males. A graph of median ages (Figure 1.3; see also Table 1.9) reveals population dynamics of the period. In 1870 and 1880 median ages of males dropped sharply. Among whites the decline apparently was due to casualties of the Civil War (over 15,000 Virginians died in the conflict). Also a cause for whites, but much more so for

Table 1.8. Distribution of Virginia's population by broad age groups, 1860–1950 (percent)

| Year | Below 20 | 20–44 | 45–64 | 65 & over |
|------|----------|-------|-------|-----------|
| 1860 | 54.3 | 32.7 | 10.8 | 3.1 |
| 1870 | 51.6 | 32.8 | 12.2 | 3.4 |
| 1880 | 52.1 | 32.4 | 11.6 | 3.9 |
| 1890 | 51.7 | 32.4 | 12.0 | 3.9 |
| 1900 | 49.4 | 33.8 | 12.9 | 3.9 |
| 1910 | 47.6 | 35.0 | 13.2 | 4.1 |
| 1920 | 46.0 | 35.5 | 14.2 | 4.3 |
| 1930 | 44.4 | 34.9 | 15.9 | 4.8 |
| 1940 | 39.1 | 38.3 | 16.7 | 5.8 |
| 1950 | 37.1 | 39.6 | 16.9 | 6.4 |

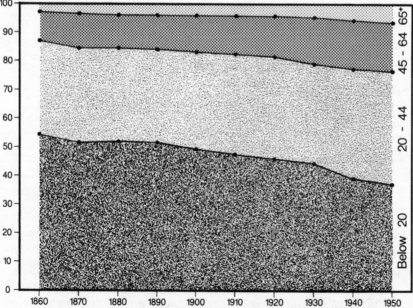

Fig. 1.2. Distribution of Virginia's population by broad age groups, 1860–1950

Table 1.9.  Median ages of Virginia's population by race and sex, 1860-1950

| Year and sex | Total | White | Nonwhite |
|---|---|---|---|
| 1860 | 18.5 | 19.2 | 17.5 |
| Male | 18.4 | 19.0 | 17.6 |
| Female | 18.5 | 19.4 | 17.4 |
| 1870 | 19.3 | 20.0 | 18.4 |
| Male | 18.6 | 19.1 | 17.7 |
| Female | 20.0 | 20.7 | 19.0 |
| 1880 | 19.0 | 20.2 | 17.3 |
| Male | 18.4 | 19.6 | 16.8 |
| Female | 19.5 | 20.7 | 17.9 |
| 1890 | 19.3 | 20.3 | 17.8 |
| Male | 19.6 | 20.0 | 17.3 |
| Female | 18.9 | 20.5 | 18.3 |
| 1900 | 20.3 | 21.2 | 19.1 |
| Male | 20.2 | 21.0 | 18.8 |
| Female | 20.5 | 21.2 | 19.3 |
| 1910 | 21.3 | 21.8 | 20.1 |
| Male | 21.3 | 21.9 | 20.0 |
| Female | 21.3 | 21.8 | 20.3 |
| 1920 | 22.2 | 22.6 | 21.4 |
| Male | 22.3 | 22.6 | 21.6 |
| Female | 22.1 | 22.5 | 21.2 |
| 1930 | 23.1 | 23.7 | 21.5 |
| Male | 23.0 | 23.6 | 21.4 |
| Female | 23.3 | 23.9 | 21.6 |
| 1940 | 25.8 | 26.5 | 23.7 |
| Male | 25.6 | 26.2 | 23.8 |
| Female | 26.0 | 26.8 | 23.7 |
| 1950 | 27.3 | 27.8 | 25.3 |
| Male | 26.9 | 27.3 | 25.4 |
| Female | 27.8 | 28.4 | 25.3 |

blacks, was out-migration. Thousands of black Virginians left the state after the war, seeking opportunities not available in the battle-devastated, land-poor area. Prosperity remained conspicuously absent in Virginia during the years of rebuilding.

As the population regained equilibrium and as life expectancy and birth rates changed, Virginia's races and sexes grew closer in climbing median ages. Between 1920 and 1930, a decade when

YEARS OF AGE

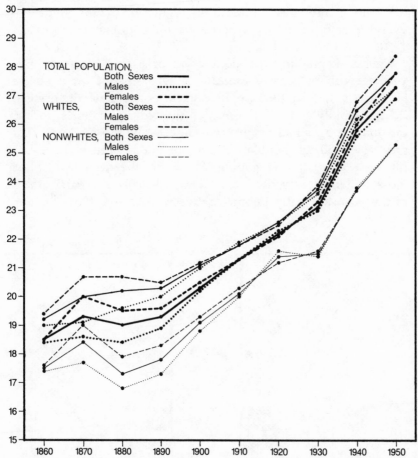

Fig. 1.3.   Median age of Virginia's population by race and sex, 1860–1950

thousands of blacks migrated to northern cities, their median age in Virginia barely increased while the white median age increased by more than one year. Sara K. Gilliam estimated that migration totaled 220,268 persons, or 11.1 percent.[11]

The largest change in age of Virginia's population during the decades occurred between 1930 and 1940, when the total population's median age rose from 23.1 to 25.8 years. In this period net migration to Virginia was positive for the first time in generations. Despite the fact that black net migration was still nega-

tive (and it has continued to the present), fewer blacks moved
out than in previous decades. In-migration, drawn in part by
World War II, continued to push up median ages from 1940 to
1950.

Figures diagraming the population of each decade by five-
year age cohorts clearly indicate in what manner it aged (see
Figures 1.4–1.7). In 1860 population proportions declined steadily and rapidly as they approached the old-age cohorts. In 1900
the younger ages had begun to decline, while those 65 and older
grew. By 1950 the population demonstrated a much older profile with fewer young people. However, the youngest cohort,
those under 5 years old, was larger, showing the early effects
of the postwar "baby boom." Between 1940 and 1950 the pop-

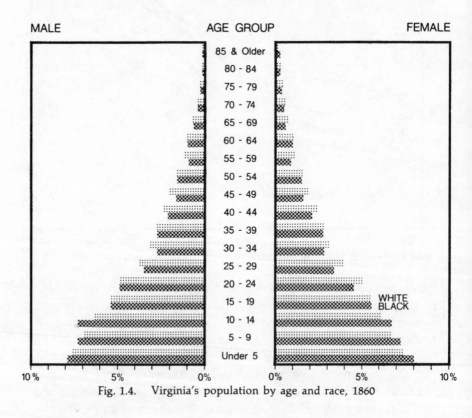

Fig. 1.4.    Virginia's population by age and race, 1860

[11] Gilliam, p. 115.

MALE                    AGE GROUP                    FEMALE

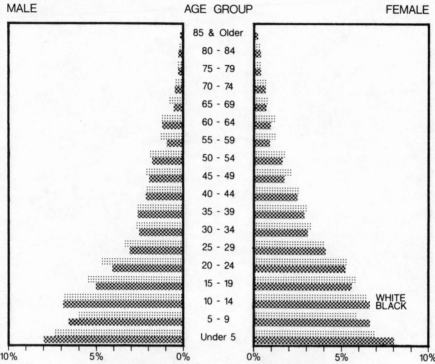

Fig. 1.5.    Virginia's population by age and race, 1870

ulation aged slightly as groups below 20 decreased about 2 percent.

The regularity of the 1860 pyramid was disrupted in 1870.
Between the ages of 20 and 44, 15 percent of the population was
male, 17.9 percent female. This difference, also reflected in the
median ages, was due in part to the death of many males in the
Civil War, and also to out-migration. Of whites in 1870, males
in this age group were 15.2 percent of the population, females
18.1 percent. Males in their thirties in 1870 were noticeably
fewer than females; ten years earlier they had comprised the
bulk of Virginia's soldiers. The 15,000 casualties accounted for
over 12 percent of the 1860 white male population aged 15-34,
or 25 percent of those aged 20-29.

The black population in 1870 had 14.5 percent males in
the 20-44 age group versus 17.8 percent females. Almost 54 per-

MALE                            AGE GROUP                            FEMALE

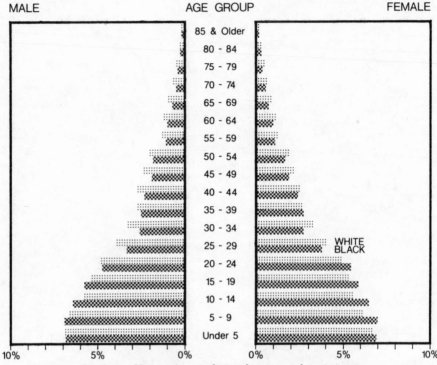

Fig. 1.6.    Virginia's population by age and race, 1900

cent of the black population was under 20 years of age, as were
50.2 percent of whites. Thus blacks, having a lower median age,
could be expected to have fewer in the 20–44 age group. Also, a
number of Virginia slaves had been sold to cotton states for an
extended period preceding the war, lowering representation of
blacks in subsequent years. A "bull market for Virginia's surplus slaves" created an annual sale in the 1830s estimated
between 6,000 and 8,500.[12] Gilliam estimated that 122,458
black persons moving from Virginia to South Central states in
1860–70 were relatives of slaves who left Virginia before the
war.[13]

From 1880 until 1920 the age distribution of Virginia's population
remained fairly regular, although the median age increased from 19
to 22.7 years. During much of this period the state's urban

[12] Dabney, p. 229.
[13] Gilliam, p. 56.

MALE                        AGE GROUP                        FEMALE

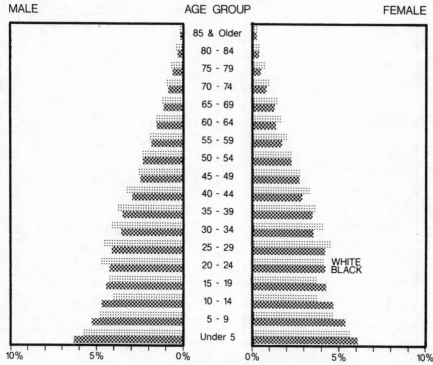

Fig. 1.7.   Virginia's population by age and race, 1950

population increased gradually, but its citizens still left in large
numbers for other areas. After 1930 the effect of positive net
migration to Virginia began to show. Younger segments of the
population occupied a smaller proportional part of the total,
as the middle ages rose. By 1950 Virginia's age distribution was
significantly different than it had been in 1860. Throughout the
decades the black distribution remained younger by virtue of
higher fertility rates, a shorter life expectancy, and greater proportional out-migration.


## Age Distribution by Place of Residence

The pyramid for United States population in 1950 is similar to
Virginia's in the same year (Figure 1.8). The basic configuration
is the same, with an indentation through the 5-19 year cohorts

MALE                        AGE GROUP                     FEMALE

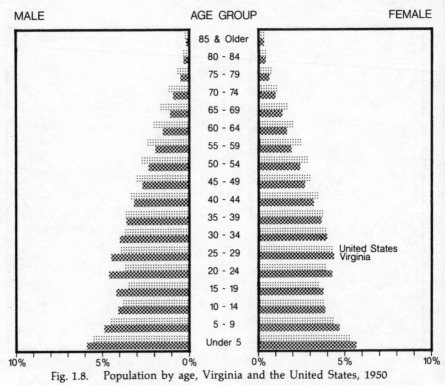

Fig. 1.8.    Population by age, Virginia and the United States, 1950

and regular decreases thereafter. Virginia's population was slightly younger, the only noticeable distinction between the age distributions.

The age distribution of Virginia's population had changed consistently from that of 1860s heavily rural, regularly tapered structure (see Figure 1.4). The effects of urbanization (and a number of natural factors) before the turn of the century, chiefly distinguished by a rise of the median age, have been noted. Some information of age by place of residence was available in the 1910 census, and already it showed a definite relationship of divergent age groups and urban–rural residence.

In 1910, and in both races, the urban population was considerably older than the rural. Just over half of the rural population was under 20 years of age, as compared to 38.3 percent of urban dwellers. Despite the younger rural population, it has a smaller reproductive potential. In the cities, 44.3 percent was aged 20–44,

12 percent more than in the countryside. Out-migration accounts for part, but not all, of the difference. In 1860, when 90.5 percent of the population was rural, 32.7 percent was 20–44 years old, practically the same proportion as fifty years later, when rural population had slipped to 76.9 percent of the total. The 1920 configuration for total population was little different from that of 1910. As in that year, the statewide pattern of younger non-white population was upheld.

In 1930 the rural category was divided into "rural farm" and "rural nonfarm" residences, recognizing the declining number of farms and an increasing suburban population. From that decade forward, age distribution of the rural nonfarm population was intermediate to those of urban and farm residents. Large differences are evident in broad age groups. On farms, 50.3 percent of the residents were under 20 years old, 28.1 percent 20–44, and 22.2 percent over 45 years. Of rural nonfarm residents, 45.5 percent were under age 20, 36 percent 20–44, and 18.4 percent 45 and older. The urban residents were still older; only 36.5 percent were under 20, 42.2 percent 20–44, and 21.2 percent 45 and older.

These general patterns continued in 1940 and 1950, and were accompanied by the overall rise of median age. By 1950 the farm population under 20 years had dropped to 43.2 percent, still more than rural nonfarm, 40.9 percent, or urban, 32.3 percent. The 20–44 age groups remained large in the cities, over 44 percent in 1940 and 1950; in the rural nonfarm section they were about 39 percent, and about 30 percent in the farming areas.

Median ages of Virginians by place of residence are available for 1940 and 1950, and demonstrate once again the differences in age structure by community class. In 1940 the state's median age was 25.8 years; that of cities was 29.1 years; of rural nonfarm residents, 24.6 years; and of farm residents, 22.9 years. For whites in the cities, it was 29.6 years; 24.9 for rural nonfarm residents; and 24 years for farm residents. For the nonwhite population, these figures were slightly lower; 27.8 years in cities; 23.4 and 20 years for rural nonfarm and farm dwellers.

In 1950 the median age of urban residents was 29.1 years, with 29.3 for whites and 28.4 for nonwhites. For a change, rural nonfarm residents were the youngest, with a 25.1 median age;

whites were 25.4 years, nonwhites 23.7. Rural farm dwellers were slightly older (25.5 years), this statistic being determined almost wholly by the white population, with a median of 27.7 years. The rise of 3.7 years in median age for farm whites between 1940 and 1950 probably reflected the aging of those left after the young moved away.

These age differences are illustrated well by population pyramids (see Figures 1.9 and 1.10). In 1940 and 1950 the urban population less than 20 years old appeared quite small, but by 1950 the infant population (under 5 years) was growing. Much of the city population pattern clearly resulted from in-migration during the rapid urban expansion heretofore mentioned.

In rural farm areas, the pattern was reversed. While the under-20 population was large (42.9 percent) and the proportions above 55 years were fairly normal, the 20–54 cohorts were severely depopulated, representing in great degree the persons who left the farms permanently. The black population again was younger.

Rural nonfarm residents in 1950 created the pyramid most regular in appearance. Two reasons may be advanced for the balance this population struck between urban and farm configurations. The first concerns original rural dwellers who maintained traditional nonfarm jobs without being greatly affected by the agricultural decline. Also, some rural areas contiguous to urban areas served as extended suburbs, with city workers commuting long distances.

Thus Virginia's population by age conformed closely to the national norm during the 1860–1950 period, and its various components reflected the economic and social changes that occurred during this interval. The accommodation of Virginia's people to conditions of economic prosperity, decline, and transition was accomplished in predictable fashion. From colonial days until 1950 Virginia achieved a distinctive history which in passing changed its way of life.

MALE                          AGE GROUP                          FEMALE

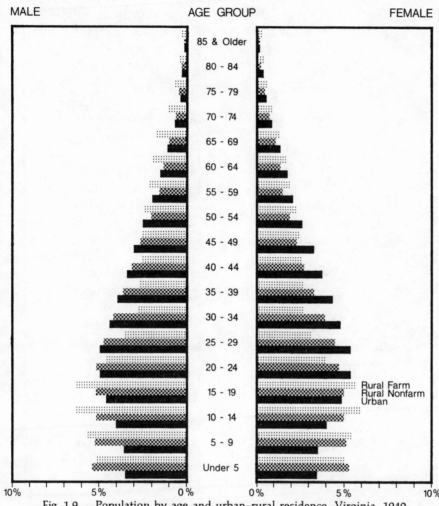

Fig. 1.9.    Population by age and urban–rural residence, Virginia, 1940

MALE                          AGE GROUP                          FEMALE

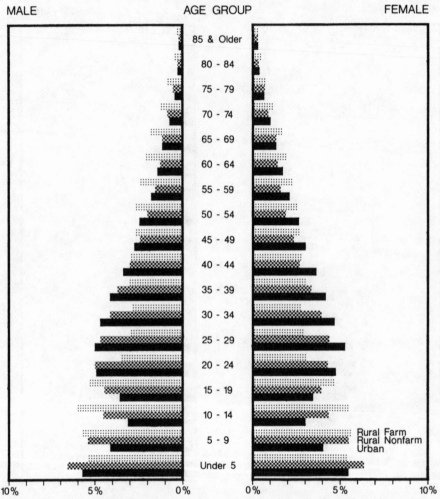

Fig. 1.10.  Virginia's population by age and urban–rural residence, 1950

PART II  The Present (1950–70)

Chapter 2

# Population Growth Rate Differentials

## Variation within Virginia

Between 1950 and 1970 the population of Virginia expanded by about 40 percent, from 3.3 to 4.7 million. This rate of increase was somewhat greater than the national level of 34 percent. In terms of total population size, Virginia ranked fifteenth among the states in 1950, and fourteenth in both 1960 and 1970. A comparison of population increases for Virginia, other states in the South Atlantic Division, and other census divisions is given in Table 2.1 and Figure 2.1.

The nation as a whole experienced a slowdown in population growth between 1950 and 1970. This is primarily due to declines in fertility which began toward the end of the earlier decade and have persisted ever since. This diminution in the rate of pop-

Table 2.1. Population growth in Virginia, the South, and the nation, 1950-70

| Area | Population (1,000s of persons) | | | Percent Change | | |
|---|---|---|---|---|---|---|
| | 1950 | 1960 | 1970 | 1950-60 | 1960-70 | 1950-70 |
| United States | 151,326 | 179,323 | 203,212 | 18.5 | 13.3 | 34.3 |
| New England | 9,314 | 10,509 | 11,842 | 12.8 | 12.7 | 27.1 |
| Middle Atlantic | 30,164 | 34,168 | 37,199 | 13.3 | 8.9 | 23.3 |
| Northeast | 39,478 | 44,678 | 49,041 | 13.2 | 9.8 | 24.2 |
| East North Central | 30,399 | 36,225 | 40,252 | 19.2 | 11.1 | 32.4 |
| West North Central | 14,061 | 15,394 | 16,319 | 9.5 | 6.0 | 16.1 |
| North Central | 44,461 | 51,619 | 56,572 | 16.1 | 9.6 | 27.2 |
| South Atlantic | 21,182 | 25,972 | 30,671 | 22.6 | 18.1 | 44.8 |
| Delaware | 318 | 446 | 548 | 40.3 | 22.8 | 72.3 |
| Maryland | 2,343 | 3,101 | 3,922 | 32.3 | 26.5 | 67.4 |
| D.C. | 802 | 764 | 757 | -4.8 | -1.0 | -5.6 |
| Virginia | 3,319 | 3,954 | 4,651 | 19.2 | 17.6 | 40.2 |
| West Virginia | 2,006 | 1,860 | 1,744 | -7.2 | -6.2 | -13.1 |
| North Central | 4,062 | 4,556 | 5,082 | 12.2 | 11.5 | 25.1 |
| South Central | 2,117 | 2,383 | 2,591 | 12.5 | 8.7 | 22.4 |
| Georgia | 3,445 | 3,943 | 4,590 | 14.5 | 16.4 | 33.2 |
| Florida | 2,771 | 4,952 | 6,789 | 78.7 | 37.1 | 145.0 |
| East South Central | 11,477 | 12,050 | 12,803 | 5.0 | 6.3 | 11.6 |
| West South Central | 14,538 | 16,951 | 19,321 | 16.6 | 14.0 | 32.9 |
| South | 47,197 | 54,973 | 62,795 | 16.5 | 14.2 | 33.1 |
| Mountain | 5,075 | 6,855 | 8,282 | 35.1 | 20.8 | 63.2 |
| Pacific | 15,115 | 21,198 | 26,523 | 40.2 | 25.1 | 75.5 |
| West | 20,190 | 28.053 | 34,804 | 38.9 | 24.1 | 72.4 |

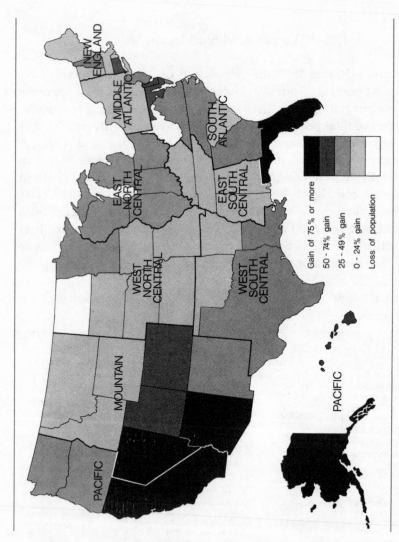

Fig. 2.1.   Rates of population growth for United States, 1950–70

ulation increase was shared by all census divisions (save the slowly growing East South Central Division) and most states, including Virginia.

The South Atlantic Division was the third–fastest–growing division over the twenty-year period, due in considerable measure to the very high growth rates occurring in Florida (145 percent). Two other states in the division, Delaware and Maryland, also experienced population growth at a higher rate than Virginia. The only other state in the entire South (which also includes the East and West South Central divisions) with greater relative growth than Virginia was Texas (45 percent).

Within Virginia population growth rates during the 1950–70 period varied rather widely. To avoid the complications created by the numerous annexations, consolidations, and incorporations in Virginia during the period (the result of Virginia's unique separation of cities and counties), the discussion of relative population change within the state will focus on the twenty–two planning districts into which the Commonwealth was divided in accordance with the Area Development Act of 1968. Changes of population and the corresponding rates of change for the districts are shown in Table 2.2 (changes in population for all cities and counties is given in Table A2.1).

Growth rates over the interval ranged from the 165–percent increase reached in Northern Virginia to the 29–percent decline recorded in the Lenowisco District, located in the extreme south-western corner of Virginia. The highest rates of growth over the period occurred in the largest metropolitan areas of the state–Richmond (Richmond Regional), Norfolk–Virginia Beach (South-eastern Virginia), and Newport News–Hampton (Peninsula). The first two of these areas grew by about 47 percent from 1950 to 1970, while the Peninsula area's population expanded by 90 percent. The only other portion of the state to grow at a rate exceeding the overall level was the RADCO district, centering on Fredericks-burg. This area is located between the Northern Virginia and Rich-mond areas and has been experiencing growth pressures from both the north and the south.

Population declines were concentrated in predominately rural portions of Virginia. Areas declining in population, besides

Table 2.2. Population change in Virginia planning districts, 1950-70

| | Area | Population (1,000s of persons) | | | Percent Change | | |
|---|---|---|---|---|---|---|---|
| | | 1950 | 1960 | 1970 | 1950-60 | 1960-70 | 1950-70 |
| 1. | Lenowisco | 120.1 | 100.2 | 84.8 | -16.5 | -15.4 | 129.4 |
| 2. | Cumberland Plateau | 133.5 | 128.0 | 112.5 | -4.1 | -12.1 | -15.7 |
| 3. | Mount Rogers | 161.5 | 160.1 | 159.4 | -0.9 | -0.4 | -1.3 |
| 4. | New River Valley | 96.9 | 97.2 | 114.8 | 0.4 | 18.1 | 18.5 |
| 5. | Fifth | 181.6 | 207.3 | 231.2 | 14.2 | 11.5 | 27.3 |
| 6. | Central Shenandoah | 151.3 | 166.6 | 186.3 | 10.1 | 11.8 | 23.2 |
| 7. | Lord Fairfax | 89.6 | 97.0 | 106.4 | 8.3 | 9.6 | 18.8 |
| 8. | Northern Virginia | 347.1 | 601.8 | 921.3 | 73.4 | 53.1 | 165.4 |
| 9. | Rappahannock-Rapidan | 61.1 | 65.6 | 72.2 | 6.5 | 10.1 | 17.2 |
| 10. | Thomas Jefferson | 91.4 | 98.0 | 115.2 | 7.2 | 17.5 | 26.1 |
| 11. | Central Virginia | 135.3 | 150.9 | 166.0 | 11.5 | 10.0 | 22.7 |
| 12. | West Piedmont | 189.8 | 205.2 | 219.2 | 8.1 | 6.8 | 15.5 |
| 13. | Southside Virginia | 95.1 | 88.8 | 82.6 | -6.6 | -7.0 | -13.2 |
| 14. | Piedmont | 86.5 | 80.2 | 77.1 | -7.3 | -3.9 | -10.9 |
| 15. | Richmond Regional | 373.2 | 462.0 | 547.5 | 23.8 | 18.5 | 46.7 |
| 16. | RADCO | 55.2 | 64.3 | 77.4 | 16.6 | 20.4 | 40.4 |
| 17. | Northern Neck | 35.0 | 36.8 | 37.0 | 5.1 | 0.6 | 5.8 |
| 18. | Middle Peninsula | 44.6 | 45.5 | 47.6 | 2.0 | 4.6 | 6.7 |
| 19. | Crater | 125.2 | 141.5 | 161.1 | 13.0 | 13.8 | 28.6 |
| 20. | Southeastern Virginia | 525.2 | 666.8 | 769.4 | 27.0 | 15.4 | 46.5 |
| 21. | Peninsula | 168.0 | 242.9 | 319.1 | 44.5 | 31.4 | 89.9 |
| 22. | Accomack-Northampton | 51.1 | 47.6 | 43.4 | -6.9 | -8.7 | -15.0 |
| | Virginia | 3,318.7 | 3,954.4 | 4,651.5 | 19.2 | 17.6 | 40.2 |

Lenowisco, included two other districts in the Southwestern area of the state (Cumberland Plateau and Mount Rogers), two districts in the Southside area (Southside Virginia and Piedmont), and the Eastern Shore (Accomack-Northampton).

If the growth rates by decade are examined separately, an interesting pattern emerges. While it is the case that the largest metropolitan areas experienced the greatest overall growth over the entire two decades, it is also true that the rate of growth during the 1960-70 decade was somewhat lower than that of the earlier decade.[1] Conversely, many smaller urban areas, which grew at a relatively low rate over the entire period, experienced higher growth in the 1960-70 decade than in the 1950-60 decade. This was the case in the New River Valley, Central Shenandoah, Lord Fairfax, Rappahannock-Rapidan, Thomas Jefferson, RADCO, and Crater districts.

## Components of Growth

The causes of population change in a state are natural increase (that is, the difference between births and deaths) and net migration (that is, persons moving into the state and persons moving out of a state). The volume of these components will depend on the age, race, and sex structure of the population as well as the relative incidence of these events for particular age-race-sex groups.

For Virginia, as with most other states, natural increase was the more important component of population change during the 1950-70 period. As noted earlier, the state's population grew from 3,318,680 to 4,651,487 between 1950 and 1970. The number of births and deaths for each of these years in this interval is given in Table 2.3. Of the total population growth (1,332,807), a total of 1,153,812, or 87 percent, was due to natural increase. The remaining 178,895 was the total net in-migration to Virginia over the entire twenty-year period.

Analyzing the data by decades, it becomes apparent that there are considerable differences between 1950 and 1960. Total population change was 635,749 (from 3,318,680 to 3,954,429). Almost all of

[1] The other metropolitan areas of the state, Roanoke (Fifth) and Lynchburg (Central Virginia), experienced similar interdecade changes.

Table 2.3. Births, deaths, and natural increase, Virginia, 1950-70

| Year | Births | Deaths | Natural Increase |
|------|--------|--------|------------------|
| 1950 (April 1 Dec. 31) | 61,516 | 22,281 | 39,235 |
| 1951 | 86,771 | 29,462 | 57,309 |
| 1952 | 90,017 | 30,178 | 59,839 |
| 1953 | 91,831 | 30,098 | 61,733 |
| 1954 | 95,154 | 29,310 | 65,844 |
| 1955 | 94,401 | 30,373 | 64,028 |
| 1956 | 96,717 | 31,401 | 65,316 |
| 1957 | 97,284 | 32,994 | 64,290 |
| 1958 | 96,773 | 33,068 | 63,705 |
| 1959 | 96,620 | 33,291 | 63,329 |
| 1960 (Jan. 1 Mar. 30) | 23,929 | 8,600 | 15,329 |
| | | | |
| 1950-60 | 931,013 | 311,056 | 619,957 |
| | | | |
| 1960 (April 1 Dec. 31) | 71,787 | 25,800 | 45,987 |
| 1961 | 97,097 | 34,008 | 63,079 |
| 1962 | 96,565 | 35,618 | 60,947 |
| 1963 | 96,854 | 36,904 | 59,950 |
| 1964 | 96,966 | 36,525 | 60,441 |
| 1965 | 89,139 | 37,043 | 52,096 |
| 1966 | 84,538 | 37,358 | 47,180 |
| 1967 | 82,775 | 37,191 | 45,584 |
| 1968 | 82,138 | 39,687 | 42,451 |
| 1969 | 83,420 | 39,048 | 44,372 |
| 1970 (Jan. 1 Mar. 31) | 21,520 | 9,752 | 11,768 |
| | | | |
| 1960-70 | 902,789 | 368,934 | 533,855 |
| | | | |
| 1950-70 | 1,833,802 | 679,990 | 1,153,812 |

Source: Virginia State Department of Health, Annual Report, various years.

this—619,957, or 97.5 percent—was the result of natural increase. Net migration to Virginia over the decade was only 15,792. Between 1960 and 1970 total population growth was somewhat greater (697,058). Natural increase, however, accounted for a much lower share of this total; the natural increase of 533,855 during the later decade was responsible for only 76.6 percent of the total population growth. The volume of net migration during this decade (163,203) was more than ten times that of the preceding decade.

A further examination of the data in Table 2.3 suggests that although the number of births reached a maximum during the middle of the interval (say, from 1954 to 1964) and then declined rather sharply, the trend in the number of deaths was more or less constantly upward. Natural increase, the difference between the two, reached a peak in 1954, when nearly 66,000 persons were added to the state's population. By the end of the period, only 40,000 to 45,000 per year were being added by natural increase.

The reasons for the abrupt decline in fertility beginning in the middle of the 1960s and persisting until the present have been a subject of considerable controversy among demographers. It is clear that while the numbers of women in the peak reproductive years have risen over the period, birth rates measured in terms of total numbers of persons, total numbers of women aged 15–44, or by specific five–year age group have fallen sharply in the past few years.[2] In 1960 there were 114 births per 1,000 women aged 15–44; by 1970 this rate (called the *general fertility rate*) had declined by more than a quarter to 85 per 1,000. Had 1960 rates held over the period from 1960 to 1990, each woman who entered her reproductive years in 1960 would have had 1.64 daughters surviving until the beginning of their own reproductive years; by 1970 this number (called the *net reproduction rate*) had declined to 1.11.

Many explanations have been proffered to account for this sharp drop. Perhaps the most plausible ones involve a very basic change in American society, particularly among women, regarding the relative importance of child rearing to the exclusion of working. It is certainly true that fertility desires and fertility expectations of American women are much lower at the present than they were fifteen years ago.[3] To these changes must be coupled the large–scale changes in the availability and efficiency of means of contraception. Such relatively safe and highly efficient means of contraception as "the pill" and the intrauterine device (IUD) were not available in 1960.

---

[2] William J. Serow, "Fertility in Virginia, 1940–1970," *University of Virginia Newsletter*, 48 (April 1972):30.

[3] U.S. Bureau of the Census, "Fertility Expectations of American Women: June 1974," *Current Population Reports*, Series P- 20, no. 277 (Feb. 1975). Births expected for women aged 18–24 averaged 2.165 in 1974 as opposed to 2.852 in 1967.

The increase in the number of deaths is nothing more than a reflection of the increase in population. The more people there are in Virginia (or anywhere else) at one time, the more people there are who will die over the course of a given period of time, *ceteris paribus*. The number of deaths per 1,000 persons was about 8.9 in 1950 and 8.4 in 1970. This small decline might be attributed to some improvements in health conditions (such as the decline in infant mortality from a level of about 35 per 1,000 live births in 1950 to 21 in 1970) and to the relatively large growth of low-mortality age groups. In general, though, rates of mortality have remained fairly stable in recent years.

As already noted, the volume of migration rose substantially between the 1950 and 1970 decades. Unfortunately, little more can be said about migration trends in this context. Migration is not measured directly (there being no requirement that changes of residence be registered like births or deaths) but rather is taken as the residual between population change and natural increase. Hence, to measure the volume of migration over a period, one must have population counts for both the beginning and end of the period as well as data on numbers of births and deaths. In the absence of the availability of consistent annual estimates, particularly during the earlier portion of the period, it is not possible to pinpoint any fluctuation in migration. Migration data for the five-year periods 1955-60 and 1965-70 are available;[4] they show that net migration to Virginia increased by 22,752 over the period from 1955-60 to 1965-70 (from 43,294 to 66,046).[5]

## Determinants of Differential Population Change

There are a sizable number of characteristics which one might hypothesize will influence rates of fertility, mortality, and migra-

[4] U.S. Bureau of the Census, *1960 Census of Population: Mobility for States and State Economic Areas* (Washington, D.C., U.S. Government Printing Office, 1963) and *1970 Census of Population: Mobility for States and the Nation* (Washington, D.C.: U.S. Government Printing Office, 1973).

[5] Persons aged 0-4 at the time of each census are excluded from these tabulations. See William J. Serow, "Changes in the Composition of Migration for States, 1955-60 to 1965-70," *Review of Regional Studies* 5 (Fall 1975): 12-28.

tion. Perhaps the most elementary and most important of these are the basic demographic variables of age, race, and sex. Of these three, perhaps the most fundamental is age.

All the components of population change are very much a function of age. Mortality, for example, is relatively high during the first year of life, then falls precipitously to a minimum around the age of 10, followed by a gradual increase which becomes increasingly larger after age 50 or 55. The overall effect is something like a J–shaped curve. As a result of the relatively high mortality at the youngest and oldest ages, it is not surprising that most of the absolute improvements in mortality which occurred in Virginia during the 1950–70 period took place among these age groups. These changes are depicted in Table 2.4.

The largest absolute decline in mortality occurred among infants (0–1), where the rate declined over 19 percent during the period. A decline of about half this level occurred for persons aged 75 and over. Relative declines were much greater for persons 0–14 than for older age groups, but it must be remembered that mortality is very low from ages 1–14.

A conventional means of separating the effects of changes in age–specific rates and changes in the age composition of a popula-

Table 2.4.  Age-specific mortality rates, Virginia, 1950 and 1970

| Age | 1950 | 1970 | Percent Change |
|-----|------|------|----------------|
| 0-1 | 41.6 | 22.5 | -45.9 |
| 1-4 | 1.6 | 0.7 | -56.3 |
| 5-14 | 0.7 | 0.4 | -42.9 |
| 15-24 | 1.5 | 1.2 | -20.0 |
| 25-29 | 2.2 | 1.5 | -31.8 |
| 30-44 | 4.3 | 3.3 | -23.3 |
| 45-54 | 9.9 | 8.0 | -19.2 |
| 55-64 | 21.5 | 18.0 | -16.3 |
| 65-74 | 42.9 | 38.0 | -11.4 |
| 75+ | 105.5 | 96.5 | -8.5 |
| Total | 8.9 | 8.4 | -5.6 |

Source:  Robert D. Grove and Alice M. Hetzel, Vital Statistics Rates in the United States, 1940-1960 (Washington, D.C.:  U. S. Government Printing Office, 1968), Table 61; and Virginia State Department of Health, 1970 Annual Report (Richmond:  Commonwealth of Virginia, 1971), Table 29.

tion is through a process called *standardization*. Essentially this procedure involves multiplying the same population by alternative sets of age–specific rates. Since the age composition in constant, differences in the number of events (in this case, deaths) are attributable solely to differences in rates. To eliminate effects of changes in population size, two *standard populations* of 100,000 may be created, one with the age composition of the 1950 population, the other with the age composition of the 1970 population. By subjecting each of these to the same mortality schedule, one may determine the influence of changes in age structure on mortality levels. Conversely, by comparing the same population subjected to different mortality schedules, one may determine the influence of change on mortality rates on mortality levels. The data on these applications are given in Table 2.5.

Table 2.5. Effects of age composition and mortality level changes on death rates, by race and sex, Virginia, 1950 and 1970

|  | Age Structure | Mortality Level | |
|---|---|---|---|
|  |  | 1950 | 1970 |
| Total | 1950 | 889 | 720 |
|  | 1970 | 1,011 | 839 |
| White Female | 1950 | 667 | 531 |
|  | 1970 | 832 | 679 |
| Nonwhite Female | 1950 | 1,089 | 734 |
|  | 1970 | 1,236 | 871 |
| White Male | 1950 | 907 | 835 |
|  | 1970 | 962 | 900 |
| Nonwhite Male | 1950 | 1,385 | 1,191 |
|  | 1970 | 1,438 | 1,259 |

The data show that mortality rates dropped between 1950 and 1970 so as to create a decline in the overall death rate of about 20 percent. That is, if nothing had changed but the age–specific mortality schedule, the number of deaths among Virginians would have declined by about 20 percent. On the other hand, this was partially offset by changes in age structure during this period. If nothing but the age structure had changed, mortality would have increased by approximately 15 percent over the period. The actual data (the interaction of these) show that the moderate decline in mortality (from a rate of 8.9 in 1950 to 8.4 in 1970) was the result of lowered age–specific mortality rates outweighing the aging of the population.

Besides age, race and sex are also important determinants of mortality. As can be seen in Figure 2.2, women have lower mortality than men at all ages, while whites have lower mortality than nonwhites at all ages except the very oldest. Although these data are shown only for 1970, the results are applicable for any period of time, in general. An important question not answered in Figure 2.2 concerns changes in mortality levels, particularly by race. If the population is divided into four race–sex groupings (white male, white female, nonwhite male, nonwhite female), data for 1950[6] show that the overall death rate was lower for white

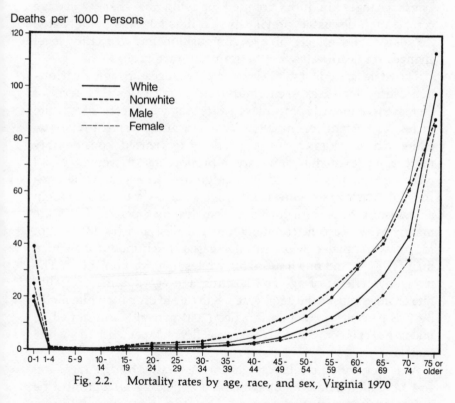

Fig. 2.2.    Mortality rates by age, race, and sex, Virginia 1970

[6] Robert D. Grove and Alice M. Hetzel, *Vital Statistics Rates in the United States, 1940–1960* (Washington, D.C.: U.S. Government Printing Office, 1968), p. 364.

females (6.7 per thousand) than for any of the other groups. White males were reported to have died at a rate of 9.1 per thousand; nonwhite females, 10.9 per thousand; and nonwhite males, 13.9 per thousand. For 1970 these rates were: white female, 6.8; white male, 9.0; nonwhite female, 8.7; nonwhite male, 12.6. Thus, on the whole, rates among whites changed very little, while rates among nonwhites dropped by about 10 percent for males and by 20 percent for females. The overall level of mortality for nonwhite females, in fact, dropped below that of white males, for the first time since reasonably complete records of deaths have been kept (the change presumably occurred sometime between 1960 and 1970, but unavailability of annual population estimates by race and sex make it impossible to judge the precise date). These changes, in turn, are tied up with the changes in age composition discussed previously. To illustrate this point, Table 2.5 also shows effects of age composition and mortality level changes on death rates for the four age–race groups.

The data in this table show that changes in age distribution caused increases in mortality rates in all cases. The level of increase was about 25 percent for white females, 7 percent for white males, 15 percent for nonwhite females, and 5 percent for nonwhite males. Women, as a whole, experienced considerably more aging than did men; larger proportions of women of all races were in higher mortality age groups. Changes in the age-specific mortality schedules were such as to lower the death rate in all cases: by 20 percent for white females; by 7 percent for white males; by 30 percent for nonwhite females; and by 13 percent for nonwhite males. Mortality decreased much more for women than for men, and much more for whites than for nonwhites. The interactive effects of age composition and age–specific mortality rate changes caused the aggregate death rate to drop for white males by (0.8 percent), nonwhite females (20.0 percent), and nonwhite males (9.1 percent) and to increase (by 1.8 percent) for white females.

As is true with mortality, migration also varies by age, race, and sex. Migration data are not available for single years but must be estimated for intercensal periods. The estimation of migration in this fashion can be accomplished in terms of age, race, and sex as follows. Beginning with the population alive at the beginning of the period, an allowance is made for expected mortality over the decade.[7] The base population (by age, race, and sex) is multiplied by the national survival rate over the decade. Similarly, registered births are also subjected to appropriate probabilities. The resulting "expected" population is then compared with the enumerated population; the difference between them is *net migration*. This procedure, however, does not permit separate estimates of in- and out-migration.[8]

The volume of net migration for the 1950–60 decade totaled 15,792, while for 1960–70 it was 163,203, as already noted. One can also determine net migration by race for each decade, as shown in Table 2.6. As can be seen, natural increase decreased for persons of all races between 1950–60 and 1960–70. Between 1950 and 1960, the white population increased by 550,066 (from 2,581,555 to 3,131,621). For the 1960–70 decade the total increase among whites was 629,893 (1970 white population: 3,761,514). Given that natural increase by decade was 470,741 and 408,849 for 1950–60 and 1960–70, respectively, it may be concluded that net migration among whites was 79,325 in the earlier decade and 221,044 in the later. For nonwhites, intercensal population increases totaled 85,683 and 64,172, respectively. Given the levels of natural increase shown in Table 2.6, net migration among nonwhites was – 63,532 between 1950 and 1960 and – 60,835 between 1960 and 1970. The rate of net migration (calculated as net migration divided by the base population) rose from 3.1 to 7.1 percent for whites and declined from – 8.6 to – 7.4 percent for nonwhites.

Published data for migration during the 1950–60 decade (by

[7] There are many possible techniques. The estimates here use the census survival rate method, which assumes that the share of a cohort surviving through the decade is identical to the national share. This method thus allows for enumeration errors. See Henry S. Shryock, Jacob S. Siegel, and Associates, *The Methods and Materials of Demography* (Washington, D.C.: U.S. Government Printing Office, 1971), p. 632.

[8] Such data are for the five-year period immediately preceding the census. Most of these data are found in the 1960 census publication *Mobility for States and State Economic Areas* and the 1970 publication *Mobility for States and the Nation* (see note 4 above).

Table 2.6.   Natural increase by race, Virginia, 1950-70

| Year | White | Nonwhite |
|------|-------|----------|
| 1950 (Apr.-Dec.) | 30,099 | 9,136 |
| 1951 | 43,953 | 13,356 |
| 1952 | 46,302 | 13,537 |
| 1953 | 47,510 | 14,223 |
| 1954 | 50,068 | 15,776 |
| 1955 | 48,241 | 15,787 |
| 1956 | 49,179 | 16,137 |
| 1957 | 48,272 | 16,018 |
| 1958 | 47,862 | 15,843 |
| 1959 | 47,631 | 15,698 |
| 1960 (Jan.-Mar.) | 11,624 | 3,704 |
| 1950-60 | 470,741 | 149,215 |
| | | |
| 1960 (Apr.-Dec.) | 34,874 | 11,114 |
| 1961 | 47,884 | 15,195 |
| 1962 | 46,784 | 14,163 |
| 1963 | 45,718 | 14,232 |
| 1964 | 45,918 | 14,523 |
| 1965 | 39,023 | 13,073 |
| 1966 | 35,649 | 11,531 |
| 1967 | 34,830 | 10,754 |
| 1968 | 33,444 | 9,007 |
| 1969 | 35,465 | 8,907 |
| 1970 (Jan.-Mar.) | 9,260 | 2,508 |
| 1960-70 | 408,849 | 125,007 |
| | | |
| 1950-70 | 879,590 | 274,222 |

Source:   Virginia State Department of Health, 1970 Annual Report, Table 4.

age, race, and sex) are available[9] but are somewhat at variance with the migration estimates given above. Differences in sources for data on births by race and differences in the population size of Virginia discovered after the 1960 population was made final account for these variations. For similar reasons, there are also minor variances between the 1960–70 estimates and published data.[10] Net migration ratios (net migration divided by population of the end of the period) for age–race–sex cohorts which incorporate these corrections are given in Table 2.7.

[9] Gladys K. Bowles and James D. Tarver, Net Migration of the Population, 1950–60, by Age, Sex and Color (Washington, D.C.: U.S. Government Printing Office, 1965), I:403.

[10] William J. Serow and Michael A. Spar, Virginia's Population: A Decade of Change. II. Net Migration for State Planning Districts (Charlottesville: Tayloe Murphy Institute, 1972), Table 3.

Table 2.7.  Net migration rates (per 1,000 people) by age, race, and sex,
Virginia, 1950-60 and 1960-70

| Age | White Male | | White Female | | Nonwhite Male | | Nonwhite Female | |
|-----|-----------|--------|--------------|--------|---------------|--------|-----------------|--------|
|     | 50-60     | 60-70  | 50-60        | 60-70  | 50-60         | 60-70  | 50-60           | 60-70  |
| 0-4   | 1.9    | -8.4  | -2.5  | -6.2  | 1.4    | -8.9   | -0.8   | -10.4  |
| 5-9   | -12.0  | 20.0  | 1.4   | 21.5  | -20.3  | -57.2  | -21.7  | -50.9  |
| 10-14 | 6.2    | 58.4  | 10.5  | 56.4  | -49.5  | -55.5  | -58.1  | -56.9  |
| 15-19 | 93.6   | 78.8  | 44.9  | 61.4  | -83.0  | -66.9  | -90.9  | -77.5  |
| 20-24 | 222.4  | 233.4 | 103.1 | 148.6 | -157.3 | -103.1 | -261.9 | -197.6 |
| 25-29 | -6.9   | 95.6  | 67.4  | 138.6 | -237.3 | -187.7 | -257.3 | -273.0 |
| 30-34 | -113.9 | -34.3 | 40.9  | 90.4  | -214.8 | -127.0 | -160.8 | -104.6 |
| 35-39 | 1.0    | 92.0  | 37.6  | 87.1  | -151.8 | 70.5   | -100.8 | -47.6  |
| 40-44 | -0.7   | 74.0  | 21.2  | 67.6  | -110.4 | -64.2  | -75.7  | -31.3  |
| 45-49 | -8.7   | 41.4  | 14.7  | 41.2  | -44.6  | -43.4  | -39.6  | -24.8  |
| 50-54 | -0.1   | 23.7  | 16.9  | 27.1  | -65.3  | -37.5  | -75.1  | -18.3  |
| 55-59 | 13.4   | 9.9   | 21.0  | 25.1  | -50.9  | -32.6  | -82.9  | -19.9  |
| 60-64 | 6.1    | 7.0   | 25.3  | 22.9  | -105.3 | -33.4  | -134.4 | -31.9  |
| 65-69 | 11.8   | 1.9   | 35.0  | 21.2  | -35.8  | -20.7  | -30.1  | -10.9  |
| 70-74 | 26.0   | 0.6   | 41.3  | 34.8  | -44.6  | -44.5  | -58.8  | -29.5  |
| 75 +  | 10.2   | -15.7 | 26.9  | 36.1  | -193.2 | -74.9  | -200.4 | -53.5  |
| Total | 17.7   | 58.3  | 29.4  | 59.9  | -84.2  | -65.4  | -89.5  | -70.6  |

Sources:  See notes 9 and 10 to chapter 2.

White age groups, in general, experienced increasing net in-migration ratios, while nonwhite age groups experienced decreasing net out-migration ratios. Migration rates, in general, regardless of direction, tended to peak during the twenties, with in-migration rates of 20 percent for white males aged 20-24 and out-migration rates of similar magnitude for nonwhite females aged both 20-24 and 25-29. One might also note that net out-migration rates for nonwhite males in these age groups were much lower than the corresponding rates for females; this may be attributable to military-induced in-migration among nonwhite males. The overall importance of age as a determinant of migration is made very clear in Figure 2.3, which shows the volume of net migration for Virginia, by age and race, for the 1960-70 decade.

Fertility, like mortality and migration, is greatly influenced by age and race. While it is technically possible to measure fertility

Thousands of Persons

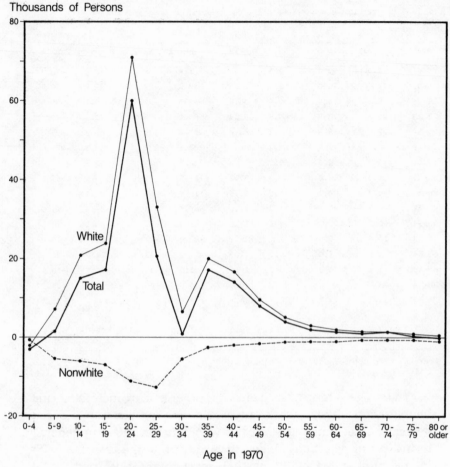

Age in 1970

Fig. 2.3.    Net migration by age and race, Virginia, 1960–70

in terms of characteristics of the father, there is, in general, little to be gained by doing so. Consequently, the discussion here will focus solely on characteristics of the mother.

Measures of fertility may be divided into measures of periodic fertility and measures of cohort fertility. *Periodic fertility* refers to the reproductive performance of the entire population (or a segment of it) at any point in time, while *cohort fertility* refers to the reproductive performance of the population (or a segment) over the course of its entire reproductive span (to date). Each of these measures will be discussed in turn.

The most frequently encountered measure of periodic fertility is the *crude birth rate*, that is, the number of births in a given year per 1,000 population. The reason for the designation *crude* is simply the failure of this measure to account for the age, sex, and racial composition of the population in question. It is readily apparent that a population with relatively more women in the reproductive years (roughly, the age group 10–49) will have a higher crude birth rate than another population with fewer such women if both populations have similar fertility patterns.

To overcome the lack of precision of the crude birth rate, several more refined measures of fertility can be employed. The simplest of these is the *general fertility rate*, which is the ratio of births in a given year to the number of women aged 15–44 (these account for almost all births). This measure recognizes differences in sex composition and, to a limited extent, differences in age composition. Still, differences in the age composition of women in their reproductive years are not shown by this measure. To provide that data, a measure called the *total fertility rate* is employed. This rate is simply the sum of the ratios of the number of births by women of a given age to the number of women of that age. The total fertility rate indicates the number of children that would be born per 1,000 women over the span of their childbearing years if the fertility rates by age were unchanged over the entire period.

Two more refined measures of fertility are available, both of which stem from the total fertility rate. These measures, the gross and the net reproduction rates, recognize that rates of reproduction hinge upon the size of the female population and, consequently, measure the reproductive performance of only the female population. The *gross reproduction rate* is simply the total fertility rate multiplied by the percentage of live births that are female. The *net reproduction rate*, which recognizes that some female children will not survive to the end of their reproductive span, is the gross reproduction rate weighted by the probability of survival to the end of the childbearing years.

Of all the measures noted above, only the crude birth rate is available on an annual basis. Although the number of births and estimated total population are available annually, there is no reliable estimate of the age composition of the population available except in the census years 1950, 1960, and 1970.

As shown in Table 2.8, movements in the crude birth rate were quite erratic from 1950 to 1970. During the early part of the 1950s, the crude birth rate remained near the post–World War II maximum (27.7 births per thousand persons in 1947). In 1956, however, a steady decline in the crude birth rate began, which accelerated in the years 1964–69. The 1969 level, 17.4, was the lowest recorded in Virginia since the compilation of reports began in 1913. The pattern for whites was nearly identical, although the lowest level of fertility among this group occurred a year earlier. Among nonwhites the pattern was slightly different. Instead of peaking in the late 1940s, fertility among nonwhites rose steadily to 1956 and 1957, when a level of 31.4 births per 1,000 population was recorded. Fertility then declined, at first slowly, then more rapidly, until a low of 20.1 was reached in 1969. In brief, for white, the crude birth rate declined consistently from a level of 24.5 in 1956 to 16.7 in 1968, a reduction of 32.7 percent. For nonwhites, fertility declined consistently from 31.4 in 1957 to 20.1 in 1969, a reduction of 36 percent. In 1956, the crude birth rate among nonwhites exceeded that of whites by 28.2 percent; by 1969, this factor had decreased to 19.6 percent.

As noted previously, the more refined measures of fertility can be computed with any degree of accuracy only in years when the census is taken since these measures require knowledge of the age distribution of the female population. The pattern of all these fertility measures, as shown in Table 2.9, paralleled those of the crude birth rate; all rates increased rather substantially from 1950 to 1960 and then declined quite sharply from 1960 to 1970. All fertility measures in 1970 were less than the corresponding data for all other years.

The net reproduction rates in 1970 for the total population, and in particular for the white population, were quite low. For whites the data show that every woman would have, on the average, only 1.05 surviving daughters. Thus, if this rate continues to hold, the

Table 2.8.  Crude birth rates (per 1,000 people)
by race, Virginia, 1950-70

| Year | Total | White | Nonwhite |
|------|-------|-------|----------|
| 1950 | 24.7 | 23.5 | 29.0 |
| 1951 | 25.5 | 24.3 | 30.0 |
| 1952 | 26.0 | 24.8 | 30.2 |
| 1953 | 26.0 | 24.8 | 30.3 |
| 1954 | 26.5 | 25.2 | 31.2 |
| 1955 | 25.8 | 24.3 | 31.2 |
| 1956 | 26.0 | 24.5 | 31.4 |
| 1957 | 25.7 | 24.1 | 31.4 |
| 1958 | 25.1 | 23.6 | 30.7 |
| 1959 | 24.7 | 23.2 | 30.3 |
| 1960 | 24.0 | 22.7 | 29.0 |
| 1961 | 24.1 | 22.8 | 28.8 |
| 1962 | 23.4 | 22.3 | 27.6 |
| 1963 | 22.9 | 21.7 | 27.6 |
| 1964 | 22.5 | 21.3 | 27.4 |
| 1965 | 20.1 | 18.9 | 25.3 |
| 1966 | 18.7 | 17.5 | 23.4 |
| 1967 | 18.0 | 16.9 | 22.3 |
| 1968 | 17.5 | 16.7 | 20.7 |
| 1969 | 17.4 | 16.8 | 20.1 |
| 1970 | 18.5 | 17.7 | 21.8 |

Source:  Virginia State Department of Health, 1970 Annual
Report, p. 40, and Statistical Annual Report 1951
(Richmond, 1951), p. 19.

Table 2.9.  General and total fertility rates and gross and net
reproduction rates by race, Virginia, 1950-70

|  | 1950* | 1960 | 1970 |
|---|---|---|---|
| **Total population** | | | |
| General fertility rate | 109.3 | 114.3 | 85.0 |
| Total fertility rate | 3,121.5 | 3,476.5 | 2,356.5 |
| Percent of births female | 0.4857% | 0.4906% | 0.4873% |
| Gross reproduction rate | 1,516.1 | 1,705.6 | 1,148.3 |
| Net reproduction rate | 1.4400 | 1.6368 | 1.1102 |
| **White population** | | | |
| General fertility rate | 102.7 | 107.1 | 80.8 |
| Total fertility rate | 2,934.0 | 3,275.5 | 2,237.2 |
| Percent of births female | 0.4834% | 0.4873% | 0.4849% |
| Gross reproduction rate | 1,418.3 | 1,596.2 | 1,084.8 |
| Net reproduction rate | 1.3604 | 1.5424 | 1.0550 |
| **Nonwhite population** | | | |
| General fertility rate | 132.7 | 143.2 | 103.7 |
| Total fertility rate | 3,727.0 | 4,254.5 | 2,817.8 |
| Percent of births female | 0.4923% | 0.5004% | 0.4955% |
| Gross reproduction rate | 1,834.8 | 2,128.8 | 1,396.2 |
| Net reprduction rate | 1.6835 | 1.9882 | 1.3221 |

Sources:  Grove and Hetzel; Virginia State Department of Health, Annual Report
(various years, 1940-70); U.S. Bureau of Census, U.S. Census of Population:
Virginia (Washington, D.C.:  U.S. Government Printing Office, 1971).

white female population of the state will eventually increase by
only about 5 percent over the course of a generation (approximately twenty-five to thirty years), not considering the impact of
migration. For nonwhites, the female population will increase by
about 32 percent. It is interesting to note that although fertility
for both races was generally lower in 1970 than in earlier years, the
difference between the reproductive performance of the races
widened since 1950. In 1950 the net reproduction rate for
nonwhites was 23.8 percent higher than the rate for whites;
in 1970 it was 25.3 percent higher.

As with changes in death rates, changes in birth rates can be
analyzed in terms of the effects of changes in age structure and
in age-specific rates (in this case, age-specific fertility rates).

Additionally, in this context, changes in the sex composition of population are also relevant, since it is only women who have children; yet the crude birth rate is a function of the entire population. To isolate the effects of these determinants, standardization is again appropriate.

Birth rates for 1950 and 1970, specific to the age and race of the mother, are shown in Table 2.10. Rates fell rather sharply over the period, with the white general fertility rate declining by 26 percent, while the nonwhite rate fell by 27 percent. The results of the standardization procedure (done in a manner precisely analogous to that of mortality) are shown in Table 2.11. The data show that changes in both age composition and in the fertility schedule acted to lower overall fertility rates. Age composition effects were fairly modest, causing a decline of about 4 or 5 percent in each racial group, while fertility schedule changes caused declines of about 16 percent for whites and 23 percent for nonwhites.

As noted previously, cohort fertility is a concept much different from periodic fertility. Cohort fertility measures the reproductive

Table 2.10. Birth rates (per 1,000 women) by age and race of mother, Virginia, 1950 and 1970

| Age | 1950 | | 1970 | |
|-----|-------|----------|-------|----------|
|     | White | Nonwhite | White | Nonwhite |
| 10-14 | 0.6 | 5.0 | 0.4 | 4.9 |
| 15-19 | 78.5 | 154.4 | 60.0 | 122.5 |
| 20-24 | 182.4 | 227.6 | 149.8 | 182.7 |
| 25-29 | 153.3 | 166.0 | 136.7 | 129.7 |
| 30-34 | 99.3 | 107.0 | 66.9 | 72.7 |
| 35-39 | 54.2 | 60.2 | 27.0 | 38.9 |
| 40-44 | 16.8 | 22.8 | 6.4 | 11.1 |
| 45-49 | 1.7 | 2.4 | 0.2 | 1.0 |
| Total 10-44 | 80.5 | 100.4 | 59.3 | 72.9 |

Sources: Grove and Hetzel, Table 22; Virginia State Department of Health, 1970 Annual Report, Table 7.

Table 2.11.  Standardized general fertility rates by race, Virginia, 1950 and 1970

|  | Age Distribution | Fertility Schedule 1950 | 1970 |
|---|---|---|---|
| White | 1950 | 80.5 | 62.1 |
|  | 1970 | 74.6 | 59.3 |
| Nonwhite | 1980 | 100.4 | 76.6 |
|  | 1970 | 94.9 | 72.9 |

performance, to date, of any group of women within the population. Changes in fertility can be observed by comparing the performance of various cohorts of women as they pass through specified age levels. One particularly important level frequently chosen for observation is the 45–49 age group, because in this age group, reproductive activity will essentially be completed, but mortality has not yet begun to reduce the size of the cohort appreciably.

Cohort fertility is usually measured as the number of live births ever experienced per 1,000 women. The data are gathered in the decennial census of population, and hence are available only in the census years of 1950, 1960, and 1970. Data in Table 2.12 show

Table 2.12.  Children ever born (per 1,000 women) by age and race of mother, Virginia, 1950-70

| Age | 1950 White | Nonwhite | 1960 White | Nonwhite | 1970 White | Nonwhite |
|---|---|---|---|---|---|---|
| 15-19 | 92 | 168 | 139 | 201 | 88 | 109 |
| 20-24 | 763 | 908 | 945 | 1,330 | 672 | 928 |
| 25-29 | 1,488 | 1,683 | 1,815 | 2,338 | 1,647 | 2,081 |
| 30-34 | 1,926 | 2,113 | 2,265 | 2,805 | 2,475 | 3,078 |
| 35-39 | 2,186 | 2,636 | 2,377 | 2,931 | 2,850 | 3,527 |
| 40-44 | 2,221 | 2,909 | 2,334 | 2,803 | 2,795 | 3,431 |
| 45-49 | 2,506 | 2,786 | 2,237 | 2,712 | 2,632 | 3,203 |
| Total | 1,545 | 1,743 | 1,706 | 2,065 | 1,620 | 2,013 |

Sources:  U.S. Bureau of Census, 1950 Census of Population:  Special Reports: Fertility (Washington, D. C.:  U.S. Government Printing Office, 1955), Table 32; 1960 Census of Population:  Virginia:  Detailed Characteristics (Washington, D.C.:  U.S. Government Printing Office, 1963), Table 113; 1970 Census of Population:  Virginia:  Detailed Characteristics (Washington, D.C.:  U.S. Government Printing Office, 1973), Table 161.

children ever born by age and race of mother for these three years. Changes in fertility can be analyzed both by following cohorts across the entire period and by examining data for specified age groups.

The number of children ever born rose for all women aged 15–49 from 1,588 per thousand in 1950 to 1,692 in 1970. This was accompanied by increases among both white and non-white women. It is hardly surprising that this would occur, given the relatively high periodic rates of fertility which characterized the earlier part of the period. This is borne out by recognizing that the number of children ever born was higher in 1960 than in either 1950 or 1970.

At the beginning of the period, cohort fertility measures were quite low because of the years of the depression and World War II; in 1950 all women 25 and over had spent some portion of their reproductive years during times of low rates of reproduction. The effects can be seen by comparing children ever born to white women aged 35–39 in 1950 to those ever born to women in the same age group in 1970. The peak years of reproduction for the former group were in the middle of the great depression (1930–35), while that of the latter was during the post-war baby boom. Actual cohort fertility (to date) for the 1970 group was 30 percent higher than that of the 1950 group. Similar effects can be seen for other age–race groups.

Another approach that may be taken with these data is to follow the various cohorts through time. The group of women aged 15–19 in 1950, for example, was the same group aged 25–29 in 1960 and aged 35–39 in 1970. Between 1950 and 1960 each white member of this cohort gave birth to 1.7 chidren, on the average, and to 1.0 children between 1960 and 1970, and each nonwhite woman to 2.2 and 1.2 children, respectively (see Figure 2.4 and Table 2.13).

The basic changes in fertility which have characterized Virginia in recent years can be seen by comparing the fertility levels in 1970 with those of previous years. Those cohorts aged under 25 were generally at lower levels of fertility (children ever born) than were earlier cohorts while passing through the same age group. The white 20–24 cohort had over 10 percent fewer births

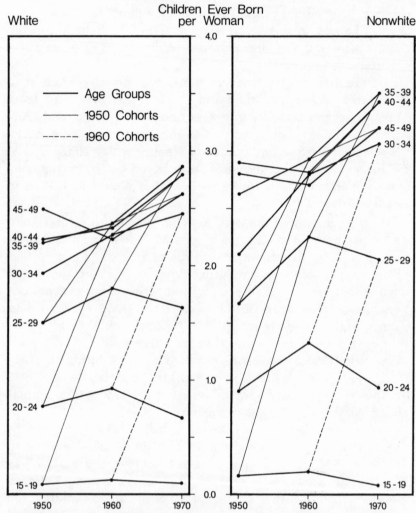

Fig. 2.4.    Children ever born per woman by age and race, Virginia, 1950–70

than did the 1950 white cohort and nearly 30 percent fewer births than did the 1960 white cohort. Among the 1970 nonwhite 20–24 cohort, fertility to date was about 2 percent higher than that of the 1950 cohort, but 30 percent lower than that of the 1960 cohort. The fertility level of the 1970 25–29 cohort was higher than the 1950 cohort but lower than that of the 1960 cohort, while all 1970 cohorts aged 30 and over surpassed

Table 2.13. Births per woman by decade, age, and race, Virginia, 1950-70

| | White | | Nonwhite | |
|---|---|---|---|---|
| Age | 1950 Cohorts (1950-60) | 1960 Cohorts (1960-70) | 1950 Cohorts (1950-60) | 1960 Cohorts (1960-70) |
| 15-19 | 1.72 | 1.52 | 2.17 | 1.88 |
| 20-24 | 1.50 | 1.53 | 1.90 | 1.75 |
| 25-29 | 0.89 | 1.04 | 1.25 | 1.19 |
| 30-34 | 0.41 | 0.53 | 0.69 | 0.63 |
| 35-39 | 0.05 | 0.26 | 0.08 | 0.27 |

Source:   Table 2.12.

the completed fertility levels of earlier cohorts. Much of the decline in fertility among the youngest 1970 childbearing cohorts is attributable to lower marriage rates for these persons and to increasing urbanization in Virginia. Before turning to the question of changing marriage rates and marital status, a word on urban-rural fertility differentials might be in order.

It has long been recognized that rural women tend to have higher fertility than their urban sisters. The reasons for this are essentially economic in nature. It used to be the case that children provided a cheap labor source to help with the family farm. Currently, as more and more of the state's population becomes urbanized, the relative cost of raising children has become much greater. Data for 1950 and 1970 showing children ever born to rural and urban Virginia women are shown in Table 2.14.

Differentials in fertility by place of residence have narrowed over the past two decades. Fertility among urban women increased by about one-fourth over the period, while rural fertility actually declined by about 5 percent. In 1950 urban fertility on the whole was about two-thirds of the rural level, while in 1970 it had reached more than four-fifths. As the data in Table 2.14 show, children ever born increased for all urban age groups older than 25. The increases were particularly substantial among women whose childbearing was reasonably complete (30 and older): 30-34, 58 percent, 35-39, 61 percent; 40-44, 49 percent; 45-49, 25 percent. For rural women, however, such large changes

Table 2.14.  Children ever born (per 1,000 women) by age and residence, Virginia, 1950 and 1970

|       | 1950 | | 1970 | |
| Age   | Urban | Rural | Urban | Rural |
|-------|-------|-------|-------|-------|
| 15-19 | 106   | 115   | 81    | 101   |
| 20-24 | 657   | 955   | 580   | 1,896 |
| 25-29 | 1,285 | 1,834 | 1,523 | 1,896 |
| 30-34 | 1,509 | 2,480 | 2,377 | 2,648 |
| 35-39 | 1,691 | 2,962 | 2,718 | 3,078 |
| 40-44 | 1,779 | 3,057 | 2,645 | 3,070 |
| 45-49 | 1,940 | 3,282 | 2,427 | 3,023 |
| Total | 1,272 | 1,933 | 1,574 | 1,914 |

Source:  Same as Table 2.12.

in completed fertility were nonexistent. The largest increase among older cohorts occurred in the 30-34 age group, and this was only 7 percent.

To explain the rather sharp relative increase in urban fertility, one must begin by remembering that 1950 levels were low due to the effects of the war and the depression. Based on the reproductive performance during the 1950-70 period, one would have to conclude that the fertility-depressing effects of the 1930s and 1940s were felt almost exclusively in urban areas and that rural people seem to be relatively unaffected by changing economic circumstances. Other explanations, such as changes in age or racial composition, do not satisfy. The share of nonwhite women among all women in the reproductive ages changed little since 1950. In that year 22 percent of urban women and 19 percent of rural women were nonwhite; in 1970 these proportions had decreased to 19 and 18 percent, respectively. Changes in age composition were actually of the sort to lower the overall level of children ever born for urban women and to cause effectively no change for rural women (see Table 2.15).

Table 2.15.  Standardized levels of children ever born to women aged 15-49 (per 1,000 women) urban-rural residence, Virginia 1950 and 1970

| | | Fertility Structure | |
|---|---|---|---|
| | Age | 1950 | 1970 |
| Urban | 1950 | 1,272 | 1,750 |
| | 1970 | 1,1171 | 1,574 |
| Rural | 1950 | 1,933 | 1,947 |
| | 1970 | 1,914 | 1,914 |

Source:   Table 2.14.

## Marriage and Divorce

An important part of the determination of fertility is the marital status of the population. Although the incidence of illegitimacy has been increasing in Virginia in recent years (see Figure 2.5), legitimate births have accounted for about 90 percent of all births recorded in the state.

In contrast to the rate of birth, the rate of marriage in Virginia followed a moderately upward course since 1950. In that year there were 36,825 marriages, for a crude marriage rate of about 10.8 per 1,000 persons. In 1970 there were 51,964 marriages in the state, generating a crude marriage rate of 11.1[11] The rate and number of divorces also increased since 1950, when 5,941 divorces (1.7 per thousand) were recorded; in 1970 there were 11,879 divorces granted in Virginia (2.5 per thousand).

The heart of the matter, though, is not the number of events at any one time, but rather, the marital condition of the female population. Marital status by age and race is shown in Table 2.16.

For white women under the age of 30, the proportion most likely to have a child (those married, with spouse present) was somewhat lower in 1970 than 1950. The proportion of single (never married) women was lower among those aged 15-24 in 1970

[11] Marriage rates are based on the number of events that take place in the state, as opposed to the number of events occurring to residents of the state, as is done with births and deaths. The number of female Virginians married in 1970 was 35,798, and that of male Virginians 33,588.

Illegitimate Births
per 1000 Legitimate Births

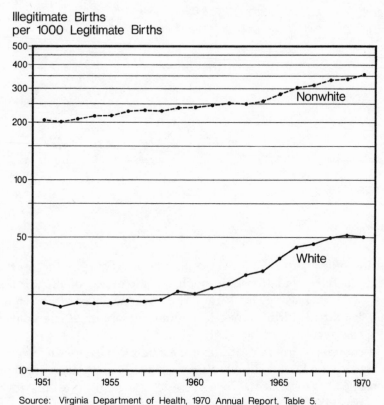

Source: Virginia Department of Health, 1970 Annual Report, Table 5.

Fig. 2.5.    Ratio of illegitimate to legitimate live births by race, Virginia, 1950–70

than in 1950, while the proportion in the "other" category (women who are or were married, but whose spouse is absent through separation, death, or divorce) rose considerably. Reflecting the increase in divorce, this latter category was actually higher for all age groups save those 45–49. However, the proportion of women who had never married was substantially lower in 1970 for all age groups 25 and over.

For nonwhite women, the proportion most likely to give birth was lower in all categories through 39. This resulted from a higher proportion of single women aged 15–29 and a higher proportion of women in the "other" category at all ages through 39. As was the case among white women, the relative number of single women declined in the older age groups.

Table 2.16.  Marital status of women by age and race, Virginia, 1950 and 1970 (percent)

| Age | White | | | | | | Nonwhite | | | | | |
| | 1950 | | | 1970 | | | 1950 | | | 1970 | | |
| | Single | Married Spouse Present | Other | Single | Married Spouse Present | Other | Single | Married Spouse Present | Other | Single | Married Spouse Present | Other |
|---|---|---|---|---|---|---|---|---|---|---|---|---|
| 15-19 | 80.1 | 17.8 | 2.1 | 83.6 | 13.1 | 3.3 | 82.6 | 14.2 | 3.2 | 90.0 | 6.4 | 3.6 |
| 20-24 | 28.2 | 65.7 | 6.1 | 30.7 | 60.2 | 9.1 | 39.3 | 47.8 | 12.9 | 42.5 | 41.4 | 16.1 |
| 25-29 | 10.2 | 82.7 | 7.1 | 9.3 | 80.8 | 9.9 | 18.4 | 63.6 | 18.0 | 19.5 | 61.0 | 19.5 |
| 30-34 | 8.1 | 84.4 | 7.5 | 5.2 | 84.9 | 9.9 | 12.8 | 68.8 | 18.4 | 11.8 | 65.5 | 22.7 |
| 35-39 | 7.6 | 83.7 | 8.7 | 4.3 | 85.5 | 10.2 | 10.2 | 66.9 | 22.9 | 8.8 | 65.2 | 26.0 |
| 40-44 | 8.1 | 81.3 | 10.6 | 4.1 | 83.0 | 12.9 | 9.2 | 63.7 | 27.1 | 7.7 | 63.7 | 28.6 |
| 45-49 | 8.5 | 76.1 | 15.4 | 4.1 | 81.8 | 14.1 | 7.5 | 59.6 | 32.9 | 7.3 | 64.4 | 28.3 |

Thus, among white women, increases in cumulative fertility may be partially explained by increases in the relative number of persons most likely to give birth. Although the rate of illegitimacy among whites more than doubled between 1950 and 1970, marital fertility accounted for 95 percent of all white fertility in 1970. Among nonwhites, the situation was somewhat different. The relative size of the population at maximum risk of childbearing declined at most age groups; fertility, however, rose fairly sharply. Some portion of this must be attributed to the rise in illegitimate fertility, which accounted for 17 percent of nonwhite births in 1951 and 26 percent in 1970.

Chapter 3

# Changes in the Distribution of Virginia's Population

## Population Redistribution in Virginia

During the two decades from April 1, 1950, to April 1, 1970, the population of Virginia increased by 40.2 percent, from 3,318,680 to 4,651,487.[1] The rate of growth was considerably faster than that recorded by the United States as a whole during the period (34.3 percent).

The rate of population growth for Virginia localities was by no means uniform. Typically, the fastest-growing areas were located in the suburban portions of Virginia's metropolitan areas, particularly those around Washington, D.C., Norfolk, Newport News–Hampton, and Richmond. The location and composition of these districts is shown in Figure 3.1. Local pockets of relatively high growth were also found in smaller urban centers of the state, particularly in and near the Shenandoah Valley. This includes cities such as Winchester, Harrisonburg, Staunton, Waynesboro, and Charlottesville.

Growth of population in the state was occurring, then, in two

---

[1] These figures differ from the official counts for 1960 and 1970 (3,966,949 and 4,648,494, respectively) due to correction for enumeration errors in both censuses. The 1960 correction was due solely to an overenumeration in Fairfax County (original count: 275,002; revised count: 262,482), while the 1970 correction was due to under-enumerations in Charlotte, Franklin and Richmond counties and the cities of Fairfax and Norton. The enumerated and revised counts for these areas are:

|  | Enumerated | Revised | Change |
|---|---|---|---|
| Charlotte County | 11,551 | 12,366 | 815 |
| Franklin County | 26,858 | 28,163 | 1,305 |
| Richmond County | 5,841 | 6,504 | 663 |
| Fairfax City | 21,970 | 22,009 | 39 |
| Norton City | 4,001 | 4,172 | 171 |
| State | 4,648,494 | 4,651,487 | 2,993 |

Not included in both cases are several enumeration errors involving the misallocation of population between two or more jurisdictions.*

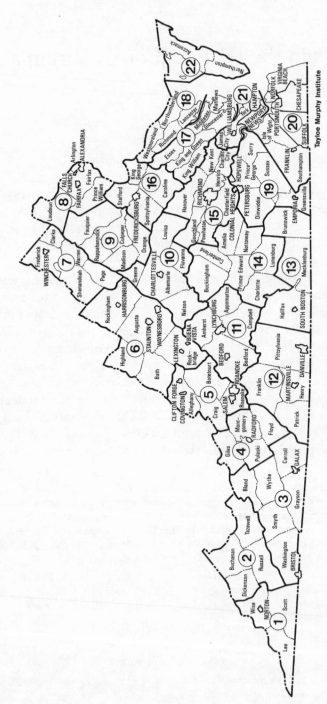

Fig. 3.1. Planning districts of Virginia

areas. First was the so-called urban corridor extending south from the Northern Virginia suburbs of Washington, D.C., to Richmond, then going southeast through the Peninsula cities of Williamsburg, Newport News, and Hampton, crossing Hampton Roads to the cities of Norfolk, Portsmouth, Chesapeake, and Virginia Beach. The other area may also be thought of as beginning in Northern Virginia, moving in a southwesterly direction through the central Piedmont and Shenandoah Valley. The overall result resembles a distorted wishbone, with the central nexus in Northern Virginia and the two arms spreading southeast and southwest from there.

The picture of the other areas in the state beyond this wishbone was quite the opposite. Generally, these areas, located in the extreme southwest, south central, and eastern portions of the state, were characterized by stagnant or declining populations. Table 3.1

Table 3.1. Components of population change in Virginia planning districts, 1960-70

| Area | Population 1960 | Population 1970 | Net Change 1960-70 | Percent Change | Percent Natural Increase | Net Migration(%) |
|------|-----------------|-----------------|--------------------|----------------|--------------------------|------------------|
| P.D. 1 | 100,212 | 84,645* | -15,567 | -15.5 | 6.0 | -21.5 |
| P.D. 2 | 128,016 | 112,497 | -15,519 | -12.1 | 9.5 | -21.6 |
| P.D. 3 | 160,065 | 159,412 | -653 | 0.4 | 7.2 | -7.6 |
| P.D. 4 | 97,223 | 114,833 | 17,600 | 18.1 | 12.4 | 5.7 |
| P.D. 5 | 297,332 | 231,175 | 23,843 | 11.5 | 8.9 | 2.6 |
| P.D. 6 | 166,585 | 186,306 | 19,721 | 11.8 | 9.7 | 2.1 |
| P.D. 7 | 97,045 | 106,372 | 9,327 | 9.6 | 9.4 | 0.2 |
| P.D. 8 | 601,811 | 921,237* | 319,426 | 53.0 | 26.5 | 26.5 |
| P.D. 9 | 65,609 | 72,222 | 6,613 | 10.1 | 9.9 | -0.2 |
| P.D. 10 | 98,049 | 115,235 | 17,186 | 17.5 | 12.1 | 5.4 |
| P.D. 11 | 150,877 | 165,997 | 15,120 | 10.0 | 9.4 | 0.6 |
| P.D. 12 | 205,213 | 217,874* | 12,661 | 6.2 | 11.3 | -5.1 |
| P.D. 13 | 88,818 | 82,563 | -6,255 | -7.0 | 7.3 | -14.3 |
| P.D. 14 | 80,205 | 76,245* | -3,960 | -4.9 | -6.0 | -10.9 |
| P.D. 15 | 461,993 | 547,542 | 85,549 | 18.5 | 12.2 | 6.3 |
| P.D. 16 | 64,302 | 77,425 | 13,123 | 20.4 | 15.5 | 4.9 |
| P.D. 17 | 36,776 | 36,348* | -428 | -1.2 | 4.9 | -6.1 |
| P.D. 18 | 45,501 | 47,609 | 2,108 | 4.6 | 5.0 | -0.4 |
| P.D. 19 | 141,471 | 161,059 | 19,588 | 13.8 | 14.0 | -0.2 |
| P.D. 20 | 666,841 | 769,371 | 102,530 | 15.4 | 16.5 | -1.1 |
| P.D. 21 | 242,874 | 319,081 | 76,207 | 31.4 | 20.9 | 10.5 |
| P.D. 22 | 47,601 | 43,446 | -4,155 | -8.7 | 4.4 | -13.1 |
| Virginia | 3,954,429 | 4,651,487 | 697,058 | 17.6 | 14.0 | 3.6 |

*Adjusted for underenumeration.

shows the 1960-70 population change and the components of change for the state's planning districts. The nexus of the wishbone may be considered to be at District 8 (Northern Virginia), which had the highest rate of population growth in the state from 1960 to 1970 (53.0 percent). The left arm of the wishbone would begin at District 9 (Rappahannock–Rapidan), go south to Districts 10 and 11 (Thomas Jefferson and Central Virginia), then west to District 6 (Central Shenandoah) and south through District 4 and 5 (New River Valley and Fifth planning districts, respectively). The right arm of the wishbone begins at District 16 (RADCO), then south to District 15 (Richmond Regional), then south and southeast through District 19 (Crater), 20, (Southeastern Virginia), and 21 (Peninsula). The districts on the left arm of the wishbone totaled 719,771 persons in 1970, an increase of 13.4 percent from the 1960 level of 634,808. The nexus of the wishbone grew from 601,811 in 1960 to 921,266 in 1970 (53.0 percent). The right arm of the wishbone included 1,577,481 persons in 1960 and 1,874,478 in 1970, an increase of 18.8 percent over the decade. In other words, Virginia's wishbone grew from 2,814,100 (71.2 percent of the state's total population) in 1960 to 3,515,515 in 1970 (75.6 percent of the state's population). The balance of the state then, 1,140,329 persons in 1960 but only 1,135,972 in 1970, had a net loss of 4,357 persons (0.4 percent).

Because the areas of high population growth in Virginia were essentially urban (or more precisely, suburban), it is not surprising that the share of population which was classified as urban rose from 47.0 percent in 1960 to 63.1 percent in 1970. The state's urban population rose by 88.1 percent from 1,560,115 in 1950 to 2,935,041 in 1970, while the rural population declined by 2.4 percent from the 1950 level of 1,758,565 to 1,716,436. It should be borne in mind that not all of this change reflected movement of population; in some cases it was merely the result of a reclassification of population from rural to urban.

Consider the case of the Norfolk-Portsmouth area (District 20). Between 1960 and 1970 the urban population grew by 144,581 persons while the rural population declined by 42,051. Part of this change was due to the formation of the cities of Chesapeake and Virginia Beach during the 1960s. Chesapeake was formed by the consolidation of the city of South Norfolk and Norfolk County; Virginia Beach, by the consolidation of the old city of Virginia Beach and Princess Anne County. In 1960 Norfolk County had 51,612 persons, of whom 28,135 were classified as urban and 23,477 were rural. To these were added 22,035 urban residents of South Norfolk. Thus, the 1960 boundaries of what is now the city of Chesapeake totaled 73,647 persons—23,477 rural and 50,170 urban. The 1970 population of Chesapeake was 89,580, of whom only 6,964 were classified as rural. Formerly rural areas became urban as the city grew and density of population increased.[2]

Two alternative ways of considering differential growth rates are a simple comparison of the rate of growth or a computation of the ratio of an area's share of state population in 1960 to its share of state population in 1970 (*population shift ratio*). These are, of course, merely two sides of the same coin. This is illustrated by Figure 3.2, which shows both variables. An area which grew slower than the entire state during the intercensal period would have a population shift ratio of less than 100. If the area had absolute population growth, its ratio would have fallen between 85.3 (the ratio of an area with constant population from 1960 to 1970) and 99.9. An area with population decline would have a ratio of less than 85.3. As can be readily seen, areas of declining population were concentrated in the southwestern, south central (Southside), and eastern parts of the state. Rates of population growth ranged from a gain of 121.5 percent in Prince William County to a loss of 21.8 percent in the city of Suffolk. The fastest-growing areas were all in metropolitan areas and were all suburban in character with the exception of the city of Hampton. Because of annexations,

[2] A similar situation was true for Virginia Beach. The 1960 data show Princess Anne County to include 77,127 persons (43,720 urban and 33,407 rural) and the old city of Virginia Beach 8,091 (all urban). The 1970 data for the new city of Virginia Beach show 166,729 urban residents and 5,377 rural residents. The analysis for Chesapeake is confused also by an annexation of 12,361 urban residents (1970 count) by the city of Portsmouth. Additionally, the 2,500 population criterion used by the census caused Pleasant Hill in Nansemond County to go from an urban to a rural status (1960 population 2,636, 1970 population 2,277) and caused Smithfield in Isle of Wight County to go from a rural status to an urban status (1960 population 917, 1970 population 2,713).

growth in many suburban localities is understated by analysis of unadjusted census data. Table 3.2 attempts to rectify this distortion by holding the boundaries at the preannexation (1960) point. The most striking difference occurs in Chesterfield County, which lost over 47,000 persons to the city of Richmond on January 1, 1970. Thus the enumerated count shows a relatively modest 7.9-percent increase for Chesterfield; adjusting for the annexation, the population of Chesterfield County (1960 boundaries) grew by nearly 75 percent. Similar, though less dramatic, changes can be seen for Albemarle and Prince George counties and the city of Chesapeake (which lost population to Portsmouth at the time of its incorporation). Incorporating the adjustments shown in Table 3.2, the fifteen fastest- and fifteen slowest-growing localities in the state are shown in Table 3.3.

## Urban-Rural Trends

Due to changes in the definition of *urban* since 1950, most of the analysis in the next three sections deals only with the 1960-70 period. Of the ninety-eight cities, counties, and city-county groupings that are being employed in this analysis, nearly half (forty-eight) were entirely rural according to the census definition The Bureau of the Census defines the *urban population* as "all persons living in urbanized areas and in places of 2,500 inhabitants or more outside urbanized areas. More specifically, the urban population consists of all persons living in (a) places of 2,500 inhabitants or more incorporated as cities, villages, boroughs . . . , and towns . . . , but excluding those living in the rural portions of extended cities; (b) unincorporated places of 2,500 inhabitants or more; and (c) other territories, incorporated or unincorporated included in urbanized areas."[3] All population not classified as urban is rural (see Figure 3.3).

Rural population may be subdivided into farm and nonfarm

[3] U.S. Bureau of the Census, *1970 Census of Population: General Social and Economic Characteristics: Virginia* (Washington, D.C.: U.S. Government Printing Office, 1972), App. pp. 1-2.

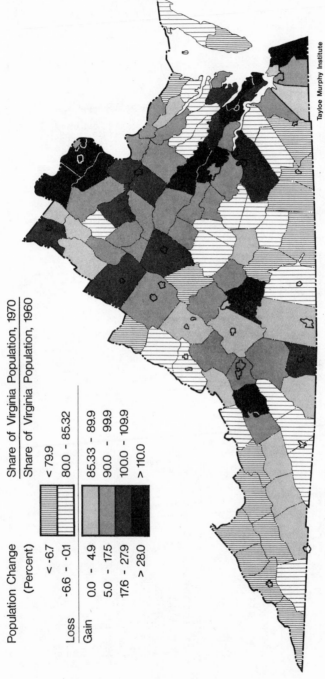

Population Change
(Percent)

Share of Virginia Population, 1970
—————————————————————
Share of Virginia Population, 1960

Loss

< -6.7       < 79.9

-6.6 - -0.1    80.0 - 85.32

Gain

0.0 - 4.9      85.33 - 89.9

5.0 - 17.5     90.0 - 99.9

17.6 - 27.9    100.0 - 109.9

> 28.0        > 110.0

Tayloe Murphy Institute

Fig. 3.2.    Relative rates of population growth by Virginia city and county, 1960–70

Table 3.2. Effect of annexation upon growth rate of involved areas, Virginia, 1960-70 (percent)

| Annexing Area | Annexed Area | Enumerated growth rate | | Actual growth rate | |
|---|---|---|---|---|---|
| | | Annexor | Annexee | Annexor* | Annexee* |
| Alexandria | Fairfax | 21.9 | 73.9 | 21.6 | 74.0 |
| Charlottesville | Albemarle | 32.1 | 22.0 | 1.1 | 51.4 |
| Clifton Forge | Alleghany | 4.4 | 2.7 | -7.9 | 8.1 |
| Danville | Pittsylvania | -0.4 | 0.8 | -1.4 | 1.7 |
| Galax | Grayson & Carroll | 19.5 | -5.0 | -14.0 | -0.7 |
| Harrisonburg | Rockingham | 22.6 | 18.3 | 3.3 | 24.0 |
| Hopewell | Prince George | 31.2 | 43.5 | 16.9 | 56.1 |
| Lynchburg | Bedford | -1.3 | 5.5 | -1.8 | 6.4 |
| Martinsville | Henry | 4.5 | 26.2 | 0.2 | 28.2 |
| Norton | Wise | -20.2 | -17.5 | -20.6 | -17.5 |
| Portsmouth | Chesapeake | -3.3 | 21.6 | -14.1 | 38.4 |
| Radford | Montgomery | 23.7 | 43.2 | 22.9 | 43.5 |
| Richmond | Chesterfield | 13.5 | 7.9 | -8.0 | 74.3 |
| Roanoke | Roanoke | -5.1 | 9.2 | -5.5 | 17.7 |
| Salem | Roanoke | 36.9 | 9.2 | 6.2 | |
| South Boston | Halifax | 15.3 | -10.6 | -8.5 | -6.4 |
| Williamsburg | York & James City | 32.7 | 54.1 | 1.8 | 60.5 |

* With 1960 boundaries.

Table 3.3. Fastest and slowest growing localities in Virginia; 1960-70 (adjusted for annexation)

| Fastest Growing | | Slowest Growing | |
|---|---|---|---|
| Locality | Percent Change, 1960-70 | Locality | Percent Change, 1960-70 |
| Prince William County[a]/ | 121.5 | Suffolk City | -21.8 |
| Virginia Beach City[b]/ | 102.5 | Highland County | -21.5 |
| Chesterfield County[c]/ | 74.3 | Lee County | -21.3 |
| Fairfax County[a, d]/ | 74.0 | Norton City | -20.6 |
| Fairfax City[a]/ | 61.7 | Dickenson County | -20.5 |
| James City-York counties[e]/ | 60.5 | Wise County | -17.5 |
| Colonial Heights City[f]/ | 57.5 | Northampton County | -14.9 |
| Prince George County[f]/ | 56.1 | Portsmouth City[b]/ | -14.4 |
| Albemarle County | 51.4 | Galax City | -14.0 |
| Loudoun County[a]/ | 51.3 | Bristol City[g]/ | -13.3 |
| Stafford County | 45.7 | Buchanan County | -12.7 |
| Montgomery County | 43.5 | Tazewell County | -11.1 |
| Chesapeake City[b]/ | 38.4 | Greensville County | -9.6 |
| Hanover County[c]/ | 36.0 | Bland County | -9.4 |
| Hampton City[e]/ | 35.3 | Northumberland County | -9.3 |

[a]/ In Washington, D. C., SMSA.
[b]/ In Norfolk-Virginia Beach-Portsmouth (Va.-N.C.) SMSA
[c]/ In Richmond SMSA.
[d]/ Adjusted for separation of city of Fairfax in 1961.
[e]/ In Newport News-Hampton SMSA.
[f]/ In Petersburg-Hopewell-Colonial Heights SMSA.
[g]/ In Kingsport-Bristol (Tenn.-Va.) SMSA.

residents.[4] According to the official 1970 enumeration of Virginia's population, the urban population was 2,931,154, the rural nonfarm population was 1,450,057, and the rural farm population was 267,283. However, the Bureau of the Census recently revised the distribution of rural farm–rural nonfarm population. The revised data show that the rural nonfarm population was 1,524,556 in 1970 and the rural farm population 192,784. Because no characteristics of these persons are available, the

[4] "The farm population consists of persons living on places of 10 or more acres from which sales of farm products amounted to $50 or more in the preceding calendar year or in places of less than 10 acres from which sales of farm products amounted to $250 or more in the preceding year" (ibid., App. p. 2). All other rural population is rural nonfarm.

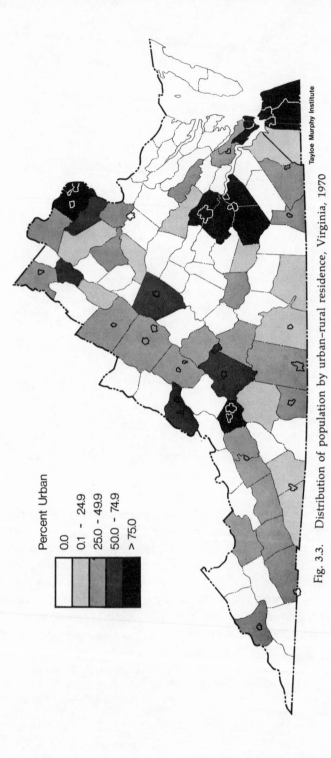

Percent Urban

0.0
0.1 - 24.9
25.0 - 49.9
50.0 - 74.9
> 75.0

Fig. 3.3.    Distribution of population by urban–rural residence, Virginia, 1970

Tayloe Murphy Institute

analysis here is based on the data originally published by the
Census Bureau. Although the absolute numbers are different,
it is unlikely that the percentage distribution of the various
demographic indicators analyzed changed to any considerable
extent. [5]

In common with the rest of the South, Virginia has lagged
behind the nation in the proportion of its population residing
in urban areas. [6] In 1950, 47.0 percent of Virginia's population
was classified as urban, as compared to the United States proportion of 64.0 percent. By 1970 Virginia's urban population had
increased to 63.1 percent of the state total, while the United States
had increased to 73.5 percent urban. In the period 1950–70
the proportion of the state's population classified as urban increased
by 34 percent, as compared to a 15–percent increase for the nation;
yet Virginia's population was still about 10 percent less urban than
the country as a whole.

As shown in Table 3.4, 55.8 percent of the state's population
was classified as urban in 1960; however, only five planning
districts (nos. 5, 8, 15, 20, and 21) were above the state
average, and eight planning districts (nos. 1, 2, 9, 13, 14,
17, 18, and 22) were below 20 percent urban. In 1970 the
same five planning districts which were above average in 1960
were still above the state average, and one additional district,
District 19, was also slightly above average. Planning Districts 5,
8, 15, 19, 20, and 21 each contain a part of a Standard Metropolitan Statistical Area (SMSA), which explains their high
proportion of urban population. Each of the eight planning
districts below 20 percent urban in 1960 remained below 20 percent
in 1970.

During this decade seventeen of the state's twenty-two planning districts increased their proportions, three planning districts
(nos. 3, 7, and 21) decreased, and two planning districts (nos.
17 and 22) remained the same (at zero percent urban).

[5] See U.S. Bureau of the Census, *Rural Population by Farm-Nonfarm Residence for
Counties in the United States: 1970* (Washington, D.C.: U.S. Government Printing
Office, 1972).

[6] The reader should be aware that a given area may change from 100 percent
rural to 100 percent urban if it becomes part of an urbanized area.

Table 3.4.   Urban-Rural mix in Virginia planning districts, 1960-70

| Area | 1960 Population Urban | 1960 Population Rural | 1970 Population Urban | 1970 Population Rural | Percent Urban 1960 | Percent Urban 1970 |
|------|-------|-------|-------|-------|------|------|
| P.D. 1 | 12,315 | 87,897 | 11,216 | 73,600 | 12.3 | 13.2 |
| P.D. 2 | 12,198 | 115,818 | 14,297 | 98,220 | 9.5 | 12.7 |
| P.D. 3 | 44,019 | 116,046 | 42,265 | 117,147 | 27.5 | 26.5 |
| P.D. 4 | 33,071 | 64,162 | 39,116 | 75,717 | 34.0 | 34.1 |
| P.D. 5 | 141,082 | 66,250 | 172,182 | 58,993 | 68.0 | 74.5 |
| P.D. 6 | 63,679 | 102,906 | 72,466 | 113,620 | 38.2 | 39.0 |
| P.D. 7 | 26,073 | 70,972 | 26,466 | 79,906 | 26.9 | 24.9 |
| P.D. 8 | 493,474 | 108,337 | 811,932 | 109,305 | 82.0 | 88.1 |
| P.D. 9 | 6,477 | 59,132 | 12,851 | 59,371 | 9.9 | 17.8 |
| P.D. 10 | 29,427 | 68,622 | 38,880 | 76,355 | 30.0 | 33.7 |
| P.D. 11 | 68,539 | 82,338 | 79,561 | 86,436 | 45.4 | 47.9 |
| P.D. 12 | 72,109 | 133,104 | 79,119 | 140,060 | 35.1 | 36.1 |
| P.D. 13 | 11,750 | 77,068 | 13,656 | 68,907 | 13.2 | 16.5 |
| P.D. 14 | 7,952 | 72,253 | 7,743 | 69,317 | 9.9 | 10.0 |
| P.D. 15 | 339,209 | 122,784 | 429,048 | 118,494 | 73.4 | 78.4 |
| P.D. 16 | 13,639 | 50,663 | 14,450 | 62,975 | 21.2 | 22.9 |
| P.D. 17 | -- | 36,776 | -- | 37,011 | 0 | 0 |
| P.D. 18 | -- | 45,501 | 2,600 | 45,009 | 0 | 5.5 |
| P.D. 19 | 69,767 | 71,704 | 101,922 | 59,137 | 49.3 | 63.3 |
| P.D. 20 | 543,129 | 123,712 | 687,710 | 81,661 | 81.4 | 89.4 |
| P.D. 21 | 215,706 | 27,168 | 277,332 | 41,749 | 88.8 | 86.9 |
| P.D. 22 | -- | 47,601 | -- | 43,446 | 0 | 0 |
| Virginia | 2,204,913 | 1,749,516 | 2,935,012 | 1,716,436 | 55.8 | 63.1 |

The greatest increase occurred in Planning District 19, which changed from 49.3 percent urban in 1960 to 63.3 percent urban in 1970. The majority of this change was located in Prince George and Dinwiddie counties. Both of these counties were 100 percent rural in 1960; in 1970 they were considered to be 42.7 and 38.0 percent urban, respectively.

Planning District 20, the most highly urbanized district in the state in 1970, changed from 81.4 percent urban in 1960 to 89.4 percent urban in 1970. This change was primarily located in two cities, Chesapeake and Virginia Beach. The city of Chesapeake increased from 68.1 percent urban in 1960 92.2 percent in 1970, and the city of Virginia Beach increased from 59.6 percent in 1960 to 96.9 percent in 1970.

## Metropolitan–Nonmetropolitan Comparisons

The metropolitan population is that living within the boundaries of a Standard Metropolitan Statistical Area. This analysis deals only with those areas which were metropolitan at the time of the 1970 census (see Table 3.5). Since then, there have been numerous additions of localities to existing Virginia metropolitan areas, as well as the creation of a new area located in Virginia and Tennessee.[7]

As would be expected, the metropolitan areas were rather heavily urbanized. In 1970 the total metropolitan population in Virginia was 2,846,034 (or 61.2 percent of the state total). Of this, 1,124,889 (39.5 percent) were located in central cities; 1,374,223 (48.3 percent) lived in other urban portions of metropolitan areas;

[7] The newly designated metropolitan localities are:

| Additions to existing areas | Total population | Central city | Other urban | Rural nonfarm | Rural farm |
|---|---|---|---|---|---|
| Lynchburg | | | | | |
|   Appomattox Co. | 9,784 | 0 | 0 | 8,351 | 1,433 |
| Newport News–Hampton SMSA | | | | | |
|   Gloucester Co. | 14,059 | 0 | 0 | 13,351 | 708 |
|   James City Co. | 17,853 | 0 | 1,400 | 15,976 | 477 |
|   Williamsburg City | 9,069 | 0 | 9,069 | 0 | 0 |
| Norfolk–Virginia Beach–Portsmouth SMSA | | | | | |
|   Nansemond City | 35,166 | 0 | 0 | 31,501 | 3,665 |
|   Suffolk City | 9,858 | 0 | 9,858 | 0 | 0 |
| Richmond SMSA | | | | | |
|   Charles City Co. | 6,158 | 0 | 0 | 5,701 | 457 |
|   Goochland Co. | 10,069 | 0 | 0 | 9,555 | 514 |
|   Powhatan Co. | 7,696 | 0 | 0 | 6,950 | 746 |
| Roanoke SMSA | | | | | |
|   Botetourt Co. | 18,193 | 0 | 0 | 16,165 | 2,028 |
|   Craig Co. | 3,524 | 0 | 0 | 2,845 | 679 |
| *New areas* | | | | | |
| Kingsport–Bristol, Tenn.–Va. SMSA (Va. Portion) | | | | | |
|   Scott Co. | 24,376 | 0 | 0 | 16,089 | 8,287 |
|   Washington Co. | 40,835 | 0 | 4,704 | 27,978 | 8,153 |
|   Bristol City | 14,857 | 14,857 | 0 | 0 | 0 |

Note: Nansemond County was incorporated as a city on July 1, 1972.

Table 3.5. Metropolitan-nonmetropolitan population (by 1970
difinitions) by race, Virginia, 1960-70

|  | Total | White | Black | Other |
|---|---|---|---|---|
| **1970** | | | | |
| Total | 4,648,494 | 3,761,514 | 861,368 | 25,612 |
| Metropolitan | 2,846,034 | 2,311,839 | 512,420 | 21,775 |
| Central city | 1,124,889 | 758,893 | 356,451 | 9,545 |
| Other | 1,721,145 | 1,552,946 | 155,969 | 12,230 |
| Nonmetropolitan | 1,802,460 | 1,449,675 | 348,948 | 3,837 |
| **1960** | | | | |
| Total | 3,966,949 | 3,142,443 | 816,258 | 8,248 |
| Metropolitan | 2,226,505 | 1,772,959 | 447,124 | 6,422 |
| Central city | 1,041,760 | 725,907 | 312,620 | 3,233 |
| Other | 1,184,475 | 1,047,052 | 134,504 | 3,189 |
| Nonmetropolitan | 1,740,444 | 1,369,484 | 369,134 | 1,826 |
| **Percent Change 1960-70** | | | | |
| Total | 17.18% | 19.70% | 5.53% | 210.52% |
| Metropolitan | 27.83 | 30.39 | 14.60 | 239.07 |
| Central city | 7.98 | 4.54 | 14.01 | 195.24 |
| Other | 45.28 | 48.32 | 15.96 | 283.51 |
| Nonmetropolitan | 3.56 | 5.86 | -5.47 | 110.13 |

309,737 (10.9 percent) lived in rural areas (but not on a farm); and the remaining 37,185 (1.3 percent) lived on farms located within metropolitan areas. Those 1,802,460 Virginians not living in metropolitan areas comprised the nonmetropolitan population. Of these, 23.9 percent lived in urban, nonmetropolitan areas; 63.3 percent lived in rural nonfarm areas; and 12.8 percent were farm residents.

The metropolitan population of Virginia (1970 boundaries) increased by some 27.6 percent from 1960 to 1970. In 1960 a total of 2,229,574 persons lived in⁻areas classified as metropolitan in 1970. The overall increase of 616,460 persons living in these areas by 1970 represented 88.4 percent of Virginia's overall population growth. Conversely, the population of nonmetropolitan Virginia grew by only 4.5 percent, from 1,724,855 in 1960 to the 1970 level of 1,802,460.

The rate of growth was by no means uniform for all metropolitan areas. Although all seven areas recorded increases of population of 10 percent or more, the actual changes ranged from 11.5 percent in the Lynchburg SMSA to 50.0 percent in the Virginia portion of the Washington, D.C., SMSA; relatively slow growth was also recorded in the Roanoke SMSA (14.3 percent). Growth at rates higher than that recorded for the entire state (17.6 percent) occurred not only near Washington but also in the Newport News–Hampton SMSA (30.1 percent), the Petersburg–Hopewell–Colonial Heights SMSA (20.7 percent), and the Richmond SMSA (18.9 percent). Growth in the Norfolk–Virginia Beach–Portsmouth SMSA took place at a rate equal to that of the entire state.

## Central City–Suburban Comparisons

In 1960, 1,058,652 persons, or 47.5 percent of the metropolitan population, resided in the central cities. By 1970 the number had increased to 1,148,360, but the proportion had declined to 40.3 percent. In a sense, this considerably understates suburban growth because of the sizable annexations which took place in Portsmouth and Richmond. If the annexed portion of these areas is subtracted, the overall central city population in 1970 would have been 1,088,737, an increase of only 2.8 percent over the 1960 level. Bearing these corrections for annexation in mind, the only sizable increases in central city population occurred in the Peninsula cities of Newport News and Hampton (21.6 and 35.3 percent, respectively) and the smaller cities of Colonial Heights and Hopewell (57.5 and 31.2 percent, respectively). The population of the city of Norfolk grew by only 1.0 percent during the decade, from 304,869 to 307,951. Fairly small declines were recorded in Lynchburg (–1.3 percent), Petersburg (–1.8 percent), and Roanoke (–5.1 percent). More considerable declines occurred in Richmond (–8.0 percent) and Portsmouth (–14.1 percent) if the effects of annexation in these cities are taken into account.

Growth in suburban areas was uniformly high, with only a few exceptions. Two of these were Arlington County and the city of Falls Church, in Northern Virginia, and had as many characteristics of the central city as they did of the typical suburb. The rate of growth in these jurisdictions was 6.7 and 5.7 percent, respectively. With the exception of Amherst County in the Lynchburg SMSA (13.6–percent increase) and Dinwiddie

County in the Petersburg–Hopewell–Colonial Heights SMSA (12.9 percent), the rate of growth in all other suburban portions of Virginia metropolitan areas exceeded 20 percent.[8]

## Racial Composition and Degree of Urbanization

This section examines the racial composition of the state in 1970 in terms of relative numbers of whites and nonwhites classified as urban and rural, as metropolitan and nonmetropolitan, and as central city and suburban residents. Due to the overall racial composition of Virginia, most of the focus is placed on white–black relationships. Brief mention is made, however, of the population of other races and of the Spanish–speaking population.

### Urban–Rural Residence

It has previously been established that 2,934,841 of Virginia's 4,648,494 (enumerated) residents were urban dwellers. Of these, 2,395,091 (81.6 percent) were white, 518,008 (17.7 percent) were black, and 21,742 (0.7 percent) were members of other racial categories. By comparing these data to the overall racial composition of the state (80.9, 18.5, and 0.6 percent, respectively), it is evident that the white and other race categories were somewhat more urbanized than was the black population. Conversely, blacks comprised a relatively larger share of the total rural population (343,360 out of 1,713,653, or 20.0 percent) than did either whites (1,366,423, or 79.8 percent) or persons of other races (3,870, or 0.2 percent).

The Spanish–speaking population was overwhelmingly urban (42,673 of 48,742, or 87.5 percent); most of the remainder was rural nonfarm (10.9 percent), with only a small fraction being farm residents (1.6 percent). In summary, the urban–rural residence pattern of Virginia, by race, shows that, for whites, 63.6 percent lived in urban areas, 30.7 percent lived in rural areas but not

[8] This allows for the loss of 47,262 persons from Chesterfield County by means of annexation by the city of Richmond on January 1, 1970.

on farms, and 5.7 percent lived on farms. For blacks, 60.1 percent were urban, 33.5 percent were rural nonfarm, and 6.4 percent were rural farm. Finally, for persons of other races, these shares were 86.2, 11.6, and 0.2 percent, respectively.

## Metropolitan–Nonmetropolitan Residence

The overall racial composition of the metropolitan population was quite similar to that of the urban population, although the share of the population which was white (81.2 percent) was slightly lower, while the shares of blacks (18.0 percent) and persons of other races (0.8 percent) were slightly higher. Comparing the urban and rural portions of metropolitan areas, the urban sector (2,502,373, or 87.9 percent of the total metropolitan population of 2,846,034) was 81.0 percent white, 18.2 percent black, and 0.8 percent of other races. The small rural portions of metropoitan areas (343,661) was somewhat more heavily white (82.7 percent), with correspondingly smaller shares of blacks (16.9 percent) and persons of other races (0.4 percent).

The nonmetropolitan population (1,802,460), not surprisingly, showed a greater share of blacks (19.4 percent) than did the metropolitan population; conversely the share of whites (80.4 percent) and persons of other races (0.2 percent) was somewhat smaller in nonmetropolitan areas. In further contrast to metropolitan areas, the white nonmetropolitan population was more heavily urbanized than the black nonmetropolitan population. For the urban portions of the nonmetropolitan population, the proportion white was 85.1 percent, compared with only 79.0 percent for the rural portions of the nonmetropolitan population. The situation was the reverse for the black population; blacks comprised 14.7 percent of the urban nonmetropolitan population but 20.8 percent of the rural portion. Persons of other races represented 0.3 percent of the urban portion and 0.2 percent of the rural portion.

A trend which has become rather evident in many portions of the nation is the so-called flight to the suburbs by white residents, leaving central cities with a large number of non-white residents. In 1970 in Virginia 758,893 of 1,124,889 residents of central cities were white. This represents only 67.5 percent of the total. Blacks represented 31.7 percent of the central city population, while persons of other races accounted for the remaining 0.8 percent. In what might be called the suburbs (that is, non-central city portions of metropolitan areas), 90.2 percent of the population was white, 9.1 percent was black, and 0.7 percent was of other racial groups. Between 1960 and 1970 the white population of central cities (1970 definition)[9] grew by 4.5 percent, while the black population increased by 14.0 percent. The white population of central cities would in fact have decreased had it not been for the annexation of 45,739 whites (and 1,523 others) by the city of Richmond in January 1970.

The situation in suburban areas was quite different. The white population of these areas grew by 48.3 percent from 1960 to 1970 while the black population grew by 16.0 percent. In 1960 there were 3.97 whites to every one black in Virginia's metropolitan areas. This ratio was 2.32 in central cities and 7.78 in the suburbs. In 1970 the overall ratio had risen to 4.51; however, the ratio in the central city had fallen to 2.13, while that of the suburbs had risen to 9.96. Of the total population increase recorded among the white population in Virginia (619,071 persons), 81.7 percent occurred in the suburban portions of the state's metropolitan areas and 5.3 percent occurred in the central cities. Of the total increase recorded among the black population (45,110 persons), 97.2 percent occurred in central cities and 47.6 percent occurred in suburban areas. The nonmetropolitan black population declined by 44.8 percent (see Table 3.5).

The number of persons of races other than black or white in Virginia more than tripled from 1960 to 1970. This racial group was heavily metropolitan to begin with, and its growth rate was much greater in metropolitan areas (239 percent) than in

[9] For census purposes, the following cities were the central cities of their respective SMSAs on April 1, 1970: Lynchburg, Hampton, Newport News, Norfolk, Portsmouth, Colonial Heights, Petersburg, Richmond, and Roanoke. Since then, Virginia Beach has been added as a central city to the Norfolk–Portsmouth SMSA, and Hopewell has been added as a central city to the Petersburg–Colonial Heights SMSA.

nonmetropolitan areas (110 percent). Within metropolitan areas, growth was much greater in the suburbs (284 percent) than in the central cities (195 percent).

Finally, almost all (88.9 percent) of Virginia's 48,742 Spanish-speaking persons lived in metropolitan areas. Of those 43,353 residing in metropolitan areas, only 27.0 percent (11,716) resided in the central city.

## Trends in Residence by Size of Place

Data using comparable definitions of places are available for the years 1950, 1960, and 1970. Figure 3.4 and Table 3.6 summarize the trends in distribution of population by size of place during this period. What is most evident is the steadily decreasing share of the population that does not live in a community. The proportion was 48.9 percent in 1950; it fell to 46.4 percent in 1960, and even further to 40.8 percent in 1970.

There should be more than the usual caution exercised in analyzing these data for Virginia due to annexation and the creation of new cities through consolidation of city-county groups. The four considerations that have taken place since 1950[10] are treated here as though they had existed from

---

[10] In addition to the Chesapeake and Virginia Beach consolidations mentioned previously, consolidations took place between the city of Hampton and Elizabeth City County in 1952 and between the cities of Newport News and Warwick in 1958. The 1950 enumerated population for these areas was as follows:

| | | | |
|---|---|---|---|
| *Norfolk County | 99,937 | *Virginia Beach | 5,390 |
| *South Norfolk | 10,434 | *Princess Anne County | 36,887 |
| **Chesapeake | 110,371 | **Virginia Beach | 42,277 |
| *Hampton | 5,966 | *Newport News | 42,277 |
| *Elizabeth City Co. | 55,028 | *Warwick | 39,875 |
| **Hampton | 60,994 | **Newport News | 82,233 |

*Old definition.
**Current definition.

Note: There were annexations by the cities of Norfolk and Portsmouth from the cities of Chesapeake and Virginia Beach since 1950.

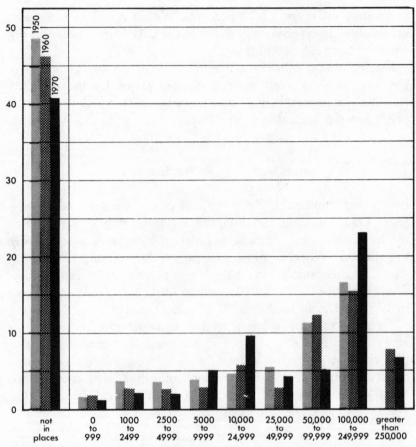

Fig. 3.4.    Distribution of population by size of place, Virginia, 1950–70

the start, so that the data in published census reports were
changed as follows: for 1960 one place of 10–25,000 population
(the city of South Norfolk) and one place of 5–10,000 (the city
of Virginia Beach) were deleted, and two places of 50–100,000
population (present-day cities of Chesapeake and Virginia
Beach) were added. For 1950 two places of 5–10,000 (the
cities of Hampton and Virginia Beach), one place of 10–25,000
(the city of South Norfolk), and one place of 25–50,000
(the city of Newport News) were deleted; added to the 1950
listing were one place of 25–50,000 (Virginia Beach–Princess

Table 3.6.  Distribution of population by size of place, Virginia, 1950-70

| Population Size | 1950 | | 1960 | | 1970 | |
|---|---|---|---|---|---|---|
| | Percentage of Total Population | Cumulative Percentage | Percentage of Total Population | Cumulative Percentage | Percentage of Total Population | Cumulative Percentage |
| 250,000 + | 0 | 0 | 7.71 | 7.71 | 6.62 | 6.62 |
| 100,000-249,999 | 16.70 | 16.70 | 15.42 | 23.13 | 23.17 | 29.79 |
| 50,000-99,999 | 11.36 | 28.06 | 12.38 | 35.51 | 5.07 | 34.86 |
| 25,000-49,999 | 5.61 | 33.67 | 2.84 | 38.35 | 4.29 | 39.15 |
| 10,000-24,999 | 4.64 | 38.31 | 5.76 | 44.11 | 9.65 | 48.80 |
| 5,000-9,999 | 3.89 | 42.20 | 2.75 | 46.86 | 5.06 | 53.86 |
| 2,500-4,999 | 3.60 | 45.80 | 2.59 | 49.45 | 2.01 | 55.87 |
| 1,000-2,499 | 3.71 | 49.51 | 2.75 | 52.20 | 2.11 | 57.98 |
| 0-999 | 1.59 | 51.10 | 1.43 | 53.63 | 1.23 | 59.21 |
| Not in communities | 48.90 | 100.00 | 46.37 | 100.00 | 40.79 | 100.00 |

Anne County), two places of 50–100,000 (Hampton–Elizabeth City County and Newport News–Warwick County), and one place of 100,000–250,000 (South Norfolk–Norfolk County).

The data in Table 3.6 show sizable increases in the share of population living in places of 100,000 or more persons. In 1950 about one-sixth of Virginia's population lived in places of this size group; by 1970 the proportion had grown to nearly one-third. Most of the increase was due to expansion of population in cities of 100,000–250,000 people. The number of such places grew from three in 1950 (Norfolk, Richmond, and what is now Chesapeake) to seven in 1970 (Richmond, Newport News, Hampton, Portsmouth, Virginia Beach, Alexandria, and Arlington County).[11] Population in places of 25,000–100,000 declined from 1950 to 1970 primarily due to population growth in cities which were in this category in 1950. Such was the case of Newport News, Hampton, Portsmouth, Virginia Beach, and Alexandria. There was also considerable expansion of population in places of 5,000–25,000 people. A great deal of this expansion is attributable to the creation of new subdivisions in outlying portions of metropolitan areas, especially in Chesterfield, Fairfax, Henrico, Loudoun, and Prince William counties. On the other hand, population in places of 1,000–5,000 persons steadily declined, because of the expansion of subdivisions into larger-size categories and the decline of isolated rural communities. The latter factor, as well as some annexation by small towns, may also explain the expansion of population in places with less than 1,000 persons.[12]

[11] Arlington County, which has no incorporated places, is defined in its entirety by the Bureau of Census as an urban place.

[12] An examination of places with 0–999 population reveals that 1 did not exist in 1960; 6 had over 1,000 population in 1960 but declined in size into this category by 1970; 49 increased in size but did not surpass 1,000 persons, (of these, annexation occurred in 11 localities); 58 declined in size; and 2 remained the same.

# Chapter 4

# Demographic and Social Characteristics

## Changes in Age Composition

Of all the sets of variables which result from census enumeration, one of the most crucial and at the same time most useful for policy makers and planners is the age composition of the population. It is well known among students of population that the age composition of a population is a direct function of the rates of fertility, mortality, and migration which that population has experienced in the past. Changes in these rates will have quite predictable and often significant impact on the age composition of an area.

Throughout the fifties a high fertility rate was maintained as the postwar baby boom peaked in 1958. Consequently in 1960 the segment of Virginia's population under 20 years old was larger than it had been in 1950. While not much change was reflected in the 0-4 cohort (an increase of 0.1 percent), the 5-9 cohort increased in its proportion of population 1.2 percent, and the 10-14 cohort 1.7 percent. The rate of absolute change for all ages in the state was 19.5 percent, and the 0-4 absolute change was very close to this (20.1 percent). However, the population increases in the 5-9 cohort (33.6 percent) and in the 10-14 cohort (44.9 percent) were far above the state average.

Cohorts including ages 20 through 39 increased less than the overall state rate, thus reducing their relative share of the population. Increases for all other cohorts were above the state norm, but only three were more than 10 percent greater. The 45-49 age group grew 31.2 percent; the 70-74 cohort, 33.7 percent; and that of 75 years and older, 47.2 percent.

Changes in the age composition of Virginia from 1960 to 1970 reflect considerable change in the state's levels of fertility and migration. The low fertility of the latter portion of the decade (relative to the previous fifteen to twenty years)[1] resulted in

[1] Serow, "Fertility in Virginia, 1940-1970."

a much smaller share of the population aged 0–4 in 1970 than in 1960 (8.4 and 11.6 percent, respectively). There were some 66,000 fewer persons in the 1970 cohort than in the 1960 cohort. Close examination of census data reveals that much of Virginia's total population increase occurred among persons aged 10–29. Altogether, the state's population grew by 682,000 persons (using official rather than corrected counts). Of this increase, 436,000 was represented by persons in this twenty–year age group. In 1960 persons 10–29 accounted for 31.7 percent of the population; in 1970, 36.4 percent. This great upsurge was due to two factors: the relatively high fertility of the 1950s and late 1940s (the postwar baby boom) and the relatively large amount of in–migration by young adults into the state during the decade. Net migration into Virginia was about 162,000 from 1960 to 1970. Of these, 113,000 were persons aged 10–29.[2]

In addition to the 10–29 age group, there was also substantial growth of population in all cohorts aged 45 and over (see Table 4.1 and Figure 4.1). Although the relative growth rate of the population 45 and over was rather high (27.2 percent), the absolute growth (273,000 persons) was not enough to prevent the greater growth of the 10–29 age group from lowering the median age of population from 27.1 years in 1960 to 26.8 years in 1970. The growth of the older segment of the population is likely to continue in the future. Barring dramatic upsurges in fertility and increases to the already high rate of net in–migration, the population of the state is likely to become somewhat older in ensuing years.

The *dependency ratio* is a device for measuring the ratio of non–producers to producers within a particular population. Dividing the two nonproducing age groups of 0–14 and 65–plus by the producing population, aged 15–64, yields the dependency ratio, which is conventionally multiplied by 100 to convert the ratio to a percentage. This measure is considered crude because

[2] These data are from Serow and Spar, *Virginia's Population: A Decade of Change. II. Net Migration for State Planning Districts*, p. 7. Estimates which vary slightly from these are found in Richard A. Engels, et al., *Net Migration in the Southeast, 1960–1970* (Knoxville and Memphis: University of Tennessee and Memphis State University, 1973). The total net migration to Virginia is estimated in the latter study to be some 153,000. Of this, 105,000 stems from the 10–29 age group.

Table 4.1. Age distribution of Virginia's population, 1950–70

| Age Group | 1950 | | 1960 | | 1970 | | Percent change | |
|---|---|---|---|---|---|---|---|---|
| | Number | Percent | Number | Percent | Number | Percent | 1950–60 | 1960–70 |
| 0–4 | 381,478 | 11.5 | 458,260 | 11.6 | 392,093 | 8.4 | 20.1 | -14.4 |
| 5–9 | 316,410 | 9.5 | 422,588 | 10.7 | 456,958 | 9.8 | 33.6 | 8.1 |
| 10–14 | 267,612 | 8.1 | 387,818 | 9.8 | 474,282 | 10.2 | 44.9 | 22.3 |
| 15–19 | 266,370 | 8.0 | 324,407 | 8.2 | 440,872 | 9.5 | 21.8 | 35.9 |
| 20–24 | 291,406 | 8.8 | 284,758 | 7.2 | 439,818 | 9.5 | -2.3 | 54.5 |
| 25–29 | 294,692 | 8.9 | 257,127 | 6.5 | 335,045 | 7.2 | -12.8 | 30.3 |
| 30–34 | 266,516 | 8.0 | 274,494 | 6.9 | 280,402 | 6.0 | 3.0 | 2.2 |
| 35–39 | 248,017 | 7.5 | 290,914 | 7.3 | 269,296 | 5.8 | 12.3 | -7.4 |
| 40–44 | 211,251 | 6.4 | 260,871 | 6.6 | 280,666 | 6.0 | 23.5 | 7.6 |
| 45–49 | 177,199 | 5.3 | 232,466 | 5.9 | 282,485 | 6.1 | 31.2 | 21.5 |
| 50–54 | 154,449 | 4.7 | 193,343 | 4.9 | 247,903 | 5.3 | 25.2 | 28.2 |
| 55–59 | 126,100 | 3.8 | 161,673 | 4.1 | 210,620 | 4.5 | 28.2 | 30.3 |
| 60–64 | 102,656 | 3.1 | 129,260 | 3.3 | 172,033 | 3.7 | 25.9 | 33.1 |
| 65–69 | 87,527 | 2.6 | 110,198 | 2.8 | 134,140 | 2.9 | 25.9 | 21.7 |
| 70–74 | 60,556 | 1.8 | 80,980 | 2.0 | 99,014 | 2.1 | 33.7 | 22.3 |
| 75+ | 66,441 | 2.0 | 97,792 | 2.5 | 132,867 | 2.9 | 47.2 | 35.9 |
| Total | 3,318,680 | 100.0 | 3,966,949 | 100.0 | 4,648,494 | 100.0 | 19.5 | 17.2 |
| Median age | 27.3 | | 27.1 | | 26.8 | | | |

AGE GROUP

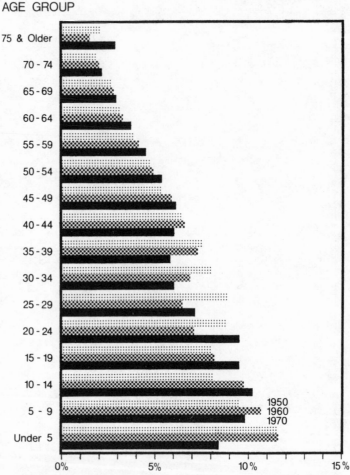

Fig. 4.1.    Percentage age composition of Virginia, 1950–70

not all persons 15–64 are acutally producers (e.g., some married
women and students) and many persons over 64 are still eco-
nomically active. The measure is, nevertheless, valuable in mak-
ing comparisons between units and in describing trends for a
single unit over time.

The total dependency ratio may be made more useful if it is
subdivided into components. Thus the *youth dependency ratio* is the
quotient of the 0–14 population divided by the 15–64 population;

the *aged dependency ratio* is the quotient of the 65-plus population divided by the 15-64 population.

Table 4.2 lists total, youth, and aged dependency ratios for Virginia in 1950, 1960, and 1970 and for Virginia planning districts, the United States, and the South Atlantic Division in 1970. There is little difference between the dependency ratio and its components among Virginia, the South Atlantic states, and the entire nation.

In 1950 the total dependency ratio for Virginia was 55.2. It was lower for whites (53.5) and higher for nonwhites (61.4). By 1960 the total dependency ratios, respectively, were 69.2, 68.5, and 83.7. Thus, while each ratio increased considerably, the relationship by race remained.

The state youth dependency ratio in 1950 was 45.2, and was also lower for whites (43.3) than for nonwhites (52.1). Conversely, the aged dependency ratio (with the total figure at 10.0) was higher for whites (10.2) than for nonwhites (9.3). These differences by age reflect the younger nature of the nonwhite population.

In 1960 all youth dependency ratios had risen concurrently with a drop in the median age (from 27.3 to 27.1 years). The total youth dependency ratio in 1960 was 54.4, an increase of 20.4 percent from 1950. For whites, it was 53.9, an increase of 24.5 percent; for nonwhites, 65.3, an increase of 25.3 percent.

Between 1960 and 1970 total dependency ratios declined for both the white and nonwhite populations of the state. For whites, the total dependency ratio decreased from 68.5 in 1960 to 54.3 in 1970, a decrease of 20.7 percent. The nonwhite dependency ratio decreased from 83.7 to 69.8, a decrease of 16.6 percent.

The youth dependency ratio, 54.4 in 1960, decreased to 44.7 in 1970. The white youth dependency ratio declined by more than 20 percent to 42.0. For nonwhites this ratio declined at a lesser rate to 57.3. Similarly, the aged dependency ratio dropped from 1960 to 1970 16.2 percent, to 10.0. The white dependency ratio dropped from 14.6 to 12.3 and the nonwhite ratio from 18.4 to 12.5.

The changes in dependency ratios, rising from 1950 to 1960 and declining to near-1950 levels in 1970, reflect changes in the

Table 4.2. Dependency Ratios by race in Virginia, 1950-70 and in its planning districts, 1970

| Area and Race | Population Age 0-14 | Age 15-64 | Age 65+ | Youth Dependency Ratio | Aged Dependency Ratio | Total Dependency Ratio |
|---|---|---|---|---|---|---|
| P.D. 1 | 22,918 | 51,941 | 9,786 | 44.1 | 18.8 | 62.9 |
| White | 22,243 | 50,760 | 9,552 | 43.8 | 18.8 | 62.9 |
| Nonwhite | 663 | 1,150 | 222 | 57.6 | 19.3 | 76.9 |
| P.D. 2 | 34,589 | 68,657 | 9,251 | 50.4 | 13.5 | 63.9 |
| White | 33,887 | 67,345 | 8,962 | 50.3 | 13.3 | 63.6 |
| Nonwhite | 675 | 1,250 | 278 | 54.0 | 22.2 | 76.2 |
| P.D. 3 | 41,564 | 100,282 | 17,566 | 41.4 | 17.5 | 58.9 |
| White | 40,121 | 97,342 | 17,005 | 41.2 | 17.5 | 58.7 |
| Nonwhite | 1,410 | 2,848 | 540 | 49.5 | 19.0 | 68.5 |
| P.D. 4 | 28,709 | 76,680 | 9,444 | 37.4 | 12.3 | 49.7 |
| White | 27,194 | 73,481 | 8,925 | 37.0 | 12.2 | 49.2 |
| Nonwhite | 1,436 | 2,974 | 504 | 48.3 | 17.0 | 65.3 |
| P.D. 5 | 61,514 | 144,925 | 24,736 | 42.4 | 17.1 | 59.5 |
| White | 53,517 | 130,279 | 22,059 | 41.4 | 16.9 | 58.0 |
| Nonwhite | 7,907 | 14,435 | 2,646 | 54.8 | 18.3 | 73.1 |
| P.D. 6 | 49,025 | 119,172 | 18,109 | 41.1 | 15.2 | 56.3 |
| White | 45,969 | 112,954 | 16,911 | 40.7 | 15.0 | 55.7 |
| Nonwhite | 2,943 | 5,988 | 1,168 | 49.2 | 19.5 | 68.7 |
| P.D. 7 | 29,118 | 65,460 | 11,794 | 44.5 | 18.0 | 62.5 |
| White | 27,561 | 62,472 | 11,270 | 44.1 | 18.0 | 62.1 |
| Nonwhite | 1,528 | 2,923 | 516 | 52.3 | 17.6 | 69.9 |
| P.D. 8 | 275,572 | 603,799 | 41,866 | 45.6 | 6.9 | 52.5 |
| White | 255,654 | 565,068 | 39,165 | 45.2 | 6.9 | 52.1 |
| Nonwhite | 17,578 | 32,949 | 2,497 | 53.4 | 7.6 | 61.0 |
| P.D. 9 | 21,280 | 42,953 | 7,989 | 49.5 | 18.6 | 68.1 |
| White | 15,485 | 34,271 | 6,501 | 45.2 | 19.0 | 64.2 |
| Nonwhite | 5,761 | 8,597 | 1,477 | 67.0 | 17.2 | 84.2 |
| P.D. 10 | 30,988 | 72,909 | 11,338 | 42.5 | 15.6 | 58.1 |
| White | 23,163 | 59,662 | 9,009 | 38.8 | 15.1 | 53.9 |
| Nonwhite | 7,737 | 12,896 | 2,305 | 60.0 | 17.9 | 77.9 |
| P.D. 11 | 45,750 | 103,276 | 16,971 | 44.3 | 16.4 | 60.7 |
| White | 34,387 | 84,281 | 13,928 | 40.8 | 16.5 | 57.3 |
| Nonwhite | 11,239 | 18,792 | 3,014 | 59.8 | 16.0 | 75.8 |

Table 4.2. (cont.)

| Area and Race | Age 0-14 | Population Age 15-64 | Age 65+ | Youth Dependency Ratio | Aged Dependency Ratio | Total Dependency Ratio |
|---|---|---|---|---|---|---|
| P.D. 12 | 62,614 | 136,169 | 19,091 | 46.0 | 14.0 | 60.0 |
| White | 43,316 | 106,181 | 15,502 | 40.8 | 14.6 | 55.4 |
| Nonwhite | 19,255 | 29,850 | 3,567 | 64.5 | 12.0 | 76.5 |
| P.D. 13 | 24,271 | 49,885 | 8,407 | 48.6 | 16.8 | 65.4 |
| White | 11,454 | 29,482 | 5,340 | 38.8 | 18.1 | 56.9 |
| Nonwhite | 12,781 | 20,323 | 3,059 | 62.9 | 15.0 | 77.9 |
| P.D. 14 | 21,685 | 45,413 | 9,147 | 47.8 | 20.1 | 67.9 |
| White | 10,269 | 28,099 | 5,934 | 36.6 | 21.1 | 57.7 |
| Nonwhite | 11,388 | 17,246 | 3,199 | 66.0 | 18.6 | 84.6 |
| P.D. 15 | 151,026 | 349,059 | 47,457 | 43.3 | 13.6 | 56.9 |
| White | 104,289 | 259,850 | 36,790 | 40.1 | 14.2 | 54.3 |
| Nonwhite | 46,049 | 87,738 | 10,503 | 52.5 | 12.0 | 64.5 |
| P.D. 16 | 22,500 | 48,551 | 6,374 | 46.3 | 13.1 | 59.4 |
| White | 16,009 | 38,385 | 5,121 | 41.7 | 13.3 | 55.0 |
| Nonwhite | 6,380 | 9,932 | 1,233 | 64.2 | 12.4 | 76.6 |
| P.D. 17 | 9,804 | 21,276 | 5,268 | 46.1 | 24.7 | 70.8 |
| White | 4,515 | 13,207 | 3,949 | 34.2 | 29.9 | 64.1 |
| Nonwhite | 5,282 | 8,035 | 1,311 | 65.7 | 16.3 | 82.0 |
| P.D. 18 | 12,974 | 28,278 | 6,357 | 45.9 | 22.5 | 68.4 |
| White | 7,428 | 19,081 | 4,589 | 38.9 | 24.0 | 62.9 |
| Nonwhite | 5,504 | 9,075 | 1,729 | 60.6 | 19.0 | 79.6 |
| P.D. 19 | 46,228 | 102,361 | 12,470 | 45.2 | 12.2 | 57.4 |
| White | 25,972 | 66,729 | 7,943 | 38.9 | 11.9 | 50.8 |
| Nonwhite | 20,120 | 34,981 | 4,506 | 57.5 | 12.9 | 70.4 |
| P.D. 20 | 224,899 | 495,750 | 48,722 | 45.4 | 9.8 | 55.2 |
| White | 148,273 | 365,124 | 34,529 | 40.6 | 9.5 | 50.1 |
| Nonwhite | 74,211 | 124,912 | 13,985 | 59.4 | 11.2 | 70.6 |
| P.D. 21 | 95,807 | 206,180 | 17,094 | 46.5 | 8.3 | 54.8 |
| White | 67,521 | 154,899 | 12,321 | 43.6 | 8.0 | 51.6 |
| Nonwhite | 27,742 | 49,624 | 4,727 | 55.9 | 9.5 | 65.4 |
| P.D. 22 | 11,597 | 25,374 | 6,475 | 45.7 | 25.5 | 71.2 |
| White | 5,133 | 15,307 | 4,595 | 33.5 | 30.0 | 63.5 |
| Nonwhite | 6,438 | 10,001 | 1,856 | 64.4 | 18.6 | 83.0 |

Table 4.2. (cont.)

| Area and Race | Age 0-14 | Population Age 15-64 | Age 65+ | Youth Dependency Ratio | Aged Dependency Ratio | Total Dependency Ratio |
|---|---|---|---|---|---|---|
| Virginia | | | | | | |
| 1950 | 965,500 | 2,138,656 | 214,524 | 45.2 | 10.0 | 55.2 |
| White | 727,668 | 1,681,798 | 172,089 | 43.3 | 10.2 | 53.5 |
| Nonwhite | 237,832 | 456,838 | 42,435 | 52.1 | 9.3 | 61.4 |
| 1960 | 1,265,495 | 2,399,999 | 288,935 | 54.4 | 14.8 | 69.2 |
| White | 959,617 | 1,937,667 | 234,337 | 53.9 | 14.6 | 68.5 |
| Nonwhite | 305,878 | 462,332 | 54,598 | 65.3 | 18.4 | 83.7 |
| 1970 | 1,323,333 | 2,959,140 | 366,021 | 44.7 | 12.4 | 57.1 |
| White | 1,024,146 | 2,436,841 | 300,527 | 42.0 | 12.3 | 54.3 |
| Nonwhite | 299,187 | 522,299 | 65,494 | 57.3 | 12.5 | 69.8 |
| United States | 57,909,564 | 125,206,543 | 20,049,592 | 46.2 | 16.0 | 62.2 |
| White | 49,881,044 | 112,128,390 | 18,483,695 | 44.5 | 16.5 | 61.0 |
| Nonwhite | 8,028,520 | 13,078,153 | 1,565,897 | 61.4 | 12.0 | 73.4 |
| South Atlantic Division | 8,681,014 | 19,058,043 | 2,932,280 | 45.6 | 15.4 | 61.0 |
| White | 6,403,411 | 15,352,117 | 2,492,099 | 41.7 | 16.2 | 57.9 |
| Nonwhite | 2,277,603 | 3,705,926 | 440,181 | 61.4 | 11.9 | 73.3 |

age components of the ratios. In 1960 the population younger than 15 years and older than 64 had increased proportionately, and the 15–64 group had decreased from 1950. However by 1970, the below–15 segment had decreased in relative size, the 15–64 segment grew substantially, while the 65 and older portion increased once again.

Total dependency ratios ranged from a low of 49.7 in Planning District 4 to a high of 71.2 in District 22. For the white population this range was 49.2 (District 4) to 64.2 (District 9). For the nonwhite population total dependency ranged between 61.0 (District 8) and 84.6 (District 14). For the entire state, nonwhite total dependency ratios were 28.5 perent higher than white total dependency ratios.

Youth dependency ratios ranged from 37.4 (District 4) to 50.4 (District 2). For the white population the range was 33.5 (District 22) to 50.3 (District 2); for the nonwhite population the range was 7.6 (District 8) to 22.2 (District 2). Aged dependency ratios for nonwhites were approximately 2 percent higher than those for whites in the state.

It has been noted that age composition differences are a function of past demographic history. There are several points which should be kept in mind. First, any factor which selectively increases (or decreases) the population in a particular age category will simultaneously decrease (or increase) the population proportions in other age categories. If two or more factors are operating simultaneously on several age categories, it is much more difficult to predict the resulting distribution, since it would be necessary to know the relative weight of each factor.

A primary factor influencing the proportion of individuals in the 0–14 age category is the birth rate. As the birth rate increases, one would expect to find higher proportions in the 0–14 age group. Birth rates, in turn, may be quite high in areas with high rates of in-migration, since migrants tend to be primarily in the 20–29 age group, which is also the age group with highest age-specific fertility rates.

An important factor influencing the proportion of the population in the 15–64 age group is migration. If an area is experiencing high rates of out-migration, the selective age characteristics of the migrants will decrease the population in this age category. Conversely, in-migration will cause the proportion of the population in this category to increase.

A second factor influencing the 15-64 age category is the presence of colleges and military installations in a particular area. If a planning district has a relatively small population (e.g., District 4), the presence of a college/university complex may raise the proportion of the population in the 15-64 age category.

It is more difficult to locate factors influencing the proportions in the 65-plus age category; in fact, proportions here are likely to represent "residuals" created by other factors such as net migration and fertility rates. If an area is experiencing low or moderate fertility rates and net out-migration, the proportions in the 65-plus age category will necessarily be high. An additional factor which may have some direct effect on this age category is selective migration of the aged for retirement purposes. This factor is, however, difficult to document.

In Planning District 8, the Virginia suburbs of Washington, D.C., there were high proportions of the white population in the 0-14 and 15-64 age categories and a low proportion in the 65- plus age group in 1970. This area was characterized by high rates of in-migration and natural increase.

In Planning District 4 there were a low proportion of whites in the 0-14 age category and slightly above-average proportions in the 15-64 and 65-plus age categories. The area was characterized by near average in-migration and natural increase (as compared to the state average). In this case it may well be that the presence of Virginia Polytechnic Institute and State University in the area caused the high proportion in the 15-64 age category.

Planning District 22 was characterized by negative rates of natural increase and net migration. This is reflected in Table 4.2 by the small proportions in the 0-14 and 15-64 age categories, resulting in a very high aged dependency ratio, 105 percent higher than the state average.

Considering just the white population of the state, small proportions in the 65-plus age category were located in Planning Districts 8, 19, 20, and 21 (as shown by the low aged dependency ratios). Each of these areas was either completely or partly metropolitan in character. Additionally, these four planning districts contained the bulk of the state's military population, who are aged 15–64. Each of these planning districts had net inmigration of whites and relatively high rates of natural increase. These two factors may well account for the relatively small proportion in the 65–plus age category.

As a final note to dependency ratios, it would be appropriate to discuss differences between the urban and rural portions of the state's population. One would hypothesize that the total dependency ratio would be considerably higher in rural areas due to higher fertility and a persistent pattern of out-migration. Not only would one expect the total ratio to be high, but both the youth and aged ratios as well. Examination of the data confirms all these hypotheses. For the rural portion of Virginia, the total dependency ratio in 1970 was 63.36, with a youth dependency ratio of 48.25 and an aged dependency ratio of 15.11; for the urban portion, the total dependency ratio was only 53.65, with youth and aged dependency ratios of 42.78 and 10.87, respectively. Unless the rural–urban migration pattern is altered, this gap is likely to widen in future years. This, in turn, suggests the need for provision of additional employment opportunities in rural areas in an effort to reduce the typical pattern of out-migration shortly after the completion of secondary or higher-level education.

## Sex Composition

The *sex ratio* is the number of males per 100 females within a given population. If the number of males equals the number of females, the sex ratio is 100. If there are more males than females in an area, the ratio is above 100; if more females than males, below 100.

Virginia's sex ratio in 1950 was 101.9, higher than the national ratio of 98.6 and that of the South Atlantic Division, 98.2. The state sex ratio for whites was 102.5; the national ratio, 99.0; and the divisional, 99.3. Nonwhite sex ratios were somewhat lower: 100.1 in Virginia, 95.7 in the nation, and 94.9 in the South Atlantic Division.

Urban areas had the lowest sex ratios in 1950 and rural farm areas the highest, with rural nonfarm residences intermediate. Sex ratios for nonwhites were generally more extreme (that is, farther from 100.0) than those for whites. Ratios in the South Atlantic Division were consistently lower than those of the nation, which in turn were lower than Virginia's. The state's ratio was higher than that of any other in the South Atlantic Division; the low extreme was 89.1 in the District of Columbia.

Between 1950 and 1960 Virginia's sex ratio dropped from 101.9 to 99.3; the United States sex ratio from 98.6 to 97.1; and the South Atlantic's from 98.2 to 97.1. Sex ratios declined for both whites and nonwhites. In Virginia the white ratio decreased from 102.5 to 99.9; the nonwhite, from 100.1 to 98.3. The decrease occurred similarly nationwide and in the South Atlantic area.

In 1960 the sex ratio for the United States was 97.1, indicating a slight excess of females over males. Within the South Atlantic Division sex ratios ranged from a high of 99.3 (Virginia) to a low of 88.3 (District of Columbia; see Table 4.3).

Between 1960 and 1970 sex ratios declined in each state in the division and in the United States as a whole. In 1970 Virginia and the District of Columbia still had the highest and lowest sex ratios in the division, although each was lower than in 1960. The trend in the United States toward lower sex ratios is a product of increasing life expectancy and differential mortality between males and females. As life expectancy increases, the number of individuals in the upper age brackets increases. This increase is not proportional between the sexes however. Age-specific mortality rates are higher for males than females at every age. The cumulative effect of these higher male age-specific mortality rates produces a smaller number of males (relative to females) reaching advanced ages, and thus a progressively lower sex ratio.

Virginia's high sex ratio in 1950, 1960, and 1970 would seem to be the result of the presence in the state of a relatively large military population (for example, in 1970 the military population was 171,983 males and 3,729 females. If the military were removed from the entire population, the sex ratio would decline from

Table 4.3.  Sex ratio by race and residence, Virginia, United States, and South Atlantic Division, 1950-70

| | Virginia | United States | South Atlantic |
|---|---|---|---|
| **1950** | | | |
| **All races** | | | |
| Total | 101.9 | 98.6 | 98.2 |
| Urban | 96.7 | 94.6 | 92.3 |
| Rural nonfarm | 106.6 | 103.6 | 103.6 |
| Rural farm | 107.1 | 110.1 | 105.5 |
| **White** | | | |
| Total | 102.5 | 99.0 | 99.3 |
| Urban | 98.1 | 94.9 | 93.5 |
| Rural nonfarm | 106.3 | 103.6 | 104.3 |
| Rural farm | 106.8 | 111.4 | 107.0 |
| **Nonwhite** | | | |
| Total | 100.1 | 95.7 | 94.9 |
| Urban | 91.8 | 91.6 | 88.6 |
| Rural nonfarm | 107.1 | 102.7 | 99.8 |
| Rural farm | 107.8 | 102.7 | 102.2 |
| Delaware | 97.9 | | |
| Maryland | 99.2 | | |
| D.C. | 89.1 | | |
| Virginia | 101.9 | | |
| W. Virginia | 100.7 | | |
| N. Carolina | 98.6 | | |
| S. Carolina | 96.7 | | |
| Georgia | 96.2 | | |
| Florida | 97.3 | | |
| **1960** | | | |
| **All races** | | | |
| Total | 99.6 | 97.1 | 97.1 |
| Urban | 96.5 | 94.1 | 92.7 |
| Rural nonfarm | 102.6 | 103.2 | 103.2 |
| Rural farm | 104.3 | 107.7 | |
| **White** | | | |
| Total | 99.9 | 97.4 | 97.9 |
| Urban | 97.2 | 94.4 | 93.6 |
| Rural nonfarm | 102.2 | 103.2 | 104.0 |
| Rural farm | 104.0 | 108.4 | |

Table 4.3. (continued)

| | Virginia | United States | South Atlantic |
|---|---|---|---|
| Nonwhite | | | |
|    Total | 98.3 | 94.7 | 94.3 |
|    Urban | 92.7 | 91.8 | 90.0 |
|    Rural nonfarm | 104.0 | 102.6 | |
|    Rural farm | 105.1 | 102.4 | 100.5 |
| | | | |
| Delaware | 98.2 | | |
| Maryland | 97.8 | | |
| D.C. | 88.3 | | |
| Virginia | 99.6 | | |
| W. Virginia | 96.8 | | |
| N. Carolina | 97.3 | | |
| S. Carolina | 97.4 | | |
| Georgia | 95.5 | | |
| Florida | 96.9 | | |
| | | | |
| 1970 | | | |
| All races | | | |
|    Total | 97.7 | 94.8 | 95.0 |
|    Urban | 96.5 | 93.0 | 93.1 |
|    Rural* | 99.7 | 100.1 | 98.4 |
| | | | |
| White | | | |
|    Total | 98.3 | 95.3 | 95.9 |
|    Urban | 97.6 | 93.5 | 94.2 |
|    Rural* | 99.6 | 100.2 | 98.8 |
| | | | |
| Nonwhite | | | |
|    Total | 95.1 | 91.9 | 91.7 |
|    Urban | 92.1 | 90.2 | 89.4 |
|    Rural* | 100.1 | 99.0 | 96.5 |
| | | | |
| Delaware | 95.2 | | |
| Maryland | 95.5 | | |
| D.C. | 86.8 | | |
| Virginia | 97.7 | | |
| W. Virginia | 93.9 | | |
| N. Carolina | 95.9 | | |
| S. Carolina | 96.5 | | |
| Georgia | 94.6 | | |
| Florida | 93.2 | | |

* Due to census processing errors, it was necessary to combine rural farm and rural nonfarm population.

97.7 to 90.5. Undoubtedly, controlling for the military population would similarly affect sex ratios in the other states in the South Atlantic Division.

Sex ratios for the total population of each planning district in 1970, subdivided by race, are presented in Table 4.4. For the total population sex ratios varied between 91.0 (Planning District 15) and 106.7 (District 20). In addition to District 20, Districts 4, 10, 19, and 21 had sex ratios above 100 (100.3, 102.5, 105.5, 103.8, respectively). Sex ratios for the white population in Virginia ranged from a low of 90.8 in District 22 to a high of 111.6 in District 20. Districts 4 (100.4), 10 (104.0), 19 (107.9), and 21 (106.9) had sex ratios above 100. For the nonwhite population sex ratios varied from a low of 81.6 (District 2) to a high of 107.0 (District 8). District 19 also had a sex ratio over 100 (101.4). Districts 1, 3, and 15 had sex ratios below 90 (86.2, 88.7, 89.0, respectively).

The high sex ratios in Planning Districts 4, 10, 19, 20, and 21 can be explained by two independent factors. In Districts 19, 20, and 21 the presence of large numbers of military personnel (estimated by the Census Bureau as 12,714, 93,940, and 26,616, respectively) served to produce high sex ratios, since most of the military personnel were male.

In Districts 4 and 10 the presence of Virginia Polytechnic Institute and State University and the University of Virginia (both with predominantly male enrollments at that time) served to raise sex ratios above 100. Planning District 8 seems a partial exception to the previous considerations. Although the sex ratio for the district was 97.2 (slightly below the state average), a large resident military population of 53,072 was found there. Analysis of the population by race, however, explains this exception. The sex ratio for nonwhites in District 8 was very high, 107.0. This was a direct effect of the military population. The nonwhite population in the district was, however, a very small percentage of the total population, 5.75 percent. Thus the remaining white population was large enough to absorb the white military population without a noticeable effect on the sex ratio. This view is supported when the "percent military" in Planning Districts 8, 19, 20, and 21 is calculated. District 8 had the lowest percent, 5.82, while Districts

Table 4.4. Sex ratios in Virginia Planning Districts, by race 1970

| Area and Race | Population Male | Female | Sex Ratio |
|---|---|---|---|
| P.D. 1 | 41,014 | 43,631 | 94.0 |
| White | 40,044 | 42,511 | 94.2 |
| Nonwhite | 942 | 1,093 | 86.2 |
| P.D. 2 | 55,412 | 57,085 | 97.1 |
| White | 54,377 | 55,817 | 97.4 |
| Nonwhite | 990 | 1,213 | 81.6 |
| P.D. 3 | 76,931 | 82,481 | 93.3 |
| White | 74,609 | 79,859 | 93.4 |
| Nonwhite | 2,255 | 2,543 | 88.7 |
| P.D. 4 | 57,493 | 57,340 | 100.3 |
| White | 54,913 | 54,687 | 100.4 |
| Nonwhite | 2,406 | 2,508 | 95.9 |
| P.D. 5 | 110,747 | 120,428 | 92.0 |
| White | 98,713 | 107,142 | 92.1 |
| Nonwhite | 11,873 | 13,115 | 90.5 |
| P.D. 6 | 90,072 | 96,234 | 93.6 |
| White | 85,011 | 90,823 | 93.6 |
| Nonwhite | 4,867 | 5,232 | 93.0 |
| P.D. 7 | 51,649 | 54,723 | 94.4 |
| White | 49,176 | 52,172 | 94.3 |
| Nonwhite | 2,435 | 2,532 | 96.2 |
| P.D. 8 | 454,010 | 467,227 | 97.2 |
| White | 422,893 | 436,994 | 96.8 |
| Nonwhite | 27,410 | 25,614 | 107.0 |
| P.D. 9 | 35,743 | 36,479 | 98.0 |
| White | 27,772 | 28,485 | 97.5 |
| Nonwhite | 7,904 | 7,931 | 99.7 |
| P.D. 10 | 58,328 | 56,907 | 102.5 |
| White | 46,824 | 45,010 | 104.0 |
| Nonwhite | 11,304 | 11,634 | 97.2 |
| P.D. 11 | 79,690 | 86,307 | 92.3 |
| White | 63,643 | 68,953 | 92.3 |
| Nonwhite | 15,880 | 17,165 | 92.5 |
| P.D. 12 | 105,371 | 112,503 | 93.7 |
| White | 80,075 | 84,924 | 94.3 |
| Nonwhite | 25,208 | 27,464 | 91.8 |
| P.D. 13 | 40,246 | 42,317 | 95.1 |
| White | 22,463 | 23,813 | 94.3 |
| Nonwhite | 17,728 | 18,435 | 96.2 |
| P.D. 14 | 36,849 | 39,396 | 93.5 |
| White | 21,148 | 23,154 | 91.3 |
| Nonwhite | 15,647 | 16,186 | 96.7 |

Table 4.4.   (continued)

| Area and Race | Population Male | Female | Sex Ratio |
|---|---|---|---|
| P.D. 15 | 260,867 | 286,675 | 91.0 |
| White | 191,774 | 209,155 | 91.7 |
| Nonwhite | 67,943 | 76,347 | 89.0 |
| P.D. 16 | 37,947 | 39,478 | 96.1 |
| White | 29,013 | 30,502 | 95.1 |
| Nonwhite | 8,765 | 8,780 | 99.8 |
| P.D. 17 | 17,656 | 18,692 | 94.5 |
| White | 10,412 | 11,259 | 92.5 |
| Nonwhite | 7,222 | 7,406 | 97.5 |
| P.D. 18 | 23,453 | 24,156 | 97.1 |
| White | 15,266 | 15,832 | 96.4 |
| Nonwhite | 8,091 | 8,217 | 98.5 |
| P.D. 19 | 82,698 | 78,361 | 105.5 |
| White | 52,234 | 48,410 | 107.9 |
| Nonwhite | 30,015 | 29,592 | 101.4 |
| P.D. 20 | 397,088 | 372,283 | 106.7 |
| White | 288,958 | 258,968 | 111.6 |
| Nonwhite | 103,084 | 110,024 | 93.7 |
| P.D. 21 | 162,528 | 156,553 | 103.8 |
| White | 121,288 | 113,453 | 106.9 |
| Nonwhite | 40,148 | 41,945 | 95.7 |
| P.D. 22 | 20,706 | 22,740 | 91.1 |
| White | 11,915 | 13,120 | 90.8 |
| Nonwhite | 8,730 | 9,565 | 91.3 |
| Virginia | 2,296,498 | 2,351,996 | 97.6 |

19, 20, and 21 had percents of 7.89, 12.20, and 8.34. Thus, the effect of the military population on the sex ratio was less in District 8 and greatest in District 20.

## Racial Composition

Virginia, along with other southern states, has always had a relatively large share of blacks among its population. The reason for this, of course, was the persistence of slavery within the South long after it had vanished farther north. Although the out-migration of the southern black has been one of the major features of United States demographic history of the present century,[3] Virginia

[3] See, for example, Daniel O. Price, *Changing Characteristics of the Negro Population* (Washington, D.C., U.S. Government Printing Office, 1969), pp. 9–40.

and other southern states continue to have a relatively high proportion of blacks (see Table 4.5). However, the proportion of
blacks in Virginia and the South declined during the 1950–70
period, while it rose somewhat for the nation as a whole. As
was demonstrated in chapter 2, the reason for this was the
persistence of out–migration of blacks from Virginia. Between
1960 and 1970 recorded natural increase (births less deaths) among
Virginia's nonwhite population [4] totaled slightly more than 125,000,
a reduction of about 15 percent from the 149,000 recorded during the
previous decade. All in all, natural increase among nonwhites was
more than 274,000 during this period. However, the absolute size
of the nonwhite population increased by only 127,000, so that
net out–migration of nonwhites over this score of years was
nearly 150,000. During the same period, the white population
increased by 1,180,000; 880,000 of this was the result of natural
increase and some 300,000 due to net in–migration.

The distribution of nonwhites across the state in 1970 was
rather uneven. As Table 4.6 shows, disproportionately large shares
of blacks were located in the eastern portion of the state,
with relatively few in the western and northern portions. The point
of division seems to run south from the Washington suburbs to
Danville. Along this line, blacks were found in about the same
degree as was true for the entire state (Districts 9–12 and 16);
to the west of this line, nonwhites were relatively few in number;
to the east, these numbers were relatively large.

The concentration ratio in Table 4.6 is simply the ratio of
share of nonwhite to share of total population in 1970. In
the far southwestern portion of the state, the values of this ratio
were extremely low, amounting to at most a sixth of what
might be termed *expected nonwhite population* (that which would result
if population were evenly distributed by race). The ratio tended
to be highest in the southern and easternmost portions of the state.
Interestingly, those portions of the state with the lowest and
highest concentration of nonwhites have been those with the
greatest losses of population in recent decades.

[4] Births and deaths are not available for blacks and other nonwhites separately.
Consequently, it is necessary to include members of other nonwhite races in the
following discussion.

Table 4.5. Racial composition of Virginia, South Atlantic states, and
United States, 1950-70  (percent)

| Area and Race | 1950 | 1960 | 1970 |
|---|---|---|---|
| Virginia |  |  |  |
| White | 77.8 | 79.2 | 80.9 |
| Black | 22.1 | 20.6 | 18.5 |
| Other | 0.1 | 0.2 | 0.6 |
| South Atlantic |  |  |  |
| White | 75.7 | 77.2 | 78.6 |
| Black | 24.1 | 22.5 | 20.8 |
| Other | 0.2 | 0.3 | 0.6 |
| United States |  |  |  |
| White | 89.5 | 88.8 | 87.5 |
| Black | 10.0 | 10.6 | 11.1 |
| Other | 0.5 | 0.6 | 1.4 |

Table 4.6.  Percent ages of total and nonwhite population in planning
districts, Virginia 1970

| Planning District | Percentage of Total Population | Percent age of Nonwhites | Concentration Ratio |
|---|---|---|---|
| 1. Lenowisco | 1.82 | 0.16 | .09 |
| 2. Cumberland Plateau | 2.42 | 0.26 | .11 |
| 3. Mount Rogers | 3.43 | 0.55 | .16 |
| 4. New River Valley | 2.47 | 0.59 | .24 |
| 5. Fifth | 4.97 | 2.84 | .57 |
| 6. Central Shenandoah | 4.01 | 1.18 | .24 |
| 7. Lord Fairfax | 2.29 | 0.57 | .25 |
| 8. Northern Virginia | 19.81 | 6.89 | .35 |
| 9. Rappahannock-Rapidan | 1.55 | 1.79 | 1.15 |
| 10. Thomas Jefferson | 2.48 | 2.63 | 1.06 |
| 11. Central Virginia | 3.57 | 3.75 | 1.05 |
| 12. West Piedmont | 4.68 | 5.85 | 1.25 |
| 13. Southside | 1.77 | 4.07 | 2.30 |
| 14. Piedmont | 1.64 | 3.59 | 2.19 |
| 15. Richmond Regional | 11.77 | 16.45 | 1.40 |
| 16. RADCO | 1.66 | 2.01 | 1.21 |
| 17. Northern Neck | 0.78 | 1.65 | 2.12 |
| 18. Middle Penninsula | 1.02 | 1.85 | 1.81 |
| 19. Crater | 3.46 | 6.78 | 1.96 |
| 20. Southeastern Virginia | 16.54 | 24.85 | 1.50 |
| 21. Peninsula | 6.86 | 9.47 | 1.38 |
| 22. Accomack-Northampton | 0.93 | 2.07 | 2.23 |

Changes in the racial composition of localities in the state between 1960 and 1970 are depicted in Figure 4.2. There were relatively few areas where the share of nonwhite population increased. They consisted of (a) a few areas with relatively low proportions of blacks, located in the western portion of the state (Buchanan, Smyth, Grayson, Highland, Augusta, and Shenandoah counties); (b) large urban areas (Richmond, Norfolk–Portsmouth), reflecting the increasing concentration of nonwhites in cities; (c) a few rural areas where losses of black population were relatively less than those of the white population. A list of all localities with components of population change by race is given in Table A4.1.

## Educational Characteristics

The median number of school years completed by Virginians aged 25 and over rose 3.2 years between 1950 and 1970. In 1950 the median (the point on the exact center of the distribution) was 8.5 years, slightly more than a grade school education. This figure increased steadily, and by 1970 it reached 11.7 years, nearly a complete high school education (see Table 4.7).

Between 1950 and 1970 there was a significant decline in the number of persons having only an eighth–grade education. In each decade the share of the population with no more than an eighth-grade education declined about 10 percent, but in absolute numbers the greatest decline (15.6 percent) occurred between 1960 and 1970.

The number of persons in Virginia who received no more than a high school diploma increased by 135 percent between 1950 and 1970. The greatest increase (65 percent) occurred between 1950 and 1960. In 1960, 20.7 percent of the population had earned just a high school diploma, and by 1970, 25.2 percent had done so.

The most spectacular increase occurred among those who completed at least four years of college. Only 6.5 percent of the population in 1950 had earned at least a college degree, compared to 8.4 percent in 1960 and 12.3 percent in 1970. In absolute numbers, the number of persons who earned at least an undergraduate degree increased by 166.2 percent between 1950 and 1970.

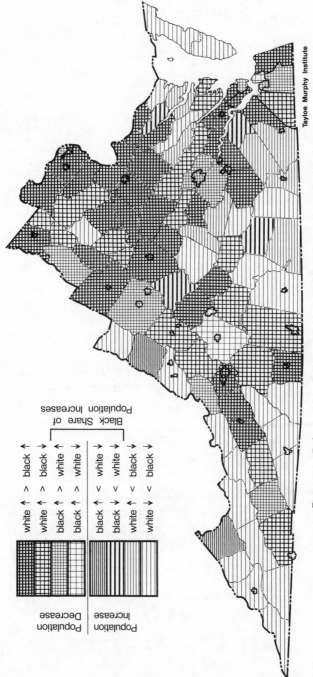

Fig. 4.2. Relative population change by race, Virginia, 1960-70

Tayloe Murphy Institute

Table 4.7. Number of school years completed by persons aged 25 and over, Virginia 1950-70

| Years of School Completed | 1950 Number | 1950 Percentage of Total | 1960 Number | 1960 Percentage of Total | 1970 Number | 1970 Percentage of Total | Percent change 1950-60 | Percent change 1960-70 | Percent change 1950-70 |
|---|---|---|---|---|---|---|---|---|---|
| 0 | 59,265 | 3.4 | 55,356 | 2.7 | 39,708 | 1.6 | -6.6 | -28.3 | -33.0 |
| 1-4 | 256,105 | 14.7 | 218,164 | 10.5 | 147,707 | 6.0 | -14.8 | 32.3 | -42.3 |
| 5-6 | 257,715 | 14.8 | 254,124 | 12.2 | 203,066 | 8.3 | -1.4 | -20.1 | -21.2 |
| 7 | 231,070 | 13.2 | 228,146 | 11.0 | 212,938 | 8.7 | -1.3 | -6.7 | -7.9 |
| 8 | 157,770 | 8.8 | 178,316 | 8.6 | 184,978 | 7.6 | 16.7 | 3.7 | 21.0 |
| Total grade school | 897,660 | 51.5 | 878,750 | 42.3 | 748,689 | 30.6 | -2.4 | -15.6 | -17.6 |
| 9-11 | 281,225 | 16.1 | 358,614 | 17.2 | 488,962 | 20.0 | 27.5 | 36.4 | 73.9 |
| 12 | 261,855 | 15.0 | 432,107 | 20.7 | 616,942 | 25.2 | 65.0 | 42.8 | 135.6 |
| Total high school | 543,080 | 31.1 | 790,721 | 37.9 | 1,105,904 | 45.2 | 45.6 | 39.9 | 103.6 |
| 13-15 | 132,855 | 7.6 | 183,428 | 8.8 | 250,838 | 10.3 | 38.1 | 36.8 | 88.8 |
| 16+ | 113,070 | 6.5 | 174,904 | 8.4 | 300,943 | 12.3 | 54.7 | 72.1 | 166.2 |
| Total post-secondary | 245,925 | 14.1 | 358,332 | 17.2 | 551,781 | 22.6 | 45.7 | 54.0 | 124.4 |
| Total | 1,745,930 | 100.0 | 2,083,159 | 100.0 | 2,446,082 | 100.0 | | | |
| Median no. of years completed | 8.5 | | 9.5 | | 11.7 | | 16.5 | 18.2 | 37.7 |

Increases in educational attainment for the population as a whole may be considered the result of two discrete factors: changes in demographic-variables, particularly age composition, and increases in the length of the educational career within cohorts. In order to untangle these skeins, the data in Table 4.8 show educational attainment by age groups for 1950 and 1970. For each group, median school years completed rose substantially, with an absolute increase of three years occurring for ages 35–39.

Table 4.8. Median years of school completed by age, Virginia, 1950 and 1970

| | 1950 | | 1970 | |
| Age | Median Years | Percentage of Population | Median Years | Percentage of Population |
|---|---|---|---|---|
| 25–29 | 10.8 | 16.4 | 12.5 | 13.6 |
| 30–34 | 10.2 | 14.8 | 12.3 | 11.5 |
| 35–39 | 9.2 | 13.7 | 12.2 | 11.1 |
| 40–44 | 8.6 | 11.7 | 12.0 | 11.5 |
| 45–54 | 7.9 | 18.5 | 11.5 | 21.6 |
| 55–64 | 7.5 | 12.9 | 9.6 | 15.7 |
| 65–74 | 6.6 | 8.2 | 8.3 | 9.6 |
| 75+ | 6.7 | 3.7 | 7.8 | 5.4 |
| Total | 8.5 | 100.0 | 11.7 | 100.0 |

As discussed previously, the population grew somewhat older during the period. Considering that median educational attainment is an inverse function of age (the medians decline consistently with age), the actual increase in median school years completed by Virginia's population between 1950 and 1970 is understated. In fact, if the 1950 age distribution still held in 1970, median school years as of 1970 would have been nearly 13 years. The marked increase in education over this twenty–year period is perhaps best underscored by noting that the 1970 median for all cohorts under age 45 equaled or exceeded the completion of a secondary education.

The upgrading of educational attainment for the state's population reflected other factors in addition to compulsory school
attendance laws. Changes in the economic structure of the state
(to be discussed in the following chapter) put a premium on
increased training before and during an individual's working life.
Additionally, the data in Table 4.8 indicate that some selectivity
has taken place in changes in the composition of cohorts over
time. For example, the cohort aged 45–54 in 1950 was basically
the same as that aged 65–74 in 1970. During this period, some
members of the cohort died or moved out of Virginia, while
other persons of this age group moved into Virginia. In 1950
the median years of school completed by this cohort was 7.9
years; in 1970, 8.3 years. Hence, both mortality and migration
have been selective by education; part of this is, of course,
due to mortality differentials by race and sex. Blacks are more
likely to have died than whites during this period, and educational
attainment is higher, on the average, for whites. Similarly, men
are more likely to have died than women during this period,
and educational attainment is higher, on the average, for women.
Similar statements also hold for migration differentials.

A comparison of trends in educational attainment in Virginia with
those of the South and the entire nation (Table 4.9) shows that the
white population of the state and the South, which was about 0.5
years behind the nation in 1950, made large strides toward
equality; by 1970 Virginia's whites had achieved parity with all
American whites, while South Atlantic whites lagged only one-
tenth of a year behind. For nonwhites (blacks only in 1970), the
situation was much less sanguine. Educational attainment of

Table 4.9.  Median years of school completed by race, Virginia,
South Atlantic Division, and United States, 1950-70

| Year | Virginia | | South Atlantic | | United States | |
|------|----------|----------|----------|----------|----------|----------|
|      | White | Nonwhite | White | Nonwhite | White | Nonwhite |
| 1950 | 9.3 | 6.1 | 9.2 | 5.9 | 9.7 | 6.9 |
| 1960 | 10.8 | 7.2 | 10.7 | 7.1 | 10.9 | 8.2 |
| 1970 | 12.1 | 8.5* | 12.0 | 8.8* | 12.1 | 9.7* |

*Black only.

nonwhites in Virginia and in the South continued to lag behind national averages; and in the case of Virginia, the absolute difference widened between 1950 (0.8 years) and 1970 (1.2 years). The increase in median school years completed between 1950 and 1970 for nonwhites was 2.4 years in Virginia, but 2.8 years in the entire nation and 2.9 years in the South Atlantic Division. This would suggest that out-migration rates of nonwhites from Virginia tend to increase with the level of education. It is possible, although not provable, that the closing of public schools in some portions of Virginia during the period of "massive resistance" to school integration explains some portion of this differential.

An examination of educational attainment in Virginia (Table 4.10) shows that in 1970 the state median number of school years completed, 11.7, was higher than the figure recorded in any single planning district, with the exception of Northern Virginia (13.1 years) and Peninsula (12.0 years). Generally, this statistic was higher in metropolitan areas; the five planning districts which had the highest median number of school years completed was either fully or predominately metropolitan.

The distribution of persons over age 25 by years of school completed in Northern Virginia was also quite different from that of the remainder of the state. This area had the lowest percentage of persons with no education (0.48 percent) and the lowest percentage of persons with some education but less than a high school diploma (24.68 percent), but the highest proportion of persons with a high school diploma (31.92 percent), those with one to three years of postsecondary education (16.14 percent), and those with four or more years of college (26.78 percent). Although Northern Virginia accounted for only 19.6 percent of all persons in the state aged 25 and over, 42.4 percent of all such persons with four or more years of postsecondary education lived there.

This is indicative of the tendency for well-educated persons to be grouped in metropolitan areas. The state total of 12.30 percent of the population aged 25 and over with four or more years of post-high school education experience may have been somewhat inflated by Northern Virginia. If all of the state except Northern Virginia were considered, only 8.76 percent of all persons over age 25 would have four or more years of education beyond the high school

Table 4.10. Education characteristics of Virginia, planning districts, 1970

| Area | Population Aged 25+ | Median Years of School | Percentage with | | | | | | Median School Years | |
|---|---|---|---|---|---|---|---|---|---|---|
| | | | No School | 1-11 Years | 12 Years | 13-15 Years | 16 Years | 17+ Years | Males | Females |
| Lenowisco | 47,563 | 8.1 | 2.91 | 73.34 | 15.84 | 3.98 | 2.75 | 1.17 | 7.8 | 8.3 |
| Cumberland Plateau | 57,963 | 8.1 | 3.09 | 73.43 | 14.49 | 5.60 | 2.42 | 0.98 | 7.7 | 8.4 |
| Mount Rogers | 91,271 | 9.1 | 2.11 | 69.17 | 17.20 | 6.70 | 3.21 | 1.61 | 8.6 | 9.5 |
| New River Valley | 57,894 | 10.5 | 1.78 | 57.66 | 22.08 | 8.21 | 5.35 | 4.91 | 10.3 | 10.7 |
| Fifth | 131,889 | 11.6 | 1.11 | 49.37 | 29.34 | 11.02 | 6.24 | 2.93 | 11.4 | 11.8 |
| Central Shenandoah | 101,761 | 10.8 | 1.68 | 55.37 | 24.59 | 8.96 | 5.56 | 3.84 | 10.4 | 11.2 |
| Lord Fairfax | 60,671 | 10.2 | 1.49 | 61.23 | 24.39 | 7.21 | 3.81 | 1.88 | 9.6 | 10.7 |
| Northern Virginia | 480,573 | 13.1 | 0.48 | 24.68 | 31.92 | 16.14 | 14.26 | 12.52 | 13.7 | 12.6 |
| Rappahannock-Rapidan | 39,457 | 9.7 | 3.01 | 60.37 | 22.08 | 7.64 | 4.64 | 2.26 | 9.0 | 10.4 |
| Thomas Jefferson | 61,077 | 11.0 | 3.22 | 52.99 | 20.09 | 8.96 | 7.16 | 8.54 | 10.6 | 11.3 |
| Central Virginia | 91,565 | 10.2 | 3.69 | 57.77 | 22.49 | 8.00 | 5.17 | 2.92 | 9.7 | 10.6 |
| West Piedmont | 117,957 | 9.6 | 2.67 | 64.62 | 20.89 | 6.40 | 3.62 | 1.80 | 9.2 | 9.9 |
| Southside | 44,123 | 9.1 | 2.63 | 69.14 | 17.37 | 6.12 | 3.08 | 1.66 | 8.3 | 9.9 |
| Piedmont | 40,859 | 9.0 | 3.78 | 67.79 | 15.89 | 6.38 | 4.03 | 2.13 | 8.2 | 9.8 |
| Richmond Regional | 300,035 | 11.4 | 1.16 | 52.72 | 23.26 | 10.78 | 7.62 | 4.45 | 11.2 | 11.6 |
| Radco | 39,511 | 10.8 | 1.45 | 57.82 | 24.73 | 6.77 | 5.28 | 3.95 | 10.4 | 11.2 |
| Northern Neck | 21,247 | 9.4 | 2.38 | 64.20 | 20.52 | 6.83 | 3.77 | 2.30 | 8.5 | 10.2 |
| Middle Peninsula | 27,642 | 10.1 | 1.90 | 60.17 | 23.15 | 7.85 | 4.57 | 2.38 | 9.2 | 11.0 |
| Crater | 80,480 | 10.4 | 2.50 | 58.52 | 23.08 | 8.28 | 5.27 | 2.36 | 10.2 | 10.6 |
| Southeastern Virginia | 371,988 | 11.3 | 1.49 | 52.59 | 27.30 | 9.72 | 5.69 | 3.22 | 11.2 | 11.4 |
| Peninsula | 154,781 | 12.0 | 1.28 | 46.49 | 29.02 | 11.17 | 7.60 | 4.45 | 12.1 | 12.0 |
| Accomack-Northampton | 25,685 | 9.4 | 2.89 | 66.02 | 19.14 | 7.12 | 3.27 | 1.55 | 8.7 | 10.0 |
| Virginia | 2,446,082 | 11.7 | 1.62 | 50.60 | 25.22 | 10.25 | 7.22 | 5.08 | 11.4 | 11.8 |

level. Individual planning districts which exceeded this total by more than 10 percent (i.e., with at least 9.64 percent of the population aged 25 and over having four or more years of postsecondary education) include New River Planning District (no. 4), with 10.26 percent; Thomas Jefferson Planning District (no. 10), with 15.70 percent; Richmond Regional Planning District (no. 15), with 12.07 percent; and Peninsula Planning District (no. 21), with 12.05 percent. These areas include two large metropolitan areas (Richmond and Newport News–Hampton) and two relatively large university communities (Blacksburg and Charlottesville).

The median number of school years completed differed by sex. For the state and for a majority of the planning districts, the median level of educational achievement was higher among females than males. However, in the two planning districts with a median level of education greater than the state average, this relationship was reversed; that is, the median level was higher for males.

In comparing educational achievement by sex, there was a higher proportion of males with no education (1.95 percent) and less than a full high school education (51.51 percent) than females (1.32 and 49.76 percent, respectively). On the other hand, there was also a greater proportion of males with four or more years of post secondary education (15.60 percent) than females (9.30 percent). In brief, the educational composition of males was more skewed at both ends of its distribution than that of females.

## Marital and Household Status

### Marital Status

Marriage trends by race, sex, and age fluctuated considerably between 1950 and 1970. Fewer men (of all races) were single in 1960 (27.5 percent) than in 1950 (29.7 percent). By 1970, however, the proportion of single men had climbed back to 29.4 percent. Most of the change was effected by those currently married rather than by those separated, divorced, or widowed.

The currently married category for men rose from 63.4 percent in 1950 to 66.1 percent in 1960, dropping to 64.1 percent by 1970. In the same three periods 6.9, 6.4, and 6.5 percent of men were separated, divorced, or widowed.

Women did not follow this pattern. While rates of single and married women fluctuated about the same amount as those of men, the proportion of separated, divorced, and widowed women rose from 15.9 to 17.4 percent in 20 years. Throughout the period, fewer women were single, and also fewer were currently married than men, and a considerably high proportion were separated, divorced, and widowed (see Table 4.11).

Table 4.11.  Marital status by sex, Virginia, 1950-70 (percent)

|  | 1950 | | 1960 | | 1970 | |
|---|---|---|---|---|---|---|
|  | Male | Female | Male | Female | Male | Female |
| Single | 29.7 | 21.0 | 27.5 | 19.4 | 29.4 | 22.0 |
| Currently married | 63.0 | 63.1 | 66.1 | 64.3 | 64.1 | 66.0 |
| Separated, widowed, divorced | 6.9 | 15.9 | 6.4 | 16..3 | 6.5 | 17.4 |

Large differences in white and nonwhite marital status were noted for each decade. Generally, larger percentages of nonwhite men and women remained single or were separated, divorced, or widowed at each census. However, although actual variances by race were large, the direction of change from decade to decade was almost constant with that of the total population.

Rates for white men changed very little over twenty years. The proportion of single men fell from 28.6 percent in 1950 to 26.1 percent in 1960 and rose slightly to 27.8 percent in 1970. Those currently married increased from 65.9 percent in 1950 to 68.7 percent in 1960, falling off to 66.6 percent in 1970. The number of those separated, divorced, and widowed climbed from 5.5 percent in 1950 to 5.6 percent in 1970.

Rates for nonwhite men changed in greater amount than those for whites and, as noted, were quite different in composition from those of whites. In 1950, 33.8 percent of nonwhite men were single;

in 1960, 33.4 percent; and in 1970, 37 percent. The proportion
of those separated, divorced, and widowed dropped from 11.8
percent in 1950 to 11 percent in 1970. Fewer nonwhite
men were married in 1970 (52 percent) than in 1950 (54.4 percent).
Part of the reason for the differences between races lies in
the greater proportion of younger men among nonwhites.

In 1950, 19.9 percent of white women were unmarried. This share
dropped to 18.3 percent in 1960 and rose to 20.4 percent in 1970.
The proportion of separated, divorced, and widowed white women
also rose, and to much greater extent than that of white men.
In 1950, 14.1 percent of women were in this category;
in 1970, 16.1 percent. Number of women currently married
dropped from 66 percent to 63.5 percent.

Again, the rates for nonwhites were quite different than for
whites. Whereas 63.5 percent of white women were married by
1970, only 47.8 percent of nonwhite women were. This latter rate
had declined from 53 percent in 1950. More nonwhite women
were single: 24.8 percent in 1950, 24 percent in 1960, and 28.7
percent in 1970. The rate of separated, divorced, and widowed,
while higher than that of white women, did not rise as
much, increasing from 22.2 percent in 1950 to 23.5 percent in
1970 (see table 4.12). Again, age composition differences are
important in explaining the differences between races.

Changes by marital status were not universal among age groups,
nor were changes by age constant by sex or race (see Table
A4.2). As a rule, however, most changes in status were accounted
for by persons between 15 and 44 years of age. An individual's
major decisions about his life take place during these years.
Changing patterns of marital status also hold implications for birth
rates and for household status.

It has been demonstrated that for the total population, marital
rates for men changed very little and those for women somewhat
more. Large changes were apparent for men in the 30–44 age
group. Over twenty years, from 1950 to 1970, the proportion of
single individuals dropped from 11.2 to 8.2 percent. Simultaneously, the proportion of this age group currently married rose
from 83.4 to 86 percent.

The largest increase in the currently married share for men was

Table 4.12.  Marital status by sex and race, Virginia, 1950-70 (percent)

|  | 1950 | | 1960 | | 1970 | |
|---|---|---|---|---|---|---|
|  | Male | Female | Male | Female | Male | Female |
| **White** | | | | | | |
| Single | 28.6 | 19.9 | 26.1 | 18.3 | 27.8 | 20.4 |
| Currently married | 65.9 | 66.0 | 68.7 | 66.9 | 66.6 | 63.5 |
| Separated, widowed, divorced | 5.5 | 14.1 | 5.2 | 14.8 | 5.6 | 16.1 |
| **Nonwhite** | | | | | | |
| Single | 33.8 | 24.8 | 33.4 | 24.0 | 37.0 | 28.7 |
| Currently married | 54.4 | 53.0 | 55.3 | 53.3 | 52.0 | 47.8 |
| Separated, widowed, divorced | 11.8 | 22.2 | 11.3 | 22.7 | 11.0 | 23.5 |

recorded in the 65 and older category, where the proportion rose from 66.5 to 71.2 percent. This change may reflect the decline in mortality, as well as some decrease in the proportion separated or divorced.

Although men between 15 and 29 did not experience much change in marital status, women did; in fact, it was in this group that the largest fluctuations occurred. The number of single women rose from 39.5 to 46 percent; those currently married dropped from 56.4 to 49.5 percent; the number separated, divorced, and widowed changed very slightly, increasing 0.4 percent. Changes were slight in the 30-44 group, except that the percent single dropped 3 percent. The other categories absorbed the difference in nearly equal amounts. Large changes in the 45-64 group occurred, however. The relative number of single women dropped 2.2 percent, that of married women rose from 66.9 to 72.3 percent, and the number separated, divorced, and widowed dropped from 25.2 to 22 percent. The decrease in the number of single women indicates that not all of the change may be attributed to increased longevity. In fact, of women 65 and older, the most heavily widowed population, the proportion of those widowed, separated, and divorced remained about 59 percent throughout.

Due to the greater changes in marital rates among the nonwhite population, the changes within age groups were larger than those of whites. For instance, while almost no change was recorded for white men of 15 to 29 years in the twenty years, all those proportions changed dramatically for nonwhite men. In 1970 5 percent more were single than in 1950; 4 percent fewer were married; and 1 percent fewer were separated, divorced, and widowed.

White women in the 15–29 group experienced considerable change. The number of remaining single climbed 6 percent, to 43.2 percent; those currently married dropped from 59.7 to 52.8 percent; and those separated, divorced, and widowed increased their number by 0.7 percent, to 4 percent. Changes were even greater among nonwhite women. The proportion of single women rose from 47.1 to 58.1 percent; declines were noted among married women, from 45.5 to 35.2 percent, and among those separated, divorced, and widowed, from 4.7 to 6.7 percent.

White and nonwhite men experienced almost equal amounts of change in the 30–44 age cohort. In each case the proportion of currently married men rose slightly, with each complementary category absorbing the difference about equally. In 1970, 88.2 percent of white men aged 30–44 years were married, 6.9 percent single, and 4.9 percent separated, divorced, or widowed. For nonwhite men, 74.1 percent were married and 15.2 percent single.

Smaller changes were noted among women aged 30–44 than in the 15–29 group. In 1970, 4.5 percent of white women were single, down somewhat from 1950 level of 7.9 percent. Rates of those currently married rose from 85.1 to 87 percent, and of those separated, divorced, and widowed from 7 to 8.5 percent. The proportion of nonwhite single women also dropped, but not so much, from 10.9 to 9.4 percent. Relative number of married women also dropped, very slightly, to 69.2 percent. The proportion who were separated, divorced, and widowed rose slightly, from 18.7 to 24.4 percent.

Small changes in marital status were recorded for men of 45 to 64 years. The proportion of married white men rose slightly; so proportions of single and separated, divorced, or widowed men dropped. The amount of change for nonwhite men was about the same throughout. The major difference to be noted is that fewer nonwhite men were married in the first place; so other categories were adjusted proportionately.

Change was somewhat greater among women of this age. The proportion of white women currently married rose from 69.6 to 74.9 percent. Likewise, the proportion of married nonwhite women rose, from 56.8 to 60 percent. The number of separated, divorced, and widowed nonwhite women dropped from 37 to 32.6 percent, while the share of single women increased from 5.9 to 7.4 percent.

In the elderly population far greater changes were reflected for men, both white and nonwhite, than for women in the separated, divorced, and widowed category. For white men 65 and over, the rate declined from 24.2 to 19.7 percent; for nonwhite men, from 34.2 to 30.5 percent. This is an indicator of increased life expectancy, as it was primarily women who benefited from increased longevity. In the separated, divorced, and widowed category, which after age 65 is changed mainly through widowhood, white women experienced an increase, from 57.2 to 58.1 percent. Not so for nonwhite women, however, whose rate of separated, divorced, and widowed went from 67.2 to 63.5 percent in twenty years.

It has been demonstrated that changes in marital status were not predictable for the entire population but were dependent on characteristics of age, sex and race. The generally stable status for men did not reveal the declining popularity of marriage among nonwhite men between 15 and 29 years and the decreasing likelihood of remaining single among white men of all ages. The slight increase of 1 percent among all single women likewise did not represent the increased frequency of remaining unmarried among all women aged 15 to 29. Also, the total increase of 1.5 percent of women separated, divorced, and widowed did not indicate that most of this change occurred among women—white and nonwhite—between 30 and 44 years of age. Nor do the overall figures indicate that marriage was much less frequently the choice in the nonwhite population. While marriage as an institution persisted among Virginians, the data suggest that it came later in life and was more prone to dissolution through divorce.

## Household Status

Between 1950 and 1970 the share of population in households in Virginia remained essentially constant. The composition of households, however, changed a great deal during the period. The number of persons per household declined from 3.8 in 1950 to 3.2 in 1970, indicating a declining birth rate and more nuclear families.

Supporting this conclusion are data showing composition of households (Table 4.13). In 1950, 10.3 percent of household members were relatives other than the head of household (always the husband if he is present) or wife or child of the head. In 1960 the proportion had declined to 8.1 percent; in 1970, 5.7 percent. Similarly, the proportion of persons not related to the head of household dropped from 3.1 to 1.8 percent.

Table 4.13. Household composition of the population, Virginia, 1950-70 (percent)

|                        | 1950 | 1960 | 1970 |
|------------------------|------|------|------|
| Head of household      | 26.7 | 28.3 | 31.2 |
| Wife of head           | 21.2 | 21.6 | 22.4 |
| Child of head          | 38.7 | 40.2 | 38.9 |
| Other relative of head | 10.3 | 8.1  | 5.7  |
| Nonrelative of head    | 3.1  | 1.9  | 1.8  |
| Persons per household  | 3.8  | 3.5  | 3.2  |

Despite the decline of other persons in the household, which would increase the relative number of children, *ceteris paribus*, their proportion increased only 0.2 percent in twenty years, to 38.9 percent. Actually, there were more children per household in 1960 (40.2 percent) than in 1950 (38.7 percent), reflecting the high birth rate of the 1950s. The sharp decline or fertility of the 1960s is represented by the 1970 data.

The proportion of "wife of head" in the households remained about the same; so the result was that, proportionately, more persons in households were heads. Their number increased from 26.7 percent in 1950 to 28.3 percent in 1960 to 31.2 percent in 1970. A great deal of this increase parallels the rise in the number of single-person households.

In 1950 the proportions of family and nonfamily heads were not reported. In 1960, 88.7 percent of all household heads were family heads; of them, 8.7 percent were female. The remaining 11.3 percent were primary individuals in nonfamily households; 66 percent of these heads were female. In 1970, 83.3 percent of all heads were family heads, 11.2 percent of whom were female, an increase of 2.5 percent from 1960. The remaining 16.7 percent were primary individuals, 62.9 percent of whom were female.

The proportion of women who were heads of household grew over the period, with the largest increases occurring between the ages of 15 and 34. (This is also the age group which increasingly chose to remain single, and which had larger separated, divorced, and widowed rates over the years). In 1970, 8.4 percent of all household heads were between 15 and 24 years of age, an increase from the 5.2 percent figure of 1950. Fewer households heads (40.2 percent) were between 25 and 44 years old, however; their proportion declined from 47.4 percent in 1950. The number of heads over 45 years old increased from 47.4 percent in 1950 to 49.7 percent in 1960 to 51.3 percent in 1970 (see Tables 4.14 and A4.3).

Household characteristics differed widely by race, with nonwhite households exhibiting larger families with more children and more relatives. Both white and nonwhite households followed the trend to smaller sizes over the years. In nonwhite households there was a much higher percentage of relatives of head other than wife or children. In 1950, 16.6 percent of household members were in this category; in 1970, 12 percent. Comparable figures for white households were 8.5 and 4.4 percent.

In 1950 the number of persons per white household was 3.6; in 1960, 3.4; and in 1950, 3.1. Nonwhite households had more people: 4.2 in 1950 and 1960, and 3.8 in 1970. The

Table 4.14. Household status by race, Virginia, 1950-70

|  | 1950 | 1960 | 1970 |
|---|---|---|---|
| Household population |  |  |  |
| Total | 3,136,235 | 3,787,952 | 4,453,480 |
| White | 2,437,120 | 2,998,671 | 3,607,333 |
| Nonwhite | 699,115 | 789,281 | 846,167 |
| Percentage of population in households |  |  |  |
| Total | 94.7 | 95.8 | 95.8 |
| White | 94.4 | 95.8 | 95.8 |
| Nonwhite | 94.9 | 96.0 | 95.9 |
| Number of households |  |  |  |
| Total | 837,275 | 1,072,840 | 1,395,401 |
| White | 672,440 | 882,853 | 1,169,028 |
| Nonwhite | 164,835 | 189,987 | 226,373 |
| Persons per household |  |  |  |
| Total | 3.8 | 3.5 | 3.2 |
| White | 3.6 | 3.4 | 3.1 |
| Nonwhite | 4.2 | 4.5 | 3.8 |
| Percentage of households with only one member |  |  |  |
| Total | NA | 11.3 | 16.7 |
| White | NA | 10.7 | 16.5 |
| Nonwhite | NA | 14.2 | 18.4 |

difference is reflected by the increasing proportion of children in the nonwhite household. In 1950 children comprised 38.7 percent of the white household and 38.9 percent of the nonwhite. In 1970 they were 38 percent of the white household but 43.3 percent of the nonwhite.

The "wife of head" category, which applies only when the husband is present, remained about 8 percent higher in white households than in nonwhite. Nonwhite households had a higher percentage of female heads: in 1950, 12.8 percent of white heads were female; among nonwhites 22.4 percent were female. The proportion of female heads increased over the years, but in 1970 many more nonwhite households (28.9 percent) than white (18.1 percent) were headed by a female.

In 1960, when heads of household were isolated by type (family and nonfamily), 9.1 percent of white families were headed by a female, and 19.7 percent of nonwhite families. In contrast, white primary individuals were much more likely to be female (69 percent) than were nonwhite primary individuals (54 percent). In 1970, 23.3 percent of nonwhite family heads were female, and 8.8 percent of white family heads. Of white primary individuals, 65.9 percent were female; of nonwhite, 54 percent.

As noted, there was progressive increase of households headed by females from 1950 to 1970. In all age categories more women headed households in 1970 than in 1950, but greatest gains were in younger, newly established households. Thus trends throughout the period have been to smaller households, more people living alone, and more families headed by females. A decreasing birth rate is depicted by smaller households and a nearly constant share of children in households. In nonwhite households the tendency is a higher proportion of children and female heads. In all households, regardless of race, more female heads were present in 1970 than in 1950. Household statistics serve as good indicators of changing life styles, the demand for housing, education, and other services, and the increasing frequency of occurrence of the nuclear family.

# Chapter 5

# Economic Change in Virginia

## Economic Changes between 1950 and 1970

Between 1950 and 1970 there were significant changes in the socioeconomic status of Virginia residents. This section reviews trends for the state in the areas of labor force composition and income.

## Labor Force Composition

The socioeconomic changes that occurred in Virginia between 1950 and 1970 were reflected in the changing composition of Virginia's labor force. These changes may be viewed in three ways: the demographic, occupational, and industrial composition of the labor force.

*Demographic Composition.* In 1950 there were 1,305,611 persons in Virginia's labor force. The number increased to 1,532,599 by 1960. A greater increase had occurred by 1970, bringing the total Virginia labor force to 1,956,894, an increase of 49.9 percent over 1950.

The portion of the population in the military increased slightly between 1950 and 1970. Of the 1950 population aged 14 and over, 4.5 percent (108,935 persons) was in the military, compared to 4.8 percent (133,082) of the 1960 population and 5.1 percent (175,718) of the 1970 population. Similarly, the civilian labor force increased from 49.8 percent (1,196,676 persons) in 1950 to 50.8 percent (1,399,517) in 1960 and 52.1 percent (1,781,176) in 1970. In 1950 the civilian labor force was 72.7 percent male and 27.3 percent female, but by 1960 the female share increased to 33.7 percent and by 1970 to 39.4 percent.

The *civilian labor force participation rate* (that is, the number of persons in the civilian labor force divided by the total population aged 14 and over) increased gradually from 49.8

percent in 1950 to 50.8 percent in 1960 and 52.1 percent in 1970.

In 1950 the overall rate of participation was higher for nonwhites (53.9 percent) than white (48.6 percent). The nonwhite male rate (74.0 percent) was higher than the white male rate (71.3 percent); the nonwhite female rate (33.8 percent) was higher than the white female rate (25.6 percent). Though the 1960 nonwhite labor force participation rate was still higher than the white rate, the white male rate (68.5 percent) surpassed the nonwhite male rate (66.9 percent) while the white female rate (32.6 percent) lagged behind the nonwhite female rate (39.0 percent). By 1970 the overall white rate (52.2 percent) was higher than the nonwhite rate (51.6 percent). The difference in the male rates had widened; the white male rate was 65.5 percent, and the nonwhite male rate was 58.0 percent. The difference between the female rates had narrowed; the white female rate was 39.4 percent and the nonwhite female rate was 40.3 percent.

Though the male labor force participation rate was consistently higher than the female rate between 1950 and 1970, there was a significant decrease in the span between the two. The rate for males was much higher than the rate for females in 1950 (71.8 percent for males and 27.4 percent for females), but by 1960 the male rate had declined slightly to 68.2 percent while the rate for females had risen considerably to 33.9 percent. By 1970 the male rate of participation had dropped to 63.7 percent while the female rate had risen to 40.1 percent.

The decrease in participation among males could be the result of the increasing incidence of Armed Forces service (8.6 percent of male Virginians in the entire labor force were military in 1950, compared with 13.7 percent in 1970) and increasing attendance at postsecondary educational institutions (13.8 percent of all Virginians aged 18–24 were enrolled in school in 1950 compared with 26.2 percent in 1970).[1]

---

[1] Another factor might well be the consistently increasing incidence of retirement at age 65 and even at younger ages. Seymour Wolfbein's *Work in American Society* (Glenview, Ill.: Scott, Foresman, 1971) shows that the retirement rate for men aged 65 had nearly tripled between 1950 and 1960: "The evidence for the 1960's indicates that this had continued to be the case in more recent years

Labor force participation among females was higher at all ages in 1970 than 1950, particularly for women over age 25 and most especially for women between the ages of 45 and 64 (see Figure 5.1). This suggests that married women tended to return to the labor force at a much greater rate in 1970 than 1950 (see Table 5.1).

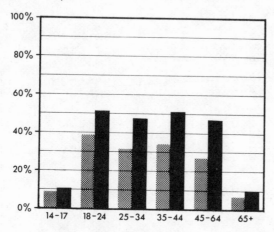

BLACK BARS REPRESENT 1970 PARTICIPATION RATES, WHILE GREY SHOWS 1950 RATES.

Fig. 5.1.    Female labor force participation rates by age, Virginia, 1950 and 1970

The civilian unemployment rate rose from 3.9 percent in 1950 to 4.2 percent in 1960 but dropped to 3 percent by 1970. Between 1950 and 1970 the male unemployment rate was consistently lower than the female rate and the white rate remained markedly lower than the nonwhite rate. However, the urban rate, which was notably higher than the rural rate in 1950, decreased by 1960 while the rural rate increased. Both urban and rural rates decreased by 1970, though the urban rate remained lower than the rural rate.

*Occupational Composition.* The most remarkable change in the occupational composition of Virginia's labor force between 1950

with growing indications, however, that more and more men are beginning to retire at even earlier ages than 65" (p. 170).

Table 5.1. Demographic characteristics of Virginia's labor force, 1950-70

| Year | Total Number | Total Percent | White Male Number | White Male Percent | White Female Number | White Female Percent | Nonwhite Male Number | Nonwhite Male Percent | Nonwhite Female Number | Nonwhite Female Percent |
|---|---|---|---|---|---|---|---|---|---|---|
| **1950** | | | | | | | | | | |
| Total Population 14+ | 2,404,426 | 100.0 | 954,534 | 39.7 | 937,160 | 40.0 | 256,265 | 10.7 | 256,467 | 10.7 |
| Number in Labor Force | 1,305,611 | 100.0 | 777,349 | 59.5 | 244,168 | 18.7 | 196,945 | 15.1 | 87,149 | 6.7 |
| Labor Force Participation Rate | | 49.8 | | 71.3 | | 25.6 | | 74.0 | | 33.8 |
| Number in Military | 108,935 | 100.0 | 97,195 | 89.2 | 4,063 | 3.7 | 7,436 | 6.8 | 241 | 0.2 |
| Civilian Labor Force | 1,196,676 | 100.0 | 680,154 | 56.8 | 240,105 | 20.1 | 189,509 | 15.8 | 86,908 | 7.3 |
| Employed Civilian | 1,150,164 | 100.0 | 659,781 | 57.4 | 232,752 | 20.2 | 177,481 | 10.2 | 80,150 | 7.0 |
| Unemployment Rate | | 3.9 | | 3.0 | | 3.1 | | 6.3 | | 7.8 |
| **1960** | | | | | | | | | | |
| Total Population 14+ | 2,753,069 | 100.0 | 1,098,198 | 39.9 | 1,121,750 | 40.8 | 262,322 | 9.5 | 270,799 | 9.8 |
| Number in Labor Force | 1,532,599 | 100.0 | 874,224 | 57.0 | 367,985 | 24.0 | 184,641 | 12.1 | 105,749 | 6.9 |
| Labor Force Participation Rate | | 50.8 | | 68.5 | | 32.6 | | 66.9 | | 39.0 |
| Number in Military | 133,082 | 100.0 | 121,635 | 91.4 | 2,124 | 2.0 | 9,169 | 8.1 | 154 | 0.1 |
| Civilian Labor Force | 1,399,517 | 100.0 | 752,589 | 53.8 | 365,861 | 26.1 | 175,472 | 12.5 | 105,595 | 7.5 |
| Employed Civilian | 1,340,800 | 100.0 | 726,226 | 54.2 | 353,516 | 26.4 | 163,324 | 12.2 | 97,734 | 7.3 |
| Unemployment Rate | | 4.2 | | 3.5 | | 3.4 | | 6.9 | | 7.4 |
| **1970** | | | | | | | | | | |
| Total Population 14+ | 3,418,599 | 100.0 | 1,379,460 | 40.4 | 1,431,984 | 41.9 | 291,658 | 8.5 | 315,497 | 9.2 |
| Number in Labor Force | 1,956,894 | 100.0 | 1,058,161 | 54.1 | 567,235 | 29.0 | 193,815 | 10.0 | 137,683 | 7.0 |
| Labor Force Participation Rate | | 52.1 | | 65.5 | | 39.4 | | 58.0 | | 40.3 |
| Number in Military | 175,718 | 100.0 | 154,256 | 87.8 | 3,298 | 1.9 | 17,727 | 10.1 | 437 | 0.2 |
| Civilian Labor Force | 1,781,176 | 100.0 | 903,905 | 50.8 | 563,937 | 31.7 | 176,088 | 9.9 | 137,246 | 7.7 |
| Employed Civilian | 1,727,111 | 100.0 | 885,555 | 51.3 | 545,247 | 31.6 | 169,009 | 9.8 | 127,300 | 7.4 |
| Unemployment Rate | | 3.0 | | 2.0 | | 3.3 | | 4.0 | | 7.2 |

| | 1950 Number | 1950 Percent | 1960 Number | 1960 Percent | 1970 Number | 1970 Percent | % Change 1950-1970 |
|---|---|---|---|---|---|---|---|
| Total Population 14+ | 2,404,426 | 100.0 | 2,753,069 | 100.0 | 3,418,599 | 100.0 | 42.2 |
| Number in Labor Force | 1,305,611 | 54.3 | 1,532,599 | 55.7 | 1,956,894 | 57.2 | 49.9 |
| Number in Military | 108,935 | 4.5 | 133,082 | 4.8 | 175,718 | 5.1 | 61.3 |
| Civilian Labor Force | 1,196,676 | 49.8 | 1,399,517 | 50.8 | 1,781,176 | 52.1 | 48.8 |
| Employed Civilian | 1,150,164 | 47.8 | 1,340,800 | 48.7 | 1,727,111 | 50.5 | 50.2 |

and 1970 was the widespread shift from agriculture to other areas of the economy. In 1950 14.3 percent of the state labor force was in agriculture (farmers, farm managers, farm foremen, and farm laborers). By 1960 only 7.2 percent was employed in agriculture. In 1970 agricultural employment accounted for a mere 2.5 percent of Virginia's labor force. The number of persons in agricultural occupations declined by 80 percent during this period.

The greatest increase in employment between 1950 and 1970 was in the white–collar segment of the labor force. In 1950, 33.5 percent of employment was in white–collar occupations (professional, managerial, clerical, sales). By 1960 these workers accounted for 40.1 percent of the labor force, an increase over 1950 of 40 percent. White–collar workers continued to increase in number, and in 1970 806,837 persons (46.7 percent of the entire labor force) were white–collar workers. The rate of increase over the twenty–year period for all white–collar workers was 109.5 percent: among professionals, it was 177.4 percent; among managers, 58.1 percent; among sales personnel, 49.3 percent; and among clerical employees, 129.4 percent. Growth in the latter area was concomitant with the pronounced upsurge in labor force participation by women.

There was a significant increase in the number of blue–collar workers in Virginia's labor force between 1950 and 1970, although the share of employment in this sector decreased because of the relatively greater increase in white–collar employment. In 1950, 46.9 percent of the labor force was in blue–collar occupations (operators, craftsmen, service workers). By 1960 these workers numbered 600,121, an increase of 11.3 percent of 1950, but they accounted for only 44.4 percent of the entire labor force. Blue–collar workers numbered 746,428 in 1970, an increase of 24.4 percent over 1960, but the share of this group in the total labor force declined slightly to 43.2 percent.

Within the blue–collar employment sector, the number of craftsmen and service workers increased substantially between 1950 and 1970. The number of operators increased moderately while the number of nonfarm laborers declined.

The number of persons employed in the private household sector increased 14.7 percent, from 43,999 in 1950 to 59,461 in 1960.

In both years this group accounted for a small share in Virginia's labor force (3.8 percent in 1950 and 3.4 percent in 1960). Between 1960 and 1970 the number of private household workers declined by 28.8 percent to slightly less than 36,000 persons, representing only 2.1 percent of the state's labor force. Over the two-decade period, employment in private households diminished by 18.3 percent, or 8,062 persons. Data summarizing changes in the occupational distribution of Virginia's work force are given in Table 5.2.

Table 5.2.  Occupational distribution of Virginia's employed labor force, 1950-70

|  | 1950 | | 1960 | | 1970 | |
|---|---|---|---|---|---|---|
|  | Number | Percent | Number | Percent | Number | Percent |
| Professional | 94,690 | 8.2 | 153,729 | 11.5 | 262,677 | 15.2 |
| Managerial | 89,230 | 7.8 | 106,297 | 7.9 | 141,070 | 8.2 |
| Clerical | 128,273 | 11.2 | 188,234 | 14.0 | 294,256 | 17.0 |
| Sales | 72,872 | 6.3 | 93,967 | 7.0 | 108,834 | 6.3 |
| Craftsmen | 152,294 | 13.2 | 177,549 | 13.2 | 231,612 | 13.4 |
| Operatives | 223,106 | 19.4 | 240,899 | 18.0 | 278,034 | 16.1 |
| Nonfarm Laborers | 88,125 | 7.7 | 76,519 | 5.7 | 77,428 | 4.5 |
| Farmers | 102,057 | 8.9 | 58,945 | 4.4 | 23,399 | 1.4 |
| Farm Laborers | 62,616 | 5.4 | 36,275 | 2.7 | 19,747 | 1.1 |
| Service Workers | 75,746 | 6.6 | 101,526 | 7.6 | 159,354 | 9.2 |
| Private Household Workers | 43,999 | 3.8 | 50,697 | 3.4 | 35,937 | 2.1 |
| Not Reported | 17,156 | 1.5 | 56,163 | 4.2 | 94,784 | 5.5 |
| Total | 1,150,164 | 100.0 | 1,340,800 | 100.0 | 1,727,132 | 100.0 |

*Industrial Composition.* The shift in the industrial composition of Virginia's labor force parallels the occupational data. Occupational data tell what members of the labor force do; industrial data describe the principal good or service produced by employers of the labor force. Data summarizing the industrial composition of Virginia's labor force are given in Table 5.3.

In the years 1950, 1960, and 1970 the largest single sector was manufacturing. This sector grew from 236,703 employees in 1950 (20.58 percent of employment) to 364,010 employees in 1970 (21.23 percent of employment). The overall increase in this sector was 53.78 percent from 1950 to 1970. Employment in durable goods manufacturing grew faster than employment in nondurable goods manufacturing. In 1950 the latter accounted for 61.7 percent of all employment in manufacturing. By 1970 it had fallen to 55.7 percent.

Over the twenty-year period, the fastest-growing sector was

Table 5.3. Industrial composition of Virginia's employed work force, 1950-70

| Industrial Category | 1950 Number | Percent | 1960 Number | Percent | 1970 Number* | Percent | Percent Change 1950-1970 |
|---|---|---|---|---|---|---|---|
| 1. Agriculture, forestry, and fisheries | 174,078 | 15.14 | 104,673 | 7.81 | 51,508 | 3.01 | -70.41 |
| 2. Mining | 28,985 | 2.52 | 19,277 | 1.44 | 15,969 | 0.93 | -44.91 |
| 3. Construction | 82,592 | 7.18 | 91,134 | 6.80 | 117,555 | 6.86 | 42.33 |
| 4. Durable goods manufacturing | 90,664 | 7.88 | 124,155 | 9.26 | 161,150 | 9.40 | 77.74 |
| 5. Nondurable goods manufacturing | 146,040 | 12.70 | 175,780 | 13.11 | 202,860 | 11.83 | 38.91 |
| 6. Transportation, communications, other public utilities | 91,118 | 7.92 | 93,172 | 6.95 | 109,208 | 6.37 | 19.85 |
| 7. Wholesale trade | 31,613 | 2.75 | 37,411 | 2.79 | 54,196 | 3.16 | 71.44 |
| 8. Retail trade | 156,007 | 13.56 | 191,844 | 14.31 | 235,906 | 13.76 | 51.22 |
| 9. Finance, insurance, and real estate | 30,084 | 2.62 | 47,123 | 3.51 | 71,748 | 4.19 | 138.49 |
| 10. Business and repair service | 20,620 | 1.79 | 28,069 | 2.09 | 41,908 | 2.44 | 103.24 |
| 11. Personal services | 84,969 | 7.39 | 95,632 | 7.13 | 83,830 | 4.89 | -1.34 |
| 12. Entertainment and recreation services | 6,913 | 0.60 | 7,705 | 0.57 | 10,122 | 0.59 | 46.42 |
| 13. Professional and related services | 89,403 | 7.77 | 150,640 | 11.24 | 269,618 | 15.73 | 201.58 |
| 14. Public Administration | 99,246 | 8.63 | 130,569 | 9.74 | 187,580 | 10.94 | 89.01 |
| Not reported | 17,832 | 1.55 | 43,616 | 3.25 | 101,092 | 5.90 | 466.90 |
| Total | 1,150,164 | 100.00 | 1,340,800 | 100.00 | 1,714,250 | 100.00 | 49.04 |

*Persons aged 16 years and over. A total of 12,882 persons aged 14-15 years are included in the occupational data of Table 5.2 but excluded here. Some 1,061 of these persons are employed in agriculture; the remaining 11,821 in other industries. Thus, of total employment in Virginia in 1970 of 1,727,132, some 52,569 or 3.04 percent are employed in the agricultural sector.

professional and related services. Employment in this sector increased by 201.53 percent from 1950 to 1970. Other sectors which grew at a rate faster than the overall level (49.04 percent in the twenty-year period) include finance, insurance, and real estate (138.49 percent); business and repair services (103.24 percent); public administration (89.01 percent); wholesale trade (71.44 percent); and retail trade (51.22 percent).

Industries that experienced growth but at a rate lower than the state total include entertainment and recreation services (46.42 percent); construction (42.33 percent); and transportation, communication, and other public utilities (19.58 percent). Finally, employment diminished in three sectors: personal services (1.34 percent), mining (44.91 percent), and fisheries (70.41 percent).

Income

Significant changed occurred in the income level of Virginians between 1950 and 1970. In general, income increased sharply, but at a slightly slower pace between 1960 and 1970. In 1950 the median income per family was $2,644, and by 1960 it had increased by 87.7 percent to $4,964. An additional increase of 82.3 percent between 1960 and 1970 created a median income of $9,049 in 1969. These data are in *current dollars*; that is, they are not adjusted for the dimunition of purchasing power resulting from the inflation that has been experienced in recent years. If family income is converted to constant (1967) dollars, the median family income would have been $3,704 in 1950 and $8,244 in 1970. Thus, in terms of the real purchasing power of family income, the change from 1950 to 1970 was 122.6 percent (see Table 5.4).

Nearly one-fifth of all Virginia families received less than $1,000 of income in 1950. By 1960 this share of families dropped to 8.9 percent, and in 1969 only 2.8 percent had an income of less than $1,000. Furthermore, in 1950 only 2.5 percent of Virginia families had incomes of $10,000 or more. The number grew to 13.2 percent by 1960, and in 1969 43.7 percent of Virginia families had incomes of at least $10,000.

Table 5.4.  Distribution of income of Virginia Families, 1950-70

| Income Category | 1950 Number | 1950 Percent | 1960 Number | 1960 Percent | 1970 Number | 1970 Percent | Percent Change 1950-60 | Percent Change 1960-70 | Percent Change 1950-70 |
|---|---|---|---|---|---|---|---|---|---|
| less than $1,000 | 137,500 | 18.5 | 80,229 | 8.4 | 32,818 | 2.8 | -41.6 | -59.1 | -76.1 |
| $1,000-$1,999 | 137,930 | 18.6 | 85,883 | 9.0 | 43,531 | 3.7 | -37.7 | -49.3 | -68.4 |
| $2,000-$2,999 | 149,545 | 20.1 | 100,017 | 10.5 | 51,495 | 4.4 | -33.1 | -48.5 | -65.5 |
| $3,000-$3,999 | 119,115 | 16.0 | 106,901 | 11.2 | 61,252 | 5.3 | -10.2 | -42.7 | -48.5 |
| $4,000-$4,999 | 70,830 | 9.5 | 108,185 | 11.3 | 67,059 | 5.8 | 52.7 | -38.0 | -5.3 |
| $5,000-$5,999 | 47,225 | 6.4 | 102,826 | 10.8 | 76,385 | 6.6 | 117.7 | -25.7 | 61.7 |
| $6,000-$6,999 | 28,730 | 3.9 | 84,835 | 8.9 | 79,682 | 6.9 | 195.2 | -6.0 | 177.3 |
| $7,000-$9,999 | 33,880 | 4.6 | 159,398 | 16.7 | 241,612 | 20.8 | 370.4 | 51.5 | 613.1 |
| $10,000+ | 18,645 | 2.5 | 126,446 | 13.2 | 508,422 | 43.7 | 578.1 | 302.0 | 2,626.8 |
| Total | 743,400 | 100.0 | 954,720 | 100.0 | 1,162,256 | 100.0 | 87.7 | 82.2 | 242.2 |
| Median | $2,644 | | $4,964 | | $9,049 | | | | |

In 1970 for the first time data showing the incidence of poverty in the state were made available. *Poverty* is defined as a level of income below the guidelines established by the Social Security Administration. The poverty level varies according to household size, age, and sex of head and farm–nonfarm residence (see Table 5.5). The value of this threshold ranged in 1970 from $6,665 for a nonfarm family of seven with a male head to $1,489 for a single female aged 65 and over living on a farm.

In Virginia 12.3 percent of all families received income which placed them below the poverty guidelines. This amounted to

Table 5.5.  Poverty income criteria for families by number of children under age 18, sex and age of head, and farm or nonfarm residence

| Family Size | None | 1 | 2 | 3 | 4 | 5 | 6 or more |
|---|---|---|---|---|---|---|---|
| | | | Number of Children | | | | |
| **Male Head—Nonfarm** | | | | | | | |
| 1.  Under 65 years old... | $1,975 | --- | --- | --- | --- | --- | --- |
| 65 years old and over | 1,774 | --- | --- | --- | --- | --- | --- |
| 2.  Under 65 years old... | 2,469 | $2,766 | --- | --- | --- | --- | --- |
| 65 years old and over | 2,216 | 2,766 | --- | --- | --- | --- | --- |
| 3.......................... | 2,875 | 2,968 | $3,137 | --- | --- | --- | --- |
| 4.......................... | 3,790 | 3,847 | 3,715 | $3,902 | --- | --- | --- |
| 5.......................... | 4,574 | 4,630 | 4,481 | 4,368 | $4,462 | --- | --- |
| 6.......................... | 5,247 | 5,265 | 5,153 | 5,041 | 4,891 | $4,967 | --- |
| 7 or more................ | 6,609 | 6,665 | 6,535 | 6,422 | 6,274 | 6,049 | $5,994 |
| **Male Head—Farm** | | | | | | | |
| 1.  Under 65 years old... | $1,679 | --- | --- | --- | --- | --- | --- |
| 65 years old and over | 1,508 | --- | --- | --- | --- | --- | --- |
| 2.  Under 65 years old... | 2,099 | $2,351 | --- | --- | --- | --- | --- |
| 65 years old and over | 1,884 | 2,351 | --- | --- | --- | --- | --- |
| 3.......................... | 2,444 | 2,523 | $2,666 | --- | --- | --- | --- |
| 4.......................... | 3,222 | 3,270 | 3,158 | $3,317 | --- | --- | --- |
| 5.......................... | 3,888 | 3,936 | 3,809 | 3,713 | $3,793 | --- | --- |
| 6.......................... | 4,460 | 4,475 | 4,380 | 4,285 | 4,157 | $4,222 | --- |
| 7 or more................ | 5,618 | 5,665 | 5,555 | 5,459 | 5,333 | 5,142 | $5,095 |
| **Female Head—Nonfarm** | | | | | | | |
| 1.  Under 65 years old... | $1,826 | --- | --- | --- | --- | --- | --- |
| 65 years old and over | 1,752 | --- | --- | --- | --- | --- | --- |
| 2.  Under 65 years old... | 2,282 | $2,491 | --- | --- | --- | --- | --- |
| 65 years old and over | 2,190 | 2,491 | --- | --- | --- | --- | --- |
| 3.......................... | 2,781 | 2,651 | $2,931 | --- | --- | --- | --- |
| 4.......................... | 3,641 | 3,771 | 3,753 | $3,715 | --- | --- | --- |
| 5.......................... | 4,368 | 4,500 | 4,481 | 4,444 | $4,294 | --- | --- |
| 6.......................... | 5,096 | 5,191 | 5,153 | 5,115 | 4,948 | $4,798 | --- |
| 7 or more................ | 6,403 | 6,497 | 6,478 | 6,422 | 6,255 | 6,124 | $5,825 |
| **Female Head—Farm** | | | | | | | |
| 1.  Under 65 years old... | $1,552 | --- | --- | --- | --- | --- | --- |
| 65 years old and over | 1,489 | --- | --- | --- | --- | --- | --- |
| 2.  Under 65 years old... | 1,940 | $2,117 | --- | --- | --- | --- | --- |
| 65 years old and over | 1,862 | 2,117 | --- | --- | --- | --- | --- |
| 3.......................... | 2,364 | 2,253 | $2,491 | --- | --- | --- | --- |
| 4.......................... | 3,095 | 3,205 | 3,190 | $3,158 | --- | --- | --- |
| 5.......................... | 3,713 | 3,825 | 3,809 | 3,777 | $3,650 | --- | --- |
| 6.......................... | 4,332 | 4,412 | 4,380 | 4,348 | 4,206 | $4,078 | --- |
| 7 or more................ | 5,443 | 5,522 | 5,506 | 5,459 | 5,317 | 5,205 | $4,951 |

Source:  U. S. Bureau of the Census, Public Use Samples of Basic Records from the 1970 Census:  Description and Technical Documentation (Washington, D. C.: U.S. Government Printing Office, 1972), p. 122.

143,005 families or 575,330 persons. Among these families, mean income was only $2,025. Additionally, 115,285 single persons living alone received income below the poverty level; these 115,285 represented 36.9 percent of all individuals living by themselves in one-person households. All told, the 1970 census showed that some 690,615 Virginians were in a poverty status; this was 14.9 percent of the state's enumerated 4,648,494 persons.

The incidence of poverty is strongly influenced by the race, age, and sex of the family head and by the place of residence. In 1970 there were more poor families with a white head (88,065) than a nonwhite head (54,940); however, only 9.0 percent of all families with a white head had incomes below the poverty level compared to 29.2 percent of families with a nonwhite head. Only 10.6 percent of families with a head less than 65 were termed poor, compared to 25.7 percent of families with head aged 65 and over; only 11.6 percent of all families, but 24.2 percent of poor families, were headed by a person aged 65 and over. Of the 47,505 families (33.2 percent of all families) headed by a female, some 36.8 percent were below the poverty level compared to 9.2 percent of families with a male head. Though only 37.2 percent of all families in the state lived in rural areas, rural families comprised 53.8 percent (76,916) of all poor families. Only 9.1 percent of urban families had incomes below the poverty level compared to 17.8 percent of rural families.

## The Economic Situation in Virginia in 1970

The remainder of this chapter is devoted to a detailed analysis of these characteristics within Virginia for 1970. Individual sections discuss employment and labor force, occupational and industrial composition of the labor force, income, and urban-rural and metropolitan-nonmetropolitan comparisons.

Employment and the Labor Force

*Labor Force Participation.* The *labor force participation rate* used in this section is the percentage of the population aged 16 and over which is in the civilian labor force.[2] Labor force participation in an area is dependent upon the relative number of job opportunities and intervening variables, such as military service or college enrollment, which tend to limit labor force participation. Additionally, the age composition of a population can have a significant effect upon the labor force participation rate. For example, a high proportion of persons aged 65 and over would contribute to a low labor force participation rate.

In Virginia 67.9 percent of all males aged 16 and over and 42.1 percent of all similarly aged females were in the labor force as of April 1, 1970. The amount of variation across the state was considerable. The planning district with the lowest labor force participation rate among males was the Southeastern Virginia Planning District (no. 20), which includes the Norfolk–Virginia Beach–Portsmouth metropolitan area; there only 53.9 percent of all males aged 16 and over participated in the labor force (see Table 5.6). The reason for the low rate was the high concentration of military personnel in the area, which by definition are not accounted for in the labor force participation rate. This factor was also very evident in the Crater Planning District (no. 19), site of Fort Lee, where the male labor force participation rate was 57.9 percent, and in the Peninsula Planning District (no. 21), where it was only 59.7 percent.

The effect of a large university in a relatively small area was quite evident in the New River Valley Planning District (no. 4), site of Virginia Polytechnic Institute and State University, and the Thomas Jefferson Planning District (no. 10), site of the University of Virginia. In these areas, male college students accounted for

[2] Rates in this section pertain strictly to the population aged 16 and over. In the introductory section, where changes in the past two decades were considered, the base of analysis was the population aged 14 and over. Consequently, the rates mentioned here are not strictly comparable with those analyzed in the first section. This difference is due to changes in published census data in the 1970 census.

Table 5.6. Employment and labor force characteristics of Virginia planning districts, 1970

| Area | Total Population Aged 16+ | Civilian Labor Force | Labor Force Participation Rate | Percent of Civilian Labor Force Unemployed |
|------|------|------|------|------|
| Lenowisco | | | | |
| Male | 28,220 | 17,740 | 62.9 | 4.3 |
| Female | 31,538 | 7,235 | 22.9 | 5.4 |
| Total | 59,758 | 24,975 | 41.8 | 4.5 |
| Cumberland Plateau | | | | |
| Male | 36,685 | 23,511 | 64.1 | 3.8 |
| Female | 38,626 | 9,016 | 23.3 | 6.1 |
| Total | 75,311 | 32,527 | 43.2 | 4.4 |
| Mount Rogers | | | | |
| Male | 54,057 | 38,230 | 70.7 | 3.8 |
| Female | 60,363 | 23,187 | 38.4 | 4.6 |
| Total | 114,420 | 61,417 | 53.7 | 4.1 |
| New River Valley | | | | |
| Male | 41,529 | 28,523 | 68.7 | 3.2 |
| Female | 42,419 | 17,012 | 40.1 | 5.4 |
| Total | 83,948 | 45,535 | 54.2 | 4.0 |
| Fifth | | | | |
| Male | 77,030 | 59,172 | 76.8 | 1.8 |
| Female | 88,301 | 36,565 | 41.4 | 3.4 |
| Total | 165,331 | 95,737 | 57.9 | 2.4 |
| Central Shenandoah | | | | |
| Male | 63,233 | 47,511 | 75.1 | 2.1 |
| Female | 70,510 | 30,364 | 43.1 | 3.4 |
| Total | 133,743 | 77,875 | 58.2 | 2.6 |
| Lord Fairfax | | | | |
| Male | 35,900 | 27,642 | 77.0 | 2.4 |
| Female | 39,466 | 16,589 | 42.0 | 4.6 |
| Total | 75,366 | 44,231 | 58.7 | 3.2 |
| Northern Virginia | | | | |
| Male | 304,090 | 213,967 | 70.4 | 1.9 |
| Female | 322,913 | 153,106 | 47.4 | 2.6 |
| Total | 627,003 | 367,073 | 58.5 | 2.2 |
| Rappahannock-Rapidan | | | | |
| Male | 24,146 | 18,269 | 75.7 | 1.9 |
| Female | 25,072 | 9,736 | 38.8 | 2.8 |
| Total | 49,218 | 28,005 | 56.9 | 2.2 |
| Thomas Jefferson | | | | |
| Male | 41,516 | 28,067 | 67.6 | 2.4 |
| Female | 40,471 | 18,057 | 44.6 | 2.6 |
| Total | 81,987 | 46,124 | 56.3 | 2.5 |
| Central Virginia | | | | |
| Male | 54,578 | 41,132 | 75.4 | 2.0 |
| Female | 62,077 | 27,177 | 43.8 | 3.0 |
| Total | 116,655 | 68,309 | 58.6 | 2.4 |
| West Piedmont | | | | |
| Male | 71,535 | 55,780 | 78.0 | 1.8 |
| Female | 79,130 | 36,900 | 46.6 | 4.7 |
| Total | 150,665 | 92,680 | 61.5 | 2.9 |
| Southside | | | | |
| Male | 26,867 | 19,083 | 71.0 | 2.6 |
| Female | 29,284 | 11,826 | 40.4 | 6.0 |
| Total | 56,151 | 30,909 | 55.1 | 3.9 |

Table 5.6.   (continued)

| Area | Total Population Aged 16+ | Civilian Labor Force | Labor Force Participation Rate | Percent of Civilian Labor Force Unemployed |
|------|--------------------------|----------------------|-------------------------------|--------------------------------------------|
| Piedmont | | | | |
| Male | 25,019 | 17,312 | 69.2 | 2.8 |
| Female | 27,891 | 10,673 | 38.3 | 5.2 |
| Total | 52,910 | 27,985 | 52.9 | 3.7 |
| Richmond Regional | | | | |
| Male | 178,292 | 137,686 | 77.2 | 1.7 |
| Female | 207,335 | 97,458 | 47.0 | 2.9 |
| Total | 385,627 | 235,144 | 61.0 | 2.2 |
| RADCO | | | | |
| Male | 25,657 | 17,970 | 70.0 | 1.5 |
| Female | 27,563 | 10,588 | 38.4 | 3.2 |
| Total | 53,220 | 28,558 | 53.7 | 2.1 |
| Northern Neck | | | | |
| Male | 12,215 | 8,232 | 67.4 | 5.2 |
| Female | 13,373 | 5,052 | 37.8 | 7.1 |
| Total | 25,588 | 13,284 | 51.9 | 6.0 |
| Middle Peninsula | | | | |
| Male | 16,264 | 11,819 | 72.7 | 1.7 |
| Female | 17,430 | 6,229 | 35.7 | 4.5 |
| Total | 33,694 | 18,048 | 53.6 | 2.7 |
| Crater | | | | |
| Male | 57,525 | 33,293 | 57.9 | 2.2 |
| Female | ·53,732 | 22,200 | 41.3 | 4.5 |
| Total | 111,257 | 55,493 | 49.9 | 3.1 |
| Southeastern Virginia | | | | |
| Male | 275,727 | 148,568 | 53.9 | 2.5 |
| Female | 253,957 | 97,769 | 38.5 | 5.9 |
| Total | 529,684 | 246,337 | 46.5 | 3.9 |
| Peninsula | | | | |
| Male | 110,693 | 66,035 | 59.7 | 2.5 |
| Female | 106,353 | 43,315 | 40.7 | 5.1 |
| Total | 217,046 | 109,350 | 50.4 | 3.6 |
| Accomack-Northampton | | | | |
| Male | 14,181 | 10,033 | 70.8 | 4.7 |
| Female | 16,638 | 7,111 | 42.7 | 13.7 |
| Total | 30,819 | 17,144 | 55.6 | 8.4 |
| State | | | | |
| Male | 1,574,959 | 1,069,536 | 67.9 | 2.3 |
| Female | 1,654,442 | 697,204 | 42.1 | 4.0 |
| Total | 3,229,401 | 1,766,740 | 54.7 | 3.0 |

approximately 20 percent of all males over the age of 15. Consequently, labor force participation rates in these two areas were relatively low—68.7 percent in Planning District 4 and 67.6 percent in District 10.

Several areas with a relatively large number of older persons in the population also had low labor force participation rates. This was particularly true in the Lenowisco Planning District (no. 1), where 10.6 percent of all males were aged 65 and over and the labor force participation rate was only 62.9 percent; Piedmont Planning District (no. 14), with 11.0 and 69.2 percent respectively; Northern Neck Planning District (no. 17), with 13.2 and 67.4

percent; and to a lesser extent, the Accomack–Northampton Planning District (no. 22, with 13.2 and 70.8 percent.

Labor force participation rates among females were somewhat less than those for males in all cases. The state labor force participation rate among women aged 16 and over was 42.1 percent, or nearly two-thirds of the observed male rate of 67.9 percent. As noted in the introductory section the labor force participation rate for women increased considerably between 1950 and 1970.

As was true of males, there was considerable variation in labor force participation among females. In areas with a high concentration of white–collar employment, rates of labor force participation among women also tend to be high. The highest rates were found in two large metropolitan areas—the Virginia portion of the Washington, D.C., SMSA (Planning District 8) with 47.4 percent and Planning District 15 (which encompasses the Richmond SMSA) with 47.0 percent. Yet, the second largest metropolitan area in the state, Norfolk–Virginia Beach–Portsmouth (contained in Planning District 20) had a low rate of 38.5 percent.

As for males, college attendance and advanced age (over 65) depressed the female labor force participation rate. Also, the presence of preschool children in a household tended to decrease the rate. College attendance appears to have been a significant factor in the Piedmont Planning District (no. 14), site of Longwood College in Farmville, with 38.3 percent; the RADCO Planning District (no. 16), site of Mary Washington College in Fredericksburg, with 38.4 percent; and perhaps New River Valley Planning District (no. 4), site of Virginia Polytechnic Institute and State University and Radford College, with 40.1 percent. As was the case for males, college enrollment had a relatively large effect when the number of female college students was large relative to the population as a whole.

The effect of a relatively large number of aged persons in the population was evident in the Lenowisco Planning District (no. 1), where 12.6 percent of the female population was aged 65 and over and the female labor force participation rate was 22.9 percent; the Mount Rogers District (no. 3), with 12.3 and 38.4 percent, respectively; Rappahannock–Rapidan District (no. 9), with 12.4 and 38.8 percent; the Piedmont District (no. 14), with 13.1

and 38.3 percent; the Northern Neck District (no. 17), with 15.5 and 37.8 percent; and the Middle Peninsula District (no. 18), with 14.9 and 35.7 percent. However, in the Eastern Shore District (no. 22), which had the highest percentage among all planning districts of women aged 65 and over (16.8 percent), the female labor force participation was a high 42.7 percent.

The effect of the presence of young children is generally to depress labor force participation among females. As the data in Table 5.7 show, the labor force participation rate of women with children under 5 years of age was 33.8 percent, while that for women without young children was 44.2 percent. A similar relationship held in most planning districts of the state. In those districts where the relationship was reversed, it is possible that the age distribution of women with young children was sufficiently different from that of women without young children to produce this result. That is, in these areas, women with young children may have tended to be in the peak age groups of labor force participation, while those without young children may have tended to be in age groups characterized by lower rates of labor force participation.

As expected, areas with a high concentration of women with children under age 6 generally had a low overall rate of labor force participation. There was one significant exception. The Northern Virginia area, with the second highest incidence of women with young children (21.7 percent), had the highest rate of female labor force participation, 47.4 percent. A contributing factor to this anomaly may have been the wide differential in labor force participation rates between women with and without young children. Women with children between the ages of 0 and 5 had a relatively low rate of participation, only 29.4 percent. On the other hand, over half of the women without young children, 52.4 percent, were participating in the labor force. This disparity was also in evidence in the Cumberland Plateau, Southeastern Virginia, and Peninsula planning districts (nos. 2, 20, and 21), although the overall rates of participation were much lower in these three areas.

In summary, several intervening variables, including military service, college attendance, old age, and maternity, limit labor force

Table 5.7. Labor force participation rates of women by presence of children aged 0-5 in Virginia planning districts, 1970

| Area | Women Aged 16+ | Labor Force Participation Rate | Number With Children 0-5 | Number In Labor Force | Labor Force Participation Rate Women With Children 0-5 | Women Without Children 0-5 | Number In Labor Force | Labor Force Participation Rate | Labor Force Participation Rate For Women Without Young Children / Labor Force Participation Rate For Women With Young Children | Percent Women 16+ With Children 0-5 |
|---|---|---|---|---|---|---|---|---|---|---|
| Lenowisco | 31,538 | 22.9 | 5,593 | 1,007 | 18.0 | 25,945 | 6,228 | 24.0 | 1.3333 | 17.7 |
| Cumberland Plateau | 38,626 | 23.3 | 7,957 | 1,187 | 14.9 | 30,669 | 7,829 | 25.5 | 1.7111 | 20.6 |
| Mount Rogers | 60,363 | 38.4 | 10,478 | 4,094 | 39.1 | 49,885 | 19,093 | 38.3 | .9795 | 17.4 |
| New River Valley | 42,419 | 40.1 | 8,132 | 2,995 | 36.8 | 34,287 | 14,017 | 40.9 | 1.1100 | 19.2 |
| Fifth | 88,301 | 41.4 | 15,291 | 5,081 | 33.2 | 73,010 | 31,484 | 43.1 | 1.2976 | 17.3 |
| Central Shenandoah | 70,510 | 43.1 | 12,163 | 4,903 | 40.3 | 58,347 | 25,461 | 43.6 | 1.0826 | 17.3 |
| Lord Fairfax | 39,466 | 42.0 | 7,031 | 2,707 | 38.5 | 32,435 | 13,882 | 42.8 | 1.1117 | 17.8 |
| Northern Virginia | 322,913 | 47.4 | 70,088 | 20,570 | 29.4 | 252,825 | 132,536 | 52.4 | 1.7860 | 21.7 |
| Rappahannock-Rapidan | 25,072 | 38.8 | 4,721 | 1,589 | 33.7 | 20,351 | 8,147 | 40.0 | 1.1892 | 18.8 |
| Thomas Jefferson | 40,471 | 44.6 | 7,608 | 3,072 | 40.4 | 32,863 | 14,985 | 45.6 | 1.1293 | 18.8 |
| Central Virginia | 62,077 | 43.8 | 10,837 | 4,561 | 42.1 | 51,240 | 22,616 | 44.1 | 1.0487 | 17.5 |
| West Piedmont | 79,130 | 46.6 | 14,947 | 7,281 | 48.7 | 64,183 | 29,619 | 46.2 | .9474 | 18.9 |
| Southside | 29,284 | 40.4 | 5,099 | 2,345 | 46.0 | 24,185 | 9,481 | 39.2 | .8523 | 17.4 |
| Piedmont | 27,891 | 38.3 | 4,629 | 2,093 | 45.2 | 23,262 | 8,580 | 36.9 | .8157 | 16.6 |
| Richmond Regional | 207,335 | 47.0 | 36,612 | 13,914 | 38.0 | 170,723 | 83,544 | 48.9 | 1.2879 | 17.7 |
| RADCO | 27,563 | 38.4 | 5,536 | 1,887 | 34.1 | 22,027 | 8,701 | 39.5 | 1.1587 | 20.1 |
| Northern Neck | 13,373 | 37.8 | 1,843 | 789 | 42.8 | 11,530 | 4,263 | 37.0 | .8636 | 13.8 |
| Middle Peninsula | 17,430 | 35.7 | 2,847 | 911 | 32.0 | 14,583 | 5,318 | 36.5 | 1.1397 | 16.3 |
| Crater | 53,732 | 41.3 | 10,838 | 4,280 | 39.5 | 42,894 | 17,920 | 41.8 | 1.0580 | 20.2 |
| Southeastern Virginia | 253,957 | 38.5 | 53,773 | 15,405 | 28.7 | 200,184 | 82,364 | 41.1 | 1.4360 | 21.1 |
| Peninsula | 106,353 | 40.7 | 23,599 | 7,085 | 30.0 | 82,754 | 36,230 | 43.8 | 1.4584 | 22.2 |
| Accomack-Northampton | 16,638 | 42.7 | 2,364 | 1,102 | 46.6 | 14,274 | 4,747 | 33.3 | .7134 | 14.2 |
| State | 1,654,442 | 42.1 | 321,986 | 108,858 | 33.8 | 1,332,456 | 588,346 | 44.2 | 1.3061 | 19.5 |

participation. In an effort to remove these factors from analysis and determine what might be called a *true labor force participation rate* (and possibly a measure of job opportunity in areas across the state), the data in Table 5.8 show the number of Virginians over age 16, the number in military service, the number in colleges, the number over age 65, and half of those women with children under 6. The latter element clearly introduces some bias, since the assumption is made without empirical basis that half of these women would participate if they had the opportunity. This is a source of bias because the actual rate is nearly 50 percent in the West Piedmont, Southside, Piedmont, and Accomack-Northampton districts (nos. 12, 13, 14, and 22) but less than 30 percent in the Lenowisco, Cumberland Plateau, Northern Virginia, and Southeastern Virginia districts (nos. 1, 2, 8 and 20).

The data in Table 5.8 show that the true state labor force participation rate was 73.84 percent. While the assumptions implicit in the derivation of this figure—namely that those in the military, in college, or over age 65 were not in the labor force—are clearly invalid to some extent[3], the exclusion of these categories as well as some women with young children removed most of the obvious factors which inhibit labor force participation.

The data in Table 5.8 show that removal of persons relatively unlikely to be in the labor force considerably increased the overall labor force participation rate for the state (from 54.7 to 73.8 percent) and in all areas of the state. The two planning districts in extreme Southwest Virginia had exceptionally low rates of labor force participation, suggesting that there was a dearth of job opportunities in the area. To a lesser extent, this also appears to have been true in the Mount Rogers, Southside, Northern Neck, and Middle Peninsula districts (nos. 3, 13, 17, and 18). In areas with a heavy concentration of military personnel, the rate was also relatively low, perhaps suggesting the

[3] The method of collecting the census prevented a person in military service from being included in the civilian labor force. However, college students working full or part time or looking for work were included, as were all persons aged 65 and over either working or actively seeking work.

Table 5.8. True labor force participation rates in Virginia planning districts, 1970

| Area | Total Population Aged 16+ (1) | Number In Military Service (2) | Number In College (3) | Number Aged 65 and Over (4) | One-half of Women With Children Under Six (5) | Potential Labor Force Members (1-[2+3+4+5]) (6) | Civilian Labor Force (7) | True Labor Force Participation Rate [7÷6] (8) |
|---|---|---|---|---|---|---|---|---|
| Lenowisco | 59,758 | 43 | 783 | 9,843 | 2,797 | 46,292 | 24,975 | 53.95 |
| Cumberland Plateau | 75,311 | 26 | 1,416 | 9,225 | 3,979 | 60,665 | 32,527 | 53.62 |
| Mount Rogers | 114,420 | 51 | 2,908 | 17,643 | 5,239 | 88,579 | 61,417 | 69.34 |
| New River Valley | 83,948 | 100 | 12,477 | 9,483 | 4,066 | 57,822 | 45,535 | 78.75 |
| Fifth | 165,331 | 156 | 5,078 | 24,836 | 7,646 | 127,615 | 95,737 | 75.02 |
| Central Shenandoah | 133,743 | 149 | 8,826 | 18,219 | 6,082 | 100,467 | 77,875 | 77.51 |
| Lord Fairfax | 75,366 | 49 | 1,123 | 11,724 | 3,516 | 58,954 | 44,231 | 75.03 |
| Northern Virginia | 627,003 | 49,110 | 26,797 | 42,615 | 35,044 | 473,437 | 367,073 | 77.53 |
| Rappahannock-Rapidan | 49,218 | 701 | 276 | 8,025 | 2,361 | 37,855 | 28,005 | 73.98 |
| Thomas Jefferson | 81,987 | 192 | 8,506 | 11,328 | 3,804 | 58,157 | 46,124 | 79.31 |
| Central Virginia | 116,655 | 211 | 4,595 | 17,015 | 5,419 | 89,415 | 68,309 | 76.40 |
| West Piedmont | 150,665 | 39 | 3,982 | 19,134 | 7,474 | 120,036 | 92,680 | 77.21 |
| Southside | 56,151 | 15 | 701 | 8,352 | 2,550 | 44,533 | 30,909 | 69.41 |
| Piedmont | 52,910 | 200 | 2,347 | 9,186 | 2,315 | 38,862 | 27,985 | 72.01 |
| Richmond Regional | 385,627 | 972 | 20,610 | 47,707 | 18,306 | 298,032 | 235,144 | 78.90 |
| RADCO | 53,220 | 2,510 | 2,690 | 6,477 | 2,768 | 38,775 | 28,558 | 73.65 |
| Northern Neck | 25,588 | 30 | 80 | 5,235 | 922 | 19,321 | 13,284 | 68.75 |
| Middle Peninsula | 33,694 | 77 | 418 | 6,361 | 1,424 | 25,414 | 18,048 | 71.02 |
| Crater | 111,257 | 11,887 | 2,060 | 12,558 | 5,419 | 79,333 | 55,493 | 69.95 |
| Southeastern Virginia | 529,684 | 82,846 | 15,381 | 49,049 | 26,887 | 355,521 | 246,337 | 69.29 |
| Peninsula | 217,049 | 26,045 | 11,424 | 16,928 | 11,800 | 150,849 | 109,350 | 72.49 |
| Accomack-Northampton | 30,819 | 210 | 170 | 6,549 | 1,182 | 22,708 | 17,144 | 75.50 |
| State | 3,229,401 | 175,629 | 132,659 | 367,492 | 160,993 | 2,392,628 | 1,766,740 | 73.84 |

military dependents were less likely to participate in the labor force than were civilians of comparable status.

*Unemployment.* An *unemployed person* is defined as a civilian who has no job, is actively seeking work, and is available when a job is found.[4] The *rate of unemployment* is defined as the percentage of persons in the labor force who are actively seeking work. For the entire state, 3.0 percent of all members of the labor force aged 16 and over were unemployed as of April 1, 1970. As has been the case in recent years, the rate of unemployment was significantly higher among females (4.0 percent) than among males (2.3 percent). Part of the reason for this difference may have been the fact that females tend to move in and out of the labor force more frequently than males. Consequently, there were relatively more females newly entering the labor market and still in search of employment.

Areal differentials show that some portions of the state experienced much higher unemployment than others. In 1970 the Accomack–Northampton Planning District (no. 22) had by far the highest rate of unemployment in the state, 8.4 percent. This was primarily due to the very high rate of unemployment among females in this area, 13.7 percent. This rate was nearly twice as high as the next greatest incidence of female unemployment, 7.1 percent in the Northern Neck District (no. 17). Even so, the rate of unemployment among males in Planning District 22, 4.7 percent, was second only to the rate observed among males in District 17, 5.2 percent. As might be anticipated from this discussion, District 17 had the second highest incidence of unemployment in 1970, 6.0 percent. Unemployment also was relatively high in the four planning districts in the southwestern portion of the state (Districts 1, 2, 3, and 4, with observed rates of 4.5, 4.4, 4.1, and 4.0 percent), in the Southside and Piedmont areas (Districts 13 and 14, with 3.9 and 3.7 percent), and in the Hampton Roads area (District 20 and 21, with 3.9 and 3.6 percent). These data are summarized in Table 5.6 and Figure 5.2.

---

[4] U.S. Department of Labor, Bureau of Labor Statistics, *How the Government Measures Unemployment* (Washington, D.C.: U.S. Government Printing Office, 1967), p. 3.

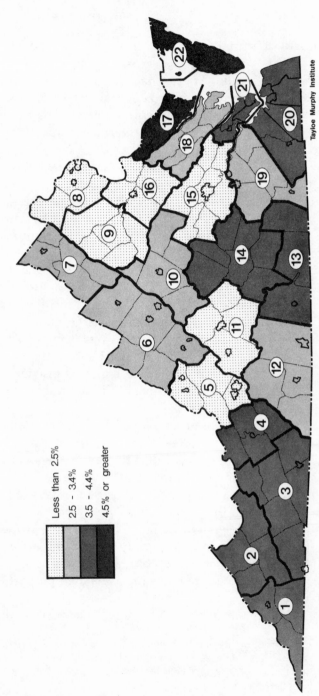

Less than 2.5%

2.5 - 3.4%

3.5 - 4.4%

4.5% or greater

Tayloe Murphy Institute

Fig. 5.2.  Rate of unemployment among the civilian labor force, Virginia planning districts, 1970

Occupational and Industrial Composition of the Labor Force

The occupational composition states what sort of work the individual does, while the industrial composition shows what sort of
product or service is produced by firms employing members of the
labor force. These variables tend to be extermely important for
social science analysis. As Alba Edwards noted in 1940: "More than
anything else, perhaps, a man's occupation determines his cause
and his contribution in life. . . . Indeed, there is no other
single characteristic that tells so much about a man and his
status—social, intellectual, and economic—as does his occupation."[5] This is principally true due to the high correlation
between income and occupational status.

*Occupational Composition.* The 1970 census of population furnished
detailed information regarding the occupational composition of the
labor force. To facilitate this analysis, the large number of
occupational categories was collapsed into four groups: white
collar, blue collar, agriculture, and service. A complete listing
of the component occupations of these four groups is provided in
Table 5.9. This table also shows the number of Virginians employed
in these groups as of April 1, 1970.

For the state 48.9 percent of all employed Virginians over the
age of 15 were engaged in white-collar occupations in 1970.
As expected, the percentage was considerably higher among
females (61.2 percent) than among males (41.1 percent).

Data on the occupational composition of an area's labor force
tell a great deal about the economy of an area. An area
specializing in trade and services tends to have a high proportion of white-collar workers, an area specializing in manufacturing
tends to have a high proportion of blue-collar workers, and
an area specializing in agriculture tends to have a high proportion
of agricultural workers.

The data presented in table 5.10 show that white-collar

[5] Alba M. Edwards, Preface to *Comparative Occupational Statistics for the United States:
1870 to 1940* (Washington, D.C.: U.S. Government Printing Office, 1940),
p. xi, quoted in Donald J. Bogue, *Principles of Demography* (New York:
John Wiley and Sons, 1969), p. 252.

Table 5.9.  Detailed composition of the occupational distribution of
Virginia's labor force, 1970

| Category | Employment in 1970 (Persons 16 Years of Age and Over) |
|---|---|
| White Collar | 839,597 |
| Professional | 274,778 |
| Engineers | 29,754 |
| Physicians, Dentists, and other Practitioners | 10,072 |
| Other Health Workers | 25,366 |
| Teachers (Elementary and Secondary) | 57,417 |
| Technicians (Non-Health) | 25,602 |
| Other Professionals | 126,567 |
| Managers and Administrators (Nonfarm) | 146,148 |
| Salaried | 123,802 |
| Manufacturing | 13,794 |
| Retail Trade | 27,925 |
| Other Industries | 82,083 |
| Self-Employed | 22,346 |
| Retail Trade | 12,346 |
| Other Industries | 10,000 |
| Sales Workers | 111,564 |
| Manufacturing and Wholesale Trade | 21,433 |
| Retail Trade | 65,911 |
| Other Industries | 24,220 |
| Clerical and Kindred Workers | 307,107 |
| Bookkeepers | 29,904 |
| Secretaries, Stenographers, Typists | 98,332 |
| Other Clerical Workers | 178,871 |
| | |
| Blue Collar | 621,245 |
| Craftsmen, Foremen, and Kindred Workers | 244,240 |
| Automobile Mechanics | 20,218 |
| Other Mechanics | 35,538 |
| Machinists | 7,907 |
| Other Metal Craftsmen | 10,714 |
| Carpenters | 23,150 |
| Construction Craftsmen, except Carpenters | 53,200 |
| Other Craftsmen | 93,513 |
| Operatives, except Transport | 224,758 |
| Durable Goods Manufacturing | 58,261 |
| Nondurable Goods Manufacturing | 109,069 |
| Nonmanufacturing Industries | 57,428 |
| Transport Equipment Operatives | 69,586 |
| Truck Drivers | 32,076 |
| Other Transport Equipment Operatives | 37,510 |
| Laborers, except Farm | 82,661 |
| Construction Laborers | 18,414 |
| Freight, Stock, and Material Handlers | 27,415 |
| Other Non-farm Laborers | 36,832 |
| | |
| Agriculture | 46,167 |
| Farmers and Farm Managers | 25,362 |
| Farm Laborers and Farm Foremen | 20,805 |
| | |
| Service | 207,241 |
| Service Workers, except Private Household | 169,049 |
| Cleaning Service Workers | 37,307 |
| Food Service Workers | 51,807 |
| Health Service Workers | 23,596 |
| Personal Service Workers | 24,100 |
| Protective Service Workers | 20,738 |
| Private Household Workers | 38,192 |
| | |
| Total | 1,714,250 |

Table 5.10.  Occupational distribution of employed civilian labor force by sex in Virginia planning districts, 1970

| Area | Percent White Collar | Percent Blue Collar | Percent Agriculture | Percent Service |
|---|---|---|---|---|
| Lenowisco | | | | |
| Male | 23.9 | 62.8 | 8.0 | 5.3 |
| Female | 51.5 | 20.3 | 1.5 | 26.7 |
| Total | 31.7 | 50.6 | 6.1 | 11.5 |
| Cumberland Plateau | | | | |
| Male | 21.1 | 69.4 | 6.0 | 3.5 |
| Female | 53.8 | 27.0 | 0.4 | 18.9 |
| Total | 30.0 | 57.8 | 4.5 | 7.7 |
| Mount Rogers | | | | |
| Male | 25.5 | 59.3 | 9.2 | 6.1 |
| Female | 38.8 | 43.3 | 1.0 | 16.8 |
| Total | 30.4 | 53.2 | 6.2 | 10.2 |
| New River Valley | | | | |
| Male | 32.8 | 54.7 | 4.4 | 8.2 |
| Female | 44.5 | 34.3 | 0.6 | 20.8 |
| Total | 37.0 | 47.1 | 3.0 | 12.8 |
| Fifth | | | | |
| Male | 40.1 | 51.5 | 1.4 | 7.0 |
| Female | 59.9 | 19.3 | 0.2 | 20.6 |
| Total | 47.6 | 39.3 | 1.0 | 12.1 |
| Central Shenandoah | | | | |
| Male | 32.2 | 52.6 | 7.9 | 7.4 |
| Female | 46.6 | 29.6 | 0.8 | 22.9 |
| Total | 37.8 | 43.8 | 5.1 | 13.4 |
| Lord Fairfax | | | | |
| Male | 29.0 | 58.1 | 7.4 | 5.6 |
| Female | 44.8 | 33.1 | 1.0 | 21.2 |
| Total | 34.9 | 48.8 | 5.0 | 11.3 |
| Northern Virginia | | | | |
| Male | 65.4 | 26.8 | 0.9 | 6.9 |
| Female | 82.5 | 4.4 | 0.1 | 13.1 |
| Total | 72.6 | 17.4 | 0.6 | 9.5 |
| Rappahannock-Rapidan | | | | |
| Male | 26.7 | 51.4 | 15.5 | 6.3 |
| Female | 46.0 | 21.8 | 1.7 | 30.6 |
| Total | 33.5 | 41.2 | 10.7 | 14.7 |
| Thomas Jefferson | | | | |
| Male | 39.3 | 46.5 | 5.9 | 8.3 |
| Female | 58.7 | 19.8 | 0.6 | 21.0 |
| Total | 47.0 | 36.0 | 3.8 | 13.3 |
| Central Virginia | | | | |
| Male | 34.0 | 55.2 | 4.7 | 6.2 |
| Female | 48.3 | 29.3 | 0.5 | 21.9 |
| Total | 39.6 | 45.0 | 3.0 | 12.4 |
| West Piedmont | | | | |
| Male | 24.6 | 62.9 | 7.1 | 5.4 |
| Female | 38.1 | 45.5 | 0.7 | 15.7 |
| Total | 29.8 | 56.1 | 4.6 | 9.4 |
| Southside | | | | |
| Male | 25.0 | 55.0 | 16.2 | 3.9 |
| Female | 39.0 | 38.4 | 1.8 | 20.9 |
| Total | 30.2 | 48.8 | 10.8 | 10.3 |
| Piedmont | | | | |
| Male | 22.4 | 56.6 | 16.4 | 4.7 |
| Female | 40.2 | 34.7 | 1.6 | 23.6 |
| Total | 29.1 | 48.4 | 10.8 | 11.8 |
| Richmond Regional | | | | |
| Male | 45.8 | 45.3 | 1.3 | 7.6 |
| Female | 65.7 | 14.3 | 0.3 | 19.7 |
| Total | 54.0 | 32.6 | 0.9 | 12.6 |

Table 5.10.  (continued)

| Area | Percent White Collar | Percent Blue Collar | Percent Agriculture | Percent Service |
|------|------|------|------|------|
| **RADCO** | | | | |
| Male | 32.8 | 56.7 | 3.5 | 7.0 |
| Female | 55.6 | 18.9 | 0.5 | 25.0 |
| Total | 41.3 | 42.9 | 2.4 | 13.5 |
| Northern Neck | | | | |
| Male | 26.5 | 57.3 | 10.7 | 5.5 |
| Female | 42.9 | 34.5 | 1.6 | 21.0 |
| Total | 32.6 | 48.7 | 7.3 | 11.3 |
| Middle Peninsula | | | | |
| Male | 28.1 | 60.8 | 6.0 | 5.1 |
| Female | 51.5 | 17.7 | 2.6 | 28.2 |
| Total | 36.0 | 46.2 | 4.9 | 12.9 |
| Crater | | | | |
| Male | 31.4 | 54.8 | 5.7 | 8.2 |
| Female | 50.7 | 21.4 | 0.4 | 27.5 |
| Total | 38.9 | 41.7 | 3.6 | 15.8 |
| Southeastern Virginia | | | | |
| Male | 38.3 | 51.1 | 2.3 | 8.3 |
| Female | 63.6 | 11.7 | 0.4 | 24.4 |
| Total | 48.1 | 35.8 | 1.5 | 14.6 |
| Peninsula | | | | |
| Male | 42.6 | 47.6 | 0.7 | 9.1 |
| Female | 65.1 | 10.6 | 0.1 | 24.3 |
| Total | 51.4 | 33.1 | 0.5 | 15.0 |
| Accomack-Northampton | | | | |
| Male | 26.0 | 51.8 | 15.9 | 6.3 |
| Female | 36.9 | 32.6 | 8.3 | 22.2 |
| Total | 30.3 | 44.3 | 13.0 | 12.5 |
| State | | | | |
| Male | 41.1 | 47.7 | 4.1 | 7.1 |
| Female | 61.2 | 18.4 | 0.5 | 20.0 |
| Total | 48.9 | 36.3 | 2.7 | 12.1 |

employment was noticeably high in metropolitan areas, particularly in the Northern Virginia, Richmond, and Newport News–
Hampton areas, where it accounted for more than half of
total employment. In two other planning districts essentially
metropolitan in character (Fifth and Southeastern Virginia),
it accounted for nearly half of the total. This was to be expected
since metropolitan areas almost always serve as trade and financial
centers. The only nonmetropolitan area where the proportion of
white–collar employment was large was the Thomas Jefferson
Planning District (no. 10). Since the city of Charlottesville is the
center of a relatively large trading area and is the location of a large
university, this result was not especially surprising.

Blue–collar employment accounted for more than half of all
employment in four planning districts (Lenowisco, Cumberland
Plateau, Mount Rogers, and West Piedmont) and was the largest
single group in all districts except the six mentioned in the
previous paragraph. Areas with particularly heavy concentrations

of blue-collar employment were typified by a high concentration of manufacturing (for example, Planning District 12 comprising the Danville-Martinsville area) or extractive industries, particularly mining (notably Planning Districts 1, 2, and 3 in Southwest Virginia).

Virginia, like most of the rest of the United States, has seen a considerable decline in the number of farmers and farm workers over the past several decades. In 1970 only 46,167 pesons, or 2.7 percent of the employed labor force over 15 years of age, were engaged in agricultural occupations. The extent of the decline in agricultural employment during the twentieth century is shown in Figure 5.3.

Throughout the present century the share of the labor force in agriculture has been steadily diminishing. Agricultural employment reached a peak in 1910, when about 305,000 of Virginia's 739,000 employed persons (aged 16 and over) were engaged in agricultural pursuits. In eighty years Virginia's labor force went from nearly half agricultural (43.7 percent in 1900) to the minimal proportion of 2.7 percent recorded in 1970. While the number of employed persons aged 16 and over increased by 183 percent between 1900 and 1970, the number of persons employed in agriculture declined by 83 percent.

In Virginia, agriculture accounted for more than 10 percent of the labor force in only four planning districts: Rappahannock Rapidan (19.7 percent), West Piedmont (10.8 percent), Piedmont (10.8 percent), and Accomack-Northampton (13.0 percent). In most other nonmetropolitan districts, it accounted for about 4 to 6 percent of the employed labor force, while in metropolitan districts it was generally around 1 percent or less. In brief, even in rural areas of the state it appears that the importance of agriculture as a source of employment is diminishing.

The final occupational category of Virginia's labor force in this analysis is service workers. This category accounted for 12.1 percent of the state's labor force and does not vary to any considerable extent across the state. A minimum share of 7.7 percent was recorded in the Cumberland Plateau District, and a maximum of 15.8 percent was found in Crater District. With the exception of workers in private households, this category is likely to experience continued growth as the economy of the state

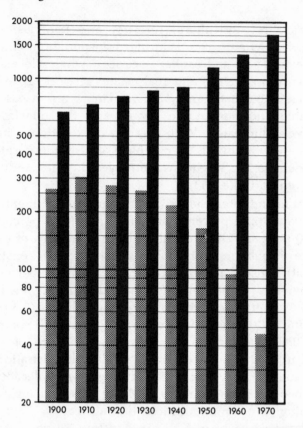

BLACK BARS REPRESENT TOTAL LABOR FORCE, WHILE GREY SHOWS
THE AGRICULTURAL PORTION.

NUMBER OF PEOPLE IN LABOR FORCE IS GIVEN IN UNITS OF
1000 LABORERS.

Fig. 5.3.   Virginia's employed labor force and
agricultural labor force, 1900–1970

provides more and more discretionary time and income to Virginia
workers.

*Industrial Composition.* The industrial composition of the labor
force is predicated in terms of the product or service provided
by industries employing the Virginia labor force. The Standard
Industrial Classification Code (SICC)[6] uses ten broad groups to

[6] Executive Office of the President, Bureau of the Budget, *Standard Industrial Classification Manual* (Washington, 1967), pp. v–vii.

classify industry: agriculture, forestry, and fisheries; mining; contract construction; manufacturing; transportation, communication, electric, gas, and sanitary services; wholesale and retail trade; finance, insurance, and real estate; services; government; and nonclassifiable. In the analysis here manufacturing was divided into durable and nondurable goods, and the nonclassifiable category was eliminated. With these two exceptions, the SICC categories were followed. A complete list of these categories and the number of Virginians employed in each industry in 1970 is given in Table 5.11.

As the table indicates, the bulk of Virginia employment in 1970 was in services (25.4 percent), manufacturing (22.4 percent), and trade (18.0 percent). Other significant concentrations of employment were in public administration (11.4 percent), construction (7.4 percent), transportation and communications (6.8 percent), and financial services (4.4 percent). As expected, relatively few persons were employed in agriculture, forestry, and fisheries (3.3 percent) or in mining (1.0 percent). Comparing this data with comparable data for 1960 (see Figures 5.4 and 5.5), the share of persons employed in 1960 in services, trade, public administration, construction, and financial services rose during the next decade, while that of people in agriculture, mining, manufacturing, and transportation and communications diminished.

Overall, employment in Virginia rose by 27.9 percent in this period. Relatively greater gains occurred in financial services (60.0 percent), services (54.2 percent), public administration (49.2 percent), construction (39.1 percent), durable goods manufacturing (36.2 percent), and wholesale and retail trade (34.3 percent). Relatively smaller gains occurred in transportation and communications (24.4 percent) and nondurable goods manufacturing (22.4 percent), while absolute declines were experienced in the agricultural (– 45.3 percent) and mining (– 11.5 percent) sectors.

Using the ten categories outlined previously, the 1970 industrial composition of the labor force in the twenty–two planning districts is given in Table 5.12. The data show considerable variability among planning districts in the industrial composition of the labor force. Agriculture, for example, employed almost 18 percent of the 1970 labor force in the Accomack–Northampton

Table 5.11.  Detailed composition of the industrial distribution of Virginia's
labor force, 1970

| Category | Employment in 1970 (Persons Aged 16 and over) |
|---|---|
| 1.  Agriculture, Forestry and Fisheries | 57,262 |
| 2.  Mining | 17,067 |
| 3.  Construction | 126,803 |
| 4.  Durable Goods Manufacturing | 169,044 |
|     a.  Furniture and Lumber and Wood Products | 44,038 |
|     b.  Primary Metal Industries | 8,974 |
|     c.  Fabricated Metal Industries | 16,541 |
|     d.  Machinery, Except Electrical | 11,521 |
|     e.  Electrical Machinery, Equipment, Supplies | 26,121 |
|     f.  Motor Vehicles and Other Transportation Equipment | 38,002 |
|     g.  Other Durable Goods | 23,847 |
| 5.  Nondurable Goods Manufacturing | 215,178 |
|     a.  Food and Kindred Products | 27,157 |
|     b.  Textile Mill and Other Fabricated Textile Products | 80,789 |
|     c.  Printing, Publishing, and Allied Industries | 20,921 |
|     d.  Chemical and Allied Products | 34,418 |
|     e.  Other Nondurable Goods | 51,893 |
| 6.  Transportation, Communication, Electric, Gas and Sanitary Services | 115,948 |
|     a.  Railroads and Railway Express Service | 19,059 |
|     b.  Trucking Service and Warehousing | 22,189 |
|     c.  Other Transportation | 26,364 |
|     d.  Communications | 23,935 |
|     e.  Utilities and Sanitary Services | 24,401 |
| 7.  Wholesale and Retail Trade | 307,797 |
|     a.  Wholesale Trade | 56,768 |
|     b.  Food, Bakery, and Dairy Stores | 38,596 |
|     c.  Eating and Drinking Places | 39,112 |
|     d.  General Merchandise Retailing | 46,455 |
|     e.  Motor Vehicle Retailing and Service Stations | 39,849 |
|     f.  Other Retail Trade | 87,017 |
| 8.  Finance, Insurance, and Real Estate | 75,420 |
|     a.  Banking and Credit Agencies | 27,829 |
|     b.  Insurance, Real Estate, and Other Finance | 47,591 |
| 9.  Services | 434,970 |
|     a.  Business Services | 25,386 |
|     b.  Repair Services | 19,154 |
|     c.  Private Households | 37,722 |
|     d.  Other Personal Services | 53,941 |
|     e.  Entertainment and Recreation Services | 11,064 |
|     f.  Hospitals | 54,438 |
|     g.  Other Health Services | 29,078 |
|     h.  Elementary and Secondary Schools and Colleges | 127,497 |
|     i.  Other Education and Kindred Services | 8,004 |
|     j.  Welfare, Religious, and Non-profit Membership Organizations | 26,642 |
|     k.  Legal, Engineering, and Miscellaneous Professional Services | 42,044 |
| 10.  Public Administration | 194,761 |
| Total | 1,714,250 |

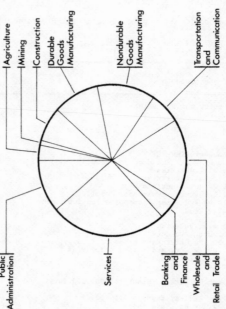

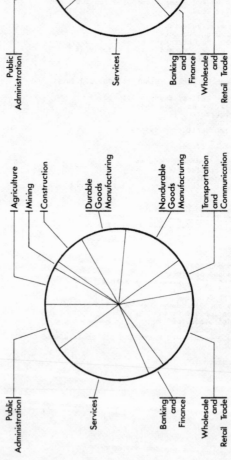

Fig. 5.4. Industrial composition of Virginia's employed labor force, 1960

Fig. 5.5. Industrial composition of Virginia's employed labor force, 1970

Table 5.12.  Industrial composition of labor force in Virginia planning districts, 1970

| Area | Agriculture, Forestry, and Fisheries | Mining | Construction | Durable Goods Manufacturing | Nondurable Goods Manufacturing | Transportation, Communication, Utilities | Wholesale and Retail Trade | Banking and Financial Services | Services | Public Administration | Total |
|---|---|---|---|---|---|---|---|---|---|---|---|
| Lenowisco Percent of Labor Force | 6.70 | 14.47 | 9.43 | 4.07 | 14.00 | 5.87 | 18.46 | 1.60 | 22.17 | 3.23 | 100.00 |
| Cumberland Plateau Percent of Labor Force | 4.86 | 29.06 | 6.82 | 6.38 | 7.52 | 6.55 | 16.99 | 1.79 | 17.28 | 2.75 | 100.00 |
| Mount Rogers Percent of Labor Force | 6.64 | 1.11 | 8.29 | 16.52 | 24.33 | 4.41 | 15.39 | 1.92 | 18.65 | 2.75 | 100.00 |
| New River Valley Percent of Labor Force | 3.42 | 0.39 | 6.93 | 13.57 | 24.98 | 4.32 | 13.52 | 2.09 | 27.79 | 2.99 | 100.00 |
| Fifth Percent of Labor Force | 1.40 | 0.33 | 6.47 | 10.48 | 13.30 | 13.46 | 21.53 | 4.45 | 24.84 | 3.74 | 100.00 |
| Central Shenandoah Percent of Labor Force | 6.20 | 0.36 | 7.51 | 12.33 | 21.33 | 4.99 | 16.10 | 2.17 | 26.51 | 2.49 | 100.00 |
| Lord Fairfax Percent of Labor Force | 6.02 | 0.48 | 10.84 | 8.78 | 21.95 | 6.44 | 19.56 | 2.67 | 19.54 | 3.71 | 100.00 |
| Northern Virginia Percent of Labor Force | 0.96 | 0.14 | 6.27 | 3.49 | 2.94 | 7.06 | 16.24 | 6.28 | 28.45 | 28.17 | 100.00 |
| Rappahannock-Rapidan Percent of Labor Force | 12.94 | 0.76 | 14.43 | 10.18 | 8.25 | 5.41 | 15.54 | 3.41 | 23.27 | 5.83 | 100.00 |
| Thomas Jefferson Percent of Labor Force | 4.78 | 0.92 | 8.93 | 12.00 | 9.62 | 5.72 | 15.20 | 4.66 | 34.22 | 3.96 | 100.00 |
| Central Virginia Percent of Labor Force | 3.39 | 0.33 | 6.92 | 20.99 | 18.77 | 5.15 | 15.33 | 3.47 | 22.91 | 2.74 | 100.00 |
| West Piedmont Percent of Labor Force | 4.83 | 0.13 | 6.23 | 17.75 | 31.92 | 4.23 | 13.63 | 2.38 | 16.68 | 2.22 | 100.00 |
| Southside Percent of Labor Force | 11.36 | 0.62 | 8.16 | 12.03 | 25.29 | 4.08 | 15.09 | 1.78 | 18.87 | 2.71 | 100.00 |
| Piedmont Percent of Labor Force | 11.81 | 0.89 | 8.18 | 13.34 | 16.30 | 6.20 | 14.70 | 1.76 | 22.46 | 4.36 | 100.00 |
| Richmond Regional Percent of Labor Force | 1.27 | 0.22 | 7.29 | 6.12 | 15.04 | 7.88 | 20.50 | 7.21 | 26.98 | 7.48 | 100.00 |
| RADCO Percent of Labor Force | 3.04 | 0.38 | 12.17 | 6.35 | 11.16 | 5.43 | 18.70 | 2.69 | 25.25 | 14.84 | 100.00 |
| Northern Neck Percent of Labor Force | 13.00 | 0.17 | 9.60 | 7.64 | 14.36 | 4.87 | 19.57 | 3.00 | 21.89 | 5.90 | 100.00 |
| Middle Peninsula Percent of Labor Force | 8.64 | 0.19 | 9.33 | 12.50 | 10.49 | 4.62 | 18.40 | 2.80 | 23.32 | 9.71 | 100.00 |
| Crater Percent of Labor Force | 4.05 | 0.31 | 6.56 | 6.78 | 24.37 | 5.06 | 17.33 | 2.39 | 24.34 | 8.80 | 100.00 |
| Southeastern Virginia Percent of Labor Force | 2.06 | 0.08 | 7.82 | 11.03 | 6.15 | 7.85 | 22.17 | 4.66 | 26.15 | 12.02 | 100.00 |
| Peninsula Percent of Labor Force | 1.01 | 0.04 | 6.25 | 19.36 | 3.96 | 5.79 | 18.05 | 3.45 | 27.92 | 14.18 | 100.00 |
| Accomack-Northampton Percent of Labor Force | 17.95 | 0.12 | 7.18 | 3.01 | 17.79 | 5.70 | 20.22 | 1.84 | 20.32 | 5.86 | 100.00 |
| State Percent of Labor Force | 3.34 | 1.00 | 7.40 | 9.86 | 12.55 | 6.76 | 17.96 | 4.40 | 25.37 | 11.36 | 100.00 |

Planning District (no. 22), and more than 10 percent in the Rappahannock–Rapidan, Southside, Piedmont, and Northern Neck districts (nos. 9, 13, 14, and 17). On the other hand, in most urban areas of the state between 1 and 2 percent of the labor force was employed in agricultural industries.

The concentration of mining industries within a couple of planning districts was even more pronounced. Mining employed over 29 percent of the labor force in the Cumberland Plateau Planning District (no. 2) and almost 15 percent in the Lenowisco District (no. 1). With the exception of the Mount Rogers District (no. 3), with 1.11 percent, mining employed less than 1 percent of the labor force in all other planning districts in 1970.

Few other industries show such pronounced concentration, although, as expected, metropolitan areas, which in the South tend to be commercial and administrative centers, tended to have more workers employed in banking and financial services and other services and fewer workers employed in manufacturing than did nonmetropolitan areas.

Another area of pronounced concentration was public administration. Employment in this sector was primarily located in the Northern Virginia Planning District (no. 8), where it accounted for over 28 percent of employment and, to a lesser extent in the Peninsula and Southeastern Virginia (nos. 21 and 20), where it accounted for 12 and 14 percent, respectively. All told, these three areas, with 43 percent of all employment in the state, accounted for nearly three-fourths (74.24 percent) of the employment in the public administration sector. Somewhat surprisingly, Planning District 15, including the state capital of Richmond, had only 7.48 percent of its labor force employed by this sector, because of the relatively low number of federal employees in the area.

The concentration pattern of employment by industry is contained in the data in Table 5.13. This table shows a summary of the rank order of each industry in each county. Highly concentrated industries, such as mining and public administration, were highly ranked in a few counties and ranked near the bottom in many of the rest. Industries that are not highly concentrated tended to have a more or less constant rank in the majority

Table 5.13. Rank order distribution of employment by industrial category in Virginia cities and counties, 1970

| | Agriculture | Mining | Construction | Durable Goods Manufacturing | Nondurable Goods Manufacturing | Transportation, Communication, Utilities | Wholesale and Retail Trade | Banking and Financial Services | Services | Public Administration | Total |
|---|---|---|---|---|---|---|---|---|---|---|---|
| 1 | 1 | 4 | 0 | 7 | 38 | 0 | 11 | 0 | 71 | 2 | 134 |
| 2 | 6 | 0 | 1 | 19 | 16 | 1 | 44 | 0 | 41 | 6 | 134 |
| 3 | 9 | 2 | 8 | 19 | 28 | 5 | 38 | 0 | 18 | 7 | 134 |
| 4 | 11 | 1 | 27 | 27 | 14 | 7 | 30 | 3 | 3 | 11 | 134 |
| 5 | 17 | 0 | 49½ | 13 | 11 | 24 | 8 | 2 | | 9 | 134 |
| 6 | 22½ | 0 | 38½ | 16 | 5 | 30½ | 3 | 7 | ½ | 11 | 134 |
| 7 | 9½ | 0 | 5 | 13 | 12 | 46½ | 0 | 20½ | ½ | 27½ | 134 |
| 8 | 9 | 3 | 5 | 17 | 8 | 18 | 0 | 31½ | 0 | 42½ | 134 |
| 9 | 43 | 6 | 0 | 3 | 2 | 2 | 0 | 60 | 0 | 18 | 134 |
| 10 | 6 | 118 | 0 | 0 | 0 | 0 | 0 | 10 | 0 | 0 | 134 |
| Total | 134 | 134 | 134 | 134 | 134 | 134 | 134 | 134 | 134 | 134 | 1,340 |

Note: Each cell represents the number of cities and counties in which employment in a specific sector ranks in a specific order among all employing industries. For example, mining is the leading sector in four jurisdictions, is third in two, fourth in one, eighth in three, ninth in six, and tenth in 118.

of planning districts. This pattern held in the construction, transportation and communication, wholesale and retail trade, banking, and services sectors.

Another and perhaps more useful way of determining the regional concentration of the labor force in certain industries is through the use of a location quotient. The location quotient for any industry, $i$, in any planning district, $j$, $L_{i,j}$, is the ratio of employment in that sector and in that planning district, $E_{ij}$ considered as a percentage of total employment in that planning district, $E_j$ to employment in that sector for the entire state, $E_{i,v}$, considered as a percentage of total employment in the state $E_v$. Mathematically, this may be defined as:

$$L_{i,j} = \frac{E_{i,j}/E_j}{E_{i,v}/E_v} . [7]$$

Thus, if 10 percent of the state's labor force is employed in sector $i$ and 15 percent of the labor force in planning district $j$ is employed in this sector, $L_{i,j}$ would equal 1.5. Location quotients for all industrial groups in all planning districts are given in Table 5.14.

In evaluating the results of the location quotient analysis, it is important to realize that the data on employment by industrial groups are tabulated on a residence basis; that is, the individual worker is counted in the area where he lives rather than the area where he works. Due to the relatively high level of interarea commuting (46.7 percent of Virginia's labor force worked outside the city or county in residence in 1970), the computation on a city–county level would be essentially mean-ingless. However, by grouping cities and counties into planning districts, much of the effect of commuting is removed.

The location quotients given in Table 5.14 are functions not only of industrial concentration but of size differentials among planning districts as well. For example, in agriculture, sixteen

[7] Alternatively, the location quotient may be viewed as any district's share of total state employment in a given sector divided by that district's share of total employment in the state. Mathematically, this would simply be: $L_{i,j} = (E_{i,j}/E_{i,v})/(E_j/E_v)$.

Table 5.14. Location quotients for employment by industrial category, Virginia planning district, 1970

| Area | Agriculture | Mining | Construction | Durable Goods Manufacturing | Nondurable Goods Manufacturing | Transportation, Communication, Utilities | Wholesale and Retail Trade | Banking and Financial Services | Services | Public Administration |
|---|---|---|---|---|---|---|---|---|---|---|
| Lenowisco | 2.0061 | 14.4700 | 1.2743 | .4128 | 1.1155 | .8683 | 1.0278 | .3636 | .8739 | .2843 |
| Cumberland Plateau | 1.4540 | 29.0600 | .9216 | .6471 | .5992 | .9689 | .9460 | .4068 | .6811 | .2421 |
| Mount Rogers | 1.9877 | 1.1100 | 1.1203 | 1.6755 | 1.9386 | .6524 | .8569 | .4364 | .7351 | .2421 |
| New River Valley | 1.0225 | .3900 | .9365 | 1.3763 | 1.9904 | .6391 | .7528 | .4750 | 1.0954 | .2632 |
| Fifth | .4191 | .3300 | .8743 | 1.0629 | 1.0598 | 1.9911 | 1.1988 | 1.0114 | .9791 | .3292 |
| Central Shenandoah | 1.8575 | .3600 | 1.0149 | 1.2505 | 1.6996 | .7382 | .8964 | .4932 | 1.0049 | .2192 |
| Lord Fairfax | 1.8018 | .4800 | 1.4649 | .8905 | 1.7490 | .9527 | 1.0891 | .6068 | .7702 | .3266 |
| Northern Virginia | .2875 | .1400 | .8473 | .3540 | .2343 | 1.0444 | .9042 | 1.4273 | 1.1214 | 2.4798 |
| Rappahannock-Rapidan | 3.8727 | .7600 | 1.9500 | 1.0325 | .6574 | .8003 | .8653 | 1.7750 | .9172 | .5132 |
| Thomas Jefferson | 1.4298 | .9200 | 1.2068 | 1.2170 | .7665 | .8462 | .8463 | 1.0591 | 1.3488 | .3486 |
| Central Virginia | 1.0151 | .3300 | .9351 | 2.1288 | 1.4956 | .7618 | .8536 | .7886 | .9030 | .2412 |
| West Piedmont | 1.4474 | .1300 | .8419 | 1.8002 | 2.5434 | .6257 | .7589 | .5409 | .6575 | .1954 |
| Southside | 3.4009 | .6200 | 1.1027 | 1.2201 | 2.0151 | .6036 | .8402 | .4045 | .7438 | .3286 |
| Piedmont | 3.5342 | .8900 | 1.1054 | 1.3529 | 1.2988 | .9172 | .8185 | .4000 | .8853 | .3838 |
| Richmond Regional | .3815 | .2200 | .9851 | .6207 | 1.1984 | 1.1657 | 1.1414 | 1.6386 | 1.0635 | 1.3063 |
| RADCO | .9102 | .3800 | 1.6446 | .6440 | .8892 | .8033 | 1.0412 | .6114 | .9953 | .5194 |
| Northern Neck | 3.8913 | .1700 | 1.2973 | .7748 | 1.1442 | .7204 | 1.0896 | .6818 | .8628 | .8548 |
| Middle Peninsula | 2.5857 | .1900 | 1.2608 | 1.2677 | .8359 | .6834 | 1.0245 | .6364 | .9192 | .7747 |
| Crater | 1.2126 | .3100 | .8865 | .6876 | 1.9418 | .7485 | .9649 | .5432 | .9594 | .7747 |
| Southeastern Virginia | .6158 | .0800 | 1.0568 | 1.1187 | .4900 | 1.1612 | 1.2344 | 1.0591 | 1.0307 | 1.0581 |
| Peninsula | .3018 | .0400 | .8446 | 1.9635 | .3155 | .8565 | 1.0050 | .7841 | 1.1005 | 1.2482 |
| Accomack-Northampton | 5.3739 | .1200 | .9703 | .3053 | 1.4175 | .8432 | 1.1258 | .4182 | .8009 | .5158 |

of the twenty-two planning districts had location quotients in excess of 1.0. This means relatively more persons were employed in the agricultural sphere in those districts than in the state as a whole. However, five of the six remaining districts are the largest and most metropolitan districts in the state. As would be expected, agriculture was not a major source of employment. The remaining district, Planning District 16, centering on Fredericksburg, had a quotient of 0.91. Since this area is located between the suburban portions of two large metropolitan areas (Washington to the north and Richmond to the south), it may be beginning to take on the suburban characteristics of its neighbors, as the process of urbanization continues. It is, for example, not uncommon to see subdivisions in Fredericksburg or Stafford County advertised in the real estate pages of Washington newspapers.

Despite the relatively high number of districts with agricultural quotients in excess of unity, the quotients were especially high (greater than 2.0) in seven districts: the Lenowisco District (no. 1) in Southwest Virginia; the Rappahannock–Rapidan District (no. 9), immediately southwest of the Washington metropolitan area; the Piedmont and Southside districts (nos. 13 and 14); the Northern Neck and Middle Peninsula districts (nos. 17 and 18); and the Accomack–Northampton District (no. 22).

The most concentrated industry was clearly mining, with extremely high location quotients found in the Lenowisco and Cumberland Plateau planning districts (14.47 and 29.06, respectively), a quotient slightly over unity (1.11) in the Mount Rogers District, and quotients less than unity in all other districts. Substantial concentration was also found in the banking sector (five of twenty-two districts with quotients over unity), transportation (four districts with quotients over unity), and public administration (four districts with quotients over unity).

In order to give some indication of the differing industrial composition of Virginia planning districts, Table 5.15 shows the four most significant sectors (in terms of location coefficient) for each planning district. The purpose of this table is to show how different the concentration patterns of industry throughout the state are. For example, Northern Virginia, with its concentrations

Table 5.15. Leading areas of relative concentration of employment in Virginia planning districts, 1970 (location quotients in parentheses)

| District | 1st Sector | 2nd Sector | 3rd Sector | 4th Sector |
|---|---|---|---|---|
| Lenowisco (P.D. 1) | Mining (14.47) | Agriculture (2.01) | Construction (1.27) | Nondurable goods manufacturing (1.16) |
| Cumberland Plateau (P.D. 2) | Mining (29.06) | Agriculture (1.45) | Transportation (.97) | Trade (.95) |
| Mount Rogers (P.D. 3) | Agriculture (1.99) | Nondurable goods manufacturing (1.94) | Durable goods manufacturing (1.68) | Construction (1.12) |
| New River Valley (P.D. 4) | Nondurable goods manufacturing (1.99) | Durable goods manufacturing (1.38) | Services (1.10) | Agriculture (1.02) |
| Fifth (P.D. 5) | Transportation (1.99) | Trade (1.20) | Durable goods manufacturing (1.06) | Nondurable goods manufacturing (1.06) |
| Central Shenandoah (P.D. 6) | Agriculture (1.86) | Nondurable goods manufacturing (1.70) | Durable goods manufacturing (1.25) | Services (1.04) |
| Lord Fairfax (P.D. 7) | Agriculture (1.80) | Nondurable goods manufacturing (1.75) | Construction (1.46) | Trade (1.09) |
| Northern Virginia (P.D. 8) | Public administration (2.48) | Banking (1.43) | Services (1.12) | Transportation (1.04) |
| Rappahannock-Rapidan (P.D. 9) | Agriculture (3.87) | Construction (1.95) | Durable goods manufacturing (1.03) | Services (.92) |
| Thomas Jefferson (P.D. 10) | Agriculture (1.43) | Services (1.35) | Durable goods manufacturing (1.22) | Construction (1.21) |
| Central Virginia (P.D. 11) | Durable goods manufacturing (2.13) | Nondurable goods manufacturing (1.50) | Agriculture (1.02) | Construction (.94) |
| West Piedmont (P.D. 12) | Nondurable goods manufacturing (2.54) | Durable goods manufacturing (1.80) | Agriculture (1.45) | Construction (.84) |
| Southside (P.D. 13) | Agriculture (3.40) | Nondurable goods manufacturing (2.02) | Durable goods manufacturing (1.22) | Construction (1.10) |
| Piedmont (P.D. 14) | Agriculture (3.53) | Durable goods manufacturing (1.35) | Nondurable goods manufacturing (1.30) | Construction (1.11) |
| Richmond Regional (P.D. 15) | Banking (1.64) | Nondurable goods manufacturing (1.20) | Transportation (1.17) | Trade (1.14) |
| RADCO (P.D. 16) | Construction (1.64) | Public administration (1.31) | Trade (1.04) | Service (1.00) |
| Northern Neck (P.D. 17) | Agriculture (3.89) | Construction (1.30) | Nondurable goods manufacturing (1.14) | Trade (1.09) |
| Middle Peninsula (P.D. 18) | Agriculture (2.59) | Durable goods manufacturing (1.27) | Construction (1.26) | Trade (1.02) |
| Crater (P.D. 19) | Nondurable goods manufacturing (1.94) | Agriculture (1.21) | Trade (.96) | Services (.96) |
| Southeastern Virginia (P.D. 20) | Trade (1.23) | Transportation (1.16) | Durable goods manufacturing (1.12) | Banking (1.06) |
| Peninsula (P.D. 21) | Durable goods manufacturing (1.96) | Public administration (1.25) | Services (1.10) | Trade (1.01) |
| Accomack-Northampton (P.D. 22) | Agriculture (5.37) | Nondurable goods manufacturing (1.42) | Trade (1.13) | Construction (.97) |

of public administration, banking and financial services, other services, and transportation is obviously quite different from areas with concentration in agriculture, manufacturing, and construction.

The data in Table 5.15 are also useful in evaluating those areas which are heavily dependent upon one or two industries for employment. The most obvious example is the Cumberland Plateau Planning District, which was characterized by an extraordinarily high location quotient for mining, a moderately high quotient for agriculture, and relatively low quotients (less than unity) for other industries.

Income

Three aspects of income are considered in this section: the mean level of family income, the incidence of poverty, and the distribution of income.

*Mean Family Income.* Mean family income is the arithmetic average of the reported level of income for all families in an area under study. Data on these levels in 1969 in all twenty-two planning districts are presented in Table 5.16. The data show a substantial amount of variation, ranging from a low of $6,302 in extreme Southwest Virginia to a high of $15,347 in Northern Virginia. Once again, the latter area is most atypical of the balance of the state. The mean level of family income in Northern Virginia was nearly $4,000 higher than in the second-place district, the Richmond Planning District (no. 15). These two districts and the Peninsula district (no. 21) were the only ones in the state with mean income above that recorded for the state as a whole.

As expected, the urbanized and metropolitan areas had somewhat higher levels of mean family income than did rural areas. In addition to the areas mentioned above, the areas around Roanoke (District 5), Harrisonburg–Staunton–Waynesboro (District 6), Charlottesville (District 10), Lynchburg (District 11), Fredericksburg (District 16), Petersburg–Hopewell–Colonial Heights (Dis-

Table 5.16. Mean family income and incidence of poverty in Virginia planning district, 1970

| Area | Number of Families | Mean Income | Number of Poor Families | Mean Income of Poor Families | Mean Income Deficit | Percent of Families in Poverty | Number of Poor Persons | Percent of Population in Poverty | Deficit/ Income Ratio of Poor Families | Mean Income as a Percent of State Total |
|---|---|---|---|---|---|---|---|---|---|---|
| Lenowisco Planning District 1 | 22,647 | $ 6,302 | 6,743 | $1,906 | $1,478 | 29.77 | 28,655 | 33.85 | .7754 | .5963 |
| Cumberland Plateau Planning District 2 | 28,637 | 7,020 | 7,356 | 2,106 | 1,515 | 25.69 | 32,717 | 29.08 | .7194 | .6643 |
| Mount Rogers Planning District 3 | 42,299 | 7,398 | 7,572 | 2,006 | 1,316 | 17.90 | 32,579 | 20.44 | .6560 | .7000 |
| New River Valley Planning District 4 | 28,763 | 8,904 | 3,577 | 1,972 | 1,247 | 12.44 | 16,037 | 13.97 | .6324 | .8425 |
| Fifth Planning District 5 | 61,607 | 9,894 | 5,825 | 2,082 | 1,293 | 9.46 | 27,616 | 11.95 | .6210 | .9362 |
| Central Shenandoah Planning District 6 | 46,916 | 9,116 | 5,400 | 2,093 | 1,297 | 11.51 | 25,622 | 13.75 | .6197 | .8626 |
| Lord Fairfax Planning District 7 | 28,408 | 8,288 | 3,656 | 2,058 | 1,275 | 12.87 | 16,536 | 15.55 | .6195 | .7843 |
| Northern Virginia Planning District 8 | 231,308 | 15,347 | 10,120 | 1,696 | 1,775 | 4.38 | 50,006 | 5.43 | 1.0466 | 1.4522 |
| Rappahannock-Rapidan Planning District 9 | 18,192 | 8,773 | 3,412 | 2,131 | 1,484 | 18.76 | 16,480 | 22.82 | .6755 | .8301 |
| Thomas Jefferson Planning District 10 | 28,032 | 9,518 | 4,496 | 2,131 | 1,459 | 16.04 | 23,884 | 20.73 | .6847 | .9006 |
| Central Virginia Planning District 11 | 41,825 | 9,411 | 4,999 | 2,173 | 1,375 | 11.95 | 24,778 | 14.93 | .6328 | .8905 |
| West Piedmont Planning District 12 | 56,556 | 8,531 | 8,034 | 2,203 | 1,368 | 14.21 | 38,645 | 17.66 | .6210 | .8072 |
| Southside Planning District 13 | 20,710 | 7,179 | 5,057 | 2,193 | 1,495 | 24.42 | 25,230 | 30.56 | .6817 | .6793 |
| Piedmont Planning District 14 | 18,395 | 7,418 | 4,493 | 2,151 | 1,522 | 24.43 | 22,121 | 29.01 | .7076 | .7019 |
| Richmond Regional Planning District 15 | 139,318 | 11,362 | 13,154 | 2,126 | 1,544 | 9.44 | 68,504 | 12.51 | .7262 | 1.0751 |
| RADCO Planning District 16 | 18,950 | 9,461 | 2,365 | 2,137 | 1,406 | 12.48 | 11,256 | 14.54 | .6579 | .8952 |
| Northern Neck Planning District 17 | 9,704 | 7,390 | 2,399 | 2,078 | 1,497 | 24.72 | 11,540 | 31.88 | .7204 | .6993 |
| Middle Peninsula Planning District 18 | 12,428 | 8,463 | 2,256 | 2,164 | 1,547 | 18.15 | 10,138 | 21.29 | .7149 | .8008 |
| Crater Planning District 19 | 37,218 | 9,216 | 5,346 | 2,178 | 1,623 | 14.36 | 27,600 | 17.14 | .7452 | .8721 |
| Southeastern Virginia Planning District 20 | 181,748 | 9,703 | 25,950 | 1,908 | 1,794 | 14.28 | 126,650 | 16.46 | .9403 | .9181 |
| Peninsula Planning District 21 | 77,346 | 10,721 | 7,817 | 1,897 | 1,776 | 10.11 | 37,703 | 11.82 | .9362 | 1.0145 |
| Accomack-Northampton Planning District 22 | 11,249 | 6,386 | 3,044 | 1,888 | 1,596 | 27.06 | 14,680 | 33.79 | .8453 | .6043 |
| Total | 1,116,256 | $10,568 | 143,005 | $2,025 | $1,548 | 12.30 | 690,615 | 14.86 | .7644 | 1.0000 |

trict 19), and Norfolk–Virginia Beach–Portsmouth (District 20) all had mean family income levels of $9,000 or greater. Additionally, the Radford–Montgomery County area (District 4) was close to this level ($8,904). Relatively low levels of income were found in the Southwestern (District 1, 2, and 3), Southside (Districts 13 and 14), Upper Peninsula (Districts 17 and 18) and Eastern Shore (District 22) areas. The level of mean family income for all planning districts is shown in graphic form in Figure 5.6.

Level of mean income does not take into account areal differences in the cost of living. Thus, mean family income in Northern Virginia was $9,000 higher than in extreme Southwestern Virginia, but this does not necessarily mean that the purchasing power of Northern Virginia families exceeded that of Southwest Virginia families by this amount. Regrettably, there are no comparable indices which show the relative cost of living in these two (or any other) areas.[8]

*Incidence of Poverty.* Data on the incidence of poverty correct this data deficiency to a limited extent. The incidence of poverty tells how many families received income less than the appropriate levels as developed by the Social Security Administration. The data on the incidence of poverty for females and individuals (also in Table 5.16) show that, in general, the lower the level of mean family income in an area, the higher the percentage of families in poverty. As Figure 5.7 shows, the relationship between the two variables was quite high. The simple coefficient of correlation (a measure of the association of two variables) was a latively high −0.859. (The negative sign indicates that the variables tend to move in the opposite direction.) Consequently, districts with low levels of income tended to have the highest incidence of poverty among families and individuals. In six of the twenty-two planning districts (Lenowisco, Cumberland Plateau, Southside, Piedmont, Northern Neck, and Accomack–North-

[8] An exception is found in the comparative retail food prices for the Norfolk–Virginia Beach–Portsmouth, Richmond, and Northern Virginia areas issued monthly by the Virginia Department of Labor and Industry. Retail price indices for metropolitan areas are found in Eleanor G. May and Raoul J. Kister, *The Cost of Living in Virginia Metropolitan Areas, 1975* (Charlottesville: Tayloe Murphy Institute, 1976).

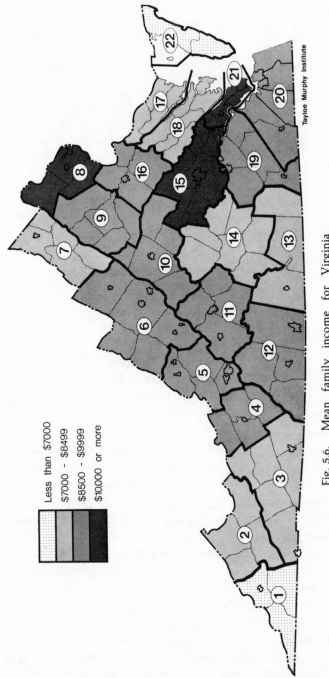

Less than $7000

$7000 - $8499

$8500 - $9999

$10,000 or more

Fig. 5.6. Mean family income for Virginia planning district, 1969

Tayloe Murphy Institute

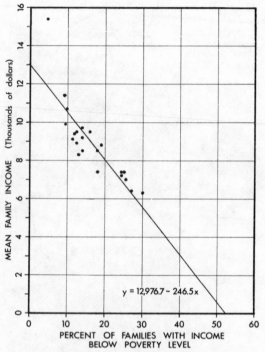

Fig. 5.7. Statistical relationship between mean
family income and percentage of families with
income below the poverty level

ampton), about one-fourth of all families were classified as
receiving a level of income below the poverty criterion.

The data in Table 5.16 also show the mean income deficit of
families below the poverty level of income. This figure represents
the average amount that each poor family would require to move
beyond the poverty level. The table also shows this number
expressed as a percentage of the mean income of poverty families.
The purpose of this ratio is to show the relative amount of
increased income required, on the average, to remove all families
from the poverty classification.

These two sets of data provide some interesting contrasts
to the data on mean family income and incidence of poverty. The
Northern Virginia area, which had by far the highest mean
family income and lowest incidence of poor families, also showed

the lowest mean income for families below the poverty level ($1,696) and the highest ratio of mean deficit to mean family income for poor families (1.05). In other words, in order to raise all poor families in Northern Virginia above the poverty level, their average income would have to increase by more than 100% (from $1,696 to $3,471). Other relatively high income areas which would also require large increases in average income include both planning districts in the Tidewater area. These districts ranked third (Peninsula Planning District) and fifth (Southeastern Virginia District) in terms of mean family income and third and second, respectively, in terms of the relative income increase required to remove all families from poverty (the ratios are 0.936 and 0.940, respectively).

*Distribution of Income.* The distribution of family income provides data on the number of families receiving income within a specified range. The data in Table 5.17 show the percentage of families in each planning district that received income within ranges beginning at less than $1,000 and ending at $50,000 and over.

As was expected, areas with a high average income also had a large number of families with a relatively high income. For example, in the Northern Virginia area, over 12 percent of all families had incomes in excess of $25,000, compared to low income areas such as the Southwest, Southside, and Eastern Shore, where this percentage varied from 1 percent to 1.5 percent as a rule. To get some idea of how different the extremes in income distribution were and how these in turn differed from the state distribution, consider Figure 5.8, which shows the cumulative percentage of all families receiving less than specified levels of income for Northern Virginia, the extreme Southwest, and Virginia as a whole. About 46 percent of all families in extreme Southwest Virginia had income of less than $5,000, compared with about 22 percent of all Virginia families and about 8 percent of Northern Virginia families. On the other hand, only about 10 percent of Southwest families had income of $10,000 or greater, compared with 32 percent of all Virginia families, and 60 percent of Northern Virginia families.

In discussing income distribution, a logical area for inquiry

Table 5.17. Distribution of family income in Virginia planning districts, 1970 (percent)

| Area | Less Than $1,000 | $1,000-1,999 | $2,000-2,999 | $3,000-3,999 | $4,000-4,999 | $5,000-5,999 | $6,000-6,999 | $7,000-7,999 | $8,000-8,999 | $9,000-9,999 | $10,000-11,999 | $12,000-14,999 | $15,000-24,999 | $25,000-49,999 | $50,000+ |
|---|---|---|---|---|---|---|---|---|---|---|---|---|---|---|---|
| Lenowisco Planning District 1 | 6.86 | 11.20 | 9.64 | 10.24 | 7.99 | 8.59 | 7.59 | 7.44 | 6.88 | 5.24 | 7.99 | 5.59 | 3.82 | 0.77 | 0.15 |
| Cumberland Plateau Planning District 2 | 4.63 | 8.82 | 8.41 | 9.18 | 8.90 | 8.64 | 7.99 | 7.95 | 7.78 | 6.50 | 9.15 | 6.50 | 4.34 | 0.90 | 0.30 |
| Mount Rogers Planning District 3 | 3.53 | 6.48 | 7.05 | 8.49 | 9.55 | 9.92 | 9.25 | 9.00 | 7.93 | 6.55 | 9.09 | 6.55 | 5.23 | 1.18 | 0.19 |
| New River Valley Planning District 4 | 2.43 | 4.64 | 5.10 | 5.83 | 6.17 | 8.30 | 9.38 | 8.36 | 8.43 | 7.37 | 12.29 | 9.86 | 9.82 | 1.72 | 0.29 |
| Fifth Planning District 5 | 1.72 | 3.17 | 4.31 | 5.56 | 5.61 | 6.91 | 7.80 | 7.92 | 8.31 | 7.55 | 13.90 | 12.51 | 11.74 | 2.40 | 0.58 |
| Central Shenandoah Planning District 6 | 2.05 | 4.17 | 4.86 | 6.29 | 6.60 | 8.11 | 8.14 | 8.92 | 8.29 | 7.06 | 11.99 | 11.62 | 9.49 | 2.08 | 0.36 |
| Lord Fairfax Planning District 7 | 2.46 | 4.39 | 5.34 | 6.17 | 7.33 | 8.69 | 9.71 | 8.91 | 8.30 | 7.46 | 11.90 | 9.52 | 7.53 | 1.85 | 0.44 |
| Northern Virginia Planning District 8 | 1.51 | 1.08 | 1.43 | 1.99 | 2.47 | 3.14 | 3.62 | 4.54 | 4.84 | 5.11 | 10.74 | 15.44 | 32.00 | 11.07 | 1.00 |
| Rappahannock-Rapidan Planning District 9 | 3.56 | 5.45 | 5.89 | 7.38 | 8.38 | 8.47 | 8.91 | 7.60 | 7.81 | 5.57 | 10.25 | 9.39 | 8.49 | 2.22 | 0.62 |
| Thomas Jefferson Planning District 10 | 2.94 | 5.28 | 5.72 | 6.51 | 6.80 | 7.84 | 7.53 | 7.34 | 6.76 | 6.29 | 11.54 | 10.75 | 10.67 | 3.29 | 0.68 |
| Central Virginia Planning District 11 | 2.04 | 4.06 | 5.08 | 6.08 | 6.20 | 7.39 | 7.29 | 7.77 | 7.96 | 7.23 | 13.68 | 12.35 | 10.26 | 2.19 | 0.43 |
| West Piedmont Planning District 12 | 2.41 | 5.01 | 5.18 | 5.94 | 7.89 | 8.51 | 8.75 | 8.32 | 7.90 | 7.85 | 12.90 | 9.87 | 7.75 | 1.47 | 0.24 |
| Southside Planning District 13 | 4.06 | 8.30 | 8.90 | 9.23 | 9.04 | 8.56 | 8.17 | 7.66 | 7.09 | 5.56 | 9.33 | 7.61 | 5.26 | 1.06 | 0.17 |
| Piedmont Planning District 14 | 4.82 | 7.97 | 8.57 | 8.43 | 9.49 | 9.56 | 8.18 | 6.83 | 5.99 | 6.07 | 8.98 | 7.82 | 5.80 | 1.04 | 0.45 |
| Richmond Regional Planning District 15 | 2.08 | 2.56 | 3.59 | 4.30 | 5.20 | 5.55 | 6.17 | 6.92 | 7.16 | 7.23 | 13.70 | 14.84 | 16.08 | 3.62 | 1.00 |
| RADCO Planning District 16 | 2.42 | 4.47 | 4.18 | 5.14 | 5.64 | 7.66 | 8.92 | 9.09 | 8.41 | 6.55 | 10.84 | 12.22 | 12.06 | 1.84 | 0.54 |
| Northern Neck Planning District 17 | 4.94 | 8.57 | 8.88 | 10.50 | 8.63 | 8.82 | 7.57 | 7.24 | 6.46 | 5.35 | 7.44 | 6.43 | 6.87 | 1.83 | 0.45 |
| Middle Peninsula Planning District 18 | 3.47 | 6.06 | 7.00 | 7.91 | 7.26 | 8.48 | 7.29 | 7.84 | 7.35 | 6.91 | 9.82 | 10.16 | 8.59 | 1.42 | 0.44 |
| Crater Planning District 19 | 3.29 | 3.89 | 4.84 | 6.09 | 6.00 | 7.49 | 7.86 | 8.26 | 7.50 | 7.42 | 12.12 | 11.81 | 11.23 | 1.89 | 0.31 |
| Southeastern Virginia Planning District 20 | 4.20 | 3.50 | 4.57 | 5.48 | 6.08 | 6.97 | 7.34 | 7.87 | 7.38 | 6.86 | 12.05 | 12.32 | 12.58 | 2.25 | 0.55 |
| Peninsula Planning District 21 | 3.03 | 2.34 | 3.51 | 4.27 | 5.08 | 6.10 | 6.91 | 7.25 | 7.69 | 7.33 | 13.11 | 13.99 | 16.33 | 2.53 | 0.54 |
| Accomack-Northampton Planning District 22 | 5.65 | 8.40 | 10.55 | 11.23 | 10.24 | 10.28 | 7.40 | 7.81 | 5.76 | 4.57 | 6.57 | 5.08 | 5.40 | 1.07 | 0.00 |
| State | 2.82 | 3.75 | 4.43 | 5.27 | 5.77 | 6.57 | 6.86 | 7.18 | 7.03 | 6.58 | 11.73 | 12.20 | 15.23 | 3.97 | 0.61 |

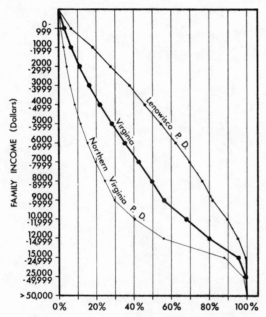

Fig. 5.8.    Cumulative income distribution,
Lenowisco Planning District, Northern Virginia Planning District, and Virginia, 1969

is the equality of income distribution. A common means of
measuring equality of income distribution which relates the
percentage of total units receiving income (families in this case) is
the Lorenz curve, a hypothetical example of which is shown in
Figure 5.9. The line labeled $L_1$ in this figure may be called the
line of equality. If all families received the same amount of
income, this would be the Lorenz curve. According to $L_1$, 10 percent
of all families receive 10 percent of total income, 20 percent
of all families receive 20 percent of total income, and so on. The
actual situation is more probably typified by line $L_2$. In
this case, the lowest 10 percent of all families receive 1 percent
of total income, the lowest 20 percent receive 4 percent of total
income, and so on.

An important use of the Lorenz curve is to determine the
index of income concentration. This may be defined as the ratio
of the area, $A$, between the diagonal, $L_1$, and the Lorenz

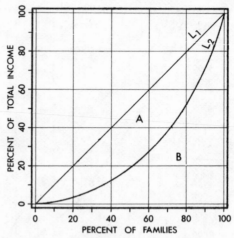

Fig. 5.9.    Hypothetical Lorenz curve

curve, $L_2$ to the total area under the diagonal, area $A$ plus
area $B$. Algebraically, this index equals:

$$I = \frac{A}{A+B}.$$

The value of the index ranges from a minimum of almost 1.0,
the situation where one family received all the income in a given
area, to 0.0, where all families would receive an equal income.
In other words, the higher the value of the index, the more
heavily concentrated income is in that particular area.

Unfortunately, these data are not available on the planning
district level. The values of the index for those portions of the
state for which these data have been computed are shown in Table
5.18. As the data show, urban and rural nonfarm areas appear
to have had relatively less inequality in income distribution than
did rural farm areas. This relationship was true for the state
as a whole and for a metropolitan–nonmetropolitan classification.
It is also interesting to note that, perhaps not surprisingly,
suburban areas showed relatively less income inequality than did
central cities. In each SMSA, the suburban portion (in the
case of the Norfolk area, the cities of Virginia Beach and
Chesapeake) showed a lower index of income concentration than
did the central city (with the exception of Colonial Heights,
which is essentially suburban in character).

Table 5.18. Index of income concentration
in selected areas of Virginia, 1970

| Area | Index |
|---|---|
| Virginia | .379 |
| Urban | .364 |
| Rural Nonfarm | .365 |
| Rural Farm | .423 |
| Metropolitan | .359 |
| Central Cities | .366 |
| Other Urban | .338 |
| Rural Nonfarm | .336 |
| Rural Farm | .401 |
| Nonmetropolitan | .369 |
| Urban | .360 |
| Rural Nonfarm | .360 |
| Rural Farm | .420 |
| Lynchburg SMSA | .347 |
| Lynchburg City | .387 |
| Urban Balance | .279 |
| Newport News-Hampton SMSA | .332 |
| Hampton City | .319 |
| Newport News City | .343 |
| Urban Balance | .287 |
| Norfolk-Virginia Beach-Portsmouth | .360 |
| Chesapeake City | .305 |
| Norfolk City | .384 |
| Portsmouth City | .353 |
| Virginia Beach City | .335 |
| Petersburg-Hopewell-Colonial Heights SMSA | .334 |
| Colonial Heights City | .277 |
| Petersburg City | .366 |
| Urban Balance | .304 |
| Richmond SMSA | .341 |
| Richmond City | .393 |
| Urban Balance | .292 |
| Roanoke SMSA | .342 |
| Roanoke City | .363 |
| Urban Balance | .301 |
| Northern Virginia | .342 |
| Alexandria City | .369 |
| Arlington County | .379 |
| Urban Balance | .321 |

Urban–Rural Comparisons

In 1970, 2.9 million, or 63.1 percent, of Virginia's 4.6 million persons lived in urban areas. Although the definition of *urban* as used by the Bureau of the Census is rather cumbersome, the urban population essentially includes almost all residents of defined metropolitan areas (both city and suburban portions) and residents of incorporated or unincorporated places of 2,500 or more inhabitants. The balance of the population is rural. The rural population, in turn, is divided into residents of farms (rural farms) and residents of other rural places (rural nonfarm). Of Virginia's 1.7 million rural persons, 1.5 million, 84.4 percent, were classified as rural nonfarm.[9]

*Employment and Labor Force.* Table 5.19 presents data on the composition of the labor force in Virginia's urban and rural areas. Labor force participation was higher among both sexes in urban areas than it was in rural areas. In urban areas, 82.0 percent of all males aged 16 and over and 44.8 percent of all females in this group were in the labor force in 1970. For rural nonfarm areas, these rates were 73.4 percent for males and 39.1 percent for females; in rural farm areas, they were 72.8 and 32.2 percent, respectively. In urban areas, the total labor force was 1,293,232, of whom 475,636, or 36.8 percent, were female. For rural nonfarm residents, the total labor force included 547,706 persons, of whom 193,912 (35.4 percent) were female. Finally among the rural farm population, the labor force comprised 101,431 individuals, of whom 31,385, or 30.9 percent, were female.

A sizable portion of the labor force in urban areas included individuals in military service. Among males, 16.2 percent

[9] The Bureau of the Census recently revised the distribution of rural farm–rural nonfarm population. The revised data show the rural nonfarm population was 1,524,556 in 1970 and the rural farm population to be 192,784. Because no characteristics of these persons are available, the analysis in this chapter is based on the data originally published by the Bureau. Although the absolute numbers will change, it is unlikely that the percentage distribution of the various socioeconomic indicators discussed in this chapter will change to any considerable extent. See U.S. Bureau of the Census, *Rural Population by Farm–Nonfarm Residence for Counties in the United States: 1970.*

of all residents aged 16 and over were in the armed forces. These individuals accounted for 19.8 percent of the male urban labor force. Naturally, among females the incidence of military personnel was much lower—only 0.7 percent of the total labor force. The military was a far less significant factor in rural areas. Among the rural nonfarm labor force, only 2.8 percent of the males and 0.1 percent of the females in the labor force were military. Among the rural farm labor force, the rates were lower still—0.4 percent of males and 0.02 percent of females.

Those persons in the labor force not in the military comprise the civilian labor force. It is this datum which provides the base for measuring unemployment. A person who is not employed but is actively seeking work (and will accept it) is considered unemployed. In 1970 the rate of unemployment was lower for the urban labor force (2.8 percent of the civilian labor force) than it was for the rural nonfarm (3.4 percent), but higher than that of the rural farm labor force (2.5 percent). The rate of unemployment among women was higher than it was for men in all three categories: urban rates of unemployment were 2.2 percent for males and 3.7 percent for females; rural nonfarm rates were 2.6 percent and 4.8 percent, respectively; and rural farm rates were 1.8 percent and 4.0 percent, respectively.

Somewhat surprising in light of the higher rates of labor force participation among urban women is the fact that the presence of young children (those aged 0 to 5) appeared to be a greater disincentive for labor force participation among urban women than among rural women. As the data in Table 5.19 show, labor force participation rates for women with children in this age group were higher among rural nonfarm (35.6 percent) and rural farm (33.6 percent) women than among urban women (32.9 percent). The relationship changed somewhat for women with children between the ages of 6 and 17 (and no children aged 0 to 5); about one half of rural nonfarm and urban women with children in this age group but only 43 percent of rural farm women with such children were in the labor force.

Finally, for women without children under 18 years of age, the pattern was the same as for all women—the highest rate of participation was among urban women (46.6 percent), followed by

Table 5.19. Employment and labor force characteristics of Virginia by urban-rural residence, 1970

|  | Urban | Rural Nonfarm | Rural Farm |
|---|---|---|---|
| **Male** | | | |
| Population 16 and Over | 996,919 | 481,825 | 96,215 |
| Labor Force | 817,596 | 353,794 | 70,046 |
| Military | 161,708 | 9,899 | 293 |
| Civilian Labor Force | 655,888 | 343,895 | 69,753 |
| Employed | 641,630 | 334,977 | 68,500 |
| Unemployed | 14,258 | 8,918 | 1,253 |
| **Female** | | | |
| Population 16 and Over | 1,062,045 | 495,343 | 97,054 |
| Labor Force | 475,636 | 193,912 | 31,385 |
| Military | 3,535 | 187 | 7 |
| Civilian Labor Force | 472,101 | 193,725 | 31,378 |
| Employed | 454,560 | 184,464 | 30,119 |
| Unemployed | 17,541 | 9,261 | 1,259 |
| **Percent With Children Aged 0-5 in Labor Force** | 32.9 | 35.6 | 33.6 |
| **Percent With Children Aged 6-17 in Labor Force** | 50.7 | 50.9 | 42.9 |
| **Percent With No Children Under 18 in Labor Force** | 46.6 | 35.9 | 28.7 |

rural nonfarm women (35.9 percent) and rural farm women (28.7 percent). Rates in all three residence categories were lower for women without children under age 18 than they were for women with children aged 6-17 (and among rural farm women with children aged 0-5). This was presumably due to decreasing labor force participation with age (see Figure 5.10).

*Occupational Distribution.* The distribution of Virginia's labor force by occupation in 1970 is presented for the urban, rural nonfarm, and rural farm segments in Table 5.20. The data represent the employed civilian labor force in each instance. As is to be expected, there was considerable variation in the occupational composition. In urban areas, white-collar workers accounted for three-fifths of the labor force. This percentage was somewhat lower in rural areas, totaling a third of employment in rural nonfarm areas and a quarter of employment in rural farm areas.

Blue-collar and agricultural employment was of relatively greater importance in rural areas. Blue-collar workers comprised less than a third of the urban labor force, compared with half

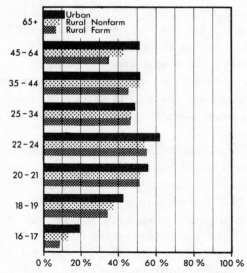

Fig. 5.10. Labor force participation rates of Virginia women by age and urban–rural residence, 1970

Table 5.20. Occupational distribution of Virginia's labor force by urban-rural residence, 1970

|  | Urban | Rural Nonfarm | Rural Farm |
|---|---|---|---|
| Professional | 211,987 | 55,216 | 7,575 |
| Managerial | 105,386 | 35,728 | 5,034 |
| Sales | 83,142 | 24,661 | 3,761 |
| Clerical | 235,467 | 62,574 | 9,066 |
|   Total White Collar | 635,982 | 178,179 | 25,436 |
| Craftsmen | 142,908 | 89,168 | 12,164 |
| Operatives | 100,216 | 107,738 | 16,804 |
| Transport Operatives | 37,244 | 27,838 | 4,504 |
| Nonfarm Laborers | 39,075 | 37,654 | 5,932 |
|   Total Blue Collar | 319,443 | 262,398 | 39,404 |
| Farmers | 1,149 | 5,020 | 19,193 |
| Farm Laborers | 2,053 | 12,435 | 6,316 |
|   Total Agricultural | 3,203 | 17,455 | 25,509 |
| Service | 115,779 | 47,236 | 6,034 |
| Private Household | 21,783 | 14,173 | 2,236 |
|   Total Service | 137,562 | 61,409 | 8,270 |
| TOTAL | 1,096,190 | 519,441 | 98,619 |

of the rural nonfarm and two-fifths of the rural farm labor force. Obviously, agricultural employment was a much larger share of the labor force among the rural farm population than among either the rural nonfarm or urban populations.

Finally, there was not a great deal of variation in the relative number of individuals engaged in service occupations, although the share in farm areas was somewhat lower than in rural nonfarm and urban areas.

Looking at the matter from a slightly different perspective, urban areas contained 63.9 percent of the state's employed labor force and accounted for 75.7 percent of white-collar employment 51.4 percent of blue-collar employment, 66 percent of service employment, and only 6.9 percent of agricultural employment. Rural nonfarm workers comprised 30.3 percent of total employment, but only 21.2 and 29.6 percent of white-collar and service employment, respectively.

Finally, while rural farm areas contained only 5.8 percent of the state's employed civilian labor force, these areas contained fully 55.3 percent of the agricultural labor force. Additionally, rural farm areas accounted for 3.0 percent of white-collar employment, 6.3 percent of blue-collar employment, and 4.0 percent of service employment.

*Industrial Composition.* Data that depict the industrial composition of Virginia's employed civilian labor force are presented in Table 5.21. These data show, on a place-of-residence basis, the number of workers classified by the principal good or service produced by their employer. Such data can be very useful in comparative analyses of the economy of given areas or sectors of the state. The presentation of data specific to urban-rural residence should show the pattern of concentration of different industries within the state of Virginia.

The data show considerable variation in the industrial mix of the labor force in urban, rural nonfarm, and rural farm areas. Nearly two-thirds of the urban labor force was concentrated into three industrial categories: services (28.1 percent of the labor force), wholesale and retail trade (19.4 percent), and public administration (14.7 percent). Among rural nonfarm workers, services again

Table 5.21.  Industrial composition of Virginia's labor force by urban-rural
residence, 1970

|  | Urban | Rural<br>Nonfarm | Rural<br>Farm |
|---|---|---|---|
| Industry |  |  |  |
| Agriculture, Forestry, Fisheries | 7,044 | 23,485 | 26,733 |
| Mining | 2,367 | 13,534 | 1,166 |
| Construction | 68,170 | 50,932 | 7,701 |
| Durable Goods Manufacturing | 92,794 | 66,321 | 9,929 |
| Nondurable Goods Manufacturing | 103,811 | 95,849 | 15,518 |
| Transportation, Communication,<br>    and Utilities | 80,790 | 30,765 | 4,393 |
| Wholesale and Retail Trade | 213,049 | 83,365 | 11,383 |
| Finance, Insurance, and Real Estate | 60,072 | 13,420 | 1,928 |
| Services | 307,487 | 111,292 | 16,191 |
| Public Administration | 160,606 | 30,748 | 3,677 |
| TOTAL | 1,096,190 | 519,441 | 98,619 |

accounted for the largest single share of the labor force,
with 21.4 percent. Second was nondurable goods manufacturing
with 18.5 percent, followed by trade with 16.1 percent of the
labor force. Together, these three sectors employed 55.9 percent
of the rural nonfarm labor force. The leading sector in farm areas
was agriculture, with 27.1 percent. The next two sectors were
trade, employing 16.4 percent and nondurable goods manufacturing with 15.7 percent. These three sectors collectively employed
59.3 percent of the rural farm labor force.

If the sectors are ranked in relative importance for each of
the three residential categories, the result is that urban areas
showed the highest rank for five categories (transportation,
trade, finance, service, and public administration) and the lowest
rank for the other five categories. Rural nonfarm areas had the
highest rank in mining, durable goods manufacturing, nondurable
goods manufacturing, and construction and were second highest in
the other six categories. Rural farm areas were highest in
agricultural and second highest in mining, construction, and both
manufacturing sectors. The relative industrial mix of all three
areas (urban, rural nonfarm, and rural farm) is shown graphically
in Figures 5.11, 5.12, and 5.13.

In order to evaluate the significance of these apparent differences in the industrial mix of the urban and rural portions of
the state, location quotients were constructed. It will be recalled
that a location quotient for any industry, $L_i$, in any geographical

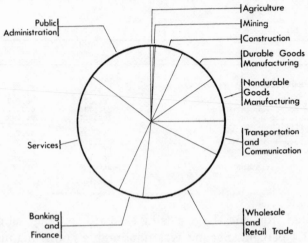

Fig. 5.11. Industrial composition of Virginia's urban labor force, 1970

area, $j$, $L_{i,j}$, may be defined as the ratio of employment in that industrial sector and geographical area, $E_{i,j}$ taken as a percentage of total employment in the area, $E_j$, to total employment in that sector in the entire state, $E_{i,v}$, considered as a percentage of total employment in the state, $E_v$, or:

$$L_{i,j} = \frac{E_{i,j}/E_j}{E_{i,v}/E_v}$$

The location quotients for all industrial sectors, classified by urban, rural nonfarm, and rural farm residence, are given in Table 5.22.

A quotient in excess of unity means that employment in that sector was more heavily concentrated in the geographical area under study than it was in the entire state. The data show several distinct patterns of concentration. Agriculture and mining were quite noticeably concentrated in one area (rural farm and rural nonfarm, respectively), with the other rural area having, in each case, a moderate concentration as well. This was true primarily because urban employment in these industrial sectors was negligible.

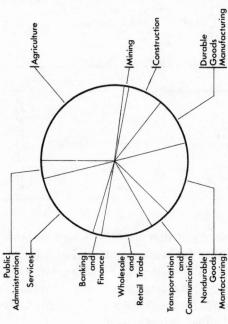

Fig. 5.13. Industrial composition of Virginia's rural farm labor force, 1970

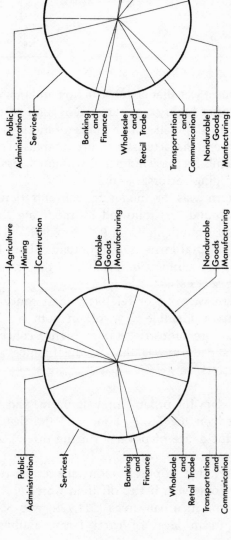

Fig. 5.12. Industrial composition of Virginia's rural nonfarm labor force, 1970

Table 5.22. Location quotients of industrial composition of Virginia's labor force, by urban-rural residence, 1970

|  | Urban | Rural Nonfarm | Rural Farm |
|---|---|---|---|
| Agriculture | .19 | 1.35 | 8.12 |
| Mining | .22 | 2.61 | 1.18 |
| Construction | .84 | 1.33 | 1.05 |
| Durable Goods Manufacturing | .86 | 1.30 | 1.02 |
| Nondurable Goods Manufacturing | .75 | 1.47 | 1.25 |
| Transportation, Communication, and Utilities | 1.09 | .88 | .66 |
| Trade | 1.08 | .89 | .64 |
| Finance | 1.25 | .59 | .45 |
| Services | 1.11 | .84 | .65 |
| Public Administration | 1.29 | .52 | .33 |

The second pattern was that of construction and manufacturing, which were both most highly concentrated in rural nonfarm areas (ranging from 1.3 to 1.5), with minor concentrations in rural farm areas. Shortages were characteristic of urban areas. The range of values of the quotients for these industries was much less than in the agriculture and mining sectors.

The third pattern was of moderate concentration in urban areas (quotients around 1.1) followed by moderate shortages in rural nonfarm areas (quotients from 0.85 to 0.90) and somewhat greater shortages in rural farm areas (quotients about 0.65). This pattern was followed almost identically in the transportation, trade, and service sectors.

The final pattern was one of relatively high concentration in urban areas with considerable drop-off in both rural areas. In other words, these are industries rather highly concentrated in urban areas. This pattern was that of the finance and public administration sectors.

*Income.* Income data for urban, rural nonfarm, and rural farm areas are analyzed on the level of income, the distribution of income, and the incidence of poverty for the three geographical areas under study.

The data indicate that in purely monetary terms, residents of urban areas were somewhat better off than were rural residents. Mean family income in urban areas ($11,779) was 36.3 percent higher than the mean level of rural farm families ($7,920).

These differences do not reflect differences in cost of living and
patterns of consumption, nor do they reflect the great incidence of
self–sufficiency in food presumably found in rural areas. However,
data on the incidence of poverty do reflect these differentials
to some extent, since the poverty threshold criteria do allow
for farm–nonfarm differentials (as well as age and sex of head
of household and family size).

Examination of the data in Table 5.23 shows that even adjusting for these differences, the incidence of poverty was much
higher in rural areas than in urban areas. Among rural nonfarm
families, some 17.3 percent received income in 1969 less than
the poverty level. At 20.2 percent, this rate was even higher for
rural farm families. But in urban areas, it was only 9.1 percent.

Table 5.23. Mean family income and incidence of poverty for Virginia families
by urban-rural residence, 1970

|  | Urban | Rural Nonfarm | Rural Farm |
|---|---|---|---|
| Number of Families | 729,703 | 361,472 | 71,081 |
| Mean Income | $11,779 | $8,645 | $7,920 |
| Number of Poor Families | 66,089 | 62,593 | 14,323 |
| Mean Income of Poor Families | $1,925 | $2,195 | $1,746 |
| Mean Income Deficit | $1,654 | $1,503 | $1,254 |
| Percent of Families in Poverty | 9.1 | 17.3 | 20.2 |
| Number of Poor Unrelated Individuals | 70,585 | 38,721 | 5,979 |
| Percent of Individuals in Poverty | 30.5 | 55.5 | 52.0 |
| Deficit/Income Ratio for Poor Families | .86 | .68 | .72 |
| Mean Income as a Percent of State Total | 111.5% | 81.8% | 74.9% |

The pattern was similar for unrelated individuals (that is, single
persons living alone, constituting a one–person household; this
does not include the institutional population). In the aggregate,
poverty was greater among these persons, but the incidence in
urban areas of the state (30.5 percent) was substantially lower
than it was in rural nonfarm (55.5 percent) and rural farm (52.0
percent) areas.

Although the incidence of poverty was less among the urban
population, it would appear that poor families there were relatively
worse off than poor rural families. Mean income of poor urban
families would have to increase by 86 percent, on the average,
if all families were to move to the poverty threshold. Among poor
rural nonfarm families, this increase would have to be only

68 percent, on the average, while for poor rural farm families income would have to rise by some 72 percent. In urban areas, the mean level of income of poor families was only 16.3 percent of that of all families; for rural nonfarm and rural farm families, the corresponding percentages are 25.4 and 22.0 percent, respectively.

The other aspect of income to be considered is the distribution of family income. Table 5.24 presents this distribution for selected intervals for urban, rural nonfarm, and rural farm families. These data show that a much greater share of rural families received relatively low levels of income than was true of urban families.

Table 5.24. Income distribution of Virginia families by urban-rural residence, 1970

| Income | Urban | Rural Nonfarm | Rural Farm |
|---|---|---|---|
| Less than $1,000 | 17,858 | 11,611 | 3,349 |
| $1,000-$1,999 | 17,858 | 19,617 | 6,056 |
| $2,000-$2,999 | 24,138 | 20,963 | 6,394 |
| $3,000-$3,999 | 30,354 | 24,818 | 6,080 |
| $4,000-$4,999 | 34,351 | 26,768 | 5,940 |
| $5,000-$5,999 | 40,582 | 29,886 | 5,917 |
| $6,000-$6,999 | 44,666 | 29,729 | 5,287 |
| $7,000-$7,999 | 49,049 | 29,465 | 4,933 |
| $8,000-$8,999 | 49,311 | 27,970 | 4,424 |
| $9,000-$9,999 | 48,015 | 24,578 | 3,867 |
| $10,000-$11,999 | 89,542 | 40,523 | 6,237 |
| $12,000-$14,999 | 100,620 | 35,926 | 5,304 |
| $15,000-$24,999 | 139,694 | 31,813 | 5,528 |
| $25,000-$49,999 | 38,301 | 6,429 | 1,389 |
| $50,000+ | 5,364 | 1,376 | 376 |
| TOTAL | 729,703 | 361,472 | 71,081 |

Only 17.1 percent of all urban families received less than $5,000, compared with 28.7 percent of rural nonfarm and 39.1 percent of rural farm families. On the other hand, the share of urban families with incomes between $10,000 and $14,999 (26.1 percent) and $15,000 and over (25.1 percent) was much higher than the respective shares among either rural nonfarm (21.2 and 11.0 percent) or rural farm (16.2 and 10.3 percent) families. The complete percentage distribution of income is shown graphically in Figure 5.14.

Lorenz curves for Virginia's urban, rural farm, and rural nonfarm families are shown in Figure 5.15. The curves for the urban and

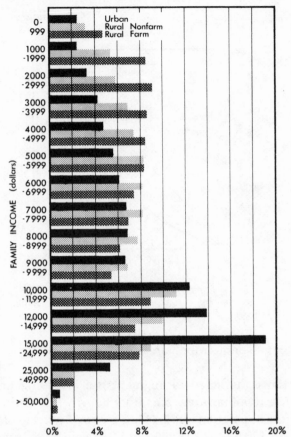

Fig. 5.14. Percentage distribution of Virginia families by income and urban–rural residence, 1969

rural nonfarm populations are practically identical, as are the indices of income concentration in these areas—0.366 for urban families and 0.365 for rural nonfarm families. However, the curve for rural farm families shows that the degree of inequality of income distribution in this group was somewhat greater. This is confirmed by the relatively high index of income concentration, 0.423. Thus, while there was an uneven distribution of income in each area (a perfectly even income distribution is possible only in theory), the degree of inequality was somewhat greater among rural farm families than among either urban or rural nonfarm families.

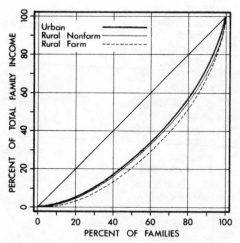

Fig. 5.15.  Lorenz curve for distribution of family income by urban–rural residence, Virginia, 1969

## Metropolitan–Nonmetropolitan Comparisons

This section is designed to augment the foregoing urban–rural analysis. Metropolitan areas are rather heavily urban—in 1970 total metropolitan population was 2,846,034 (or 61.2 percent of the state's population). Of this, 1,124,889 (39.5 percent of all metropolitan population) were located in central cities; 1,374,223 (48.3 percent) lived in other urban portions of metropolitan areas; 390,737 (10.9 percent) lived in rural nonfarm areas. Table 5.25 lists the components of Virginia's metropolitan areas and classifies the population as central city, other urban, rural nonfarm, or rural farm.

There were 1,802,460 Virginians living in nonmetropolitan areas. Of these persons, 23.9 percent lived in nonmetropolitan urban areas, 63.3 percent lived in rural nonfarm areas, and 12.8 percent lived in rural farm areas.[10]

[10] The complete census count was used to make these tabulations, although the rural farm–rural nonfarm distinction is estimated on the basis of sample (fourth-count) data. Due to small discrepancies between the complete count and sample data, the totals which appear in Tables 5.26 and 5.27 will not necessarily agree with the numbers presented in the text. The overall differences are so small that they are of no importance.

Table 5.25. Geographic composition of Virginia's metropolitan population, by urban-rural residence, 1970

| | Total | Central City | Other Urban | Rural Nonfarm | Rural Farm |
|---|---|---|---|---|---|
| Lynchburg SMSA | 123,474 | 54,083 | 18,945 | 41,690 | 8,756 |
| Lynchburg City | 54,083 | 54,083 | | | |
| Amherst County | 26,072 | | 7,758 | 13,733 | 4,581 |
| Campbell County | 43,319 | | 11,187 | 27,957 | 4,175 |
| Newport News-Hampton | 292,159 | 258,956 | 7,843 | 23,741 | 1,619 |
| Hampton City | 120,779 | 120,779 | | | |
| Newport News City | 138,177 | 138,177 | | | |
| York County | 33,203 | | 7,843 | 23,741 | 1,619 |
| Norfolk-Virginia Beach | 680,600 | 418,914 | 249,216 | 10,499 | 1,971 |
| Chesapeake City | 89,580 | | 82,641 | 5,745 | 1,194 |
| Norfolk City | 307,951 | 307,951 | | | |
| Portsmouth City | 110,963 | 110,963 | | | |
| Virginia Beach City | 172,106 | | 166,575 | 4,754 | 777 |
| Petersburg-Colonial | 128,809 | 51,200 | 45,422 | 27,050 | 5,137 |
| Heights-Hopewell | 15,097 | 15,097 | | | |
| Colonial Heights City | 36,103 | 36,103 | | | |
| Petersburg City | 23,471 | | 23,471 | | |
| Hopewell City | 25,046 | | 9,516 | 12,025 | 3,505 |
| Dinwiddie County | 29,092 | | 12,435 | 15,025 | 1,632 |
| Prince George County | | | | | |
| Richmond SMSA | 518,319 | 249,621 | 179,427 | 78,676 | 10,595 |
| Richmond City | 249,621 | 249,621 | | | |
| Chesterfield County | 76,855 | | 41,806 | 32,613 | 2,436 |
| Hanover County | 37,479 | | 8,294 | 23,068 | 6,117 |
| Henrico County | 154,364 | | 129,327 | 22,995 | 2,042 |
| Roanoke SMSA | 181,436 | 92,115 | 64,506 | 23,449 | 1,366 |
| Roanoke City | 92,115 | 92,115 | | | |
| Salem City | 21,982 | | 21,982 | | |
| Roanoke County | 67,339 | | 42,524 | 23,449 | 1,366 |
| Washington SMSA | 921,237 | | 808,864 | 104,632 | 7,741 |
| (Virginia Portion) | 174,284 | | 174,284 | | |
| Arlington County | 455,021 | | 407,901 | 44,269 | 2,851 |
| Fairfax County | 10,024 | | 10,024 | | |
| Loudoun County | 111,102 | | 72,975 | 24,931 | 2,195 |
| Prince William County | 110,938 | | 110,938 | 35,432 | 2,695 |
| Alexandria City | 21,970 | | 21,970 | | |
| Fairfax City | 10,772 | | 10,772 | | |
| Falls Church City | | | | | |
| Total | 2,846,034 | 1,124,889 | 1,374,223 | 309,737 | 37,185 |

*Labor Force and Employment.* Table 5.26 presents a summary of labor force characteristics for Virginia's metropolitan and non-metropolitan areas. The overall rate of labor force participation among individuals aged 16 and over (including military personnel) was somewhat higher in metropolitan areas (63.8 percent) than in nonmetropolitan areas (55.2 percent). This difference was due to the much larger concentration of military personnel in the metropolitan areas. Considering the civilian labor force as a percentage of the population aged 16 and over, the rate of labor force participation was 54.68 percent in metropolitan areas and 54.75 percent in nonmetropolitan areas.

A similar correction made separately by sex shows that 65.6 percent of metropolitan males and 44.1 percent of metropolitan females were in the civilian labor force. In nonmetropolitan areas the corresponding rates of civilian labor force participation were 71.5 and 39.2 percent, respectively. It is also because of the high proportion of military personnel in metropolitan areas (and the high proportion of military personnel who were male—97.9 percent) that females comprised a relatively smaller share of the metropolitan labor force than they did of the nonmetropolitan labor force, even though female labor force participation rates were higher in metropolitan areas. Complete labor force participation rates for each sex are given in Figure 5.16.

The rate of unemployment, which is measured only for the civilian labor force, was considerably lower for metropolitan area residents. Only 2.67 percent of the civilian labor force residing in metropolitan areas was unemployed (out of work and actively seeking work) at the time of the census (April 1, 1970), compared with 3.44 percent of the nonmetropolitan civilian labor force. This was true for each sex, although unemployment among males was lower than unemployment among females.

*Occupational and Industrial Composition.* In terms of the occupational composition of the labor force, the metropolitan labor force was primarily engaged in white-collar occupations, with somewhat smaller shares of employment in blue-collar and service occupations. Employment in agricultural occupations was extremely small, as expected. Nonmetropolitan workers were

Table 5.26. Employment, labor force, and occupational and industrial
characteristics of Virginia by metropolitan-nonmetropolitan residence, 1970

|  | Metropolitan | Nonmetropolitan |
|---|---|---|
| Population Aged 16 and Over | 1,967,794 | 1,261,607 |
| In Labor Force | 1,246,298 | 696,071 |
| Labor Force Participation Rate | 63.3% | 55.2% |
| Armed Forces | 170,300 | 5,329 |
| Civilian Labor Force | 1,075,998 | 690,742 |
| Employed | 1,047,286 | 666,964 |
| Unemployed Rate | 2.67 | 3.44 |
| Percent of Labor Force Female | 35.7 | 36.9 |
| Percent of Civilian Labor Force Female | 41.0 | 37.1 |
| Percent of Employment: |  |  |
| White Collar Occupations | 58.4 | 34.2 |
| Blue Collar Occupations | 28.8 | 47.9 |
| Agricultural | 0.7 | 5.9 |
| Service | 12.1 | 12.0 |
| Percent of Employment in: |  |  |
| Agricultural Industries | 1.1 | 6.9 |
| Mining | 0.1 | 2.3 |
| Construction | 6.8 | 8.4 |
| Durable Goods Manufacturing | 8.5 | 12.1 |
| Nondurable Goods Manufacturing | 8.0 | 19.8 |
| Transportation, Communication, Utilities | 7.7 | 5.3 |
| Wholesale and Retail Trade | 19.2 | 16.0 |
| Banking and Financial Services | 5.7 | 2.4 |
| Other Services | 27.1 | 22.6 |
| Public Administration | 16.0 | 4.2 |

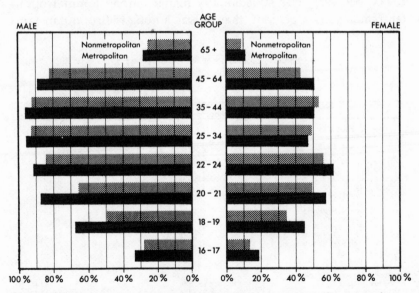

Fig. 5.16. Labor force participation rates by age, sex, and metropolitan-
nonmetropolitan residence, Virginia, 1970

engaged in blue-collar and agricultural occupations to a considerably greater extent, in white-collar occupations to a lesser extent, and in about the same proportions for service occupations.

There were considerable differences in the industrial composition of the metropolitan and nonmetropolitan labor forces. Briefly, the metropolitan labor force was engaged to a relatively greater extent than the nonmetropolitan labor force in the following industrial groups: transportation, communication, and utilities; wholesale and retail trade; banking and other financial services; other services; and public administration. For the other five industrial groups (agriculture, forestry, and fisheries; mining; construction; and durable and nondurable goods manufacturing), employment was relatively greater among the nonmetropolitan labor force.

*Income.* A summary of income statistics for metropolitan and nonmetropolitan areas is presented in Table 5.27. The data show that the proportion of families having a low income (less than $5,000 per year) was substantially higher among nonmetropolitan families (31.2 percent) than it was among metropolitan fam-

Table 5.27.  Income distribution and incidence of poverty for Virginia families by metropolitan-nonmetropolitan residence, 1970

|  | Metropolitan | Nonmetropolitan |
|---|---|---|
| Number of Families | 704,532 | 457,724 |
| Income Level |  |  |
| Less Than $1,000 | 17,357 | 15,461 |
| $1,000-$1,999 | 15,917 | 27,614 |
| $2,000-$2,999 | 21,791 | 29,704 |
| $3,000-$3,999 | 27,156 | 34,096 |
| $4,000-$4,999 | 31,236 | 35,823 |
| $5,000-$5,999 | 37,351 | 39,034 |
| $6,000-$6,999 | 40,989 | 38,693 |
| $7,000-$7,999 | 46,012 | 37,435 |
| $8,000-$8,999 | 46,734 | 34,971 |
| $9,000-$9,999 | 45,728 | 30,732 |
| $10,000-$11,999 | 87,245 | 49,057 |
| $12,000-$14,999 | 100,541 | 41,309 |
| $15,000-$24,999 | 142,258 | 34,777 |
| $25,000-$49,999 | 38,803 | 7,316 |
| $50,000+ | 5,414 | 1,702 |
| Median Income | $12,076 | $8,247 |
| Number of Families Below |  |  |
| Poverty Line | 61,586 | 81,419 |
| Mean Income | $1,914 | $2,110 |
| Mean Income Deficit | $1,697 | $1,434 |
| Deficit-Income Ratio | .887 | .680 |

ilies (16.1 percent). Additionally, the proportion of higher income families ($15,000 or more) was also considerably higher in metropolitan areas (26.5 percent) than in nonmetropolitan areas (9.6 percent). These differences were reflected in the higher level of average income found among metropolitan families ($12,076) compared with nonmetropolitan families ($8,247). The income distribution of these groups is presented graphically in Figure 5.17.

Differences in income level cannot necessarily be equated with differences in economic well-being. Again, differences in cost of living and life style have to be considered. Data which show the incidence of poverty do correct for these omissions to some extent. As the data in Table 5.27 show, the incidence of

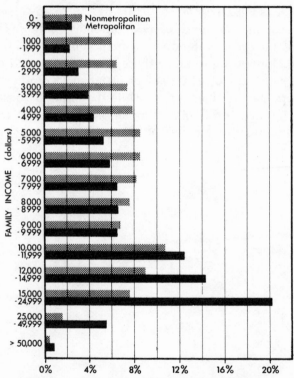

Fig. 5.17. Percentage distribution of Virginia families by income and metropolitan-nonmetropolitan residence, 1969

poverty was considerably greater among nonmetropolitan residents (17.8 percent of all families and 52.1 percent of all unrelated individuals) than it was among metropolitan residents (8.7 percent of families and 28.9 percent of unrelated individuals). However, the relative degree of poverty appears to be greater in metropolitan areas; that is, poor residents of metropolitan areas are relatively and absolutely poorer than poor persons residing in nonmetropolitan areas. The mean income among poor metropolitan families was $1,914, or 15.8 percent or the mean level of income for all metropolitan families. For these families to move to the poverty threshold, they would require, on the average, an additional $1,697, or 88.7 percent of their average earnings. The mean level of family income among poor nonmetropolitan families was greater than that of poor metropolitan families, both in an absolute sense ($2,110 vs. $1,914) and a relative sense. The $2,110 mean income level of poor nonmetropolitan families is 25.6 percent of the overall nonmetropolitan mean, and the amount that would be needed to move these poor families to the poverty threshold is $1,434, or 68.0 percent of mean income among poor nonmetropolitan families. Thus, while the poor comprise a larger share of the nonmetropolitan population, the poor in these areas appear to be relatively better off than the metropolitan poor.

PART III   The Future (1970–2000)

Chapter 6

# Alternative Scenarios

## Methodology and Assumptions

The focus in this and the following chapter is radically different from that of previous chapters. The preceding discussion concentrated on data from previous censuses and accordingly described the status of the state's population as it actually was at various dates. The reliability which generally characterizes these data is necessarily absent when discussing events which have not yet come to pass. This chapter and the next discuss the future of Virginia's population.

It is obviously necessary in such a discussion to make assumptions about the future course of fertility, mortality, and migration—the three components of population change. The coupling of any set of assumptions about these events results in a population projection. A *projection*, then, is merely the arithmetic result of applying the demographic assumptions to a given population base. The base that is employed in all of the following projections is the 1970 census of population for Virginia. A projection is neither a forecast nor a prediction, but merely a statement of what will be if events follow a postulated course. A projection, therefore, is no better or no worse than the assumptions that underlie it.

Of the components of population change, two—fertility and migration—tend to be rather volatile and difficult to predict. Fertility, for example, is currently at an all-time low. Whether it will remain at this level, or rise, or continue to decline is difficult to say. Evidence which does exist, U.S. Bureau of the Census data on fertility expectations, suggests the completed family size for current cohorts of women in the peak reproductive years (say 20 to 34) is likely to be much lower than that of earlier cohorts.[1] The reasons for this are many: new

[1]U.S. Bureau of the Census, "Fertility Expectations of American Women: June 1974," *Current Population Reports*, Series P-20, no. 277 (Feb. 1975).

roles for women in society, delay of marriage, increase of divorce, and availability of safe and reliable means of contraception, to name a few.

Migration is equally difficult to forecast. In a state such as Virginia a great deal of migration is the result of the large number of military installations located in the state. A recent study[2] has indicated that Virginia received a disporportionately large number of military migrants in recent years. The large number of federal civilian employees located in the Northern Virginia and Tidewater areas also has had a considerable impact on migration.

To allow, then, for variation in these components, six population projections with varying rates of fertility and migration have been developed. Mortality, which is relatively constant in comparison with the other components, is held constant at the 1970 level. The six projections are generated by two assumptions regarding fertility and three regarding migration. The fertility assumptions are labeled *A* and *B* in the discussion that follows. Series A assumes that 1970 fertility rates, specific to the age and race of the mother, will hold constant for the entire projection period (1970 to 2000). Series B assumes rates of fertility will decline in a linear fashion from 1970 to 1980, so that in 1980 the replacement will be reached; this level is that at which each generation will exactly reproduce itself. Allowing for fertility and mortality at their current levels, the replacement level works out to about 2.1 children born per woman. Fertility remains constant from 1980 to 2000.

The three migration assumptions are labeled Series I, II, and III. Series I assumes that 1960–70 migration rates, specific to age, race, and sex, will hold over the entire period. Series II assumes that 1960–70 rates will decline by 50 percent, in linear fashion, between 1970 and 1980, and then remain constant. Finally, Series III assumes the migration rates to decline to zero by 1980, and then hold constant.

The intention here is not to identify one of these projections as being most probable. Rather, this is an attempt to provide a fairly wide range of projections in the anticipation of "bracketing" the

[2] Willam J. Serow, "The Role of the Military in the Net Migration for States, 1965–1970," *Review of Public Data Use* 4 (May 1976): 42–48.

actual outcome. On the whole, the projections probably tend toward the conservative side, since no allowance is made for the prospect of either fertility or migration increasing beyond the 1970 level.

These projections were generated by standard demographic procedures. The base population was multiplied by age–race–sex-specific survivorship probabilities (that is, one minus the appropriate death rate) on five–year interval bases. The average population (beginning plus end divided by two) was multiplied by the age–race–sex-specific rate of net migration to obtain net migration for the cohort over each five–year interval. The number of births is obtained in somewhat more complex fashion. Each female cohort that would spend some portion of the five-year interval in the child–bearing years was used. The average size of the cohort (beginning population less half of deaths plus net migration) was subjected to an age–race-specific fertility rate. This rate was essentially an average of beginning and end of the period rates for the cohort. The result of this is the number of births. These were then separated into males and females on the basis of 1970 data given sex ratios at birth as a function of the mother's age and race.

An example of this procedure might be in order. The 1970 census recorded a total of 167,228 white females aged 15–19. The five–year survivorship probability is 0.997. Hence, the expected number of survivors would be 166,735, and the average number alive over the period is 166,982. The five–year net migration rate for this cohort (based on 1960–70 data) is 1.082. Hence, the number of persons alive in this cohort at the end of the period (in 1975) would be 180,700.

The number of persons in this cohort at risk of having a child during the period is the initial population plus half of net migration less deaths: $167,228 + 0.5(13,472 - 493) = 167,228 + 6,490 = 173,718$. Allowing for infant mortality, the annual age-specific birth rates at the beginning and end of the period would be 66.4 and 139.4 per thousand, respectively. The annual average rate would be 102.9 births per thousand. Applying this, times five, to the average number of persons in the cohort (173,718) results in 18,398 surviving births to members of the cohort during the 1970–75 period. Of these, 51.3 percent (or 45,834) would be boys. Age–specific rates of fertility, migration, and mortality utilized for the projections are given in Table A6.1.

## Differences in Population Size

The different assumptions employed in generating the alternative population projections naturally result in differences in the size and composition of the state's population over time. The total size of population for 1970 and at five–year intervals is shown in Table 6.1. For purposes of comparison, the official state population projections, prepared by the Division of State Planning and Community Affairs, are also included.[3]

Table 6.1. Alternative population projections, (in 1,000 of persons) Virginia, 1970-2000

| Series | 1970 | 1975 | 1980 | 1985 | 1990 | 1995 | 2000 |
|--------|------|------|------|------|------|------|------|
| I-A    | 4,648 | 4,979 | 5,356 | 5,754 | 6,138 | 6,512 | 6,900 |
| II-A   | 4,648 | 4,975 | 5,320 | 5,658 | 5,975 | 6,274 | 6,582 |
| III-A  | 4,648 | 4,953 | 5,245 | 5,509 | 5,744 | 5,955 | 6,160 |
| I-B    | 4,648 | 4,967 | 5,307 | 5,651 | 5,981 | 6,295 | 6,604 |
| II-B   | 4,648 | 4,953 | 5,251 | 5,527 | 5,780 | 6,009 | 6,221 |
| III-B  | 4,648 | 4,942 | 5,196 | 5,410 | 5,594 | 5,750 | 5,888 |
| DSPCA  | 4,648 | NA | 5,295 | 5,620 | 5,969 | 6,285 | 6,606 |

Source: DSPCA figures are from Commonwealth of Virginia, Division of State Planning and Community Affairs, Population Projections, Virginia Counties and Cities: 1980-2000 (Richmond: Commonwealth of Virginia, 1975).

By the end of the century, there is a range of slightly more than one million persons between the highest and lowest projections. The highest projection, Series I-A, shows a 2000 population of 6.9 million, 48 percent higher than that in 1970, while the lowest projection, Series III-B, shows a population of 5.9 million,

[3] Commonwealth of Virginia, Division of State Planning and Community Affairs, *Population Projections, Virginia Counties and Cities: 1980–2000* (Richmond: Commonwealth of Virginia, 1975).

27 percent higher. The average annual rate of increase for these projections is 1.3 percent and 0.8 percent, respectively. In the thirty-year period from 1940 to 1970, the state's population increased by 74 percent, or an annual average rate of 1.9 percent. Hence, for the final thirty years of the twentieth century the state's population growth rate is likely to be substantially less than that of the preceding thirty-year period, even under the most generous of assumptions. It should be noted that Series I-A and Series III-B are substantially higher and lower, respectively, that the remainder of the projections. The Series II-A and I-B projections (as well as the official state projections) are about 6.6 million, while Series III-A and II-B approximate 6.2 million.

The latest available population estimate for the state, July 1, 1974, indicated a total population of 4.9 million.[4] If this rate of growth continued to April 1, 1975, the state's population would have been 4,965,000. This figure is approximately the same as the Series I-B projection, lower than Series I-A and II-A, but higher than Series III-A, II-B, and III-B.

Table 6.2 shows average annual growth rate of population, for each five-year interval, for the six projections developed here as well as the official state projections. The trend in all cases is downward; that is, the growth rate of population is shown to decline as time passes. The only significant exception to this statement occurs in Series I-A, where the rate of increase for both the 1975-80 and 1980-85 periods is greater than that for 1970-75. In all other cases, the average annual growth rate for 1970-75 is not exceeded. In all cases, the growth rate for the period from 1985 to 2000 is projected to be substantially lower than that for the first fifteen years of the projection period.

## Differences in Age, Race, and Sex

In addition to producing absolute differences in population, alternative assumptions will also produce variations in the age,

[4] Sara K. Gilliam and William J. Serow, *Estimates of the Population of Virginia Counties and Cities: July 1, 1973 and July 1, 1974* (Charlottesville: Tayloe Murphy Institute, Aug. 1975).

Table 6.2. Average annual population growth rates by quinquennium, Virginia, 1970-2000

| Series | 1970 1975 | 1975 1980 | 1980 1985 | 1985 1990 | 1990 1995 | 1995 2000 |
|--------|------|------|------|------|------|------|
| I-A    | 1.39 | 1.47 | 1.44 | 1.30 | 1.19 | 1.16 |
| II-A   | 1.37 | 1.35 | 1.24 | 1.10 | 0.98 | 0.96 |
| III-A  | 1.28 | 1.15 | 0.99 | 0.84 | 0.72 | ɩ 0.68 |
| I-B    | 1.34 | 1.33 | 1.26 | 1.14 | 1.03 | 0.96 |
| II-B   | 1.28 | 1.18 | 1.03 | 0.90 | 0.78 | 0.70 |
| III-B  | 1.23 | 1.01 | 0.81 | 0.67 | 0.55 | 0.48 |
| DSPCA  | 1.31* | 1.31* | 1.20 | 1.21 | 1.04 | 1.00 |

*For the 1970-80 period.

race, and sex composition of population. In general, the most important differences are those of age, and it is on these that most of the discussion will focus.

The structure of a population at a given moment is a reflecton of its previous history of fertility, mortality, and migration. A period characterized by high birth rates will be revealed in the future by relatively large cohorts born at the time of high fertility. Virginia, for example, in 1970 had relatively large numbers of persons aged 15–19 and 10–14. These were, in part, a reflection of the high birth rates which occurred after World War II. Similarly, large amounts of migration, much of it induced by military buildups during the late 1960s, produced a large cohort of 20–24–year–olds in Virginia in 1970. The influences of mortality are not readily seen in Virginia, but one can easily imagine what the effects of a war or a plague might be in demographic terms.

The projections developed here all assume that fertility in Virginia will be somewhat lower in the future than it has been in the immediate past. As a consequence all the projections show that considerable aging will characterize the state's population between the present and the end of he century. This is due to two interrelated circumstances: most of those born during the high fertility period in the middle of the century will still be alive but growing older, while the number of births is projected to be much smaller (relative to total population) than was the case in that high fertility period. In brief, the state will have relatively large cohorts in the middle-age groups but relatively small ones in the younger groups.

This aging of population also has an impact on the sex composition of Virginia. Although sex ratios at birth are held constant for the entire projection period, the aging of the population implies that women will become an increasingly larger proportion of the state's population, simply because mortality among women is lower than that for men at all ages. As the population as a whole ages, the cumulative effects of these mortality differences become greater. Given the mortality conditions prevailing in 1970 (those which are used for all projections here), of 100,000 white females born in 1970, the number who would survive to age 65 would be 82,284. For white males, the corresponding number of survivors would be 64,271. For nonwhites, the survivors would be 64,113 for females and 43,846 for males.

The degree to which the state's racial composition will change depends on the degree to which hypothesized changes in fertility and migration rates by race differ from present levels. Fertility among nonwhites has historically been higher than among whites; in the projections described here, the changes in fertility in Series B are such that there are no changes in differential fertility from the 1970 fertility levels used in Series A. Hence, the fertility assumptions in the projections will have no influence on the racial composition of Virginia.

This is not the case with migration, however. In chapter 2 the discussion on migration noted that in recent years there has been substantial net in-migration among whites but substantial net out-migration among nonwhites. The Series I projections, since they assume continuation of the 1960-70 age-race-sex-specific migration rates, result in a continuing decline in the share of Virginia's population which is nonwhite. The Series II projections do likewise, but the rate of decline is much slower, since migration rates are forecast to be somewhat lower for all racial groups.

Finally, in the Series III projection, the nonwhite share of the state's population will rise, since net migration for all races is held at a zero level. In this case, the higher fertility among non-whites causes their share to rise.

Data on the distribution of the population by race and sex are given in Table 6.3 (complete age–race–sex profiles for each projection for all years are shown in Table A6.2). The sex distri-

Table 6.3. Sex ratio (males per 100 females) and share of population nonwhite, Virginia, 1970-2000

| Series | 1970 | 1975 | 1980 | 1985 | 1990 | 1995 | 2000 |
|--------|------|------|------|------|------|------|------|
| **I-A** | | | | | | | |
| Sex ratio | 97.7 | 97.2 | 96.7 | 96.3 | 95.9 | 95.8 | 95.7 |
| Percent Nonwhite | 19.1 | 18.2 | 17.4 | 16.6 | 15.9 | 15.2 | 14.7 |
| **II-A** | | | | | | | |
| Sex ratio | 97.7 | 97.6 | 97.5 | 97.5 | 97.6 | 97.8 | 98.3 |
| Percent Nonwhite | 19.1 | 18.3 | 17.8 | 17.6 | 17.4 | 17.2 | 17.1 |
| **III-A** | | | | | | | |
| Sex ratio | 97.7 | 97.2 | 96.7 | 96.5 | 96.2 | 96.0 | 95.9 |
| Percent Nonwhite | 19.1 | 18.5 | 18.4 | 18.8 | 19.2 | 19.8 | 20.3 |
| **I-B** | | | | | | | |
| Sex ratio | 97.7 | 97.2 | 96.6 | 96.1 | 95.6 | 95.4 | 95.2 |
| Percent Nonwhite | 19.1 | 18.2 | 17.3 | 16.5 | 15.7 | 15.1 | 14.5 |
| **II-B** | | | | | | | |
| Sex ratio | 97.7 | 97.2 | 96.7 | 96.3 | 95.9 | 95.6 | 95.4 |
| Percent Nonwhite | 19.1 | 18.3 | 17.9 | 17.6 | 17.4 | 17.2 | 17.1 |
| **III-B** | | | | | | | |
| Sex ratio | 97.7 | 97.1 | 97.6 | 96.2 | 95.9 | 95.6 | 95.5 |
| Percent Nonwhite | 19.1 | 18.4 | 18.4 | 18.7 | 19.1 | 19.6 | 20.1 |

bution of the population is conventionally expressed by the sex ratio (the number of men per 100 women). In 1970 there were slightly less than 98 men per 100 women in the state. This ratio is projected to decrease in all alternative projections save Series II-A (that with 1970 fertility levels and lower net migration). The lower fertility series (Series B) produces a uniformly lower sex ratio, due to the greater aging of population implicit in lower fertility. The sex ratio, further, is made greater by lower net migration. The reason for this is that net migration for males is heavily age dependent, with a disproportionate share of net migration occurring between the ages of 20 and 24.

As expected, the share of the population which is nonwhite is projected to increase only in those cases (Series III) where net migration reaches zero. The higher the level of net migration (in for whites, out for nonwhites), the lower the proportion of nonwhites. The differences between fertility assumptions are relatively small, but also as would be expected, the nonwhite proportion is higher in the higher fertility series (Series A).

Basic changes in Virginia's age composition which would come about under the alternative population projections are shown in Table 6.4. Differences in fertility are reflected only in the cohorts aged under 30 in the year 2000. These, of course, are those persons born since the beginning of the projection period. Hence, each projection in Series A is identical to the corresponding projections in Series B for ages 30 and older. Differences between Series I, II, and III are the result of alternative migration assumptions. Because of differences in migration, there will be induced differences in births as well. This simply reflects the fact that as an area experiences a higher level of net in- migration, the area will also have a higher level of births (absolute number) due simply to the probability of births among migrants.[5]

It is readily apparent from the data in Table 6.4 that the youngest segments of the population will be by far the slowest-growing element in the future. Even under the highest fertility and migration assumptions (Series I-A) the population aged 0-29 is projected to increase by 29 percent between 1970 until 2000, while the population aged 30 and over is projected to grow by 72 percent. Under the lowest fertility and migration assumptions (Series III-B), the rate of increase for the youngest cohorts is only 5 percent, in contrast to the 53-percent growth projected for those 30 and older. For Series I and II projections, growth is projected to be at a peak among persons aged 30-44 in 2000 (84 and 69 percent, respectively), while the Series III projections shows equally high growth for this age group and that 65 and over. Since migration rates fall rather sharply after age 30, it is not surprising that the growth rate for persons 65 and over in 2000

[5] William J. Serow, "The Potential Demographic Impact of Migration," *Review of Regional Studies* 4 (Fall 1974): 16–28.

Table 6.4.  Change in age composition (in 1,000s of persons) Virginia, 1970-2000

| Series | 1970 | 2000 | Percent Change | Series | 1970 | 2000 | Percent Change |
|--------|------|------|--------|--------|------|------|--------|
| I-A |  |  |  | I-B |  |  |  |
| 0-14 | 1,323 | 1,644 | 24 | 0-14 | 1,323 | 1,458 | 10 |
| 15-29 | 1,219 | 1,625 | 33 | 15-29 | 1,219 | 1,515 | 24 |
| 30-44 | 830 | 1,525 | 84 | 30-44 | 830 | 1,525 | 84 |
| 45-64 | 913 | 1,508 | 65 | 45-64 | 913 | 1,508 | 65 |
| 65+ | 366 | 598 | 63 | 65+ | 366 | 598 | 63 |
| Total | 4,648 | 6,900 | 48 | Total | 4,648 | 6,604 | 42 |
| II-A |  |  |  | II-B |  |  |  |
| 0-14 | 1,323 | 1,612 | 22 | 0-14 | 1,323 | 1,390 | 5 |
| 15-29 | 1,219 | 1,556 | 28 | 15-29 | 1,219 | 1,417 | 16 |
| 30-44 | 830 | 1,401 | 69 | 30-44 | 830 | 1,401 | 69 |
| 45-64 | 913 | 1,428 | 56 | 45-64 | 913 | 1,428 | 56 |
| 65+ | 366 | 585 | 60 | 65+ | 366 | 585 | 60 |
| Total | 4,648 | 6,582 | 42 | Total | 4,648 | 6,221 | 34 |
| III-A |  |  |  | III-B |  |  |  |
| 0-14 | 1,323 | 1,502 | 14 | 0-14 | 1,323 | 1,329 | 1 |
| 15-29 | 1,219 | 1,432 | 17 | 15-29 | 1,219 | 1,334 | 9 |
| 30-44 | 830 | 1,295 | 56 | 30-44 | 830 | 1,295 | 56 |
| 45-64 | 913 | 1,357 | 59 | 45-64 | 913 | 1,357 | 49 |
| 65+ | 366 | 574 | 57 | 65+ | 366 | 574 | 57 |
| Total | 4,648 | 6,160 | 33 | Total | 4,648 | 5,888 | 27 |

varies but slightly among the projections. These persons were at least 35 at the beginning of the projection period, and their peak years of migration are behind them.[6] Persons aged 30-44 in 2000 will have passed through their peak migration years during the projection period. Hence, the size of this cohort at the end of the projection period will be very sensitive to migration.

Consider that the 30-44 cohort in 2000 is identical to that aged 0-14 in 1970 (a cohort is a group of persons born in the same specified time interval, in this case from April 1,

[6] Larry H. Long, "New Estimates of Migration Expectancy in the United States," *Journal of the American Statistical Association* 68 (March 1973): 37-43. Long shows that approximately two-thirds of all moves in an individual's lifetime (about 13) take place between the ages of 0-34.

1955, to March 31, 1970). Virginia had a total of 1,323,000 persons in this age group as of the 1970 census. Changes in the size of the cohort over the projection period will be influenced by both mortality and migration. Under the highest migration assumption (Series I), this cohort grows by about 200,000 persons (to 1,525,000), an increase of 15 percent. Under the medium-level assumption, growth of the cohort is lowered to 1,401,000, or about 6 percent. Under the lowest migration assumptions the number of deaths to the cohort exceeds the level of net migration, and the size of the cohort declines by 2 percent, to 1,295,000.

A convenient method of depicting changes in the age composition over time is the dependency ratio, the ratio of the number of persons not of working age. The youth dependency ratio (YDR) here is defined as the number of young dependents, aged 0–14, divided by the persons aged 15–64, times 100. The aged dependency ratio (ADR) is the number of persons aged 65 and over, divided by the number of persons 15–64, times 100. The total dependency ratio (TDR) is merely the sum of the YDR and ADR. Dependency ratios for Virginia under the alternative population projections are given in Table 6.5.

The dependency ratio for Virginia was 57.1 in 1970. All projections show that this will decline by 6 to 12 percent by the end of the century. In all six projections, the decline is due to a sizable decrease in the YDR, offset to varying degrees by moderate increases in the ADR. As would be expected, the greatest decreases in the YDR occur in the Series B (low fertility) projections. This series also has uniformly greater increases in the ADR, again as the result of the fertility decline and its consequent effects on the age structure of the population.

Migration also has clearly evident influences on the dependency ratio. In each case, the level of dependency increases as the level of net migration decreases. Again, since migration is very much a function of age, this is hardly a surprising result.

This concludes the analysis of the demographic changes that are implicit in the alternative population projections of Virginia. Although these differences are of considerable interest in themselves, the more intriguing question concerns the consequences these demographic changes will have on social and economic conditions in the state. These will be addressed in the following chapter.

Table 6.5. Dependency ratios, Virginia, 1970–2000

| Series | | 1970 | 1975 | 1980 | 1985 | 1990 | 1995 | 2000 |
|--------|------|------|------|------|------|------|------|------|
| I-A | | | | | | | | |
| | YDR | 44.7 | 39.8 | 37.9 | 39.6 | 39.4 | 37.4 | 35.3 |
| | ADR | 12.4 | 12.1 | 12.4 | 13.0 | 13.6 | 13.5 | 12.8 |
| | TDR | 57.1 | 51.9 | 50.3 | 52.6 | 53.0 | 50.9 | 48.1 |
| II-A | | | | | | | | |
| | YDR | 44.7 | 40.2 | 38.7 | 41.0 | 40.7 | 38.7 | 36.8 |
| | ADR | 12.4 | 12.2 | 12.5 | 13.3 | 14.0 | 13.9 | 13.3 |
| | TDR | 57.1 | 52.4 | 51.2 | 54.3 | 54.7 | 52.6 | 50.1 |
| III-A | | | | | | | | |
| | YDR | 44.7 | 40.0 | 38.4 | 40.6 | 40.5 | 38.7 | 36.8 |
| | ADR | 12.4 | 12.2 | 12.6 | 13.6 | 14.5 | 14.6 | 14.1 |
| | TDR | 57.1 | 52.2 | 51.0 | 54.2 | 55.0 | 53.3 | 50.9 |
| I-B | | | | | | | | |
| | YDR | 44.7 | 39.5 | 36.5 | 36.9 | 35.9 | 34.0 | 32.1 |
| | ADR | 12.4 | 12.1 | 12.4 | 13.0 | 13.7 | 13.7 | 13.2 |
| | TDR | 57.1 | 51.6 | 48.9 | 49.9 | 49.6 | 47.7 | 45.3 |
| II-B | | | | | | | | |
| | YDR | 44.7 | 39.6 | 36.8 | 37.4 | 36.4 | 34.5 | 32.7 |
| | ADR | 12.4 | 12.2 | 12.5 | 13.3 | 14.1 | 14.2 | 13.8 |
| | TDR | 57.1 | 51.8 | 49.3 | 50.7 | 50.5 | 48.7 | 46.5 |
| III-B | | | | | | | | |
| | YDR | 44.7 | 39.6 | 37.0 | 37.8 | 36.9 | 35.1 | 33.4 |
| | ADR | 12.4 | 12.2 | 12.6 | 13.6 | 14.5 | 14.8 | 14.4 |
| | TDR | 57.1 | 51.8 | 49.6 | 51.4 | 51.4 | 49.9 | 47.8 |

Note: YDR: youth dependency ratio. ADR: aged dependency ratio.
TRD: total dependency ratio.

# Chapter 7

# Implications of Alternative Scenarios

The purpose of this chapter is to consider what kinds of economic and social differences might be expected to occur as a consequence of the alternative population projections discussed in the preceding chapter. This effort should not be construed as an exercise in soothesaying; rather, it provides a series of educated guesses as to what will happen under a series of reasonable alternative population projections. There are many possible influences on the trends illustrated below other than the demographic. A few examples of such possibilities would include the outbreak of a major war, a severe and prolonged economic depression, a renewal of the oil embargo, and the like. All these are ignored in the following analysis. What the analysis here attempts to show are, under conditions of "normalcy," the predictable and measurable effects of alternative trends in population size and composition for Virginia.

## Labor Force Size and Composition

The relative size and composition of the labor force are the direct result of the age composition of the population. The preceding chapter has provided alternative projections of the population of the state in terms of its size and composition by age, race, and sex. At this juncture, it is appropriate to apply age- and sex-specific rates of labor force participation to these alternative projection series to assess the impact of demographic change on Virginia's future labor force.

The first question to be addressed is appropriate rates of labor force participation. If one were to decide that the best course would be simply to assume continuation of the pattern for 1970, one would ignore basic changes in labor force participation which have characterized the state in recent years, discussed in chapter 5. Basically, labor force participation among males of all ages has been declining, while that of females has been increasing. Consequently, labor force rates for males were assumed to decline at a rate consistent with the 1960–70 trends until 1990, then to remain constant. The final assumption reflects a supposition that there is some degree beyond which labor force participation will not be reduced, particularly between the ages of 25 and 55.

For women, there are two variables to be considered. First is the sharp upward trend in female labor force participation; second is the recognition that childbearing and labor force participation are still often mutually exclusive activities. Hence, the basic assumption of continuation of past trends to 1990 was modified to permit differentiation for assumed fertility differences. For women of childbearing age, labor force participation was assumed higher in the lower fertility proportion series (Series B). The assumed differences were, by 2000, 1 percent for 15–19 and 35–44 age groups and 5 percent for the 20–24 and 25–34 groups. Age–sex–specific rates of labor force participation used in this study are shown in Table 7.1.

A summary of the results of the application of these rates to the alternative population projections presented in the preceding chapter is given in Table 7.2 (Table A7.1 in the appendix gives the complete scenarios). Table 7.2 shows the absolute size of the labor force, the share of the labor force which is female, the ratio of the labor force to total population, and a broad age composition of the members of the labor force.

The absolute size of the labor force will vary directly with population size. This is generally the case in the projection here, although in the earlier years the Series A labor force projections are uniformly lower than the Series B ones due to the higher rates of labor force participation for women assumed in the latter case. This latter assumption, of course, also explains the uniformly higher proportion of females in the Series B labor force in all cases. These higher rates of female labor force participation, coupled with moderate declines for the rates in the male population, suggest that the future labor force of Virginia is likely to be comprised of a larger portion of female workers. By the end of

Table 7.1. Labor force participation rates by age and sex, Virginia, 1975-2000

| Age | 1975 | | 1980 | | 1985 | | 1990-2000 | |
|---|---|---|---|---|---|---|---|---|
| Male |
| 15-19 | .382 | | .377 | | .369 | | .368 | |
| 20-24 | .847 | | .837 | | .832 | | .828 | |
| 25-34 | .943 | | .941 | | .939 | | .939 | |
| 35-44 | .944 | | .941 | | .939 | | .937 | |
| 45-54 | .911 | | .906 | | .904 | | .902 | |
| 55-59 | .835 | | .829 | | .825 | | .822 | |
| 60-64 | .689 | | .673 | | .665 | | .660 | |
| 65-69 | .374 | | .349 | | .337 | | .330 | |
| 70+ | .153 | | .132 | | .121 | | .115 | |
| Female |
| Series | A | B | A | B | A | B | A | B |
| 15-19 | .237 | .238 | .242 | .243 | .245 | .247 | .249 | .251 |
| 20-24 | .592 | .602 | .611 | .632 | .626 | .647 | .636 | .660 |
| 25-34 | .494 | .505 | .512 | .534 | .517 | .542 | .521 | .548 |
| 35-44 | .520 | .522 | .530 | .534 | .542 | .546 | .549 | .551 |
| 45-54 | .524 | .524 | .535 | .535 | .546 | .546 | .552 | .552 |
| 55-59 | .476 | .476 | .490 | .490 | .500 | .500 | .506 | .506 |
| 60-64 | .366 | .366 | .376 | .376 | .384 | .384 | .389 | .389 |
| 65-69 | .169 | .169 | .167 | .167 | .167 | .167 | .166 | .166 |
| 70+ | .060 | .060 | .057 | .057 | .056 | .056 | .054 | .054 |

the century, these projections indicate that women will account for nearly 39 percent of Virginia's labor force, as opposed to 36 percent in 1970. When it is remembered that Virginia's labor force has historically included large numbers of military personnel, these overall projections may well understate the increasing role of women in the Commonwealth's future labor force. If only the civilian labor force is considered, the female proportion was 39.5 percent in 1970. If the relative number of military personnel remains static in future decades, then the share of females in Virginia's civilian labor force will total nearly 45 percent by the end of the present century.

The share of total population represented by members of the labor force can be an important determinant of the future level of per capita income and the composition of consumer demand. Simply stated, the fewer the number of nonworkers vis-à-vis the number of workers, the higher the level of per capita income, *ceteris paribus*. The projections suggest that numbers of the

Table 7.2.  Labor force size and characteristics, Virginia, 1970-2000

| Year and Series | Labor Force (1,000s) | Percentage of Total Population | Percent Female | Percent Aged 15-34 | Percent Aged 35-64 | Percent Aged 65+ |
|---|---|---|---|---|---|---|
| 1970 | 1956.9 | 42.1 | 36.0 | 45.7 | 51.2 | 3.1 |
| 1975  IA | 2160.6 | 43.4 | 36.9 | 49.0 | 48.6 | 2.4 |
| IIA | 2162.8 | 43.5 | 36.7 | 48.7 | 48.4 | 2.9 |
| IIIA | 2156.5 | 43.5 | 36.8 | 48.6 | 48.5 | 2.9 |
| IB | 2175.6 | 43.8 | 36.9 | 48.9 | 48.3 | 2.8 |
| IIB | 2170.1 | 43.8 | 37.0 | 48.9 | 48.3 | 2.8 |
| IIIB | 2163.7 | 43.8 | 37.0 | 48.8 | 48.3 | 2.9 |
| 1980  IA | 2393.3 | 44.7 | 37.5 | 50.4 | 47.0 | 2.6 |
| IIA | 2362.1 | 44.4 | 37.5 | 50.1 | 47.2 | 2.7 |
| IIIA | 2331.4 | 44.5 | 37.5 | 49.9 | 47.4 | 2.7 |
| IB | 2410.0 | 45.4 | 38.0 | 50.7 | 46.7 | 2.6 |
| IIB | 2378.5 | 45.3 | 37.9 | 50.4 | 46.9 | 2.7 |
| IIIB | 2347.6 | 45.2 | 37.9 | 50.2 | 47.1 | 2.7 |
| 1985  IA | 2528.8 | 44.9 | 37.9 | 47.7 | 49.6 | 2.7 |
| IIA | 2513.0 | 44.4 | 37.9 | 47.3 | 50.0 | 2.7 |
| IIIA | 2447.9 | 44.4 | 37.9 | 46.8 | 50.4 | 2.8 |
| IB | 2602.4 | 46.1 | 38.4 | 48.1 | 49.3 | 2.6 |
| IIB | 2531.8 | 45.8 | 38.3 | 47.6 | 49.7 | 2.7 |
| IIIB | 2472.7 | 45.7 | 38.5 | 47.1 | 50.1 | 2.9 |
| 1990  IA | 2744.4 | 44.7 | 38.0 | 44.6 | 52.7 | 2.7 |
| IIA | 2637.9 | 44.1 | 37.8 | 44.2 | 53.1 | 2.7 |
| IIIA | 2532.3 | 44.1 | 37.9 | 43.5 | 53.6 | 2.9 |
| IB | 2768.0 | 46.3 | 38.6 | 45.0 | 52.3 | 2.7 |
| IIB | 2657.2 | 46.0 | 38.5 | 44.5 | 52.8 | 2.7 |
| IIIB | 2554.1 | 45.7 | 38.5 | 43.9 | 53.3 | 2.8 |
| 1995  IA | 2944.2 | 45.2 | 38.1 | 41.8 | 55.7 | 2.5 |
| IIA | 2801.1 | 44.6 | 37.8 | 41.6 | 55.7 | 2.7 |
| IIIA | 2646.7 | 44.4 | 38.0 | 40.9 | 56.3 | 2.8 |
| IB | 2951.4 | 46.9 | 38.9 | 41.8 | 55.6 | 2.6 |
| IIB | 2794.8 | 46.5 | 38.6 | 41.4 | 55.9 | 2.7 |
| IIIB | 2652.4 | 46.1 | 38.6 | 40.9 | 56.3 | 2.8 |
| 2000  IA | 3173.7 | 46.0 | 38.1 | 40.3 | 57.3 | 2.4 |
| IIA | 2987.2 | 45.4 | 37.7 | 40.6 | 56.9 | 2.5 |
| IIIA | 2777.5 | 45.1 | 38.0 | 39.9 | 57.5 | 2.6 |
| IB | 3145.4 | 47.6 | 38.7 | 39.7 | 57.9 | 2.4 |
| IIB | 2936.5 | 47.2 | 38.6 | 39.5 | 58.0 | 2.5 |
| IIIB | 2752.7 | 46.8 | 38.6 | 39.3 | 58.1 | 2.6 |

labor force will account for about 5 percent more of the population in 2000 than they did in 1970.

This is the direct consequence of increased female labor force participation and the changed age structure of the state's population which is likely in the future. Because of the relative decline in the number of children, which is not completely offset by increases in the relative number of persons of retirement age, the relative number of dependents in Virginia will shrink in coming years. Consequently, income of families will be divided, in the aggregate, by fewer persons, yielding a higher level of income per person. A higher level of income will also change the composition of demand away from those items which may be termed necessities and toward those which might be called discretionary or luxury items.

In 1970 each member of the labor force supported 1.4 persons other than him/her self. By the end of the century, the projections summarized in Table 7.2 suggest that this ratio will fall to as low as 1.1 or 1.2. Again, the relatively low fertility projection (Series B) consistently yields a somewhat higher proportion of the population in the labor force, due to the higher rates of female labor force participation.

Changes in the age composition of population will be reflected in changes in the age composition of the labor force. Given the gradual aging of the population of Virginia, it is not surprising that the state's labor force will also be subject to some aging. In 1970 about 46 percent of the Virginia labor force was in the 15–34 (young workers) age group, with 51 percent in the middle age group (35–64), and 3 percent over the age of 65. The projections of the future labor force suggest that by the end of the century, the proportion of younger workers will decline to about 40 percent, while that of middle–aged workers will climb to 57–58 percent. A decline in the proportion of older workers is also suggested, because the declining labor force participation of this group will outweigh the increases in their relative numbers.

## Labor Productivity

A potentially important consequence of changes in the demographic composition of the labor force is the effect of these changes on labor force productivity. In a general sense, productivity is easily definable as the amount of output produced per unit of labor input. In practice, though, productivity is extremely difficult to measure. As the economy of the nation and of the Commonwealth becomes increasingly concentrated in the tertiary (services) section rather than the primary (extractive, including agriculture) or secondary (manufacturing) sectors, the notion of output becomes somewhat problematic. How, for example, does one measure the output of a physician, attorney, or professor?

The most obvious alternative is to assume that earnings in a given period of time reflect productivity. In the absense of imperfections in the labor market, this is, of course, the case, but unfortunately, a labor market which lacks imperfections is indeed a rara avis. Variations in earnings according to the race or sex of the worker, when all other variables are ostensibly equal, are perhaps the most obvious example of such an imperfection.

Here *productivity* will be measured by the average value of hourly work as a function of age and sex. These data pertain to the 1966–67 period and are taken from a recent study by Edward F. Denison.[1] The use of hourly earnings is useful in overcoming difficulties associated with valuation in weeks worked per year, or hours worked per week, but do not per se remove the possibility of bias toward full-time workers, because their hourly wages may be higher.

The data in Table 7.3 are on a relative basis, that is, an index of the average hourly wage of each age–sex group relative to the average hourly wage of the labor force as a whole. It is important to recognize that these differences reflect actual differentials in value of work, as perceived by employers. The differences themselves do not necessarily have any direct correlation to quality of the labor input of the various demographic groups. As Denison notes in the context: "It does not matter whether

[1] Edward F. Denison, *Accounting for United States Economic Growth, 1929–1969* (Washington, D.C.: The Brookings Institution, 1974), pp. 33–35, 187–91.

Table 7.3. Average hourly earning by age and sex, relative to the total labor force, 1967 (males 35-44=100)

| Age | Male | Female |
|-----|------|--------|
| 14-19 | 27 | 37 |
| 20-24 | 58 | 45 |
| 25-34 | 86 | 52 |
| 35-44 | 100 | 51 |
| 45-64 | 95 | 52 |
| 65+ | 66 | 41 |

Source: Denison, Table F-1.

these differences result from differences in the value of the work the groups are able and willing to do . . . or from failure to use abilities that are present. Such failure may occur because abilities are not recognized or because of discrimination in hiring, training, promotion, or dismissal so that one group or another cannot reach its full work capability. Potential abilities that are unused do not affect output."[2]

To measure the effect of prospective demographic change in Virginia's labor force, under the alternative scenarios discussed previously, the indices in Table 7.3 will be multiplied by labor force composition by age and sex (shown in Table A7.1). The result will be an aggregate index of productivity for each labor force scenario which is presented relative to the 1970 base year (derived by multiplying the 1970 labor force composition by the index values in Table 7.3). The results of these computations are presented in Table 7.4. The implicit assumption made here, of course, is that the relative productivity of the age-sex groups will remain invariant over time. This is probably a weak assumption, given the efforts to insure equal employment opportunity for all segments of the labor force, but these projections do serve as a baseline to depict how alternative patterns of prospective demographic change will affect probable levels of productivity, in the absence of social and economic changes which may influence the relative internal composition of the productivity index. A

[2] Ibid., p. 33.

Table 7.4.  Index of aggregate labor productivity
by sex, Virginia 1980-2000  (1970 = 100)

| Series | 1980 | 1990 | 2000 |
|--------|------|------|------|
| Total |  |  |  |
| I-A | 98.2 | 100.5 | 100.3 |
| II-A | 98.3 | 100.6 | 100.2 |
| III-A | 98.4 | 100.7 | 100.3 |
| I-B | 98.1 | 100.2 | 100.6 |
| II-B | 98.2 | 100.3 | 100.6 |
| III-B | 98.3 | 100.4 | 100.5 |
| Male |  |  |  |
| I-A | 98.4 | 101.5 | 101.5 |
| II-A | 98.5 | 101.4 | 101.1 |
| III-A | 98.7 | 101.7 | 101.4 |
| I-B | 98.4 | 101.6 | 102.2 |
| II-B | 98.5 | 101.7 | 102.2 |
| III-B | 98.7 | 101.8 | 102.2 |
| Female |  |  |  |
| I-A | 100.4 | 101.6 | 101.0 |
| II-A | 100.4 | 101.6 | 100.9 |
| III-A | 100.4 | 101.5 | 100.8 |
| I-B | 100.8 | 101.1 | 101.2 |
| II-B | 100.8 | 101.1 | 101.1 |
| III-B | 100.8 | 101.0 | 101.0 |

continuation of past trends in the educational attainment of the labor force is but one example of these potential influences.

The index values in Table 7.4 are the result of changes in the age composition of the labor force, the sex composition of the labor force, and rates of labor force participation. The results suggest that after 1980 the combination of these forces is such as to increase, by less than 1 percent, the overall productivity index. The increases for men and women separately are much greater, but the overall increase is dampened by the increasing share of women in the labor force. Again, this should not be interpreted as implying that female workers are somehow inferior to their male counterparts. Rather, this reflects differences in wages which, in an imperfect labor market, are the consequence of a whole host of factors, of which presumed actual productivity is but one.

A few words are in order regarding the effects of the alternative demographic assumptions made in the creation of our six population scenarios. It will be recalled that Series A and Series B differed in terms of the fertility component (with the former showing somewhat higher fertility, while Series I, Series II, and Series III differed in terms of the net migration component (with the rate of net migration being higher in Series I than in Series II or Series III, and that of Series II being higher than the rate in Series III).

The Series B projections yield higher productivity indexes for males in 1990 and 2000. This is also the case for females, except in 1990. It must be recalled that the Series B female population was assumed to have higher rates of labor force participation among women in the primary childbearing years due to the lower fertility rates of this series. However, for the total labor force, the productivity index is higher for the Series A population in both 1980 and 1990. This is the result of the higher proportion of women in the Series B labor force. By 2000, one would hypothesize the age composition changes between Series A and Series B are of sufficient magnitude (and sufficiently favorable) to outweigh the increase in the share of women.

The differences between Series I, Series II, and Series III are somewhat less clear-cut. For men, and for the total population, Series III, with the lowest rate of migration, yields a marginally more productive work force in 1980 and 1990, with very little variation being present at the terminal year. For women, the alternative migration assumptions make absolutely no difference in 1980, but in 1990 and 2000 the series with the highest migration rate (Series I) is marginally more productive than the other series.

A good deal of the exploration for these differences between male and female workers lies in the relative productivity of age groups within the sexes. For male workers, the levels of productivity are much lower for those at either end of the age spectrum than for those in the middle. For women, though, the amount of variation in productivity by age is relatively slight. The lowest age category among women is 71 percent as productive as the most productive group, compared with only 27 percent among male workers. This suggests that women tend to reach peak earnings earlier in life than do men, and then remain at relatively the same level throughout their working life. This phenomenon is depicted graphically in Figure 7.1, which relates relative income of Virginians in 1969 to age and sex. *Relative income* is mean income of a particular age–sex group divided by mean income of all persons of that sex.

## School Enrollment

As already noted, one of the principal changes which will occur in Virginia's population is a major shift of the population's age composition. This section and that which follows deal with aspects directly related to the most visible of these changes: the decline in the relative numbers of persons of school age and the increase in the relative and absolute number of persons of retirement age. The present section focuses on prospective trends in school enrollment at the elementary and secondary levels, with some additional analysis of the probable course of enrollment at institutions of higher education.

Enrollment rates for persons between the ages of 7 and 16 are in excess of 90 percent and are likely to remain constant over time (Table 7.5). Enrollment for persons aged 6 is somewhat lower (according to 1970 census data), due to the fact that the census

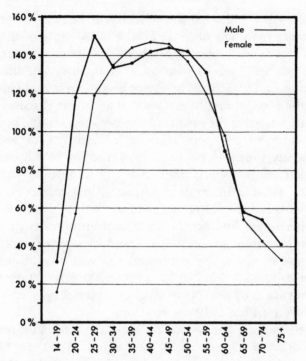

Fig. 7.1.  Relative income by age and sex,
Virginia, 1969

Table 7.5.  Enrollment rate of persons aged 5-19, grades 1-12,
Virginia, 1970

| Age | Male | | Female | |
| | Elementary | Secondary | Elementary | Secondary |
|---|---|---|---|---|
| 5-9 | 70.3 | 0.0 | 70.6 | 0.0 |
| 10-14 | 89.1 | 7.7 | 87.9 | 9.3 |
| 15-19 | 7.8 | 59.2 | 6.5 | 59.8 |

is taken in April although the school year begins in September. Hence, more than half of those aged 6 at the time of the census, were, in fact aged 5 when the school year began. After the age of 16, attendance at school is no longer mandatory, and the dropout rate from secondary schools begins to become relatively important.

Since the population projections that are being discussed in this context are based on the results of the 1970 census, the projections actually refer to the population as of April 1 of each year. Consequently, the projections of school enrollment will also pertain to this part of the year, rather than the traditional start of the academic year. For illustrative purposes, this convention should make relatively little difference.

The elementary and secondary school enrollment projections, by sex, are depicted in Table 7.6. The data refer to persons aged 5–19. These comprise the overwhelming majority of enrollment in grades 1–12 in 1970; 773,000 of 776,000 elementary students (99.6 percent) and 304,000 of 310,000 secondary students (98.1 percent) were in the 5–19 age bracket.

Total elementary and secondary enrollment for Virginia among persons aged 5–19 was 1,077,021 as of April 1, 1970. All projections indicate a decline in this figure for 1980. For 1990 all but the lowest two show moderate increases in enrollment, and all but the very lowest show enrollment increases by the end of the century. Even the highest projection, however, indicates that enrollment in 2000 will exceed the 1970 level by only 18.4 percent. By way of contrast, school enrollment grew by 89 percent from 1950 to 1970. By any reasonable standard, the marked growth in school enrollment which has characterized Virginia in previous years seems likely to be at an end. The distribution will vary greatly across the state, of course, but on the aggregate, the era of constant shortages of space and personnel in the educational sector would appear to be over. Such a situation already characterizes many of the school systems throughout the Commonwealth at present.

It is also worthy of note that the projections of school enrollment suggest that growth will be relatively less for grades 1–8 than for grades 9–12. In 1970 about 72 percent of all enroll-

Table 7.6.  Projected School enrollment of persons aged 5-19 by sex, Virginia 1980-2000

|  | Male | Female | Total |
|---|---|---|---|
| **1970** |  |  |  |
| Elementary | 397,459 | 375,280 | 772,739 |
| Secondary | 152,240 | 152,042 | 204,282 |
| Total | 549,699 | 527,322 | 1,077,021 |
| **1980** |  |  |  |
| **I-A** |  |  |  |
| Elementary | 359,700 | 342,400 | 702,100 |
| Secondary | 158,300 | 156,500 | 314,800 |
| Total | 518,000 | 498,900 | 1,016,900 |
| **II-A** |  |  |  |
| Elementary | 364,800 | 340,600 | 705,400 |
| Secondary | 156,500 | 155,200 | 311,700 |
| Total | 521,300 | 495,800 | 1,017,100 |
| **III-A** |  |  |  |
| Elementary | 355,900 | 338,900 | 694,800 |
| Secondary | 154,700 | 153,900 | 308,600 |
| Total | 510,600 | 492,800 | 1,003,400 |
| **I-B** |  |  |  |
| Elementary | 355,300 | 338,600 | 693,900 |
| Secondary | 158,300 | 156,500 | 314,800 |
| Total | 513,600 | 495,100 | 1,008,700 |
| **II-B** |  |  |  |
| Elementary | 353,500 | 336,900 | 690,400 |
| Secondary | 156,500 | 155,200 | 311,700 |
| Total | 510,000 | 492,100 | 1,002,100 |
| **III-B** |  |  |  |
| Elementary | 315,600 | 335,200 | 686,000 |
| Secondary | 154,700 | 153,900 | 308,600 |
| Total | 506,300 | 489,100 | 995,400 |
| **1990** |  |  |  |
| **I-A** |  |  |  |
| Elementary | 441,400 | 419,800 | 861,200 |
| Secondary | 160,600 | 159,300 | 319,900 |
| Total | 602,000 | 579,100 | 1,181,100 |
| **II-A** |  |  |  |
| Elementary | 449,700 | 410,900 | 860,600 |
| Secondary | 163,700 | 156,400 | 320,100 |
| Total | 613,400 | 567,300 | 1,180,700 |

Table 7.6. (continued)

|  | Male | Female | Total |
|---|---|---|---|
| **III-A** | | | |
| Elementary | 423,500 | 402,600 | 826,100 |
| Secondary | 153,000 | 153,000 | 306,000 |
| Total | 576,500 | 555,600 | 1,132,100 |
| | | | |
| **I-B** | | | |
| Elementary | 404,000 | 385,200 | 789,200 |
| Secondary | 155,300 | 154,300 | 309,200 |
| Total | 559,300 | 539,500 | 1,098,800 |
| | | | |
| **II-B** | | | |
| Elementary | 396,000 | 377,100 | 773,100 |
| Secondary | 151,600 | 151,500 | 303,100 |
| Total | 547,600 | 528,600 | 1,076,200 |
| | | | |
| **III-B** | | | |
| Elementary | 387,600 | 369,500 | 757,100 |
| Secondary | 147,800 | 148,200 | 296,000 |
| Total | 535,400 | 517,700 | 1,053,100 |
| | | | |
| **2000** | | | |
| **I-A** | | | |
| Elementary | 461,800 | 438,300 | 900,100 |
| Secondary | 188,500 | 186,300 | 374,800 |
| Total | 650,300 | 624,600 | 1,274,900 |
| | | | |
| **II-A** | | | |
| Elementary | 461,700 | 418,100 | 879,800 |
| Secondary | 186,800 | 178,300 | 365,100 |
| Total | 648,500 | 596,400 | 1,274,900 |
| | | | |
| **III-A** | | | |
| Elementary | 423,100 | 401,800 | 824,900 |
| Secondary | 171,900 | 171,400 | 343,300 |
| Total | 595,000 | 573,200 | 1,168,200 |
| | | | |
| **I-B** | | | |
| Elementary | 413,500 | 393,600 | 807,100 |
| Secondary | 169,400 | 168,100 | 337,500 |
| Total | 582,900 | 561,700 | 1,144,600 |
| | | | |
| **II-B** | | | |
| Elementary | 394,600 | 375,700 | 770,300 |
| Secondary | 159,800 | 160,900 | 320,700 |
| Total | 554,400 | 536,600 | 1,091,000 |
| | | | |
| **III-B** | | | |
| Elementary | 377,800 | 359,700 | 737,500 |
| Secondary | 154,600 | 154,600 | 309,200 |
| Total | 532,400 | 514,300 | 1,046,700 |

ment was concentrated in the eight lower grades. By 2000 this percentage will decline to slightly over 70 percent.

The relative stability of school enrollment which will characterize the state in coming years, coupled with increases in the size of the labor force, suggests that the share of public expenditures devoted to education may decline, if the kind of education available in 1970 is maintained. Alternatively, if the share of public resources devoted to education remains constant, the prospect of limited growth in enrollment may permit significant improvements in the quality of education. One way of illustrating the trend is to compare changes in the number of taxpayers with changes in school enrollment. A reasonable approximation for the former (considering only the household sector) is the size of the labor force.

As can be seen in Table 7.7, the ratio of the labor force to elementary and secondary school enrollment will rise substantially throughout the remainder of the century. No matter which alter-

Table 7.7.   Ratio of labor force to school enrollment (grades 1-12), Virginia, 1970-2000

|  | 1970 | 1980 | 1990 | 2000 |
|---|---|---|---|---|
| Series I-A | 1.82 | 2.35 | 2.32 | 2.49 |
| Series II-A | 1.82 | 2.32 | 2.23 | 2.40 |
| Series III-A | 1.82 | 2.32 | 2.24 | 2.38 |
| Series I-B | 1.82 | 2.39 | 2.52 | 2.75 |
| Series II-B | 1.82 | 2.37 | 2.47 | 2.69 |
| Series III-B | 1.82 | 2.36 | 2.43 | 2.63 |

native population projection is considered, the number of workers per student enrolled will rise by at least 0.5 in almost all cases. This data also shows clear-cut differences between the various projection series. The higher fertility case (Series A) yields a consistently lower ratio than does the lower fertility case (Series B), and similarly, the ratios decline with declines in the rate of net migration (Series I consistently exceeds Series II, which consistently exceeds Series III). Thus, low fertility–high migration is the best outcome, as this minimizes the number of children and maximizes the size of the labor force.

The question of enrollment in institutions of higher education is somewhat more difficult to interpret. Unlike elementary and secondary school enrollments, where rates of enrollment are very high and relatively invariant and the age group in attendance is relatively fixed, college enrollment rates are more variable, since attendance is a matter of choice rather than compulsion, and the age distribution of college students tends to be somewhat broader.

Additionally, if one looks at demand for higher education within a state, one should also consider that interstate migration for purposes of college attendance is a fairly widespread phenomenon, whereas such migration for elementary and secondary education is of little importance, in a relative sense.

The 1970 census showed a total of 132,659 persons under the age of 35 enrolled in Virginia's colleges and universities. The definition of *college enrollment* is a person attending a "regular" college, university, or professional school, whether by day or night, and whether full or part time. *Regular schooling* is that which leads to a degree, certificate, or some other measure of achievement and specifically excludes private tutoring and correspondence classes unless some sort of transferable credit is earned. Attendance at junior or community colleges is included in college enrollment.[3]

The development and expansion of Virginia's community college system in recent years is a well-documented phenomenon. Given the increasing emphasis placed on instruction in specific skills in these institutions, as well as the possible continuation of increasing rates of attendance of high school graduates in traditional four-year colleges and universities, it is likely that rates of college enrollment in the Commonwealth will increase in coming years.

Here it is arbitrarily assumed that enrollment rates will rise by 50 percent between 1970 and 2000, with a linear increase in the rate of enrollment. The basic 1970 rates by age, sex, and level of enrollment for 1970 and the projected levels for 1980, 1990, and 2000 are given in Table 7.8.

[3] U.S. Bureau of the Census, *1970 Census of Population: General Social and Economic Characteristics: Virginia* App. pp. 8–9.

Table 7.8.  Rates of college enrollment by age, sex, and level, Virginia, 1970-2000

| | Male | | Female | |
| | Undergraduate | Graduate | Undergraduate | Graduate |
|---|---|---|---|---|
| **1970** | | | | |
| 15-19 | 8.8 | 0.0 | 10.4 | 0.0 |
| 20-24 | 13.9 | 2.2 | 11.9 | 1.0 |
| 25-29 | 4.3 | 3.6 | 1.9 | 0.9 |
| 30-34 | 2.1 | 2.0 | 1.6 | 0.7 |
| **1980** | | | | |
| 15-19 | 10.27 | 0.0 | 12.13 | 0.0 |
| 20-24 | 16.22 | 2.57 | 13.88 | 1.17 |
| 25-29 | 5.02 | 4.20 | 2.22 | 1.05 |
| 30-34 | 2.45 | 2.33 | 1.87 | 0.82 |
| **1990** | | | | |
| 15-19 | 11.73 | 0.0 | 13.87 | 0.0 |
| 20-24 | 18.53 | 2.93 | 15.87 | 1.33 |
| 25-29 | 5.73 | 4.80 | 2.53 | 1.20 |
| 30-34 | 2.80 | 2.67 | 2.13 | 0.93 |
| **2000** | | | | |
| 15-19 | 13.2 | 0.0 | 15.60 | 0.0 |
| 20-24 | 20.85 | 3.30 | 17.85 | 1.56 |
| 25-29 | 6.45 | 5.40 | 2.85 | 1.35 |
| 30-34 | 3.15 | 3.00 | 2.4 | 1..05 |

Under the assumption of gradual increases in the rate of college enrollment, all projection series indicate that enrollments by Virginians at institutions of higher education will pass the 200,000 level by the end of the century (Table 7.9). The series range from a high of 265,000 (about twice the 1970 level) to 216,600 (about two-thirds higher than the 1970 base). Most of the enrollment increases are likely before 1980 and after 1990. In all cases, the decade from 1980 to 1990 shows the relatively small size of the 1965-70 and 1970-75 birth cohorts relative to the actual size of older cohorts and the projected size of younger cohorts. The irregularities of increase in projected enrollments are depicted even more clearly in Figure 7.2, which shows projected total enrollment, by five-year interval, for Series I-B. This series is shown because its demographic assumptions come closest to matching the realities of the 1970-75 period.

For the first ten years of the projection period, enrollment is projected to increase by 55,000; this is nearly equally divided between the 1970-75 and 1975-80 periods. However, the period

Table 7.9.  Projected college enrollment by sex, Virginia, 1980-2000

| Series and Year | | Male | Female | Undergraduate | Graduate | Total |
|---|---|---|---|---|---|---|
| | 1970 | 75,435 | 57,224 | 114,160 | 18,499 | 132,659 |
| I-A | 1980 | 109,140 | 78,758 | 158,043 | 29,855 | 187,898 |
| | 1990 | 119,183 | 84,676 | 169,064 | 34,795 | 203,859 |
| | 2000 | 153,113 | 111,943 | 224,672 | 40,384 | 265,056 |
| II-A | 1980 | 106,505 | 77,568 | 154,809 | 29,264 | 184,073 |
| | 1990 | 113,724 | 81,739 | 162,759 | 32,704 | 195,463 |
| | 2000 | 147,307 | 106,053 | 215,263 | 38,200 | 253,463 |
| III-A | 1980 | 103,906 | 76,398 | 151,623 | 28,681 | 180,304 |
| | 1990 | 106,277 | 78,868 | 154,370 | 30,775 | 185,145 |
| | 2000 | 131,795 | 100,932 | 198,305 | 34,422 | 232,727 |
| I-B | 1980 | 109,140 | 78,758 | 158,043 | 29,855 | 187,898 |
| | 1990 | 118,426 | 83,921 | 167,552 | 34,795 | 202,347 |
| | 2000 | 143,084 | 103,774 | 207,981 | 38,877 | 246,858 |
| II-B | 1980 | 106,505 | 77,568 | 154,809 | 29,264 | 184,073 |
| | 1990 | 111,794 | 80,998 | 160,088 | 32,704 | 192,792 |
| | 2000 | 132,272 | 98,295 | 194,707 | 35,860 | 230,567 |
| III-B | 1980 | 103,906 | 76,398 | 151,623 | 28,681 | 180,304 |
| | 1990 | 105,550 | 78,140 | 152,915 | 30,775 | 183,690 |
| | 2000 | 123,095 | 93,486 | 183,446 | 33,134 | 216,581 |

from 1980 to 1985 shows an increase of only 8,000 enrolled, while in the following quinquennium enrollment should rise by less than 7,000. The rate of increase picks up after 1990, with enrollments growing by 19,000 between 1990 and 1995, and by an additional 25,000 between 1995 and 2000.

One might reasonably ask to what extent are the projected enrollment increases attributable to changes in the rate of college attendance, and to what extent are they due to changes in the demographic composition of the population. The answer to this question lies in Table 7.10, which shows what might be termed *baseline* enrollment projections for the extreme series (Series I-A and III-B) for the years 1980, 1990, and 2000. These differ from those in Table 7.9 in that the baseline projections assume that 1970 enrollment rates by age and sex remain constant.

Not surprisingly, the results shown in Table 7.10 differ dramatically from those in Table 7.9. For the year 2000, for example, enrollment under the fixed schedule is one-third less than it would be under assumptions of a linear increase in enrollment rates. Under the demographic assumptions underlying the Series I-A projection, total enrollment would grow by 132,000 between 1970 and 2000 with increasing attendance rates but by

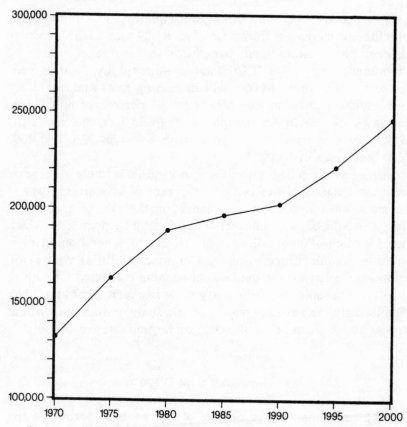

Fig. 7.2.   Illustrative projected college enrollment, Virginia, 1970–2000

Table 7.10.   Illustrative baseline projections of college enrollment, Virginia, 1980-2000

| Series | Total | Graduate | Under_graduate | %Change from 1970 T | G | U | % Change from "regular projection" |
|--------|-------|----------|----------------|------|------|------|----------------------------------|
| **1980** | | | | | | | |
| I-A | 161,020 | 25,576 | 135,444 | 21.4 | 38.3 | 18.6 | -14.3 |
| III-B | 154,512 | 24,570 | 129,942 | 16.5 | 32.8 | 13.8 | |
| **1990** | | | | | | | |
| I-A | 152,925 | 26,107 | 126,818 | 15.3 | 41.1 | 11.1 | -25.0 |
| III-B | 137,795 | 23,091 | 114,704 | 3.9 | 24.8 | 0.5 | |
| **2000** | | | | | | | |
| I-A | 176,704 | 26,922 | 149,782 | 33.2 | 45.5 | 31.2 | -33.3 |
| III-B | 144,387 | 22,089 | 122,298 | 8.8 | 19.4 | 7.1 | |

only 44,000 with constant rates. Consequently, one-third of the enrollment increases shown in Table 7.9 are attributable to demographic change and two-thirds to increasing rates of enrollment. For Series III-B, total enrollment by 2000 is projected to increase by 84,000 with increasing rates and by 12,000 with constant rates. In this case, only 15 percent of enrollment increases are due to demographic change. In fact, the Series III-B baseline projection shows enrollments lower in 1990 and 2000 than they were in 1980.

In brief, while college enrollment in Virginia is likely to increase over the balance of the century, the rate of growth appears to be much more dependent on changes in the rate of enrollment than it would be on demographic change. The degree to which the rate of enrollment will change is likely to depend on changes in the economic structure of the Commonwealth, as well as on temporal fluctuations in the level of economic activity. Growth of enrollment should be particularly slow between 1980 and 1990. Additionally, relative increases in graduate enrollment would appear to be greater than those in undergraduate enrollment.

## The Aging Population

Analogous to the relative decline of the younger portion of the population, the future population of Virginia will have larger numbers of older persons, in both relative and absolute terms. Chapter 6 discussed the growth of the senior segment of the Commonwealth's population. This section discusses some of the implications of this growth.

Many of the social and economic problems which are the by-product of population aging are national in scope. One of the more important of these, perhaps, is the issue of social security financing and the question of the future efficacy of many pension systems as they now exist. Basically, the problem is that current benefits are financed out of current contributions (hence, the designation of such systems as "pay-as-you-go"). In the future, the ratio of contributors to recipients will change considerably; under the present structure, the burden of supporting future generations of retired persons will fall more heavily on future generations of workers. A likely consequence is a change in the method of financing, away from pay-as-you-go toward general revenue financing.[4] Such problems, however, are not particularly relevant at the state level save for such areas as the state employee retirement system.

More important are economic and social structural changes in Virginia which will occur as adaptation is made to demographic reality. Many of these changes will be reflected in changes in income and consumption patterns; these will be discussed in the two following sections. As background to these, and to provide data for other analyses regarding aging in Virginia, the first task of this section is to present projections of households in Virginia, classified by age and sex of the head.

Rates of household headship by race and sex for Virginia in 1970 are given in Table 7.11. A *household* is any person or group of related persons occupying the same housing unit. Rates of household headship have been increasing in recent years due to delay in marriage and increase in the incidence of divorce, inter alia. Since, by current definition, the husband in a husband-wife family is always considered head of household, post-ponement or dissolution of marriage creates two households where there would otherwise have been one. Forecasting future trends in household headship is rather difficult due to the myriad of social and other variables involved in the determination of these trends. Consequently, household projections here assume no change in 1970 rates of household headship specific to age and sex. In light of current trends, it is most likely that actual rates will rise somewhat in the future; consequently, the household projections shown in Table 7.12 may well err on the conservative side. (Complete demographic detail of projected households is given in Table A7.2.)

---

[4] This problem is discussed in more detail in Timothy D. Hogan, "The Implications of Population Stationary for the Social Security System," *Social Science Quarterly* (June, 1974): 151–58; and Boone A. Turchi, "Stationary Populations: Pensions and the Social Security Systems," in *Zero Population Growth: Implications*, ed. J. J. Spengler (Chapel Hill, N.C.: Carolina Population Center, 1975), pp. 75–94.

Table 7.11.  Rates of household headship
by age and sex, Virginia, 1970

| Age | Male | Female |
| --- | --- | --- |
| 15-19 | 3.32 | 1.22 |
| 20-24 | 37.89 | 9.27 |
| 25-29 | 77.52 | 10.93 |
| 30-34 | 85.75 | 11.12 |
| 35-39 | 89.20 | 11.83 |
| 40-44 | 90.38 | 13.22 |
| 45-49 | 91.73 | 14.81 |
| 50-54 | 91.13 | 17.97 |
| 55-59 | 91.96 | 23.24 |
| 60-64 | 91.41 | 30.45 |
| 65-69 | 89.19 | 38.20 |
| 70-74 | 89.57 | 43.77 |
| 75-79 | 84.76 | 44.29 |
| 80-84 | 78.51 | 40.23 |
| 85+ | 57.87 | 30.18 |

Note:  These rates are the number of primary
individuals and family heads (in an age-sex
group), divided by the total number of persons
in that age-sex group.

Table 7.12. Household characteristics, Virginia, 1970-2000

| Year | Series | Number of Households | Persons Per Household | Percent Primary Individual | Percent Female Head | Age of Head (percent age distribution) | | | |
|------|--------|------|------|------|------|------|------|------|------|
| | | | | | | 15-29 | 30-44 | 45-64 | 65+ |
| 1970 | | 1,394,802* | 3.19 | 16.7 | 19.8 | 19.0 | 29.6 | 35.9 | 15.4 |
| 1980 | I-A | 1,700,476 | 3.05 | 16.8 | 19.9 | 20.8 | 31.7 | 32.4 | 15.1 |
| | II-A | 1,685,343 | 3.06 | 16.8 | 19.9 | 20.5 | 31.8 | 32.6 | 15.2 |
| | III-A | 1,669,772 | 3.04 | 16.8 | 19.9 | 20.1 | 31.8 | 32.7 | 15.3 |
| | I-B | 1,700,476 | 3.02 | 16.8 | 19.9 | 20.8 | 31.7 | 32.4 | 15.1 |
| | II-B | 1,685,343 | 3.02 | 16.8 | 19.9 | 20.5 | 31.8 | 32.6 | 15.2 |
| | III-B | 1,669,722 | 3.02 | 16.8 | 19.9 | 20.1 | 31.8 | 32.7 | 15.3 |
| 1990 | I-A | 2,011,466 | 2.96 | 16.4 | 19.9 | 17.5 | 37.2 | 29.8 | 15.6 |
| | II-A | 1,947,478 | 2.97 | 16.4 | 19.9 | 16.9 | 37.1 | 30.0 | 16.0 |
| | III-A | 1,886,161 | 2.95 | 16.6 | 20.0 | 16.2 | 37.0 | 30.3 | 16.5 |
| | I-B | 2,011,165 | 2.88 | 16.4 | 19.9 | 17.5 | 37.2 | 29.8 | 15.6 |
| | II-B | 1,946,808 | 2.88 | 16.4 | 19.9 | 16.8 | 37.1 | 30.1 | 16.0 |
| | III-B | 1,885,890 | 2.88 | 16.6 | 20.0 | 16.2 | 37.0 | 30.3 | 16.5 |
| 2000 | I-A | 2,310,397 | 2.89 | 16.4 | 20.1 | 16.5 | 33.2 | 35.6 | 14.7 |
| | II-A | 2,189,326 | 2.91 | 16.5 | 20.0 | 16.6 | 32.3 | 35.8 | 15.3 |
| | III-A | 2,056,469 | 2.90 | 16.8 | 20.3 | 15.7 | 31.9 | 36.4 | 16.0 |
| | I-B | 2,292,540 | 2.88 | 16.4 | 20.1 | 15.8 | 33.5 | 35.9 | 14.8 |
| | II-B | 2,159,791 | 2.88 | 16.6 | 20.2 | 15.5 | 32.8 | 36.3 | 15.4 |
| | III-B | 2,041,244 | 2.80 | 16.7 | 20.3 | 15.1 | 32.1 | 36.7 | 16.1 |

*Excludes households with head aged 14 and under (599 in 1970).

The number of households in Virginia is projected to rise to more than 2 million by the end of the century, an increase of at least 600,000 over the 1970 level of 1.4 million. Because fertility is projected to be lower in the future than it has been in the immediate past, the number of persons per household is projected to decline, in all cases, to a level of 2.8–2.9 by the end of the century. (The share of the total population in households was 96.9 percent in 1970; this share was assumed to hold constant throughout the projection period.)

Despite the aging of the population discussed in the preceding chapter, the share of households constituted by primary individuals (one-person households) is projected to remain constant over the period. This result may not be too surprising when it is recalled that primary individuals tend to come from the younger and older ends of the age spectrum. What happens in this context is that the relative decline in young primary individuals is offset by the relative increase in old primary individuals. In 1970 there were some 233,000 primary individuals in Virginia. Of these, 44,025 (18.9 percent) were aged 15–29, and 80,629 (34.5 percent) were aged 65 and over. Although persons in these age groups accounted for only a third of all household heads, they totaled more than half of all primary individuals. By the year 2000, however, while the number of primary individuals will rise to a maximum, in Series I–A, of 379,500 (or by 63 percent), the number of 15–29–year–old primary individuals will rise by only 38 percent, to 60,935, and the number of primary individuals aged 65 and over will grow by 70 percent, to 137,268. By 2000, under the Series I–A assumptions, young persons will comprise 16.1 percent of primary individuals, while older persons will constitute 36.2 percent.

The share of households headed by females is projected to increase only marginally by the end of the century. Because females are much more likely to be the head of a single–person household (63 percent of all primary individuals were female in 1970) than a family head (11.1 percent), the reasons for this relative stability are essentially the same as those cited above regarding primary individuals.

Considerable changes are projected to occur in the broad

age distribution of heads of households. By the end of the century, the largest relative increases are projected to occur in what might be termed younger middle–age households (head aged 30–44), followed by older middle–aged households (head aged 45–64). The share of households with an older head is not greater in 2000 than in 1970, except in the Series III projections, which assume no net migration to Virginia after 1980.

The principal factor underlying these changes are the large number of household formations undertaken by members of the postwar baby boom. The relative impact of this boom can best be seen by considering the number of births registered to Virginians for five–year age periods beginning in 1940: 1940–44, 324,351; 1945–49, 390,401; 1950–54, 445,759; 1955–59, 481,795; 1960–64, 483,079; and 1965–69, 423,614.[5] Thus, as the disproportionately large cohorts born between 1950 and 1964 set up their own households, they greatly influence the distribution by age of head of household. In 1970 the children of the baby boom were all under 20 and not yet in the household formation stage. In 1980 these cohorts will be aged 15–29; hence, the share of house–holds headed by persons in this age group increases. The data for 1990 show considerable increase (over 1980) in the share of households headed by persons age 30–44, while the 2000 data show considerable increase over 1990 in the share of households headed by persons 45–64. Persons born between 1950 and 1964 will comprise 20–21 percent of all household heads in 1980 and 35–40 percent of all household heads in both 1990 and 2000.

By way of contrast, the current household heads in those age groups (15–29, 25–39, and 35–49) comprise 19, 30, and 30 percent, respectively. In brief, then, the disproportionately large birth cohorts of the 1950s and early 1960s will be the dominant force in household formation for the remainder of the century.

The increasing share of older persons in the population suggests that a wide variety of social and economic changes are likely, as society adapts itself to meeting changes in relative needs of the population. Noted previously was the considerable slowdown in the

[5] To illustrate the degree to which fertility has fallen, births from 1970–74 totaled 386,593, or 60,000 less than the level attained for the comparable five- year period twenty years earlier.

rate of increase in the school population that will characterize
Virginia throughout the remainder of the century. On the other side
of the coin, the demand for services that are relatively more important to older persons will grow at an increasing rate. One of
the most important of these is health care. As indices for demand
for health care, two variables are significant: hospital stays (and
the duration of these stays) and visits to physicians. The
basic data (annual number of stays, length of stays, and annual
number of visits, per person, by age and sex) are shown in Table
7.13. The data are for the United States from 1963 to 1965.

Table 7.13.  Annual number of hospital stays, duration of stay, and annual
number of physician visits, by age and sex, United States, 1963-65

| Year | Sex | Hospital Stays per Person | Average Duration | Physician Visits per Person |
|------|-----|---------------------------|------------------|------------------------------|
| 0-44 | Male | .0784 | 7.9 | 3.6 |
|      | Female | .1507 | 5.6 | 4.7 |
| 45-64 | Male | .1498 | 12.1 | 4.5 |
|       | Female | .1462 | 9.8 | 5.6 |
| 65-74 | Male | .1824 | 13.1 | 5.4 |
|       | Female | .1804 | 12.2 | 6.9 |
| 75+ | Male | .2063 | 12.5 | 7.3 |
|     | Female | .1877 | 12.8 | 7.7 |

Source:  U.S. Department of Health, Education, and Welfare, National Center
for Health Statistics, Age Patterns in Medical Care, Illness, and Disability:
United States, July 1963-June 1965 (Washington, D.C.: U. S. Government Printing
Office, 19  ).

The changes in demand for these services are shown in Table
7.14. The data are presented as index numbers, with 1970 being
the base in all cases. Essentially, the data by age and sex are
multiplied by the appropriate number of stays or visits, or length
of stay, and summed for each age-sex group. The total is then
divided by the 1970 total and multiplied by 100 to yield an
index number.

In all cases, demand for these specified health services is
projected to increase at a rate greater than the total population
does. Since older persons require these services to a greater
extent, this is to be expected, given the aging of the population
that characterizes all the projections. As would be expected,

Table 7.14. Projected total demand for selected health
services, Virginia, 1980-2000 (index numbers, 1970 = 100)

| Year | Series | Hospital Stays | Days in Hospital | Physician visits | Population |
|------|--------|---------|----------|---------|------------|
| 1980 | I-A | 115.1 | 114.9 | 115.3 | 115.2 |
| | II-A | 114.2 | 114.2 | 114.5 | 114.4 |
| | III-A | 112.8 | 113.0 | 113.0 | 112.8 |
| | I-B | 114.1 | 114.1 | 114.2 | 114.2 |
| | II-B | 113.0 | 113.2 | 113.2 | 113.0 |
| | III-B | 111.9 | 112.2 | 112.1 | 111.8 |
| 1990 | I-A | 132.0 | 132.0 | 132.4 | 132.1 |
| | II-A | 128.4 | 128.7 | 128.9 | 128.5 |
| | III-A | 123.9 | 124.7 | 124.2 | 123.6 |
| | I-B | 129.0 | 129.6 | 129.3 | 128.7 |
| | II-B | 124.9 | 125.9 | 125.1 | 124.3 |
| | III-B | 121.1 | 122.4 | 121.3 | 120.3 |
| 2000 | I-A | 155.6 | 153.0 | 150.0 | 148.4 |
| | II-A | 142.6 | 146.1 | 143.0 | 141.6 |
| | III-A | 134.4 | 138.3 | 134.4 | 132.5 |
| | I-B | 149.9 | 148.5 | 144.2 | 142.1 |
| | II-B | 136.1 | 140.8 | 136.1 | 133.8 |
| | III-B | 129.2 | 134.1 | 129.1 | 126.7 |

the greater the level of population growth, the greater the
absolute increase in demand for medical services. In relative
terms, say, demand per capita, this is not the case. In this
case where there is an implicit control for population size,
the differential aging in the projections becomes relevant. If,
for example, one computes the arithmetic average of the three
index values for each projection at each point in time and divides
the average by the population growth index, the result is an

index of demand per capita. This is shown in Table 7.15. The lower fertility series (Series B) has a consistently higher level of per capita demand than the higher series (Series A). The value of the index increases as migration rates decrease for 1980 and 1990, but at the end of the century, the lowest index values occur for the intermediate migration series (Series II).

Table 7.15.   Projected per capita demand for selected health services, Virginia, 1980–2000 (index numbers, 1970 = 100)

| Series | 1980 | 1990 | 2000 |
|--------|------|------|------|
| I-A    | 99.9  | 100.02 | 103.0 |
| II-A   | 99.9  | 100.1  | 101.6 |
| III-A  | 100.1 | 100.5  | 102.4 |
| I-B    | 99.9  | 100.5  | 103.8 |
| II-B   | 100.1 | 100.8  | 102.9 |
| III-B  | 100.2 | 101.1  | 103.2 |

The aging of the population will have numerous other implications for the economic and social structure of Virginia. Many of these changes will result not only directly from age composition changes but also indirectly through the mechanism of income change, which is itself partially a function of age distribution variation. The following section, then, deals with projected income changes.

## Level of Income

The level of income is functionally related to the age and sex of a person. The income projections here are based on income for families and unrelated individuals[6] and are on 1970 census income data. There are many different ways to measure income;[7] the use of census income here reflects the availability of data showing average levels of income by age and sex of family heads or unrelated individuals (Table 7.16).

Table 7.16.  Mean income by age and sex of head of household, Virginia, 1969

| | Male | | Female | |
| | Family Head | Unrelated Individuals | Family Head | Unrelated Individuals |
| Age | | | | |
| --- | --- | --- | --- | --- |
| 15–24 | $ 7,005 | $2,364 | $3,446 | $2,017 |
| 25–34 | 10,261 | 6,505 | 4,074 | 5,511 |
| 35–44 | 12,437 | 7,798 | 5,223 | 5,011 |
| 45–64 | 12,896 | 5,952 | 6,782 | 4,561 |
| 65+ | 7,149 | 3,052 | 5,948 | 2,612 |

The intention here is to provide projections of income to allow recognition of the role of demographic change. Changes in population composition will affect the distribution of families and individuals and, hence, the level of income, both in the aggregate and on the per capita level. Changes in income over time as measured by census data are measured in current dollars; that is, they are not adjusted for fluctuations in purchasing power through differential rates of inflation. The income projections included here are in constant (1969) dollars. This is called *real income*, in that purchasing power is held to be constant over time.

[6] Unrelated individuals consist of primary individuals, as well as persons in a household not related to the head and those living in group quarters, but not in an institution. The latter group consists primarily of residents of college dormitories and military barracks. Unrelated individuals who are not primary individuals are called "secondary individuals."

[7] Differences between several alternative definitions of income are contained in John L. Knapp, *Distribution of Virginia Adjusted Gross Income by Income Class, 1972* (Charlottesville: Tayloe Murphy Institute, 1974), pps. 1–2.

The major decision to be made is the rate at which real income will change over the 1970–2000 period. Between 1947 and 1973 real income of families rose by 99.8 percent, on the average, while that of unrelated individuals rose by 111.7 percent.[8] On an average basis, this translates to an increase of 2.7 percent per year for families and 2.9 percent per year for unrelated individuals. Since the purpose here is not to forecast income per se, but rather to explore demographic variation and its probable impact on Virginia, the choice of rates of income growth itself is immaterial. Consequently, the projections that follow assume the continuation of the rates observed for the 1947–73 period, with the proviso that the rate of increase in real income for families and individuals is assumed to be unrelated to demographic variation. Additionally, as noted above, no effort is made to forecast rates of inflation, although it has been suggested that the forces which lead to aging of the population may also exacerbate inflationary pressures.[9]

Alternative levels of total, per capita, mean family and mean individual income are shown in Table 7.17. Differences in per capita income in the series occur as early as 1980, when the lower fertility projections of Series B show consistently higher levels of per capita income than do those of Series A. In 1980 the Series B per capita levels are about 1 percent higher, on the average, than those of Series A. This widens to nearly 3 percent in 1990 and to 4 percent by the end of the century. All in all, the level of per capita income in constant (1969) dollars is projected to increase by 150 to 162 percent over the thirty-year projection period. Differences in the mean level of income for families and unrelated individuals do not become at all important until the end of the century. Even at this point, differences in the number of families and individuals only occur among individuals aged 15–29; so the relative differences between the Series A and Series B projections are slight. On the average, the Series B family is projected to have an income about 0.25 percent higher than the

---

[8] U.S. Bureau of the Census, "Money Income in 1973 of Families and Persons in the United States," *Current Population Reports*, Series P-60, no. 97 (1975), Table 11.

[9] Joseph J. Spengler, "Prospective Population Changes and Price Level Tendencies," *Southern Economic Journal* 38 (April 1972): 459–67.

Table 7.17. Projected level of income, Virginia, 1970-2000
(in 1969 dollars)

| Year and Series | Per Capita | Mean Family Income | Mean Income of Individuals | Total Income (millions) |
|---|---|---|---|---|
| 1970 | $2,985 | $10,502 | $3,748 | $13,872.891 |
| 1980 | | | | |
| I-A | 4,100 | 13,577 | 5,104 | 21,959.780 |
| II-A | 4,091 | 13,587 | 5,117 | 21,765.861 |
| III-A | 4,111 | 13,595 | 5,130 | 21,561.115 |
| I-B | 4,138 | 13,577 | 5,104 | 21,959.780 |
| II-B | 4,147 | 13,587 | 5,117 | 21,765.861 |
| III-B | 4,149 | 13,595 | 5,130 | 21,561.115 |
| 1990 | | | | |
| I-A | 5,578 | 17,930 | 7,124 | 34,242.186 |
| II-A | 5,544 | 17,938 | 7,120 | 33,122.792 |
| III-A | 5,580 | 17,950 | 7,129 | 32,049.974 |
| I-B | 5,724 | 17,930 | 7,127 | 34,237.911 |
| II-B | 5,729 | 17,940 | 7,124 | 33,114.022 |
| III-B | 5,728 | 17,951 | 7,132 | 32,045.884 |
| 2000 | | | | |
| I-A | 7,536 | 23,693 | 9,308 | 51,998.318 |
| II-A | 7,478 | 23,694 | 9,260 | 49,221.511 |
| III-A | 7,487 | 23,703 | 9,249 | 46,115.018 |
| I-B | 7,818 | 23,740 | 9,399 | 51,630.635 |
| II-B | 7,809 | 23,762 | 9,368 | 48,588.111 |
| III-B | 7,779 | 23,749 | 9,337 | 45,802.639 |

Series A family. The magnitude of difference for unrelated individuals averages about 1 percent.

Differences in income created by alternative migration assumptions have considerably less input than do fertility differentials. In 1980 and 1990 the lowest migration series (Series III) has marginally higher levels of income than the two higher series, but by 2000 no clear-cut pattern of differentiation emerges. In any event, the differences between the migration series are quite small.

A useful way of considering the impact of alternative demographic assumptions on levels of income is to consider the roles that population change and economic change play independently of each other. This may be accomplished by a four-way division of total income: the base amount, that of 1969; the economic growth component, derived by holding population constant, while allowing income to increase; the demographic component, calculated by holding income constant while allowing population to change; and demographic-economic interaction, or the residual between total income change and that explained by the three other components.[10] An illustration of this technique is shown in Table 7.18, while complete results for all projections series are given in Table 7.19.

In Table 7-18, Series I-A in 1980 is chosen to illustrate the procedure. The first step is simply to take the 1970 base ($13.9 billion). Next, to measure the effect of economic change, the 1970 number of families and individuals is multiplied by 1980 income levels. This yields income in 1980 in the absence of demographic change. The contribution of economic change is simply this total (18.2 billion) less the base. The third step measures the effect of demographic change, by multiplying projected 1980 families and individuals by 1970 income. The net contribution of demographic change is the base subtracted from this amount. Finally, the sum of the net contribution of economic and demographic change is subtracted from total change. The residual ($900 million) is attributable to economic-demographic interaction. This residual is the result of growth in both income and households simultaneously.

The results of similar calculations for the alternative projection series are shown in Table 7.19 (both in absolute and percentage terms). Economic change, or increases in the level of income regardless of demographic variation, explains about half of the total projected increase in income. The share of change attributable to this source declines over time in all cases, as does that attributable to demographic change. This variable accounts for about one-third of all change between 1970 and 1980, but only a quarter from 1970 to 1990 and a fifth from 1970 to 2000. The effect of the interaction becomes increasingly important over time, rising from 10 percent in 1980 to about 30 percent of that level by the end of the century.

[10] This technique is adapted from Herman P. Miller, "Population, Pollution, and Affluence," *Business Horizons* 14 (April 1971): 5-7, 10-16.

Table 7.18.  Illustrative effects of population change and economic change on total income (Series I-A, 1980)

1. Base: $13,872.891 million (from table 7.17)

2. Economic Change (1970 population and 1980 income):

| Age | Male-Headed families (1970) | Mean income (1980) | Female-headed families (1970) | Mean Income (1980) |
|---|---|---|---|---|
| 15-24 | 83,403 | $9,141 | 8,190 | 4,497 |
| 25-34 | 232,254 | 13,390 | 22,602 | 5,316 |
| 35-44 | 231,107 | 16,230 | 26,885 | 6,816 |
| 45-64 | 377,216 | 16,829 | 45,386 | 8,850 |
| 65+ | 108,609 | 9,329 | 26,063 | 7,767 |
| Total income: | $14,984.516 million | | | $944.328 |

| Age | Male individuals (1970) | Mean income (1980) | Female individuals (1970) | Mean Income (1980) |
|---|---|---|---|---|
| 15-24 | 117,352 | $3,154 | 54,970 | 2,691 |
| 25-34 | 36,041 | 8,680 | 17,215 | 7,353 |
| 35-44 | 19,897 | 10,405 | 11,698 | 6,686 |
| 45-64 | 35,992 | 7,942 | 60,601 | 6,086 |
| 65+ | 22,992 | 4,072 | 66,789 | 3,485 |
| Total income: | $1,269.464 million | | | $954.296 |

Total: $18,152.604  net $4,279.713

3. Demographic Change (1980 population and 1970 income):

| Age | Male-headed families (1980) | Mean income (1970) | Female-headed families (1980) | Mean Income (1970) |
|---|---|---|---|---|
| 15-24 | 96,227 | $7,005 | 9,591 | $3,446 |
| 25-34 | 362,432 | 10,261 | 33,730 | 4,074 |
| 35-44 | 264,741 | 12,437 | 31,055 | 5,223 |
| 45-64 | 408,867 | 12,896 | 51,219 | 6,782 |
| 65+ | 125.72 | 7,149 | 32,391 | 5,948 |
| Total income: | $13,853.172 | | | $872.696 |

| Age | Male individuals (1980) | Mean income (1970) | Female individuals (1980) | Mean Income (1970) |
|---|---|---|---|---|
| 15-24 | 135,147 | 82,364 | 64,288 | 2,017 |
| 25-34 | 55,675 | 6,505 | 25,010 | 5,511 |
| 35-44 | 22,772 | 7,798 | 13,277 | 5,011 |
| 45-64 | 39,785 | 5,952 | 72,005 | 4,561 |
| 65+ | 26,065 | 3,052 | 83,396 | 2,612 |
| Total income: | $1,175.580 | | | $880.275 |

Total: $16,780.723  net: $2,907.832

Total income change:  21,959.780-13, 872.891=8,086.889
Explained by economic and demographic change:  4279.713 + 2,907.832=7187.545

4. Economic-Demographic Interaction:  899.344

Table 7.19.  Components of income growth, Virginia, 1980-2000  (billions of dollars)

| Series | Base | Total Change | Economic | Demographic | Interaction |
|---|---|---|---|---|---|
| **1980** | | | | | |
| I-A,I-B | 13.87 | 8.07 | 4.28 | 2.91 | 0.88 |
| II-A,II-B | 13.87 | 7.89 | 4.28 | 2.76 | 0.85 |
| III-A,III-B | 13.87 | 7.69 | 4.28 | 2.60 | 0.81 |
| **1990** | | | | | |
| I-A | 13.87 | 20.37 | 9.88 | 6.13 | 4.36 |
| II-A | 13.87 | 19.25 | 9.88 | 5.48 | 3.89 |
| III-A | 13.87 | 18.18 | 9.88 | 4.86 | 3.44 |
| I-B | 13.87 | 20.37 | 9.88 | 6.12 | 4.36 |
| III-B | 13.87 | 18.17 | 9.88 | 4.85 | 3.44 |
| **2000** | | | | | |
| I-A | 13.87 | 38.13 | 17.21 | 9.37 | 11.55 |
| II-A | 13.87 | 35.35 | 17.21 | 8.07 | 10.07 |
| III-A | 13.87 | 32.24 | 17.21 | 6.72 | 8.31 |
| I-B | 13.87 | 37.76 | 17.21 | 9.21 | 11.34 |
| II-B | 13.87 | 34.72 | 17.21 | 7.86 | 9.65 |
| III-B | 13.87 | 31.93 | 17.21 | 6.58 | 8.14 |
| **Percentage Distribution** | | | | | |
| **1980** | | | | | |
| I-A,I-B | | 100.0 | 54.0 | 36.1 | 10.9 |
| II-A,II-B | | 100.0 | 54.2 | 35.0 | 10.8 |
| III-A,III-B | | 100.0 | 55.7 | 33.8 | 10.5 |
| **1990** | | | | | |
| I-A | | 100.0 | 48.5 | 30.1 | 21.4 |
| II-A | | 100.0 | 51.3 | 28.5 | 20.2 |
| III-A | | 100.0 | 54.3 | 26.7 | 19.0 |
| I-B | | 100.0 | 48.5 | 30.1 | 21.4 |
| II-B | | 100.0 | 51.4 | 28.4 | 20.2 |
| III-B | | 100.0 | 54.4 | 26.7 | 18.9 |
| **2000** | | | | | |
| I-A | | 100.0 | 45.1 | 24.6 | 28.5 |
| II-A | | 100.0 | 48.7 | 22.8 | 28.5 |
| III-A | | 100.0 | 53.4 | 20.8 | 25.8 |
| I-B | | 100.0 | 45.6 | 24.4 | 30.0 |
| II-B | | 100.0 | 49.6 | 22.6 | 27.8 |
| III-B | | 100.0 | 53.9 | 20.6 | 25.5 |

The effects of demographic change vary, of course, with the projected numbers of families and unrelated individuals. These will, in turn, vary directly with population size. Consequently, it is not surprising that the relative and absolute importance of demographic change in explaining future growth of income is directly related to ultimate population size. If the analysis is carried one step farther to assume that change through economic-demographic interaction accrues to the economic and demographic factors in about the same proportion as change directly attributable to these factors, it becomes evident that economic change will be responsible for about two-thirds of projected income growth, while the remaining one-third will be the result of demographic change.

Changes in the level of income, coupled with change in the age structure of consumers, will result in changes in patterns of household demand by Virginians. The final section of this chapter discusses some of these changes.

## Volume and Composition of Demand

This final section discusses how prospective changes in population and in the level of income will change consumption in coming years. To some extent, this has already been discussed in other contexts; the demand for education and the demand for health services have already been discussed. These were treated primarily in terms of the effects of changes in the age consumption of the population. In addition, demand for other sorts of goods and services may be construed as being a function of the level of income as well as the size of the population, or its composition.

Consider, for example, the average family. At early stages of family formation, income will be low relative to probable future levels. Yet spending may be disproportionately high, especially if a house is purchased and offspring begin to appear. As the family ages, income will grow and the composition of demand will change. Discretionary purchases (a larger house, major appliances, more frequent travel, even college education for the children) become a more important portion of the family budget. Yet, typically, the family will also save some portion of its income, in an effort to insure adequate income for the impending retirement years. Finally, during retirement, the family (presumably devoid of its offspring, in what has been termed the "empty nest" situation) will have lower income but relatively high spending. Most of the child-related expenditures of earlier years will disappear, but costs of medical treatment, drugs, and so on typically increase as morbidity becomes more common.

Unfortunately, data on consumption by age and income are not available since the consumer expenditure survey of 1960-61. These data show, for example, how spending patterns vary with income (or age of head of household) but do not show how consumption patterns change with income or age changes.

Nevertheless, these data are used here to estimate the effects of changing levels of age and income on the level of consumption, measured on a relative basis since 1970. However, the technically minded reader should bear in mind that due to lack of data, average propensities to consume, rather than marginal data, are used here.

Data showing the percentage distribution of consumption by age of head for American households are given in Table 7.20. The data show considerable differences in consumption patterns by age. Generally, these data are consistent with the description of consumption patterns given above. Food generally increases in importance over the family life cycle, reflecting increasing family size and then decreasing income in the retirement years. Generally, demand for food is relatively inelastic with respect to income (volume consumed does not change as much as income); so as income declines, the share of expenditures devoted to food rises. The pattern for housing is similar, except that the proportion of income spent on it is relatively high at both ends of the age spectrum. Medical care, as expected, rises sharply at the end of the age spectrum, while transportation needs decline, especially after retirement. Discretionary items (part of clothing, recreation and reading, education) are at a maximum for families during the middle years of the life cycle and for individuals during the early years.

The data in Table 7.20 are aggregated over all income levels. In order to allow for income change, it is also necessary to determine how increments to income are consumed, by age groups. Such data are available, by age, for all heads of households, but unfortunately, not for families and individuals separately. The data in Table 7.21 show the average increase in amount spent on each category by age of head, per $1,000 increase in money income after taxes. To remove possible distortions, the two highest and two lowest categories are not considered. Additionally, the sum of increased consumption is forced to add up to 100%, thus excluding savings rates from this analysis.

The final data items required are the amounts of increased income that are diverted to consumption, and the amounts to taxes, savings, and other items. As additional income is earned,

Table 7.20.  Percentage distribution of consumption expenditures by age of
head of household, United states, 1960-61

|  | 15-24 | 25-34 | 35-44 | 45-64 | 65+ |
|---|---|---|---|---|---|
| **Families** | | | | | |
| Food | 21.6 | 23.7 | 25.1 | 24.4 | 26.5 |
| Tobacco | 2.0 | 1.9 | 1.8 | 1.8 | 1.4 |
| Alcoholic Beverage | 1.0 | 1.5 | 1.5 | 1.5 | 1.2 |
| Housing | 31.0 | 31.0 | 27.9 | 26.8 | 30.5 |
| Clothing | 8.8 | 9.8 | 11.4 | 10.8 | 7.3 |
| Personal Care | 2.8 | 2.8 | 2.9 | 3.0 | 2.8 |
| Medical Care | 6.1 | 6.1 | 5.9 | 7.0 | 11.2 |
| Recreation & Reading | 4.9 | 5.2 | 5.2 | 4.7 | 3.5 |
| Education | 0.9 | 0.7 | 1.1 | 1.5 | 0.3 |
| Transportation | 19.8 | 15.7 | 15.1 | 15.7 | 12.4 |
| Other | 1.0 | 1.4 | 2.1 | 2.8 | 2.9 |
| **Individuals** | | | | | |
| Food | 21.8 | 20.4 | 22.1 | 24.5 | 25.9 |
| Tobacco | 1.6 | 2.2 | 2.2 | 1.8 | 0.8 |
| Alcoholic Beverages | 3.7 | 3.8 | 4.3 | 2.5 | 0.7 |
| Housing | 24.3 | 27.0 | 31.2 | 35.0 | 42.6 |
| Clothing | 13.6 | 10.6 | 10.0 | 8.0 | 5.8 |
| Personal Care | 2.8 | 2.8 | 2.9 | 2.9 | 2.4 |
| Medical care | 3.4 | 4.1 | 4.2 | 6.2 | 9.1 |
| Recreation & Reading | 7.0 | 6.5 | 4.8 | 4.3 | 3.2 |
| Education | 2.3 | 1.2 | 0.5 | 0.1 | 0.0 |
| Transportation | 18.2 | 19.4 | 15.7 | 12.4 | 7.5 |
| Other | 1.1 | 1.9 | 2.1 | 2.2 | 2.2 |

Source:  U.S. Department of Labor, Bureau of Labor Statistics,
Survey of Consumer Expenditures, 1960-1961, Supplement 2 to BLS
Report 237-93 (Washington, D.C.:  U.S. Government Printing Office,
1966), Tables 12a and 12b.

some portion of this is devoted to tax payments. Of the remainder, which may be called disposable income, some portion is
saved or paid as interest or transfer payments. The balance is
personal consumption. Table 7.22 shows the relationship between
total income of persons, disposable income, and personal income
for selected years from 1950 to 1973.[11]

[11] It should be pointed out here that these data are based on personal income,
which differs somewhat from the money income definition employed in the projections
discussed in the text.

Table 7.21.  Average increase in consumption per $1,000 increase on income by age of head of household, United States, 1960-61

|                        | 15-24 | 25-34 | 35-44 | 45-64 | 65+   |
|------------------------|-------|-------|-------|-------|-------|
| Food                   | 174.0 | 192.5 | 201.9 | 221.5 | 203.6 |
| Tobacco                | 17.3  | 6.2   | 11.7  | 14.2  | 8.7   |
| Alcoholic Beverages    | 19.4  | 19.0  | 19.5  | 20.5  | 16.5  |
| Housing                | 304.6 | 319.1 | 279.6 | 218.5 | 253.4 |
| Clothing               | 73.2  | 105.8 | 126.1 | 117.9 | 106.3 |
| Personal Care          | 16.8  | 19.9  | 23.9  | 27.6  | 28.4  |
| Medical Care           | 65.4  | 67.6  | 57.5  | 61.4  | 100.9 |
| Recreation & Reading   | 51.8  | 70.7  | 64.9  | 56.3  | 46.5  |
| Education              | 0.9   | 6.0   | 14.1  | 17.1  | 11.5  |
| Transportation         | 258.2 | 172.7 | 182.7 | 211.1 | 206.6 |
| Other                  | 18.4  | 20.5  | 18.0  | 21.8  | 17.4  |

Source:  Same as Table 7.20, Tables 14a-g.

Table 7.22.  Relationship of personal Income, disposable personal income, and personal consumption, United States, 1950-73 (percent)

|        | 1950 | 1955 | 1960 | 1965 | 1969 | 1970 | 1971 | 1972 | 1973 |
|--------|------|------|------|------|------|------|------|------|------|
| DPI/PI | 90.9 | 88.5 | 87.3 | 87.8 | 84.5 | 85.6 | 86.4 | 84.9 | 85.2 |
| PC/DPI | 92.3 | 92.4 | 92.9 | 91.5 | 91.3 | 89.3 | 89.4 | 91.2 | 91.1 |
| PI/PC  | 83.9 | 81.8 | 81.1 | 80.3 | 77.1 | 76.4 | 77.2 | 77.4 | 77.6 |

Source:  U.S. Bureau of the Census, Statistical Abstract of the United States: 1974 (Washington, D.C.:  U.S. Government Printing Office, 1974), Tables 599, 607.

The data show that in the most recent five-year period (1969-73), consumption averaged approximately 77 percent of total personal income. The general downward trend of this ratio is also readily apparent. It is assumed here that this ratio will continue to decline at an average of 0.1 percent per year. Thus, in 1980, 76.5 percent of income will be consumed; 75.5 percent in 1990; and 74.5 percent in 2000. Again, it should be noted that the lack of data requires the use of an average concept in place of the preferable marginal concept. Further, the assumption that this ratio is constant over age groups and income levels is probably somewhat unrealistic in that income taxes are designed to be progressive (taking a larger share as income increases) and that savings rates are likely to be positive in the middle years but negative (or at least relatively low) in the younger and older years of the family life cycle.

Projected levels of consumption, by major category, are shown in Table 7.23. The data are shown as index numbers, with 1970 being set equal to 100. Total consumption (in terms of constant dollars spent) is projected to be 55 to 60 percent higher in 1980, and 225 to 270 percent higher at the end of the century. Although all major categories of consumption should increase substantially beyond 1970 levels, there is considerable variation as a result of age and income differences within the projected populations. By the end of the century, demand for inelastic items such as food and tobacco products is projected to increase at rates somewhat less than overall consumption trends, as are expenditures for personal care and miscellaneous items. Expenditures for medical care and housing are projected to grow at about the same rate as total expenditures. One might have expected the former to increase relatively quickly with the aging of the populations, but it should be remembered that children are also disproportionately large consumers of medical care, and their ranks will grow by a relatively small amount.

Items which are somewhat discretionary in nature (and hence characterized by income elasticity greater than unity)[12] are projected to grow by relatively greater amounts over the balance of the century. These include clothing, recreation and reading, education, and transportation. The projected rate of growth for education far exceeds that of all other expenditures, although it remains a comparatively small item in the total consumer budget. This again may appear to be a surprising result in light of the relatively slow growth forecast for the younger age groups, but with the increasing sophistication of Virginia's economy, a greater premium will be placed on education for all segments of the labor force. Thus, as education becomes a more or less continuous process over the entire life cycle, perhaps it is not unlikely

[12] That is, expenditures for these items increase at a rate faster than income.

Table 7.23. Projected levels of consumption, Virginia, 1980-2000 (index numbers, 1970 = 100)

| Series | Total | Food | Tobacco | Alcoholic Beverage | Housing | Clothing | Personal Care | Medical Care | Recreation & Reading | Education | Transportation | Other |
|---|---|---|---|---|---|---|---|---|---|---|---|---|
| **1980** | | | | | | | | | | | | |
| I-A & I-B | 159.1 | 155.2 | 146.8 | 167.8 | 166.0 | 163.1 | 154.5 | 162.3 | 170.1 | 203.3 | 171.5 | 154.8 |
| II-A & II-B | 157.7 | 154.0 | 145.5 | 166.3 | 164.6 | 161.7 | 153.2 | 161.0 | 168.5 | 201.4 | 170.0 | 153.6 |
| III-A & III-B | 156.2 | 152.6 | 143.9 | 164.7 | 163.0 | 160.2 | 151.9 | 159.7 | 166.9 | 199.5 | 168.3 | 152.4 |
| **1990** | | | | | | | | | | | | |
| I-A | 244.9 | 224.9 | 202.9 | 259.7 | 245.2 | 252.9 | 225.0 | 238.9 | 268.1 | 359.8 | 268.3 | 228.4 |
| II-A | 236.9 | 217.7 | 196.2 | 251.1 | 237.0 | 244.7 | 218.0 | 231.6 | 258.9 | 346.4 | 259.5 | 221.5 |
| III-A | 229.2 | 210.8 | 189.9 | 242.8 | 229.1 | 236.8 | 211.1 | 224.5 | 250.1 | 333.1 | 250.9 | 214.8 |
| I-B | 244.8 | 224.9 | 202.9 | 259.7 | 245.2 | 252.9 | 225.0 | 238.9 | 268.0 | 359.8 | 268.3 | 228.4 |
| II-B | 236.8 | 217.7 | 196.2 | 251.1 | 236.9 | 244.7 | 217.9 | 231.5 | 258.8 | 346.2 | 259.4 | 221.5 |
| III-B | 229.2 | 210.8 | 189.9 | 242.8 | 229.1 | 236.8 | 211.1 | 224.4 | 250.1 | 331.1 | 250.9 | 214.8 |
| **2000** | | | | | | | | | | | | |
| I-A | 367.3 | 333.5 | 293.7 | 401.3 | 358.6 | 386.2 | 333.0 | 357.6 | 410.3 | 583.8 | 419.7 | 344.8 |
| II-A | 347.3 | 315.4 | 277.7 | 379.3 | 338.9 | 364.7 | 315.1 | 339.1 | 387.3 | 543.0 | 397.1 | 326.5 |
| III-A | 325.4 | 295.8 | 260.1 | 354.9 | 316.8 | 341.8 | 295.9 | 318.7 | 361.9 | 504.9 | 372.0 | 307.0 |
| I-B | 364.7 | 331.4 | 291.5 | 398.3 | 355.8 | 383.9 | 331.1 | 355.3 | 407.3 | 579.2 | 416.3 | 343.0 |
| II-B | 342.8 | 311.7 | 274.0 | 374.2 | 334.1 | 360.6 | 311.7 | 335.0 | 382.0 | 533.8 | 391.5 | 323.2 |
| III-B | 323.2 | 294.0 | 258.3 | 352.3 | 314.5 | 339.8 | 294.2 | 316.7 | 359.3 | 501.1 | 369.1 | 305.4 |

that expenditures for education will rise so rapidly. A graphic summary of the change in the composition of personal consumption is shown in Figure 7.3, which depicts the estimated 1970 shares and the average projected share for the year 2000.

It should be noted that the amount of variation between projection series in terms of composition of demand is minimal; differences in the share of total consumption diverted to any category differ by no more than half a percentage point between series.

At this juncture, it is enlightening to shift from analysis of dollar volume of demand to analysis of demand for physical units. One of the most meaningful and fruitful areas for this type of analysis is housing. The number of housing units required at any point in time is basically the number of households (as noted earlier a *household* is a person or persons occupying a separate housing unit). To this should be added some additional vacant units. It is obvious, though, that the housing requirements of the population will change along with the age of the head and size of the household. This final analysis, then, will look at projected changes in households in light of the probable effects on demand for housing by type (single unit, multiunit, mobile).

As noted above, the number of households (and occupied housing units) in Virginia stood at 1.4 million in 1970. To this should be added some 102,000 vacant units, 8,000 of which are classified as seasonal or migratory units. Hence, of total "year–round units," 1.4 million were occupied and 94,000 were vacant. The vacancy rate, then, stood at 6.4 percent.

It has already been established that the number of households in Virginia will be 2.0–2.3 million by the end of the century (see Table 7.12); hence, the net change in housing stock should be in the 0.6–0.9 million range. The net change, in turn, may be regarded as the number of additions to the housing stock less removals. In addition to units required for newly formed households, additional units will have to be constructed to replace units which go out of the housing stock. This latter may be categorized as replacement demand.

The differences in projected net increase in demand for housing among the alternative population projections become increasingly great over time. These differences are shown in Table 7.24.

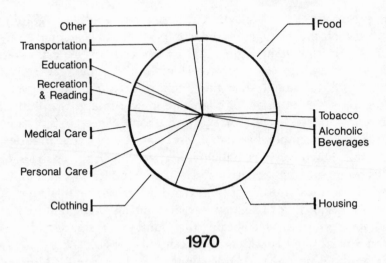

1970

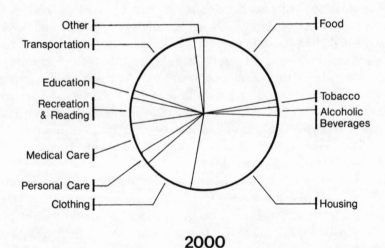

2000

Fig. 7.3.   Distribution of expenditure by category, Virginia, 1970 and 2000

Table 7.24. Projected increments in total net housing demand, Virginia, 1970-2000

| Period | Projection Series | | | | | |
|---|---|---|---|---|---|---|
| | I-A | II-A | III-A | I-B | II-B | III-B |
| 1970-80 | 305,674 | 290,541 | 274,920 | 305,674 | 290,541 | 274,920 |
| 1980-90 | 310,970 | 262,135 | 216,439 | 310,689 | 261,465 | 216,168 |
| 1990-00 | 298,951 | 241,848 | 170,308 | 281,375 | 212,983 | 155,354 |
| 1970-90 | 616,644 | 552,676 | 491,359 | 616,363 | 552,006 | 491,088 |
| 1970-2000 | 915,595 | 794,524 | 661,667 | 897,738 | 764,989 | 646,442 |

Between 1970 and 1980 the net increase in the number of households is projected to increase by 275,000–305,000; between 1970 and 1990, by 490,000–615,000; and between 1970 and 2000 by 645,000–915,000. Projected levels of migration are a much more significant determinant in this case than are fertility trends. The A and B series differ by only modest amounts in all cases, while most of the wide divergence occurs between Series I, II, and III. Since by the end of the century projected birth differentials will only affect the population under the age of 30 (and hence, only a small proportion of households), this result is not unduly surprising.

The Series I projections show that net demand, per decade, is more or less constant over the three decades of the projection period. In Series II and Series III, however, net demand declines during each decade, so that the increase required in the 1990–2000 decade is somewhat less than that required in the 1980–90 decade, which, in turn, is less than that required for the 1970–80 decade.

It has been suggested that "age is . . . [the] most important [indication of housing demand] since it services as a good indication for many related variables. For example, sex ratio, marital status, income, and assets all have age–related cycles."[13] Not only do age composition changes affect the number and size of households, but they will also play a large role in determining the type of housing unit demanded by the household. In projecting housing needs for

[13] Thomas C. Marcin, *The Effects of Declining Population Growth on the Demand for Housing* (St. Paul: North Central Forest Experiment Station, 1974), p. 1.

the United States, Thomas C. Marcin has developed "incremental occupancy rates" by age of head and household, specific to type of unit (single family, multiunit, mobile). These are presented in Table 7.25. Using these incremental rates, plus the existing housing stock by type as of 1970, it then becomes possible to trace out change in net demand for housing as a function of type of unit.

Table 7.25.   Incremental occupancy rates by age of head of household and type of unit, 1970-2000   (percent)

| Age | Single Unit | Multiunit | Mobil |
|---|---|---|---|
| 15-24 | 5 | 65 | 30 |
| 25-29 | 30 | 45 | 25 |
| 30-34 | 50 | 32 | 18 |
| 35-44 | 65 | 22 | 13 |
| 45-54 | 63 | 24 | 13 |
| 55-64 | 55 | 28 | 17 |
| 65+ | 49 | 33 | 18 |

Source:   Marcin, p. 5.

Complete data relating age of head of household to type of unit occupied for Virginia in 1970 are not available from regular census materials. To estimate these data, national public use sample data compiled by Marcin[14] were used, with state totals for occupied units by type used as controls. These base data are given in Table 7.26.

Net additional housing demand by type of units is shown in Table 7.27. This table shows that the greatest increase on a relative basis will occur for mobile units, followed by units in multiple structures (i.e., apartments), and finally by single-family units. These differences reflect not only changes in the age composition of population but also a declining preference for single-family units with corresponding increases in demand for other varieties. Much of this may well reflect, implicitly, the soaring costs of home ownership which has been widely discussed in recent years. In any event, about three-fourths of housing units occupied by Virginians in 1970 were of the single-family variety.

[14] Ibid., p. 5.

Table 7.26. Estimated number of occupied units by type and age of head, Virginia, 1970

| Age | Single Unit | Multiunit | Mobile | Total |
|-----|-------------|-----------|--------|-------|
| 15-24 | 50,805 | 55,548 | 10,782 | 117,135 |
| 25-29 | 95,239 | 44,588 | 8,429 | 148,256 |
| 30-34 | 104,621 | 26,116 | 4,514 | 135,251 |
| 35-44 | 231,602 | 40,046 | 6,073 | 277,721 |
| 45-54 | 229,594 | 45,016 | 6,178 | 280,788 |
| 55-64 | 174,129 | 38,909 | 7,312 | 220,350 |
| 65+ | 157,482 | 50,535 | 7,284 | 215,301 |
| Total | 1,043,472 | 300,758 | 50,572 | 1,394,802 |

Table 7.27. New additional housing units required, Virginia, 2000

| Series | Number | | | Percent age of 1970 Units | | |
|--------|--------|--|--|---------------------------|--|--|
| | Single Unit | Multiunit | Mobile | Single Unit | Multiunit | Mobile |
| I-A | 500,919 | 266,332 | 148,543 | 48.0 | 88.6 | 293.7 |
| II-A | 498,351 | 255,919 | 142,466 | 47.8 | 85.1 | 283.7 |
| III-A | 434,705 | 231,123 | 128,696 | 41.7 | 76.8 | 254.5 |
| I-B | 429,653 | 214,784 | 120,552 | 41.2 | 71.4 | 238.4 |
| II-B | 367,918 | 187,734 | 105,515 | 35.3 | 62.4 | 208.6 |
| III-B | 367,252 | 179,516 | 96,154 | 35.2 | 59.7 | 190.1 |

By the end of the century, this proportion should decline to 67–70 percent. Conversely, 21.6 percent of the units occupied in 1970 were in multiunit structures and 3.6 percent were mobile. By the end of the century, these shares are likely to increase to 23–24 and 7–8 percent, respectively. In general, the slower the rate of population growth, the relatively larger is the share of increased demand for single units and the smaller the share for multiunits and mobile units.

The volume of replacement demand will not depend on population growth, but rather on the age and structural characteristics of housing units in the 1970 stock. In 1970 some 161,000 occupied housing units lacked one or more plumbing facilities (piped water, flush toilet, and bathtub or shower). These units would seem to be the most likely immediate candidates for replacement.

Another means of identifying housing units which may need to be replaced is analysis of the age of housing units. If units more than fifty years old are arbitrarily so classified, then by 1990 some 413,000 units will need to be replaced, with an additional 214,000 requiring replacement between 1990 and 2000. By considering only the age of housing unit, then, replacement demand can be estimated to total nearly 630,000 units between 1970 and 2000. Consequently, the total number of housing units that will be required to satisfy the demand of new households and to replace old units will range from 1.27 to 1.55 million. If some units that do not meet the age criteria but do contain plumbing deficiencies are also discarded, then the total gross increment to the housing stock of Virginia that will be required between 1970 and 2000 will probably range from 1.4 to 1.7 million units. If recent price level tendencies for housing continue, it is likely that a substantial portion of the replacement sector will be devoted to relatively low priced units, no matter what variety.

Appendix Tables

# Appendix Tables

Table A2.1.  Population change in Virginia cities and counties, 1950-70

| Area | 1950 | 1960 | 1970 |
|------|------|------|------|
| 1. Lenowisco | 120,082 | 100,212 | 84,816 |
| Lee | 36,106 | 25,824 | 20,321 |
| Scott | 27,640 | 25,813 | 24,376 |
| Wise | 52,021 | 43,562[a,b] | 35,947 |
| Norton* | 4,315 | 5,013[a,b] | 4,172 |
| 2. Cumberland Plateau | 133,471 | 128,016 | 112,497 |
| Buchanan | 35,748 | 36,724 | 32,071 |
| Dickenson | 23,393 | 20,211 | 16,077 |
| Russell | 26,818 | 26,290 | 24,533 |
| Tazewell | 47,512 | 44,791 | 39,816 |
| 3. Mount Rogers | 161,514 | 160,065 | 159,412 |
| Bland | 6,436 | 5,982 | 5,423 |
| Carroll | 24,092 | 23,178[a] | 23,092[b] |
| Grayson | 18,734 | 17,390[a] | 15,439[b] |
| Smyth | 30,187 | 31,066 | 31,349 |
| Washington | 37,536 | 38,076 | 40,835 |
| Wythe | 23,327 | 21,975 | 22,139 |
| Bristol* | 15,954 | 17,144 | 14,857 |
| Galax* | 5,248 | 5,254[a] | 6,278[b] |
| 4. New River Valley | 96,871 | 97,233 | 114,833 |
| Floyd | 11,351 | 10,462 | 9,775 |
| Giles | 18,956 | 17,219 | 16,741 |
| Montgomery | 29,780 | 32,923 | 47,157[b] |
| Pulaski | 27,758 | 27,258 | 29,564 |
| Radford* | 9,026 | 9,371 | 11,596[b] |
| 5. Fifth | 181,559 | 207,332 | 231,175 |
| Alleghany | 17,279 | 12,128[a,b] | 12,461[b] |
| Botetourt | 15,766 | 16,175 | 18,193 |
| Craig | 3,452 | 3,356 | 3,524 |
| Roanoke | 34,663 | 45,635 | 67,339[a,b] |
| Clifton Forge* | 5,795 | 5,268 | 5,501[b] |
| Covington* | 5,860 | 11,062 | 10,060 |
| Roanoke* | 91,921 | 97,110 | 92,115[b] |
| Salem* | 13,841 | 15,110 | 14,643 |

Table A2.1   (cont.)

| Area | 1950 | 1960 | 1970 |
|------|------|------|------|
| 6. Central Shenandoah | 151,265 | 166,585 | 186,306 |
| Augusta | 34,154 | 37,363[b] | 44,220 |
| Bath | 6,296 | 5,335 | 5,192 |
| Highland | 4,069 | 3,221 | 2,529 |
| Rockbridge | 17,383 | 16,502 | 16,637[a] |
| Rockingham | 35,079 | 40,485[b] | 47,890[b] |
| Buena Vista* | 5,214 | 6,300 | 6,425[b] |
| Harrisonburg* | 10,810 | 11,916[b] | 14,605[b] |
| Lexington* | 5,976 | 7,537 | 7,597[a] |
| Staunton* | 19,927 | 22,232[b] | 24,504 |
| Waynesboro* | 12,357 | 15,694[b] | 16,707 |
| 7. Lord Fairfax | 89,574 | 97,045 | 106,372 |
| Clarke | 7,074 | 7,942 | 8,102 |
| Frederick | 17,537 | 21,941 | 28,893 |
| Page | 15,152 | 15,572 | 16,581 |
| Shenandoah | 21,169 | 21,825 | 22,852 |
| Warren | 14,801 | 14,655 | 15,301 |
| Winchester* | 13,841 | 15,110 | 14,643 |
| 8. Northern Virginia | 347,087 | 601,811 | 921,276 |
| Arlington | 135,449 | 163,401 | 174,284 |
| Fairfax | 96,611 | 248,997[b] | 455,032[a,b] |
| Loudoun | 21,147 | 24,549 | 37,150 |
| Prince William | 22,612 | 50,164 | 111,102[b] |
| Alexandria* | 61,787 | 91,023[a] | 110,927[b] |
| Fairfax* | 1,946 | 13,585 | 22,009[a] |
| Falls Church* | 7,535 | 10,192 | 10,772 |
| 9. Rappahannock-Rapidan | 61,630 | 65,609 | 72,222 |
| Culpeper | 13,242 | 15,088 | 18,218 |
| Fauquier | 21,248 | 24,066 | 26,375 |
| Madison | 8,273 | 8,187 | 8,638 |
| Orange | 12,755 | 12,900 | 13,792 |
| Rappahannock | 6,112 | 5,368 | 5,199 |
| 10. Thomas Jefferson | 91,365 | 98,049 | 115,235 |
| Albermarle | 26,662 | 30,969 | 37,780[b] |
| Fluvanna | 7,121 | 7,227 | 7,621 |
| Greene | 4,745 | 4,715 | 5,248 |
| Louisa | 12,826 | 12,959 | 14,004 |
| Nelson | 14,042 | 12,752 | 11,702 |
| Charlottesville* | 25,969 | 29,427 | 38,880[b] |

Table A2.1 (cont.)

| Area | 1950 | 1960 | 1970 |
|------|------|------|------|
| 11. Central Virginia | 135,327 | 150,877 | 165,997 |
| Amherst | 20,332 | 22,953 | 26,072 |
| Appomattox | 8,764 | 9,148 | 9.784 |
| Bedford | 25,566 | 25,107[b] | 26,728[a] |
| Campbell | 28,877 | 32,958[b] | 43,319 |
| Lynchburg* | 47,727 | 54,790[b] | 54,083 |
| Bedford* | 4,061 | 5,921 | 6,011 |
| 12. West Piedmont | 189,834 | 205,213 | 219,179 |
| Franklin | 24,560 | 25,925 | 28,163[b] |
| Henry | 31,219 | 40,335[b] | 50,901[b] |
| Patrick | 15,642 | 15,282 | 15,282 |
| Pittsylvania | 66,096 | 58,296[b] | 58,789[b] |
| Danville* | 35,066 | 46,577[b] | 46,391[b] |
| Martinsville* | 17,251 | 18,798[b] | 19,653[b] |
| 13. Southside | 95,075 | 88,818 | 82,563 |
| Brunswick | 20,136 | 17,779 | 16,172 |
| Halifax | 35,385 | 33,637[a] | 30,076[b] |
| Mecklenburg | 33,497 | 31,428 | 29,426 |
| South Boston* | 6,057 | 5,974[a] | 6,889[a] |
| 14. Piedmont | 86,498 | 80,205 | 77,060 |
| Amelia | 7,908 | 7,815 | 7,592 |
| Buckingham | 12,288 | 10,877 | 10,597 |
| Charlotte | 14,057 | 13,368 | 12,366 |
| Cumberland | 7,252 | 6,360 | 6,179 |
| Lunenburg | 14,116 | 12,523 | 11,687 |
| Nottoway | 15,479 | 15,141 | 14,260 |
| Prince Edward | 15,398 | 14,121 | 14,379 |
| 15. Richmond Regional | 373,196 | 461,993 | 547,542 |
| Charles City | 4,676 | 5,492 | 6,158 |
| Chesterfield | 40,400 | 71,197[c] | 77,045[b] |
| Goochland | 8,934 | 9,206 | 10,069 |
| Hanover | 21,985 | 27,550 | 37,479 |
| Henrico | 57,340 | 117,339 | 154,364 |
| New Kent | 3,995 | 4,504 | 5,300 |
| Powhatan | 5,556 | 6,747 | 7,696 |
| Richmond* | 230,310 | 219,958 | 249,431 |

Table A2.1  (cont.)

| Area | 1950 | 1960 | 1970 |
|------|------|------|------|
| 16. RADCO | 55,161 | 64,302 | 77,425 |
| Caroline | 12,471 | 12,725 | 13,925 |
| King George | 6,710 | 7,243 | 8,039 |
| Spotsylvania | 11,920 | 13,819[b] | 16,424 |
| Stafford | 11,902 | 16,876 | 24,587 |
| Fredericksburg* | 12,158 | 13,639[b] | 14,450 |
| 17. Northern Neck | 34,989 | 36,776 | 37,011 |
| Lancaster | 8,640 | 9,174 | 9,126 |
| Northumberland | 10,012 | 10,185 | 9,239 |
| Richmond | 6,189 | 6,375 | 6,504 |
| Westmoreland | 10,148 | 11,042 | 12,142 |
| 18. Middle Peninsula | 44,624 | 45,501 | 47,609 |
| Essex | 6,530 | 6,690 | 7,099 |
| Gloucester | 10,343 | 11,919 | 14,059 |
| King and Queen | 6,299 | 5,889 | 5,491 |
| King William | 7,589 | 7,563 | 7,497 |
| Mathews | 7,148 | 7,121 | 7,168 |
| Middlesex | 6,715 | 6,319 | 6,295 |
| 19. Carter | 125,192 | 141,471 | 161,059 |
| Dinwiddie | 18,839 | 22,183 | 25,046 |
| Greensville | 10,655 | 10,620 | 9,604[a,b] |
| Prince George | 19,679 | 20,270[b] | 29,092[b] |
| Surry | 12,785 | 12,411 | 11,464 |
| Colonial Heights* | 6,077 | 9,587[c] | 15,097 |
| Emporia* | 5,664 | 5,535 | 5,300[a,b] |
| Hopewell* | 10,219 | 17,895[b] | 23,471[b] |
| Petersburg* | 35,054 | 36,750[b] | 36,103 |
| 20. Southeastern Virginia | 525,205 | 666,841 | 769,371 |
| Isle of Wight | 14,906 | 17,164 | 18,285 |
| Southampton | 21,852 | 19,931 | 18,582[a] |
| Chesapeake*,[d] | 110,371 | 73,647[b] | 89,580[b] |
| Franklin* | 4,670 | 7,264 | 6,880[a] |
| Norfolk* | 213,513 | 304,869[b] | 307,951 |
| Portsmouth* | 80,039 | 114,773[b] | 110,963[b] |
| Suffolk*,[e] | 37,577 | 43,975 | 45,024 |
| Virginia Beach,[f] | 42,277 | 85,218[b] | 172,106 |
| 21. Peninsula | 168,029 | 242,874 | 219,081 |
| James City | 6,317 | 11,539 | 17,853[b] |
| York | 11,750 | 21,583 | 33,203[b] |
| Hampton*,[g] | 60,994 | 89,258 | 120,779 |
| Newport News*,[h] | 82,233 | 113,662 | 138,177 |
| Williamsburg* | 6,735 | 6,832 | 9,069[b] |

Table A2.1 (cont.)

| Area | 1950 | 1960 | 1970 |
|------|------|------|------|
| 22. Accomack-<br>    Northampton | 51,132 | 47,601 | 43,446 |
| Accomack | 33,832 | 30,635 | 29,004 |
| Northampton | 17,300 | 16,966 | 14,442 |

* City.

a.  City incorporated during preceding decade.

b.  Annexation during preceding decade

c.  Part of Chesterfield County annexed by Colonial Heights (District 19) be-
    tween 1950 and 1960.

d.  Chesapeake was formed by the merger of Norfolk County and the city of South Norfolk
    in 1963.  Portions of these areas were annexed by the city of Portsmouth in 1963.

e.  Suffolk was formed by the merger of

f.  Virginia Beach was formed by the merger of Princes Anne County and the city of
    Virginia Beach in 1963.

g.  Hampton was formed by the merger of Elizabeth City County and the city of Hampton
    in 1952.

h.  Newport News was formed by the merger of the cities of Newport News and Warwick
    in 1958.

Table A4.1.  Components of population change by race in Virginia cities and counties, 1960-70

White Population

| Planning Districts 1-5 | Total | | Change | Natural Increase | Net Migration |
|---|---|---|---|---|---|
| | 1960 | 1970 | | | |
| 1. Lenowisco | 98,106 | 83,352 | -14,754 | 6,987 | -21,741 |
| Lee | 25,655 | 20,220 | -5,435 | 1,003 | -6,438 |
| Scott | 25,502 | 24,158 | -1,344 | 1,984 | -3,328 |
| Wise | 42,334 | 35,052 | -7,282 | 3,600 | -10,882 |
| Norton | 4,615 | 3,922[a] | -693 | 400 | -1,093 |
| 2. Cumberland Plateau | 125,330 | 110,767 | -14,563 | 14,528 | -29,091 |
| Buchanan | 36,714 | 32,021 | -4,693 | 6,387 | -11,080 |
| Dickenson | 20,053 | 15,956 | -4,097 | 2,011 | -6,108 |
| Russell | 25,782 | 24,222 | -1,560 | 2,199 | -2,759 |
| Tazewell | 42,781 | 38,568 | -4,213 | 3,931 | -8,144 |
| 3. Mount Rogers | 155,184 | 154,930 | -254 | 12,273 | -12,527 |
| Bland | 5,783 | 5,283 | -500 | 200 | -720 |
| Carroll-Grayson-Galax[b] | 44,719 | 43,770 | -949 | 2,790 | -3,739 |
| Smyth | 30,561 | 30,781 | 220 | 2,907 | -2,687 |
| Washington | 37,119 | 40,027 | 2,298 | 3,640 | -732 |
| Wythe | 21,014 | 21,289 | 275 | 1,595 | -1,320 |
| Bristol | 15,988 | 13,780 | -2,208 | 1,121 | -3,329 |
| 4. New River Valley | 92,282 | 109,867 | 17,585 | 10,746 | 6,839 |
| Floyd | 9,929 | 9,229 | -700 | 333 | -1,033 |
| Giles | 16,777 | 16,334 | -433 | 1,591 | -2,024 |
| Montgomery | 31,394 | 45,519 | 14,125 | 5,135 | 8,990 |
| Pulaski | 25,441 | 27,731 | 2,290 | 2,804 | -514 |
| Radford | 8,741 | 11,044 | 2,303 | 883 | 1,420 |
| 5. Fifth | 182,740 | 206,113 | 23,373 | 15,666 | 7,707 |
| Alleghany-Clifton Forge[b] | 15,884 | 16,695 | 811 | 1,279 | -468 |
| Botetourt | 15,190 | 16,703 | 1,513 | 1,077 | 436 |
| Craig | 3,351 | 3,509 | 158 | 127 | 31 |
| Roanoke-Roanoke-Salem | 138,579 | 160,364 | 21,785 | 12,236 | 9,549 |
| Covington | 9,736 | 8,842 | -894 | 947 | -1,841 |

Table A4.1 (cont.)

| Nonwhite Population | | | | | |
|---|---|---|---|---|---|
| | Total | | | Natural | Net |
| Planning Districts 1-5 | 1960 | 1970 | Change | Increase | Migration |
| 1. Lenowisco | 2,106 | 1,464 | -642 | 54 | -696 |
| Lee | 169 | 101 | -68 | -13 | -55 |
| Scott | 311 | 218 | -93 | 12 | -105 |
| Wise | 1,245 | 895 | -350 | 1 | -351 |
| Norton | 381 | 250 | -131 | 54 | -185 |
| 2. Cumberland | 2,686 | 1,730 | -956 | 59 | -1,015 |
| Buchanan | 10 | 50 | 40 | 3 | 37 |
| Dickenson | 158 | 121 | -37 | 5 | -42 |
| Russell | 508 | 311 | -197 | 34 | -231 |
| Tazewell | 2,010 | 1,248 | -762 | 17 | -779 |
| 3. Mount Rogers | 4,481 | 4,482 | -399 | 275 | -674 |
| Bland | 199 | 140 | -59 | -8 | -51 |
| Carroll-Grayson-Galax[b] | 1,103 | 1,039 | -64 | 114 | -178 |
| Smyth | 505 | 568 | 63 | 35 | 28 |
| Washington | 957 | 808 | -149 | 18 | -167 |
| Wythe | 961 | 850 | -111 | 64 | -175 |
| Bristol | 1,156 | 1,077 | -79 | 52 | -131 |
| 4. New River Valley | 4,951 | 4,896 | -55 | 389 | -444 |
| Floyd | 533 | 476 | -57 | 58 | -115 |
| Giles | 442 | 397 | -45 | 61 | -106 |
| Montgomery | 1,529 | 1,638 | 109 | 71 | 38 |
| Pulaski | 1,817 | 1,833 | 16 | 183 | -167 |
| Radford | 630 | 552 | -78 | 16 | -94 |
| 5. Fifth | 24,592 | 25,062 | 470 | 2,176 | -1,697 |
| Alleghany-Clifton Forge[b] | 1,512 | 1,267 | -245 | 60 | -305 |
| Botetourt | 1,525 | 1,490 | -35 | 81 | -116 |
| Roanoke-Roanoke-Salem[c] | 20,224 | 21,072 | 848 | 1,939 | -1,091 |
| Covington | 1,326 | 1,218 | -108 | 87 | -195 |

Table A4.1 (cont.)

White Population

| Planning Districts 6-9 | 1960 Total | 1970 | Change | Natural Increase | Net Migration |
|---|---|---|---|---|---|
| 6. Central Shenandoah | 157,540 | 176,339 | 18,799 | 14,918 | 3,881 |
| Augusta | 37,728 | 42,208 | 6,480 | 3,531 | 2,949 |
| Bath | 4,835 | 4,632 | -203 | 337 | -540 |
| Highland | 3,203 | 2,515 | -688 | -51 | 637 |
| Rockbridge-Lexington[c] | 22,045 | 22,312 | 267 | 1,812 | -1,545 |
| Rockingham-Harrisonburg[b] | 50,942 | 60,989 | 10,047 | 5,286 | 4,761 |
| Buena Vista | 6,046 | 6,202 | 156 | 641 | -485 |
| Staunton | 20,029 | 21,917 | 1,888 | 1,052 | 836 |
| Waynesboro | 14,712 | 15,564 | 1,852 | 2,310 | -1,458 |
| 7. Lord Fairfax | 92,162 | 101,529 | 9,367 | 8,033 | 1,334 |
| Clarke | 6,573 | 6,888 | 315 | 430 | -115 |
| Frederick | 21,507 | 28,416 | 6,909 | 3,091 | 3,818 |
| Page | 15,094 | 16,097 | 1,003 | 1,123 | -120 |
| Shenandoah | 21,468 | 22,470 | 1,002 | 1,158 | -156 |
| Warren | 13,600 | 14,342 | 742 | 1,232 | -490 |
| Winchester | 13,920 | 13,316 | -604 | 999 | -1,603 |
| 8. Northern Virginia | 560,130 | 860,221 | 300,901 | 120,919 | 179,172 |
| Arlington | 154,172 | 161,329 | 7,157 | 24,650 | -17,493 |
| Fairfax-Fairfax[c] | 249,323[a] | 457,246 | 207,923 | 55,233 | 152,690 |
| Loudoun | 20,204 | 32,443 | 12,239 | 3,028 | 8,211 |
| Prince William | 46,032 | 104,438 | 58,406 | 18,406 | 40,194 |
| Alexandria | 80,388 | 94,233 | 13,845 | 18,406 | -4,561 |
| Falls Chruch | 10,011 | 10,532 | 521 | 1,390 | -869 |
| 9. Rappahannock-Rapidan | 49,556 | 56,297 | 6,741 | 4,205 | 2,536 |
| Culpeper | 10,945 | 13,818 | 2,873 | 838 | 2,035 |
| Fauquier | 17,818 | 20,455 | 2,637 | 2,119 | 518 |
| Madison | 6,357 | 6,857 | 500 | 416 | 84 |
| Orange | 10,013 | 10,836 | 823 | 616 | 207 |
| Rappahannock | 4,423 | 4,331 | -92 | 216 | -308 |

Table A4.1 (cont.)

Nonwhite Population

| Planning Districts 6-9 | Total | | Change | Natural Increase | Net Migration |
|---|---|---|---|---|---|
| | 1960 | 1970 | | | |
| 6. Central Shenandoah | 9,045 | 9,987 | 942 | 718 | 224 |
| Augusta | 1,635 | 2,012 | 377 | 183 | 194 |
| Bath | 500 | 560 | 60 | 0 | 60 |
| Highland | 18 | 14 | -4 | -4 | 0 |
| Rockbridge-Lexington[c] | 1,994 | 1,922 | -72 | 114 | -186 |
| Rockingham-Harrisonburg[b] | 1,459 | 1,526 | 67 | 88 | -21 |
| Buena Vista | 254 | 223 | -31 | 15 | -46 |
| Staunton | 2,203 | 2,587 | 384 | 185 | 199 |
| Waynesboro | 982 | 1,143 | 161 | 137 | 24 |
| 7. Lord Fairfax | 4,883 | 4,843 | -40 | 520 | -560 |
| Clarke | 1,369 | 1,214 | -155 | 110 | -265 |
| Frederick | 434 | 477 | 43 | 97 | -54 |
| Page | 478 | 484 | 6 | 52 | -46 |
| Shenandoah | 357 | 382 | 25 | 37 | -12 |
| Warren | 1,055 | 959 | -96 | 125 | -221 |
| Winchester | 1,190 | 1,327 | 137 | 99 | 38 |
| 8. Northern Virginia | 41,681 | 61,016 | 19,335 | 9,037 | 10,298 |
| Arlington | 9,229 | 12,955 | 3,726 | 1,965 | 1,761 |
| Fairfax-Fairfax[c] | 13,159[a] | 19,745 | 6,586 | 2,638 | 3,948 |
| Loudoun | 4,345 | 4,707 | 362 | 752 | -390 |
| Prince William | 4,132 | 6,664 | 2,532 | 1,200 | 1,332 |
| Alexandria | 10,635 | 16,705 | 6,070 | 2,455 | 3,615 |
| Falls Church | 181 | 240 | 59 | 27 | 32 |
| 9. Rappahannock-Rapidan | 16,053 | 15,925 | -128 | 2,311 | -2,439 |
| Culpeper | 4,143 | 4,400 | 257 | 715 | -458 |
| Fauquier | 6,248 | 5,920 | -328 | 859 | -1,187 |
| Madison | 1,830 | 1,781 | -49 | 216 | -265 |
| Orange | 2,887 | 2,956 | 69 | 470 | -401 |
| Rappahannock | 945 | 868 | -77 | 51 | -128 |

Table A4.1 (cont.)

White Population

| Planning Districts 10-14 | Total 1960 | 1970 | Change | Natural Increase | Net Migration |
|---|---|---|---|---|---|
| 10. Thomas Jefferson | 75,814 | 91,969 | 16,155 | 7,727 | 8,428 |
| Albemarle-Charlottesville[c] | 50,193 | 65,472 | 15,279 | 6,736 | 8,543 |
| Fluvanna | 4,502 | 4,880 | 378 | 114 | 264 |
| Greene | 4,129 | 4,681 | 552 | 479 | 73 |
| Louisa | 7,793 | 8,589 | 796 | 182 | 614 |
| Nelson | 9,197 | 8,347 | -850 | 216 | -1,066 |
| 11. Central Virginia | 118,943 | 132,791 | 13,848 | 9,924 | 3,924 |
| Amherst | 17,439 | 20,330 | 2,891 | 1,087 | 1,804 |
| Appomattox | 6,818 | 7,354 | 536 | 400 | 136 |
| Campbell | 26,004 | 36,448 | 10,444 | 4,099 | 6,345 |
| Lynchburg-Bedford-Bedford[b,c] | 68,682 | 68,659 | -23 | 4,338 | -4,361 |
| 12. West Piedmont | 153,751 | 16,894 | 13,143 | 16,123 | -2,980 |
| Franklin | 22,178 | 24,314[a] | 2,136 | 2,128 | 8 |
| Henry-Martinsville[b] | 44,328 | 53,814 | 9,486 | 7,264 | 2,222 |
| Patrick | 13,902 | 13,987 | 85 | 1,275 | -1,190 |
| Pittsylvania-Danville[b] | 73,343 | 74,779 | 1,436 | 5,456 | -4,020 |
| 13. Southside | 46,797 | 46,263 | -534 | 2,762 | -3,296 |
| Brunswick | 7,348 | 6,713 | -635 | 97 | 732 |
| Halifax-South Boston[b] | 22,732 | 22,545 | -187 | 1,654 | 1,841 |
| Mecklenburg | 16,717 | 17,005 | 288 | 1,011 | 723 |
| 14. Piedmont | 45,153 | 44,784 | -369 | 1,293 | 1,662 |
| Amelia | 3,806 | 3,985 | 179 | 145 | 34 |
| Buckingham | 6,015 | 5,891[a] | -124 | 99 | -223 |
| Charlotte | 8,037 | 7,435[a] | -602 | 349 | -951 |
| Cumberland | 2,910 | 3,211 | 301 | 98 | 203 |
| Lunenburg | 7,233 | 6,622 | -611 | 83 | -694 |
| Nottoway | 8,664 | 8,543 | -121 | 306 | -424 |
| Prince Edward | 8,488 | 9,097 | 609 | 213 | -396 |

Table A4.1 (cont.)

| Nonwhite Population Planning Districts 10-14 | Total 1960 | Total 1970 | Change | Natural Increase | Net Migration |
|---|---|---|---|---|---|
| 10. Thomas Jefferson | 22,235 | 23,266 | 1,031 | 3,051 | -2,020 |
| Albemarle-Charlottesville | 10,203 | 11,188 | 985 | 1,206 | -221 |
| Fluvanna | 2,725 | 2,741 | 16 | 478 | -462 |
| Greene | 586 | 567 | -19 | 66 | -85 |
| Louisa | 5,166 | 5,415 | 249 | 835 | -586 |
| Nelson | 3,555 | 3,355 | -200 | 466 | -666 |
| 11. Central Virginia | 31,934 | 33,206 | 1,272 | 4,448 | -3,176 |
| Amherst | 5,514 | 5,742 | 228 | 919 | -691 |
| Appomattox | 2,330 | 2,430 | 100 | 338 | -238 |
| Campbell | 6,954 | 6,871 | -83 | 1,159 | -1,242 |
| Lynchburg-Bedford-Bedford[b,c] | 17,136 | 18,163 | 1,027 | 2,032 | -1,005 |
| 12. West Piedmont | 51,462 | 52,285 | 823 | 8,900 | -8,077 |
| Franklin | 3,747 | 3,849[a] | 102 | 637 | -535 |
| Henry-Martinsville[b] | 14,805 | 16,740 | 1,935 | 3,128 | -1,193 |
| Patrick | 1,380 | 1,295 | -85 | 218 | -303 |
| Pittsylvania-Danville[b] | -31,530 | 30,401 | -1,129 | 4,917 | -6,046 |
| 13. Southside | 42,079 | 36,300 | -5,719 | 5,253 | -10,972 |
| Brunswick | 10,431 | 9,459 | -972 | 1,157 | -2,129 |
| Halifax-South Boston[b] | 16,877 | 14,420 | -2,457 | 2,186 | -4,643 |
| Mecklenburg | 14,711 | 12,421 | -2,290 | 1,910 | -4,200 |
| 14. Piedmont | 35,052 | 32,276 | -2,776 | 4,810 | -7,586 |
| Amelia | 4,009 | 3,607 | -402 | 452 | -854 |
| Buckingham | 4,862 | 4,706[a] | -156 | 915 | -1,071 |
| Charlotte | 5,331 | 4,931[a] | -400 | 855 | -1,255 |
| Cumberland | 3,450 | 2,968 | -482 | 424 | -906 |
| Lunenburg | 5,290 | 5,065 | -225 | 784 | -1,009 |
| Nottoway | 6,477 | 5,717 | -760 | 689 | -1,449 |
| Prince Edward | 5,633 | 5,282 | -351 | 691 | -1,042 |

Table A4.1 (cont.)

White Population

| Planning Districts 15-19 | Total | | Change | Natural Increase | Net Migration |
|---|---|---|---|---|---|
| | 1960 | 1970 | | | |
| 15. Richmond Regional | 333,106 | 400,903 | 67,797 | 33,651 | 34,146 |
| Charles City | 917 | 1,048 | 131 | 74 | 57 |
| Chesterfield-Richmond[b] | 189,389 | 211,869 | 22,480 | 13,714 | 8,766 |
| Goochland | 4,773 | 5,679 | 906 | 298 | 608 |
| Hanover | 20,561 | 30,681 | 10,120 | 2,415 | 7,705 |
| Henrico | 111,269 | 143,821 | 32,543 | 16,612 | 15,931 |
| New Kent | 2,126 | 2,923 | 797 | 188 | 609 |
| Powhatan | 4,071 | 4,891 | 820 | 350 | 470 |
| 16. RADCO | 47,919 | 59,485 | 11,566 | 6,381 | 5,185 |
| Caroline | 6,037 | 6,659 | 622 | 428 | 194 |
| King George | 5,283 | 5,885 | 602 | 676 | -74 |
| Spotsylvania | 10,663 | 12,807 | 2,144 | 1,281 | 863 |
| Stafford | 14,900 | 22,238 | 7,338 | 3,263 | 4,075 |
| Fredericksburg | 11,036 | 11,896 | 860 | 733 | 127 |
| 17. Northern Neck | 21,406 | 22,083 | 677 | -25 | 702 |
| Lancaster | 5,535 | 5,586 | 51 | -56 | 107 |
| Northumberland | 5,840 | 5,617 | -223 | -169 | -54 |
| Richmond | 4,159 | 4,120[a] | -39 | 201 | -240 |
| Westmoreland | 5,872 | 6,760 | 888 | -1 | 889 |
| 18. Middle | 27,893 | 31,115 | 3,222 | 524 | 2,698 |
| Essex | 3,590 | 3,893 | 384 | 157 | 227 |
| Gloucester | 8,562 | 10,918 | 2,356 | 578 | 1,778 |
| King and Queen | 2,759 | 2,654 | -105 | 50 | -155 |
| King William | 3,999 | 4,194 | 195 | 201 | -6 |
| Mathews | 5,364 | 5,504 | 140 | -328 | 468 |
| Middlesex | 3,700 | 3,952 | 252 | -134 | 386 |
| 19. Crater | 81,450 | 100,375 | 18,925 | 11,048 | 7,877 |
| Dinwiddie | 8,450 | 13,597 | 5,098 | 1,206 | 3,892 |
| Greensville-Emporia[c] | 7,281 | 7,359 | 78 | 467 | -389 |
| Prince George-Hopewell[b] | 30,349 | 42,081 | 11,732 | 6,491 | 5,241 |
| Surry | 2,196 | 2,029 | -167 | -94 | -73 |
| Sussex | 4,186 | 4,210 | 24 | 120 | -96 |
| Colonial Heights | 9,567 | 15,015 | 5,484 | 1,503 | 3,981 |
| Petersburg | 19,372 | 16,048 | -3,324 | 1,355 | -4,679 |

Table A4.1 (cont.)

| Nonwhite Population Planning Districts 15-19 | Total 1960 | 1970 | Change | Natural Increase | Net Migration |
|---|---|---|---|---|---|
| 15. Richmond Regional | 128,887 | 146,630 | 17,743 | 17,526 | 217 |
| Charles City | 4,575 | 5,110 | 535 | 863 | 328 |
| Chesterfield-Richmond[b] | 101,766 | 114,607 | 12,841 | 13,315 | 474 |
| Goochland | 4,433 | 4,390 | -43 | 644 | 687 |
| Hanover | 6,989 | 6,789 | -200 | 1,191 | 1,391 |
| Henrico | 6,070 | 10,552 | 4,482 | 958 | 3,524 |
| New Kent | 2,378 | 2,377 | -1 | 346 | -347 |
| Powhatan | 2,676 | 2,805 | 129 | 209 | -80 |
| 16. RADCO | 16,383 | 17,940 | 1,557 | 3,010 | -1,453 |
| Caroline | 6,688 | 7,266 | 578 | 1,138 | -560 |
| King George | 1,960 | 2,154 | 194 | 376 | -182 |
| Spotsylvania | 3,156 | 3,617 | 461 | 562 | -101 |
| Stafford | 1,976 | 2,349 | 373 | 526 | -153 |
| Fredericksburg | 2,603 | 2,554 | -49 | 408 | -457 |
| 17. Northern Neck | 15,370 | 14,928 | -442 | 2,151 | -2,593 |
| Lancaster | 3,639 | 3,540 | -99 | 455 | -554 |
| Northumberland | 4,345 | 3,622 | -723 | 379 | -1,105 |
| Richmond | 2,216 | 2,384[a] | 168 | 358 | -190 |
| Westmoreland | 5,170 | 5,382 | 212 | 959 | -747 |
| 18. Middle Peninsula | 17,608 | 16,494 | -1,114 | 1,690 | -2,804 |
| Essex | 3,181 | 3,206 | 25 | 480 | -455 |
| Gloucester | 3,357 | 3,141 | -216 | 213 | -429 |
| King and Queen | 3,130 | 2,837 | -293 | 277 | -570 |
| King William | 3,564 | 3,303 | -261 | 486 | -747 |
| Mathews | 1,757 | 1,664 | -93 | 58 | -151 |
| Middlesex | 2,619 | 2,343 | -276 | 176 | -452 |
| 19. Crater | 60,021 | 60,684 | 663 | 9,438 | -8,775 |
| Dinwiddie | 13,684 | 11,449 | -2,235 | 1,533 | -3,768 |
| Greensville-Emporia[c] | 8,874 | 7,545 | -1,329 | 1,357 | -2,686 |
| Prince George-Hopewell[b] | 7,816 | 10,482 | 2,666 | 1,727 | 939 |
| Surry | 4,024 | 3,853 | -171 | 553 | -724 |
| Sussex | 8,225 | 7,254 | -971 | 1,288 | -2,259 |
| Colonial Heights | 20 | 46 | 26 | 7 | 19 |
| Petersburg | 17,378 | 20,005 | 2,677 | 2,973 | -296 |

Table A4.1 (cont.)

White Population

| Planning Districts 20-22 | Total | | Change | Natural Increase | Net Migration |
|---|---|---|---|---|---|
| | 1960 | 1970 | | | |
| 20. Southeastern Virginia | 464,851 | 545,181 | 80,330 | 76,124 | 4,206 |
| Isle of Wight | 8,133 | 9,206 | 1,073 | 433 | 640 |
| Southampton-Franklin[c] | 11,536 | 11,878 | 372 | 702 | -363 |
| Chesapeake-Portsmouth[b] | 129,397 | 134,579 | 5,182 | 17,593 | -12,411 |
| Norfolk | 225,251 | 215,069 | -10,182 | 35,809 | -45,991 |
| Suffolk | 19,483 | 19,626 | 143 | 1,299 | -1,156 |
| Virginia Beach | 71,051 | 154,823 | 83,772 | 20,285 | 63,487 |
| 21. Peninsula | 174,951 | 234,848 | 59,897 | 34,632 | 25,265 |
| James City-York-Williamsburg[b] | 30,186 | 47,576 | 17,390 | 4,779 | 12,611 |
| Hampton | 70,163 | 89,376 | 19,213 | 15,770 | 3,443 |
| Newport News | 74,602 | 97,896 | 23,294 | 14,083 | 9,211 |
| 22. Accomack-Northampton | 26,557 | 24,936 | -1,621 | -578 | -1,043 |
| Accomack | 18,779 | 18,101 | -678 | -502 | -176 |
| Northampton | 7,778 | 6,835 | -943 | -76 | -867 |

Table A4.1 (cont.)

Nonwhite Population

| Planning Districts 20-22 | Total 1960 | 1970 | Change | Natural Increase | Net Migration |
|---|---|---|---|---|---|
| 20. Southeastern Virginia | 201,990 | 221,590 | 19,600 | 34,074 | -14,474 |
| Isle of Wight | 9,031 | 9,079 | 48 | 1,703 | -1,655 |
| Southampton-Franklin[c] | 15,659 | 13,584 | -2,075 | 2,404 | 4,479 |
| Chesapeake-Portsmouth[b] | 59,023 | 65,964 | 6,941 | 9,826 | -2,885 |
| Norfolk | 80,621 | 92,882 | 12,261 | 14,298 | -2,037 |
| Suffolk | 24,492 | 22,798 | -1,694 | 3,118 | -4,812 |
| Virginia Beach | 13,164 | 17,283 | 4,119 | 2,725 | 1,394 |
| 21. Peninsula | 67,923 | 84,233 | 16,310 | 12,599 | 3,711 |
| James City-York-Williamsburg[b] | 9,768 | 12,549 | 2,781 | 1,915 | 866 |
| Hampton | 19,095 | 31,403 | 12,308 | 3,499 | 8,809 |
| Newport News | 39,060 | 40,281 | 1,221 | 7,185 | -5,964 |
| 22. Accomack-Northampton | 21,044 | 18,510 | -2,534 | 2,556 | -5,090 |
| Accomack | 11,856 | 10,903 | -953 | 1,591 | -2,472 |
| Northampton | 9,188 | 7,607 | -1,581 | 1,037 | -2,618 |

a  Adjusted for enumeration error.
b  Annexation.
c  New city incorporation.

*Appendix Tables*

Table A4.2. Marital status by race, sex, and age Virginia, 1950-70 (percent)

| All Races | | Men | | | Women | |
|---|---|---|---|---|---|---|
| | Single | Cur. Mar. | Sep., Div., Wid. | Single | Cur. Mar. | Sep., Div., Wid. |
| **All ages** | | | | | | |
| 1970 | 29.4 | 64.1 | 6.5 | 22.0 | 60.6 | 17.4 |
| 1960 | 27.5 | 66.1 | 6.4 | 19.4 | 64.3 | 16.3 |
| 1950 | 29.7 | 63.4 | 6.9 | 21.0 | 63.1 | 15.9 |
| **14 years** | | | | | | |
| 1970 | 98.2 | 1.5 | 0.3 | 98.9 | 0.9 | 0.2 |
| 1960 | 99.5 | 0.4 | 0.1 | 98.9 | 1.0 | 0.1 |
| 1950 | 99.1 | 0.6 | 0.3 | 99.2 | 0.7 | 0.1 |
| **15-29 years** | | | | | | |
| 1970 | 59.7 | 38.0 | 2.3 | 46.0 | 49.5 | 4.5 |
| 1960 | 60.5 | 37.7 | 1.8 | 41.8 | 54.8 | 4.4 |
| 1950 | 59.9 | 38.0 | 2.1 | 39.5 | 56.4 | 4.1 |
| **30-44 years** | | | | | | |
| 1970 | 8.2 | 86.0 | 5.8 | 5.4 | 83.9 | 10.7 |
| 1960 | 9.5 | 86.0 | 4.5 | 6.0 | 85.4 | 8.7 |
| 1950 | 11.2 | 83.4 | 5.4 | 8.5 | 82.0 | 9.5 |
| **45-64 years** | | | | | | |
| 1970 | 6.4 | 85.1 | 8.5 | 5.7 | 72.3 | 22.0 |
| 1960 | 7.4 | 84.1 | 8.5 | 7.2 | 70.3 | 22.5 |
| 1950 | 7.6 | 82.4 | 10.0 | 7.9 | 66.9 | 25.2 |
| **65 & older** | | | | | | |
| 1970 | 7.1 | 71.2 | 21.7 | 8.1 | 32.9 | 59.0 |
| 1960 | 6.3 | 70.5 | 23.2 | 8.5 | 32.7 | 58.8 |
| 1950 | 7.2 | 66.5 | 26.3 | 8.9 | 32.0 | 59.1 |

| White | | Men | | | Women | |
|---|---|---|---|---|---|---|
| | Single | Cur. Mar. | Sep., Div., Wid. | Single | Cur. Mar. | Sep., Div., Wid. |
| **All ages** | | | | | | |
| 1970 | 27.8 | 66.6 | 6.5 | 20.4 | 63.5 | 16.1 |
| 1960 | 26.1 | 68.7 | 5.2 | 18.3 | 66.9 | 14.8 |
| 1950 | 28.6 | 65.9 | 5.5 | 19.9 | 66.0 | 14.1 |
| **14 years** | | | | | | |
| 1970 | 98.3 | 1.4 | 0.3 | 99.0 | 0.8 | 0.2 |
| 1960 | 99.5 | 0.4 | 0.1 | 98.8 | 1.1 | 0.1 |
| 1950 | 98.9 | 0.7 | 0.4 | 99.3 | 0.6 | 0.1 |
| **15-29 years** | | | | | | |
| 1970 | 57.7 | 40.0 | 2.3 | 43.2 | 52.8 | 4.0 |
| 1960 | 58.6 | 39.7 | 1.7 | 39.6 | 56.5 | 3.9 |
| 1950 | 58.8 | 39.4 | 1.8 | 37.2 | 59.7 | 3.1 |
| **30-40 years** | | | | | | |
| 1970 | 6.9 | 88.2 | 4.9 | 4.5 | 87.0 | 8.5 |
| 1960 | 9.4 | 86.9 | 3.7 | 5.3 | 88.1 | 6.6 |
| 1950 | 9.6 | 86.5 | 3.9 | 7.9 | 85.1 | 7.0 |
| **45-64 years** | | | | | | |
| 1970 | 5.4 | 87.9 | 6.7 | 5.3 | 74.9 | 19.8 |
| 1960 | 7.8 | 85.7 | 6.5 | 7.1 | 72.9 | 20.0 |
| 1950 | 7.1 | 85.3 | 7.6 | 8.4 | 69.6 | 22.0 |
| **65 years & older** | | | | | | |
| 1970 | 6.4 | 73.9 | 19.7 | 8.3 | 33.6 | 58.1 |
| 1960 | 5.9 | 79.5 | 14.6 | 9.1 | 33.3 | 57.6 |
| 1950 | 7.3 | 68.5 | 24.2 | 9.7 | 33.1 | 57.2 |

Table A4.2 (cont.)

Nonwhite

| | | Men | | | Women | |
|---|---|---|---|---|---|---|
| | Single | Cur. Mar. | Sep., Div., Wid. | Single | Cur. Mar. | Sep., Div., Wid. |
| **All ages** | | | | | | |
| 1970 | 37.0 | 52.0 | 11.0 | 28.7 | 47.8 | 23.5 |
| 1960 | 33.4 | 55.3 | 11.3 | 24.0 | 53.3 | 22.7 |
| 1950 | 33.8 | 54.4 | 11.8 | 24.8 | 53.0 | 22.2 |
| **14 years** | | | | | | |
| 1970 | 97.7 | 2.3 | 0.0 | 98.9 | 0.9 | 0.2 |
| 1960 | 99.6 | 0.3 | 0.1 | 99.3 | 0.6 | 0.1 |
| 1950 | 99.8 | 0.1 | 0.1 | 99.1 | 0.7 | 0.2 |
| **15-29 years** | | | | | | |
| 1970 | 69.1 | 28.5 | 2.4 | 58.1 | 35.2 | 6.7 |
| 1960 | 68.6 | 28.8 | 2.6 | 50.5 | 43.1 | 6.4 |
| 1950 | 64.1 | 32.5 | 3.4 | 47.1 | 45.5 | 7.4 |
| **30-44 years** | | | | | | |
| 1970 | 15.2 | 74.1 | 10.7 | 9.4 | 69.2 | 21.4 |
| 1960 | 16.7 | 72.9 | 10.4 | 9.4 | 72.3 | 18.3 |
| 1950 | 17.1 | 71.5 | 11.4 | 10.9 | 70.2 | 18.9 |
| **45-64 years** | | | | | | |
| 1970 | 11.3 | 71.1 | 17.6 | 7.4 | 60.0 | 32.6 |
| 1960 | 11.8 | 71.3 | 16.9 | 7.6 | 59.4 | 33.0 |
| 1950 | 9.6 | 71.7 | 18.7 | 5.9 | 56.8 | 37.0 |
| **65 years & older** | | | | | | |
| 1970 | 9.5 | 60.0 | 30.5 | 7.0 | 29.5 | 63.5 |
| 1960 | 7.8 | 60.7 | 31.5 | 5.7 | 29.9 | 64.4 |
| 1950 | 6.7 | 59.1 | 34.2 | 5.5 | 27.3 | 67.2 |

Table A4.3.  Household characteristics by age, race, and sex, Virginia, Virginia, 1970-70 (percent)

| | Age | Total Male | Total Female | White Male | White Female | Nonwhite Male | Nonwhite Female |
|---|---|---|---|---|---|---|---|
| **Head of household** | | | | | | | |
| 1950 | 14-24 | 4.8 | 0.4 | 5.1 | 0.4 | 3.4 | 0.5 |
| | 25-34 | 21.8 | 1.5 | 23.1 | 1.2 | 16.5 | 2.5 |
| | 35-44 | 21.9 | 2.4 | 22.5 | 1.8 | 19.5 | 4.4 |
| | 45-64 | 27.8 | 6.4 | 27.7 | 5.5 | 28.3 | 10.1 |
| | 65+ | 9.0 | 4.1 | 8.8 | 3.9 | 9.9 | 4.9 |
| | Total | 85.3 | 14.8 | 87.2 | 12.8 | 77.6 | 22.4 |
| 1960 | 14-25 | 5.0 | 0.9 | 5.3 | 1.0 | 3.4 | 0.8 |
| | 25-34 | 18.1 | 2.0 | 18.9 | 1.7 | 14.4 | 3.2 |
| | 35-44 | 21.7 | 2.7 | 22.2 | 2.2 | 19.5 | 4.6 |
| | 45-64 | 28.9 | 6.6 | 27.9 | 7.2 | 27.9 | 9.7 |
| | 65+ | 9.2 | 5.0 | 9.0 | 4.7 | 10.4 | 6.1 |
| | Total | 82.8 | 17.2 | 83.2 | 16.8 | 75.6 | 24.4 |
| 1970 | 14-24 | 6.9 | 1.6 | 7.3 | 1.5 | 4.7 | 1.8 |
| | 25-34 | 17.9 | 2.5 | 18.7 | 2.1 | 13.7 | 4.5 |
| | 35-44 | 17.4 | 2.6 | 17.8 | 2.1 | 14.9 | 5.0 |
| | 45-64 | 28.9 | 7.0 | 29.1 | 6.4 | 27.7 | 10.3 |
| | 65+ | 9.2 | 6.3 | 9.0 | 6.0 | 10.2 | 7.3 |
| | Total | 80.0 | 20.0 | 81.9 | 18.1 | 71.1 | 28.9 |
| **Family and nonfamily heads** | | | | | | | |
| 1950 | Family heads | | NOT AVAILABLE | | | | |
| | Primary ind. | | | | | | |
| 1960 | Family heads | 89.1 | 10.9 | 90.9 | 9.1 | 80.3 | 19.7 |
| | Primary ind. | 34.0 | 66.0 | 30.6 | 69.4 | 46.0 | 54.0 |
| 1970 | Family heads | 88.8 | 11.2 | 91.2 | 8.8 | 76.7 | 23.3 |
| | Primary ind. | 37.1 | 62.9 | 35.1 | 64.9 | 45.6 | 54.4 |
| **Composition of household** | | | | | | | |
| 1950 | Head | 26.7 | | 27.6 | | 23.6 | |
| | Wife of head | 21.2 | | 22.9 | | 15.4 | |
| | Child of head | 38.7 | | 38.7 | | 38.9 | |
| | Other relative | 10.3 | | 8.5 | | 16.6 | |
| | Nonrelative | 3.1 | | 2.4 | | 5.5 | |
| 1960 | | | | | | | |
| | Head | 28.3 | | 29.5 | | 24.1 | |
| | Wife of head | 21.6 | | 23.2 | | 15.5 | |
| | Child of head | 40.2 | | 39.8 | | 41.5 | |
| | Other relative | 8.1 | | 6.0 | | 15.4 | |
| | Nonrelative | 1.9 | | 1.5 | | 3.5 | |
| 1970 | | | | | | | |
| | Head | 31.2 | | 32.4 | | 26.2 | |
| | Wife of head | 22.4 | | 23.8 | | 15.8 | |
| | Child of head | 38.9 | | 38.0 | | 43.3 | |
| | Other relative | 5.7 | | 4.4 | | 12.0 | |
| | Nonrelative | 1.8 | | 1.5 | | 2.7 | |

Table A6.1. Rates of fertility, mortality, and migration

I. Fertility (births per 1,000 women per year)

| Series A | Age | All Years | Series B 1970-75 | 1970-75 | 1980- |
|---|---|---|---|---|---|
| White | 10-14 | 0.4 | 0.4 | 0.4 | 0.4 |
| | 15-19 | 60.0 | 58.5 | 55.2 | 54.0 |
| | 20-24 | 149.8 | 146.0 | 137.8 | 135.0 |
| | 25-29 | 136.7 | 133.2 | 125.8 | 123.1 |
| | 30-34 | 66.9 | 65.2 | 61.6 | 60.3 |
| | 35-39 | 27.0 | 26.3 | 24.8 | 24.3 |
| | 40-44 | 6.4 | 6.2 | 5.9 | 5.8 |
| | 45-49 | 0.2 | 0.2 | 0.2 | 0.2 |
| Nonwhite | 10-14 | 4.9 | 4.7 | 4.6 | 4.6 |
| | 15-19 | 122.5 | 119.4 | 112.7 | 110.3 |
| | 20-24 | 182.7 | 178.1 | 168.1 | 164.6 |
| | 25-29 | 129.7 | 126.4 | 119.3 | 116.8 |
| | 30-34 | 72.7 | 70.8 | 66.9 | 65.5 |
| | 35-39 | 38.9 | 37.9 | 35.8 | 35.0 |
| | 40-44 | 11.1 | 10.8 | 10.3 | 10.0 |
| | 45-49 | 1.0 | 1.0 | 1.0 | 1.0 |

Percent of births females:  nonwhite  50.45
                            white     51.27

II. Mortality (probability of surviving next five years)

| Age | White Male | White Female | Nonwhite Male | Nonwhite Female |
|---|---|---|---|---|
| 0-4 | .99616 | .99732 | .99243 | .99489 |
| 5-9 | .99762 | .99866 | .99689 | .99834 |
| 10-14 | .99558 | .99807 | .99260 | .99741 |
| 15-19 | .99275 | .99705 | .98522 | .99504 |
| 20-24 | .99203 | .99689 | .98030 | .99337 |
| 25-29 | .99134 | .99632 | .97688 | .99069 |
| 30-34 | .98960 | .99364 | .97147 | .98332 |
| 35-39 | .98416 | .99050 | .95782 | .97432 |
| 40-44 | .97233 | .98626 | .93619 | .96248 |
| 45-49 | .95347 | .97815 | .90803 | .94841 |
| 50-54 | .92517 | .96675 | .86997 | .92893 |
| 55-59 | .88221 | .95266 | .81817 | .89865 |
| 60-64 | .82527 | .92536 | .76598 | .85979 |
| 65-69 | .74544 | .87513 | .69562 | .79144 |
| 70-74 | .62987 | .79356 | .59376 | .70951 |
| 75-79 | .54638 | .73441 | .50760 | .66986 |
| 80-84 | .48543 | .63720 | .46268 | .60716 |

Table A6.1 (cont.)

III.  Net Migration    (five-year rate per 1,000 persons)

| Series I | | Series II | | | Series III | | |
|---|---|---|---|---|---|---|---|
|  | All Years | 1970 1975 | 1975 1980 | 1980- | 1970- 1975 | 1975- 1980 | 1980- |
| **White Male** | | | | | | | |
| 0-4 | -4.2 | -3.7 | -2.6 | -2.1 | -3.2 | -1.1 | 0 |
| 5-9 | 10.2 | 8.9 | 6.4 | 5.1 | 7.7 | 2.6 | 0 |
| 10-14 | 30.6 | 26.8 | 19.1 | 15.3 | 23.0 | 7.7 | 0 |
| 15-19 | 41.9 | 36.6 | 26.3 | 21.0 | 31.4 | 10.5 | 0 |
| 20-24 | 142.1 | 124.3 | 87.9 | 71.1 | 106.6 | 35.5 | 0 |
| 25-29 | 50.8 | 44.4 | 31.8 | 25.4 | 38.1 | 12.7 | 0 |
| 30-34 | -16.7 | -14.6 | -10.4 | -8.3 | -12.5 | -4.2 | 0 |
| 35-39 | 49.4 | 43.2 | 30.9 | 24.7 | 37.1 | 12.4 | 0 |
| 40-44 | 39.2 | 34.3 | 24.5 | 19.6 | 29.4 | 9.8 | 0 |
| 45-49 | 21.4 | 18.7 | 13.4 | 10.7 | 16.1 | 5.4 | 0 |
| 50-54 | 12.1 | 10.6 | 7.6 | 6.1 | 9.1 | 3.0 | 0 |
| 55-59 | 5.0 | 4.4 | 3.1 | 2.5 | 3.8 | 1.3 | 0 |
| 60-64 | 3.5 | 3.1 | 2.1 | 1.7 | 2.6 | 0.9 | 0 |
| 65-69 | 0.9 | 0.8 | 0.6 | 0.5 | 0.7 | 0.2 | 0 |
| 70-74 | 0.3 | 0.3 | 0.1 | 0.1 | 0.2 | 0.1 | 0 |
| 75-79 | -2.0 | -1.7 | -1.3 | -1.0 | -1.5 | -0.5 | 0 |
| 80-84 | -14.2 | -12.4 | -8.9 | -7.1 | -10.7 | -3.6 | 0 |
| **White Female** | | | | | | | |
| 0-4 | -3.1 | -2.7 | -1.9 | -1.5 | -2.3 | -0.8 | 0 |
| 5-9 | 10.9 | 9.5 | 6.9 | 5.5 | 8.2 | 2.7 | 0 |
| 10-14 | 29.5 | 25.8 | 18.5 | 14.8 | 22.1 | 7.4 | 0 |
| 15-19 | 32.2 | 28.2 | 20.1 | 16.1 | 24.2 | 8.1 | 0 |
| 20-24 | 83.8 | 73.3 | 52.4 | 41.9 | 62.9 | 21.0 | 0 |
| 25-29 | 77.4 | 67.7 | 48.4 | 38.7 | 58.1 | 19.4 | 0 |
| 30-34 | 48.5 | 42.4 | 30.3 | 24.2 | 36.4 | 12.1 | 0 |
| 35-39 | 46.6 | 40.8 | 29.1 | 23.3 | 35.0 | 11.7 | 0 |
| 40-44 | 35.6 | 31.1 | 22.3 | 17.8 | 26.7 | 8.9 | 0 |
| 45-49 | 21.3 | 18.6 | 13.4 | 10.7 | 16.0 | 5.3 | 0 |
| 50-54 | 13.8 | 12.1 | 8.6 | 6.9 | 10.4 | 3.5 | 0 |
| 55-59 | 12.8 | 11.2 | 8.0 | 6.4 | 9.6 | 3.2 | 0 |
| 60-64 | 11.7 | 10.2 | 7.3 | 5.8 | 8.8 | 2.9 | 0 |
| 65-69 | 10.8 | 9.4 | 6.8 | 5.4 | 8.1 | 2.7 | 0 |
| 70-74 | 17.9 | 15.7 | 11.2 | 9.0 | 13.4 | 4.5 | 0 |
| 75-79 | 18.3 | 16.0 | 11.4 | 9.1 | 13.7 | 4.6 | 0 |
| 80-84 | 18.8 | 16.4 | 11.8 | 9.4 | 14.1 | 4.7 | 0 |

Table A6.1 (cont.)

III.  Net Migration (cont.)

| Series I | | Series II | | | Series III | | |
|---|---|---|---|---|---|---|---|
| | All<br>Years | 1970<br>1975 | 1975<br>1980 | 1980- | 1970-<br>1975 | 1975-<br>1980 | 1980- |
| Nonwhite Male | | | | | | | |
| 0-4 | -4.4 | -3.8 | -2.8 | -2.2 | -3.3 | -1.1 | 0 |
| 5-9 | -27.4 | -24.0 | -17.1 | -13.7 | -20.6 | -6.9 | 0 |
| 10-14 | -26.6 | -23.3 | -16.6 | -13.3 | -20.0 | -6.7 | 0 |
| 15-19 | -31.9 | -27.9 | -20.0 | -16.0 | -23.9 | -8.0 | 0 |
| 20-24 | -47.9 | -41.9 | -29.9 | -23.9 | -35.9 | -12.0 | 0 |
| 25-29 | -82.4 | -72.1 | -51.5 | -41.2 | -61.8 | -20.6 | 0 |
| 30-34 | -59.5 | -52.0 | -37.3 | -29.8 | -44.6 | -14.9 | 0 |
| 35-39 | -33.5 | -29.3 | -20.9 | -16.7 | -25.1 | -8.4 | 0 |
| 40-44 | -30.6 | -26.8 | -19.1 | -15.3 | -23.0 | -7.7 | 0 |
| 45-49 | -21.0 | -17.4 | -13.1 | -10.5 | -15.8 | -5.3 | 0 |
| 50-54 | -18.2 | -15.9 | -11.4 | -9.1 | -13.7 | -4.6 | 0 |
| 55-59 | -15.9 | -13.9 | -10.0 | -8.0 | -11.9 | -4.0 | 0 |
| 60-64 | -16.3 | -14.3 | -10.1 | -8.1 | -12.2 | -4.1 | 0 |
| 65-69 | -10.2 | -8.9 | -6.4 | -5.1 | -7.7 | -2.6 | 0 |
| 70-74 | -21.5 | -18.8 | -13.5 | -10.8 | -16.1 | -5.4 | 0 |
| 75-79 | -28.4 | -24.8 | -17.8 | -14.2 | -21.3 | -7.1 | 0 |
| 80-84 | -42.7 | -37.4 | -26.6 | -21.3 | -32.0 | -10.7 | 0 |
| Nonwhite Female | | | | | | | |
| 0-4 | -5.2 | -4.5 | -3.3 | -2.6 | -3.9 | -1.3 | 0 |
| 5-9 | -24.5 | -21.4 | -15.4 | -12.3 | -18.4 | -6.1 | 0 |
| 10-14 | -27.3 | -23.9 | -17.0 | -13.6 | -20.5 | -6.8 | 0 |
| 15-19 | -36.6 | -32.0 | -22.9 | -18.3 | -27.5 | -9.2 | 0 |
| 20-24 | -86.2 | -75.4 | -53.9 | -43.1 | -64.7 | -21.6 | 0 |
| 25-29 | -113.7 | -99.5 | -71.1 | -56.9 | -85.3 | -28.4 | 0 |
| 30-34 | -48.5 | -42.4 | -30.3 | -24.2 | -36.4 | -12.1 | 0 |
| 35-39 | -23.0 | -21.1 | -14.4 | -11.5 | -17.3 | -5.8 | 0 |
| 40-44 | -15.3 | -13.4 | -9.6 | -7.7 | -11.5 | -3.8 | 0 |
| 45-49 | -12.2 | -10.7 | -7.6 | -6.1 | -9.2 | -3.1 | 0 |
| 50-54 | -9.0 | -7.9 | -5.6 | -4.5 | -6.8 | -2.3 | 0 |
| 55-59 | -9.8 | -8.6 | -6.1 | -4.9 | -7.4 | -2.5 | 0 |
| 60-64 | -15.6 | -13.6 | -9.8 | -7.8 | -11.7 | -3.9 | 0 |
| 65-69 | -5.4 | -4.7 | -3.4 | -2.7 | -4.1 | -1.4 | 0 |
| 70-74 | -14.4 | -12.6 | -9.0 | -7.2 | -10.8 | -3.6 | 0 |
| 75-79 | -15.1 | -13.2 | -9.4 | -7.5 | -11.3 | -3.8 | 0 |
| 80-84 | -35.5 | -31.0 | -22.3 | -17.8 | -26.6 | -8.9 | 0 |

Sources:  Section I-U.S. Bureau of Census, 1970 Census of Population, General Population
Characteristics of Virginia, Table 20; Virginia State Department of Health, Annual
Statistical Report (1970), Table 7; Section II-University of Virginia, Bureau of
Population and Economic Research, "Abridged Life Table for Virginia by Race and Sex,
1970," Tables 6,7,8,9; Section III-William J. Serow and Michael A. Spar, Virginia
Population: A Period of Change. II. Net Migration for State Planning Districts
(Charlottesville:  Tayloe Murphy Institute, 1972), Table 3.

Table A6.2.  Population by age, race, and sex, Virginia, 1970-2000

1970 - All Series

| Age | Total | White | Nonwhite | Male | Female |
|-----|-------|-------|----------|------|--------|
| 0-4 | 392,093 | 305,074 | 87,019 | 199,585 | 192,508 |
| 5-9 | 456,958 | 354,088 | 102,870 | 232,508 | 224,450 |
| 10-14 | 474,282 | 364,984 | 109,298 | 241,202 | 233,080 |
| 15-19 | 440,872 | 343,007 | 97,865 | 225,034 | 215,838 |
| 20-24 | 439,818 | 367,522 | 72,296 | 231,510 | 208,308 |
| 25-29 | 335,045 | 281,865 | 53,180 | 167,638 | 167,407 |
| 30-34 | 280,402 | 233,297 | 47,105 | 139,365 | 141,037 |
| 35-39 | 269,296 | 222,656 | 46,640 | 132,886 | 136,410 |
| 40-44 | 280,666 | 232,861 | 47,805 | 137,317 | 143,349 |
| 45-49 | 282,485 | 234,861 | 47,624 | 136,877 | 145,608 |
| 50-54 | 247,903 | 205,053 | 42,850 | 121,814 | 126,089 |
| 55-59 | 210,620 | 173,142 | 37,478 | 101,895 | 108,725 |
| 60-64 | 172,033 | 142,577 | 29,456 | 80,366 | 91,667 |
| 65-69 | 134,140 | 108,850 | 25,290 | 58,914 | 75,226 |
| 70-74 | 99,014 | 81,436 | 17,578 | 40,940 | 58,074 |
| 75-79 | 66,687 | 55,417 | 11,270 | 26,138 | 40,549 |
| 80-84 | 39,435 | 32,985 | 6,450 | 13,951 | 25,484 |
| 85+ | 26,745 | 21,839 | 4,906 | 9,181 | 17,564 |
| | | | | | |
| Total | 4,648,494 | 3,761,514 | 886,980 | 2,297,121 | 2,351,373 |

Table A6.2   (cont.)

1975 - I-A

| Age | Total | White | Nonwhite | Male | Female |
|-----|-------|-------|----------|------|--------|
| 0-4 | 449,550 | 350,800 | 98,750 | 229,200 | 220,350 |
| 5-9 | 391,500 | 307,300 | 84,200 | 199,050 | 192,450 |
| 10-14 | 463,950 | 364,050 | 99,900 | 236,100 | 227,850 |
| 15-19 | 482,350 | 377,350 | 105,000 | 246,000 | 236,350 |
| 20-24 | 470,400 | 380,000 | 90,400 | 245,500 | 224,900 |
| 25-29 | 452,900 | 388,550 | 64,350 | 236,150 | 216,750 |
| 30-34 | 334,100 | 284,550 | 49,550 | 162,000 | 172,100 |
| 35-39 | 287,250 | 242,450 | 44,800 | 142,550 | 144,700 |
| 40-44 | 272,200 | 228,050 | 44,150 | 133,850 | 138,350 |
| 45-49 | 277,550 | 232,900 | 44,650 | 134,650 | 142,900 |
| 50-54 | 273,500 | 229,850 | 43,650 | 130,400 | 143,100 |
| 55-59 | 233,850 | 195,800 | 38,050 | 111,700 | 122,150 |
| 60-64 | 191,950 | 160,300 | 31,650 | 88,700 | 103,250 |
| 65-69 | 149,950 | 126,100 | 23,850 | 65,450 | 84,500 |
| 70-74 | 108,650 | 90,050 | 18,600 | 43,200 | 65,450 |
| 75-79 | 71,250 | 59,900 | 11,350 | 25,350 | 45,900 |
| 80-84 | 40,450 | 33,950 | 6,500 | 13,650 | 26,800 |
| 85+ | 27,300 | 21,550 | 5,750 | 10,000 | 17,300 |
| Total | 4,978,650 | 4,073,500 | 905,150 | 2,453,500 | 2,525,150 |

Table A6.2 (cont.)

| 1980 - I-A | | | | | |
|---|---|---|---|---|---|
| Age | Total | White | Nonwhite | Male | Female |
| 0-4 | 504,100 | 396,300 | 107,800 | 257,050 | 247,050 |
| 5-9 | 448,950 | 353,350 | 95,600 | 228,650 | 220,300 |
| 10-14 | 397,650 | 315,900 | 81,750 | 202,200 | 195,450 |
| 15-19 | 472,350 | 376,350 | 96,000 | 241,100 | 231,250 |
| 20-24 | 515,050 | 418,050 | 97,000 | 268,650 | 246,400 |
| 25-29 | 482,300 | 401,850 | 80,450 | 249,300 | 233,000 |
| 30-34 | 451,600 | 391,700 | 59,900 | 228,350 | 223,250 |
| 35-39 | 342,750 | 295,700 | 47,050 | 165,850 | 176,900 |
| 40-44 | 290,650 | 248,350 | 42,300 | 143,800 | 146,850 |
| 45-49 | 269,400 | 228,100 | 41,300 | 131,450 | 137,950 |
| 50-54 | 268,950 | 227,950 | 41,000 | 128,450 | 140,500 |
| 55-59 | 258,500 | 219,650 | 38,850 | 119,750 | 138,750 |
| 60-64 | 213,600 | 181,350 | 32,250 | 97,450 | 116,150 |
| 65-69 | 167,500 | 141,850 | 25,650 | 72,300 | 95,200 |
| 70-74 | 121,900 | 104,400 | 17,500 | 48,100 | 73,800 |
| 75-79 | 78,450 | 66,400 | 12,050 | 26,750 | 51,700 |
| 80-84 | 43,750 | 37,150 | 6,600 | 13,450 | 30,300 |
| 85+ | 28,600 | 22,500 | 6,100 | 10,150 | 18,450 |
| Total | 5,356,050 | 4,426,900 | 929,150 | 2,632,800 | 2,723,250 |

Table A6.2   (cont.)

---

1985 - I-A

| Age | Total | White | Nonwhite | Male | Female |
|-----|-------|-------|----------|------|--------|
| 0-4 | 532,900 | 423,900 | 109,000 | 271,800 | 261,100 |
| 5-9 | 503,450 | 399,150 | 104,300 | 256,450 | 247,000 |
| 10-14 | 456,000 | 363,250 | 92,750 | 232,250 | 223,750 |
| 15-19 | 405,150 | 326,600 | 78,550 | 206,600 | 198,550 |
| 20-24 | 505,400 | 416,800 | 88,600 | 263,950 | 241,450 |
| 25-29 | 528,400 | 442,050 | 86,350 | 273,000 | 255,400 |
| 30-34 | 480,150 | 405,250 | 74,900 | 240,700 | 239,450 |
| 35-39 | 463,900 | 407,050 | 56,850 | 234,150 | 229,750 |
| 40-44 | 347,350 | 302,900 | 44,450 | 167,500 | 179,850 |
| 45-49 | 287,950 | 248,400 | 39,550 | 141,300 | 146,650 |
| 50-54 | 261,100 | 223,150 | 37,950 | 125,450 | 135,650 |
| 55-59 | 254,300 | 217,700 | 36,600 | 118,100 | 136,200 |
| 60-64 | 236,650 | 203,650 | 33,000 | 104,600 | 132,050 |
| 65-69 | 186,750 | 160,550 | 26,200 | 79,550 | 107,200 |
| 70-74 | 136,400 | 117,500 | 18,900 | 53,150 | 83,250 |
| 75-79 | 88,350 | 77,000 | 11,350 | 29,850 | 58,500 |
| 80-84 | 48,150 | 41,100 | 7,050 | 13,950 | 34,200 |
| 85+ | 31,200 | 24,800 | 6,400 | 10,300 | 20,900 |
| | | | | | |
| Total | 5,753,550 | 4,800,800 | 952,750 | 2,822,650 | 2,930,900 |

Table A6.2   (cont.)

| 1990 - I-A Age | Total | White | Nonwhite | Male | Female |
|---|---|---|---|---|---|
| 0-4 | 536,150 | 430,650 | 105,500 | 273,500 | 262,650 |
| 5-9 | 532,450 | 426,950 | 105,500 | 271,250 | 261,200 |
| 10-14 | 511,650 | 410,400 | 101,250 | 260,650 | 251,000 |
| 15-19 | 464,700 | 375,550 | 89,150 | 237,400 | 227,300 |
| 20-24 | 434,400 | 361,850 | 72,550 | 226,550 | 207,850 |
| 25-29 | 519,850 | 440,950 | 78,900 | 268,750 | 251,100 |
| 30-34 | 526,150 | 445,800 | 80,350 | 263,600 | 262,550 |
| 35-39 | 492,250 | 421,150 | 71,100 | 246,150 | 246,100 |
| 40-44 | 470,600 | 416,900 | 53,700 | 236,800 | 233,800 |
| 45-49 | 344,800 | 303,250 | 41,550 | 164,950 | 179,850 |
| 50-54 | 279,350 | 243,000 | 36,350 | 135,050 | 144,300 |
| 55-59 | 247,000 | 213,150 | 33,850 | 115,450 | 131,550 |
| 60-64 | 232,900 | 201,800 | 31,100 | 103,300 | 129,600 |
| 65-69 | 207,450 | 180,600 | 26,850 | 85,450 | 122,000 |
| 70-74 | 152,400 | 133,050 | 19,350 | 58,600 | 93,800 |
| 75-79 | 99,100 | 86,800 | 12,300 | 33,050 | 66,050 |
| 80-84 | 53,250 | 46,550 | 6,700 | 14,450 | 38,800 |
| 85+ | 33,900 | 27,150 | 6,750 | 10,400 | 23,500 |
| Total | 6,138,350 | 5,165,550 | 972,800 | 3,005,350 | 3,133,000 |

Table A6.2   (cont.)

| 1995 - I-A | | | | | |
|---|---|---|---|---|---|
| Age | Total | White | Nonwhite | Male | Female |
| 0-4 | 537,050 | 432,250 | 104,800 | 273,950 | 263,100 |
| 5-9 | 535,850 | 433,750 | 102,100 | 273,050 | 262,800 |
| 10-14 | 541,400 | 438,950 | 102,450 | 275,850 | 265,550 |
| 15-19 | 521,550 | 424,250 | 97,300 | 266,500 | 255,050 |
| 20-24 | 498,400 | _16,050 | 82,350 | 260,450 | 237,950 |
| 25-29 | 447,250 | 382,650 | 64,600 | 230,900 | 216,350 |
| 30-34 | 518,050 | 444,650 | 73,400 | 259,650 | 258,400 |
| 35-39 | 539,600 | 463,300 | 76,300 | 269,700 | 269,900 |
| 40-44 | 498,200 | 431,100 | 67,100 | 248,400 | 249,800 |
| 45-49 | 467,100 | 416,950 | 50,150 | 233,150 | 233,950 |
| 50-54 | 334,750 | 296,600 | 38,150 | 157,600 | 177,150 |
| 55-59 | 264,800 | 232,050 | 32,750 | 124,750 | 140,050 |
| 60-64 | 226,300 | 197,450 | 28,850 | 101,050 | 125,250 |
| 65-69 | 204,200 | 178,800 | 25,400 | 84,500 | 119,700 |
| 70-74 | 169,950 | 150,050 | 19,900 | 63,050 | 106,900 |
| 75-79 | 110,950 | 98,350 | 12,600 | 36,450 | 74,500 |
| 80-84 | 59,700 | 52,450 | 7,250 | 15,950 | 43,750 |
| 85+ | 37,350 | 30,600 | 6,750 | 10,650 | 26,700 |
| Total | 6,512,450 | 5,520,250 | 992,200 | 3,185,600 | 3,326,850 |

Table A6.2   (cont.)

2000 - I-A

| Age | Total | White | Nonwhite | Male | Female |
|---|---|---|---|---|---|
| 0-4 | 562,050 | 454,550 | 107,500 | 286,750 | 275,300 |
| 5-9 | 536,800 | 435,350 | 101,450 | 273,550 | 263,250 |
| 10-14 | 545,050 | 445,950 | 99,100 | 277,800 | 267,250 |
| 15-19 | 552,250 | 453,800 | 98,450 | 282,200 | 270,050 |
| 20-24 | 559,950 | 470,050 | 89,900 | 292,650 | 267,300 |
| 25-29 | 513,250 | 439,950 | 73,300 | 265,500 | 247,750 |
| 30-34 | 446,000 | 385,900 | 60,100 | 223,200 | 222,800 |
| 35-39 | 531,850 | 462,150 | 69,700 | 266,000 | 265,850 |
| 40-44 | 546,600 | 474,550 | 72,050 | 272,250 | 274,350 |
| 45-49 | 494,100 | 431,450 | 62,650 | 244,100 | 250,000 |
| 50-54 | 453,900 | 407,900 | 46,000 | 233,250 | 230,650 |
| 55-59 | 317,450 | 283,450 | 34,000 | 145,250 | 172,200 |
| 60-64 | 242,550 | 214,950 | 27,600 | 109,050 | 133,500 |
| 65-69 | 198,400 | 174,850 | 23,550 | 82,750 | 115,650 |
| 70-74 | 167,250 | 148,400 | 18,850 | 62,350 | 104,900 |
| 75-79 | 124,250 | 111,250 | 13,000 | 39,250 | 85,000 |
| 80-84 | 66,950 | 59,500 | 7,450 | 17,600 | 49,350 |
| 85+ | 41,300 | 34,300 | 7,000 | 11,450 | 29,850 |
| | | | | | |
| Total | 6,899,950 | 5,888,300 | 1,011,650 | 3,374,950 | 3,525,000 |

Table A6.2   (cont.)

**1975 - II-A**

| Age | Total | White | Nonwhite | Male | Female |
|-----|-------|-------|----------|------|--------|
| 0-4 | 458,800 | 359,550 | 99,250 | 238,850 | 219,950 |
| 5-9 | 391,350 | 306,850 | 84,500 | 199,000 | 192,350 |
| 10-14 | 462,900 | 362,700 | 100,200 | 235,550 | 227,350 |
| 15-19 | 481,100 | 375,600 | 105,500 | 245,250 | 235,850 |
| 20-24 | 466,350 | 375,150 | 91,200 | 242,700 | 223,650 |
| 25-29 | 450,850 | 385,650 | 65,200 | 235,250 | 215,600 |
| 30-34 | 333,850 | 284,000 | 49,850 | 162,400 | 171,450 |
| 35-39 | 285,950 | 241,050 | 44,900 | 141,850 | 144,100 |
| 40-44 | 271,200 | 227,000 | 44,200 | 133,400 | 137,800 |
| 45-49 | 276,100 | 231,350 | 44,750 | 134,400 | 141,700 |
| 50-54 | 273,250 | 229,500 | 43,750 | 130,300 | 142,950 |
| 55-59 | 233,650 | 195,500 | 38,150 | 111,600 | 122,050 |
| 60-64 | 191,950 | 160,200 | 31,750 | 88,750 | 103,200 |
| 65-69 | 149,850 | 126,000 | 23,850 | 65,450 | 84,400 |
| 70-74 | 108,550 | 89,950 | 18,600 | 43,200 | 65,350 |
| 75-79 | 71,150 | 59,800 | 11,350 | 25,350 | 45,800 |
| 80-84 | 40,500 | 33,950 | 6,550 | 13,700 | 26,800 |
| 85+ | 27,350 | 21,600 | 5,750 | 10,000 | 17,350 |
| | | | | | |
| Total | 4,974,700 | 4,065,400 | 909,300 | 2,457,000 | 2,517,700 |

Table A6.2 (cont.)

1980 - II-A

| Age | Total | White | Nonwhite | Male | Female |
|------|-----------|-----------|----------|-----------|-----------|
| 0-4 | 510,100 | 399,700 | 110,400 | 265,350 | 244,750 |
| 5-9 | 457,750 | 360,700 | 97,050 | 238,100 | 219,650 |
| 10-14 | 394,900 | 312,050 | 82,850 | 200,750 | 194,150 |
| 15-19 | 467,500 | 369,900 | 97,600 | 238,200 | 229,300 |
| 20-24 | 500,300 | 400,250 | 100,050 | 258,500 | 241,800 |
| 25-29 | 472,350 | 387,850 | 84,500 | 244,050 | 228,300 |
| 30-34 | 448,700 | 386,700 | 62,000 | 229,450 | 219,250 |
| 35-39 | 337,950 | 290,050 | 47,900 | 164,050 | 173,900 |
| 40-44 | 287,000 | 243,550 | 43,450 | 142,200 | 144,800 |
| 45-49 | 266,850 | 225,300 | 41,550 | 130,200 | 136,650 |
| 50-54 | 266,550 | 225,250 | 41,300 | 127,850 | 138,700 |
| 55-59 | 257,650 | 218,550 | 39,100 | 119,550 | 138,100 |
| 60-64 | 213,000 | 180,500 | 32,500 | 97,350 | 115,650 |
| 65-69 | 167,200 | 141,400 | 25,800 | 72,300 | 94,900 |
| 70-74 | 121,500 | 103,850 | 17,650 | 48,150 | 73,350 |
| 75-79 | 78,200 | 66,050 | 12,150 | 26,850 | 51,350 |
| 80-84 | 43,850 | 37,200 | 6,650 | 13,750 | 30,100 |
| 85+ | 28,550 | 22,350 | 6,200 | 10,200 | 18,350 |
| Total | 5,319,900 | 4,371,200 | 948,700 | 2,626,850 | 2,693,050 |

Table A6.2  (cont.)

1986 - II-A

| Age | Total | White | Nonwhite | Male | Female |
|-----|-------|-------|----------|------|--------|
| 0-4 | 531,900 | 416,800 | 115,100 | 276,350 | 255,550 |
| 5-9 | 508,750 | 400,500 | 108,250 | 264,400 | 244,350 |
| 10-14 | 461,600 | 366,100 | 95,500 | 239,750 | 221,850 |
| 15-19 | 397,900 | 316,850 | 81,050 | 202,450 | 195,450 |
| 20-24 | 482,250 | 388,900 | 93,350 | 248,300 | 233,950 |
| 25-29 | 504,500 | 410,600 | 93,900 | 259,000 | 245,500 |
| 30-34 | 469,100 | 388,250 | 80,850 | 238,350 | 230,750 |
| 35-39 | 452,400 | 392,650 | 59,750 | 230,850 | 221,550 |
| 40-44 | 337,550 | 291,800 | 45,550 | 163,250 | 174,300 |
| 45-49 | 280,550 | 239,600 | 40,950 | 138,600 | 141,950 |
| 50-54 | 257,450 | 219,000 | 38,450 | 123,800 | 133,650 |
| 55-59 | 251,250 | 214,200 | 37,050 | 117,350 | 133,900 |
| 60-64 | 235,300 | 201,850 | 33,450 | 104,400 | 130,900 |
| 65-69 | 185,750 | 159,250 | 26,500 | 79,450 | 106,300 |
| 70-74 | 135,600 | 116,450 | 19,150 | 53,250 | 82,350 |
| 75-79 | 87,750 | 76,200 | 11,550 | 30,000 | 57,750 |
| 80-84 | 47,750 | 40,600 | 7,150 | 14,050 | 33,700 |
| 85+ | 30,850 | 24,450 | 6,400 | 10,250 | 20,600 |
| Total | 5,658,200 | 4,664,050 | 994,150 | 2,793,850 | 2,864,350 |

*Appendix Tables*

Table A6.2   (cont.)

---

1990 - II-A

| Age | Total | White | Nonwhite | Male | Female |
|------|-----------|-----------|-----------|-----------|-----------|
| 0-4 | 528,950 | 414,650 | 114,300 | 275,300 | 253,650 |
| 5-9 | 530,450 | 417,600 | 112,850 | 275,350 | 255,100 |
| 10-14 | 512,400 | 405,800 | 106,600 | 266,300 | 246,100 |
| 15-19 | 465,100 | 371,700 | 93,400 | 241,800 | 223,300 |
| 20-24 | 410,600 | 333,050 | 77,550 | 211,100 | 199,500 |
| 25-29 | 486,650 | 399,050 | 87,600 | 249,000 | 237,650 |
| 30-34 | 501,000 | 411,100 | 89,900 | 253,000 | 248,000 |
| 35-39 | 472,200 | 394,250 | 77,950 | 239,350 | 232,850 |
| 40-44 | 451,950 | 394,900 | 57,050 | 229,850 | 222,100 |
| 45-49 | 331,950 | 288,850 | 43,100 | 159,200 | 172,750 |
| 50-54 | 270,800 | 232,950 | 37,850 | 131,900 | 138,900 |
| 55-59 | 242,750 | 208,250 | 34,500 | 113,750 | 129,000 |
| 60-64 | 229,450 | 197,650 | 31,800 | 102,600 | 126,850 |
| 65-69 | 205,650 | 178,350 | 27,300 | 85,250 | 120,400 |
| 70-74 | 150,900 | 131,200 | 19,700 | 58,550 | 92,350 |
| 75-79 | 98,050 | 85,450 | 12,600 | 33,200 | 64,850 |
| 80-84 | 52,550 | 45,750 | 6,800 | 14,600 | 37,950 |
| 85+ | 33,450 | 26,600 | 6,850 | 10,450 | 23,000 |
| Total | 5,974,850 | 4,937,150 | 1,037,700 | 2,950,550 | 3,024,300 |

Table A6.2 (cont.)

| 1995 - II-A | | | | | |
|---|---|---|---|---|---|
| Age | Total | White | Nonwhite | Male | Female |
| 0-4 | 528,000 | 414,900 | 113,100 | 276,600 | 251,400 |
| 5-9 | 527,550 | 415,450 | 112,100 | 274,350 | 253,200 |
| 10-14 | 534,150 | 423,100 | 111,050 | 277,300 | 256,850 |
| 15-19 | 516,200 | 411,950 | 104,250 | 268,500 | 247,700 |
| 20-24 | 480,300 | 390,950 | 89,350 | 252,350 | 227,950 |
| 25-29 | 414,600 | 341,800 | 72,800 | 211,750 | 202,850 |
| 30-34 | 483,400 | 399,550 | 83,850 | 243,200 | 240,200 |
| 35-39 | 504,100 | 417,450 | 86,650 | 253,900 | 250,200 |
| 40-44 | 470,900 | 396,500 | 74,400 | 237,750 | 233,150 |
| 45-49 | 444,500 | 390,800 | 53,700 | 224,300 | 220,200 |
| 50-54 | 320,700 | 280,900 | 39,800 | 151,500 | 169,200 |
| 55-59 | 255,300 | 221,400 | 33,900 | 121,200 | 134,100 |
| 60-64 | 221,750 | 192,150 | 29,600 | 99,500 | 122,250 |
| 65-69 | 200,550 | 174,500 | 26,050 | 83,900 | 116,650 |
| 70-74 | 167,600 | 147,200 | 20,400 | 62,900 | 104,700 |
| 75-79 | 109,300 | 96,350 | 12,950 | 36,500 | 72,800 |
| 80-84 | 58,700 | 51,300 | 7,400 | 16,100 | 42,600 |
| 85+ | 36,700 | 29,900 | 6,800 | 10,750 | 25,950 |
| Total | 6,274,300 | 5,196,150 | 1,078,150 | 3,102,350 | 3,171,950 |

Table A6.2  (cont.)

2000 - II-A

| Age | Total | White | Nonwhite | Male | Female |
|------|-----------|-----------|-----------|-----------|-----------|
| 0-4 | 553,950 | 432,900 | 121,050 | 292,100 | 261,850 |
| 5-9 | 526,550 | 415,700 | 110,850 | 275,600 | 250,950 |
| 10-14 | 531,250 | 420,900 | 110,350 | 276,250 | 255,000 |
| 15-19 | 538,150 | 429,550 | 108,600 | 279,600 | 258,550 |
| 20-24 | 533,000 | 433,250 | 99,750 | 280,200 | 252,800 |
| 25-29 | 484,900 | 401,050 | 83,850 | 253,250 | 231,650 |
| 30-34 | 411,850 | 342,200 | 69,650 | 206,850 | 205,000 |
| 35-39 | 486,600 | 405,750 | 80,850 | 244,200 | 242,400 |
| 40-44 | 502,650 | 419,900 | 82,750 | 252,200 | 250,450 |
| 45-49 | 462,450 | 392,400 | 70,050 | 231,600 | 230,850 |
| 50-54 | 429,300 | 379,750 | 49,550 | 213,600 | 215,700 |
| 55-59 | 302,900 | 267,200 | 35,700 | 139,350 | 163,550 |
| 60-64 | 233,300 | 204,200 | 29,100 | 106,050 | 127,250 |
| 65-69 | 193,800 | 169,550 | 24,250 | 81,400 | 112,400 |
| 70-74 | 163,400 | 143,900 | 19,500 | 62,000 | 101,400 |
| 75-79 | 121,850 | 108,400 | 13,450 | 39,250 | 82,600 |
| 80-84 | 65,550 | 57,900 | 7,650 | 17,700 | 47,850 |
| 85+ | 40,550 | 33,400 | 7,150 | 11,600 | 28,950 |
| Total | 6,582,000 | 5,457,900 | 1,124,100 | 3,262,800 | 3,319,200 |

Table A6.2 (cont.)

1975 - III-A

| Age | Total | White | Nonwhite | Male | Female |
|-----|-------|-------|----------|------|--------|
| 0-4 | 448,050 | 348,250 | 99,800 | 228,500 | 219,550 |
| 5-9 | 391,300 | 306,500 | 84,800 | 198,950 | 192,350 |
| 10-14 | 461,900 | 361,350 | 100,550 | 235,000 | 226,900 |
| 15-19 | 479,900 | 373,950 | 105,950 | 244,500 | 235,400 |
| 20-24 | 462,350 | 370,300 | 92,050 | 239,900 | 222,450 |
| 25-29 | 448,850 | 382,800 | 66,050 | 234,400 | 214,450 |
| 30-34 | 333,650 | 283,450 | 50,200 | 162,900 | 170,750 |
| 35-39 | 284,750 | 239,650 | 45,100 | 141,250 | 143,500 |
| 40-44 | 270,300 | 226,000 | 44,300 | 132,950 | 137,350 |
| 45-49 | 276,600 | 231,700 | 44,900 | 134,200 | 142,400 |
| 50-54 | 272,900 | 229,100 | 43,800 | 130,150 | 142,750 |
| 55-59 | 233,550 | 195,350 | 38,200 | 111,700 | 121,850 |
| 60-64 | 191,850 | 160,000 | 31,850 | 88,750 | 103,100 |
| 65-69 | 149,750 | 125,900 | 23,850 | 65,450 | 84,300 |
| 70-74 | 108,500 | 89,800 | 18,700 | 43,250 | 65,250 |
| 75-79 | 71,100 | 59,700 | 11,400 | 25,400 | 45,700 |
| 80-84 | 40,450 | 33,900 | 6,550 | 13,700 | 26,750 |
| 85+ | 27,400 | 21,650 | 5,750 | 10,000 | 17,400 |
| Total | 4,953,150 | 4,039,350 | 913,800 | 2,440,950 | 2,512,200 |

Table A6.2   (cont.)

1980 - III-A

| Age   | Total     | White     | Nonwhite | Male      | Female    |
|-------|-----------|-----------|----------|-----------|-----------|
| 0-4   | 495,400   | 382,300   | 113,100  | 252,650   | 242,750   |
| 5-9   | 446,500   | 348,000   | 98,500   | 227,500   | 219,000   |
| 10-14 | 392,200   | 308,200   | 84,000   | 199,350   | 192,850   |
| 15-19 | 462,800   | 363,600   | 99,200   | 235,400   | 227,400   |
| 20-24 | 485,700   | 382,550   | 103,150  | 248,450   | 237,250   |
| 25-29 | 462,650   | 374,100   | 88,550   | 238,900   | 223,750   |
| 30-34 | 445,850   | 381,750   | 64,100   | 230,550   | 215,300   |
| 35-39 | 333,150   | 284,450   | 48,700   | 162,250   | 170,900   |
| 40-44 | 282,200   | 238,850   | 43,350   | 139,450   | 142,750   |
| 45-49 | 264,500   | 222,500   | 42,000   | 129,050   | 135,450   |
| 50-54 | 266,150   | 224,550   | 41,600   | 127,250   | 138,900   |
| 55-59 | 256,800   | 217,450   | 39,350   | 119,350   | 137,450   |
| 60-64 | 212,650   | 179,900   | 32,750   | 97,400    | 115,250   |
| 65-69 | 166,850   | 140,900   | 25,950   | 72,350    | 94,500    |
| 70-74 | 121,700   | 103,900   | 17,800   | 48,200    | 73,500    |
| 75-79 | 77,950    | 65,650    | 12,300   | 26,900    | 51,050    |
| 80-84 | 43,400    | 36,750    | 6,650    | 13,500    | 29,900    |
| 85+   | 28,400    | 22,200    | 6,200    | 10,200    | 18,200    |
| Total | 5,244,850 | 4,277,600 | 967,250  | 2,578,700 | 2,666,150 |

Table A6.2  (cont.)

**1985 - III-A**

| Age | Total | White | Nonwhite | Male | Female |
|-----|-------|-------|----------|------|--------|
| 0-4 | 510,700 | 389,400 | 121,300 | 260,500 | 250,200 |
| 5-9 | 493,500 | 381,050 | 112,450 | 251,550 | 241,950 |
| 10-14 | 445,650 | 347,400 | 98,250 | 226,950 | 218,700 |
| 15-19 | 390,800 | 307,200 | 83,600 | 198,350 | 192,450 |
| 20-24 | 459,900 | 361,700 | 98,200 | 233,300 | 226,600 |
| 25-29 | 482,250 | 380,450 | 101,800 | 245,900 | 236,350 |
| 30-34 | 458,850 | 371,700 | 87,150 | 236,200 | 222,650 |
| 35-39 | 441,200 | 378,500 | 62,700 | 227,600 | 213,600 |
| 40-44 | 327,950 | 280,850 | 47,100 | 159,100 | 168,850 |
| 45-49 | 275,100 | 233,900 | 41,200 | 134,900 | 140,200 |
| 50-54 | 253,950 | 214,900 | 39,050 | 122,150 | 131,800 |
| 55-59 | 250,100 | 212,550 | 37,550 | 116,700 | 133,400 |
| 60-64 | 233,900 | 200,000 | 33,900 | 104,150 | 129,750 |
| 65-69 | 184,950 | 158,150 | 26,800 | 79,500 | 105,450 |
| 70-74 | 134,800 | 115,350 | 19,450 | 53,350 | 81,450 |
| 75-79 | 87,550 | 75,800 | 11,750 | 30,100 | 57,450 |
| 80-84 | 47,450 | 40,200 | 7,250 | 14,150 | 33,300 |
| 85+ | 30,550 | 24,150 | 6,400 | 10,300 | 20,250 |
| | | | | | |
| Total | 5,509,150 | 4,473,250 | 1,035,900 | 2,704,750 | 2,804,400 |

Table A6.2  (cont.)

1990 - III-A

| Age | Total | White | Nonwhite | Male | Female |
|-----|-------|-------|----------|------|--------|
| 0-4 | 501,050 | 377,350 | 123,700 | 255,500 | 245,550 |
| 5-9 | 508,700 | 388,150 | 120,550 | 259,300 | 249,400 |
| 10-14 | 492,500 | 380,300 | 112,200 | 250,900 | 241,600 |
| 25-19 | 444,050 | 346,250 | 97,800 | 225,800 | 218,250 |
| 20-24 | 388,350 | 305,600 | 82,750 | 196,600 | 191,750 |
| 25-29 | 456,550 | 359,650 | 96,900 | 230,850 | 225,700 |
| 30-34 | 478,200 | 378,050 | 100,150 | 243,000 | 235,200 |
| 35-39 | 453,750 | 368,550 | 85,200 | 232,950 | 220,800 |
| 40-44 | 434,300 | 373,700 | 60,600 | 223,200 | 211,100 |
| 45-49 | 319,850 | 275,100 | 44,750 | 153,900 | 165,950 |
| 50-54 | 264,200 | 225,900 | 38,300 | 127,750 | 136,450 |
| 55-59 | 238,700 | 203,400 | 35,300 | 112,100 | 126,600 |
| 60-64 | 227,800 | 195,400 | 32,400 | 101,900 | 125,900 |
| 65-69 | 203,950 | 176,150 | 27,800 | 85,100 | 118,850 |
| 70-74 | 149,700 | 129,600 | 20,100 | 58,700 | 91,000 |
| 75-79 | 97,050 | 84,150 | 12,900 | 33,350 | 63,700 |
| 80-84 | 52,200 | 45,250 | 6,950 | 14,750 | 37,450 |
| 85+ | 33,050 | 26,150 | 6,900 | 10,500 | 22,550 |
| Total | 5,743,950 | 4,638,700 | 1,105,250 | 2,816,150 | 2,927,800 |

Table A6.2  (cont.)

1995 - III-A

| Age | Total | White | Nonwhite | Male | Female |
|-----|-------|-------|----------|------|--------|
| 0-4 | 495,450 | 367,850 | 127,600 | 252,600 | 242,850 |
| 5-9 | 499,300 | 376,400 | 122,900 | 254,600 | 244,700 |
| 10-14 | 507,700 | 387,450 | 120,250 | 258,650 | 249,050 |
| 15-19 | 490,800 | 379,100 | 111,700 | 249,650 | 241,150 |
| 20-24 | 441,300 | 344,500 | 96,800 | 223,800 | 217,500 |
| 25-29 | 385,650 | 303,900 | 81,750 | 194,600 | 191,050 |
| 30-34 | 452,800 | 357,450 | 95,350 | 228,200 | 224,600 |
| 35-39 | 472,800 | 374,900 | 97,900 | 239,600 | 233,200 |
| 40-44 | 446,200 | 363,900 | 82,300 | 228,150 | 218,050 |
| 45-49 | 423,350 | 365,850 | 57,500 | 215,900 | 207,450 |
| 50-54 | 307,450 | 265,850 | 41,600 | 145,800 | 161,650 |
| 55-59 | 248,400 | 213,800 | 34,600 | 117,250 | 131,150 |
| 60-64 | 217,400 | 186,900 | 30,500 | 97,950 | 119,450 |
| 65-69 | 198,600 | 171,950 | 26,650 | 83,350 | 115,250 |
| 70-74 | 165,450 | 144,500 | 20,950 | 62,850 | 102,600 |
| 75-79 | 107,850 | 94,450 | 13,400 | 36,700 | 71,150 |
| 80-84 | 57,800 | 50,200 | 7,600 | 16,300 | 41,500 |
| 85+ | 36,350 | 29,400 | 6,950 | 10,850 | 25,500 |
| Total | 5,954,650 | 4,778,350 | 1,176,300 | 2,916,800 | 3,037,850 |

Table A6.2   (cont.)

2000 - III-A

| Age | Total | White | Nonwhite | Male | Female |
|-----|-------|-------|----------|------|--------|
| 0-4 | 510,550 | 374,300 | 136,250 | 260,250 | 250,300 |
| 5-9 | 493,450 | 366,700 | 126,750 | 251,400 | 242,050 |
| 10-14 | 498,300 | 375,700 | 122,600 | 253,950 | 244,350 |
| 15-19 | 505,900 | 386,200 | 119,700 | 257,350 | 248,550 |
| 20-24 | 487,700 | 377,150 | 110,550 | 247,400 | 240,300 |
| 25-29 | 438,200 | 342,600 | 95,600 | 221,500 | 216,700 |
| 30-34 | 382,450 | 302,000 | 80,450 | 192,350 | 190,100 |
| 35-39 | 447,650 | 354,450 | 93,200 | 224,950 | 222,700 |
| 40-44 | 464,700 | 370,100 | 94,600 | 234,550 | 230,150 |
| 45-49 | 434,350 | 356,250 | 78,100 | 220,300 | 214,050 |
| 50-54 | 406,600 | 353,200 | 53,400 | 204,600 | 202,000 |
| 55-59 | 289,250 | 251,700 | 37,550 | 133,850 | 155,400 |
| 60-64 | 226,350 | 196,450 | 29,900 | 102,500 | 123,850 |
| 65-69 | 189,450 | 164,350 | 25,100 | 80,100 | 109,350 |
| 70-74 | 161,100 | 141,000 | 20,100 | 61,600 | 99,500 |
| 75-79 | 119,600 | 105,650 | 13,950 | 39,300 | 80,300 |
| 80-84 | 64,300 | 56,400 | 7,900 | 17,900 | 46,400 |
| 85+ | 39,850 | 32,450 | 7,400 | 11,700 | 28,150 |
| | | | | | |
| Total | 6,159,750 | 4,906,650 | 1,253,100 | 3,015,550 | 3,144,200 |

Table A6.2 (cont.)

1975 - I-B

| Age | Total | White | Nonwhite | Male | Female |
|-----|-------|-------|----------|------|--------|
| 0-4 | 437,400 | 341,800 | 95,600 | 223,000 | 214,400 |
| 5-9 | 391,500 | 307,300 | 84,200 | 199,050 | 192,450 |
| 10-14 | 463,950 | 364,050 | 99,900 | 236,100 | 227,850 |
| 15-19 | 482,350 | 377,350 | 105,000 | 246,000 | 236,350 |
| 20-24 | 470,400 | 380,000 | 90,400 | 245,500 | 224,900 |
| 25-29 | 452,900 | 388,550 | 64,350 | 236,150 | 216,750 |
| 30-34 | 334,100 | 284,550 | 49,550 | 162,000 | 172,100 |
| 35-39 | 287,250 | 242,450 | 44,800 | 142,550 | 144,700 |
| 40-44 | 272,200 | 228,050 | 44,150 | 133,850 | 138,350 |
| 45-49 | 277,550 | 232,900 | 44,650 | 134,650 | 142,900 |
| 50-54 | 273,500 | 229,850 | 43,650 | 130,400 | 143,100 |
| 55-59 | 233,850 | 195,800 | 38,050 | 111,700 | 122,150 |
| 60-64 | 191,950 | 160,300 | 31,650 | 88,700 | 103,250 |
| 65-69 | 149,950 | 126,100 | 23,850 | 65,450 | 84,500 |
| 70-74 | 108,650 | 90,050 | 18,600 | 43,200 | 65,450 |
| 75-79 | 71,250 | 59,900 | 11,350 | 25,350 | 45,900 |
| 80-84 | 40,450 | 33,950 | 6,500 | 13,650 | 26,800 |
| 85+ | 27,300 | 21,550 | 5,750 | 10,000 | 17,300 |
| Total | 4,966,500 | 4,064,500 | 902,000 | 2,447,300 | 2,519,200 |

Table A6.2  (cont.)

1980 - I-B

| Age | Total | White | Nonwhite | Male | Female |
|-----|-------|-------|----------|------|--------|
| 0-4 | 466,200 | 366,500 | 99,700 | 237,400 | 228,800 |
| 5-9 | 437,350 | 344,250 | 93,100 | 222,400 | 214,950 |
| 10-14 | 397,650 | 315,900 | 81,750 | 202,200 | 195,450 |
| 15-19 | 472,350 | 376,350 | 96,000 | 241,100 | 231,250 |
| 20-24 | 515,050 | 418,050 | 97,000 | 268,650 | 246,400 |
| 25-29 | 482,300 | 401,850 | 80,450 | 249,300 | 233,000 |
| 30-34 | 451,600 | 391,700 | 59,900 | 228,350 | 223,250 |
| 35-39 | 342,750 | 295,700 | 47,050 | 165,850 | 176,900 |
| 40-44 | 290,650 | 248,350 | 42,300 | 143,800 | 146,850 |
| 45-49 | 269,400 | 228,100 | 41,300 | 131,450 | 137,950 |
| 50-54 | 268,950 | 227,950 | 41,000 | 128,450 | 140,500 |
| 55-59 | 258,500 | 219,650 | 38,850 | 119,750 | 138,750 |
| 60-64 | 213,600 | 181,350 | 32,250 | 97,450 | 116,150 |
| 65-69 | 167,500 | 141,850 | 25,650 | 72,300 | 95,200 |
| 70-74 | 121,900 | 104,400 | 17,500 | 48,100 | 73,800 |
| 75-79 | 78,450 | 66,400 | 12,050 | 26,750 | 51,700 |
| 80-84 | 43,750 | 37,150 | 6,600 | 13,450 | 30,300 |
| 85+ | 28,600 | 22,500 | 6,100 | 10,150 | 18,450 |
| Total | 5,306,550 | 4,388,000 | 918,550 | 2,606,900 | 2,699,650 |

Table A6.2 (cont.)

1985 - I-B

| Age | Total | White | Nonwhite | Male | Female |
|-----|-------|-------|----------|------|--------|
| 0-4 | 480,050 | 381,800 | 98,250 | 244,450 | 235,600 |
| 5-9 | 465,650 | 369,150 | 96,500 | 236,800 | 228,850 |
| 10-14 | 444,350 | 353,950 | 90,400 | 226,000 | 218,350 |
| 15-19 | 405,150 | 326,600 | 78,550 | 206,600 | 198,550 |
| 20-24 | 505,600 | 417,000 | 88,600 | 263,950 | 241,650 |
| 25-29 | 528,400 | 442,050 | 86,350 | 273,000 | 255,400 |
| 30-34 | 480,150 | 405,250 | 74,900 | 240,700 | 239,450 |
| 35-39 | 463,900 | 407,050 | 56,850 | 234,150 | 229,750 |
| 40-44 | 347,350 | 302,900 | 44,450 | 167,500 | 179,850 |
| 45-49 | 287,950 | 248,400 | 39,550 | 141,300 | 146,650 |
| 50-54 | 261,100 | 223,150 | 37,950 | 125,450 | 135,650 |
| 55-59 | 254,300 | 217,700 | 36,600 | 118,100 | 136,200 |
| 60-64 | 236,650 | 203,650 | 33,000 | 104,600 | 132,050 |
| 65-69 | 186,750 | 160,550 | 26,200 | 79,550 | 107,200 |
| 70-74 | 136,400 | 117,500 | 18,900 | 53,150 | 83,250 |
| 75-79 | 88,350 | 77,000 | 11,350 | 29,850 | 58,500 |
| 80-84 | 48,150 | 41,100 | 7,050 | 13,950 | 34,200 |
| 85+ | 31,200 | 24,800 | 6,400 | 10,300 | 20,900 |
| Total | 5,651,450 | 4,719,600 | 931,850 | 2,769,400 | 2,882,050 |

Table A6.2    (cont.)

| 1990 - I-B Age | Total | White | Nonwhite | Male | Female |
|---|---|---|---|---|---|
| 0-4 | 482,000 | 387,350 | 94,650 | 245,500 | 236,500 |
| 5-9 | 479,700 | 384,600 | 95,100 | 244,000 | 235,700 |
| 10-14 | 473,150 | 379,500 | 93,650 | 240,650 | 232,500 |
| 15-19 | 452,800 | 365,950 | 86,850 | 230,950 | 221,850 |
| 20-24 | 434,400 | 361,850 | 72,550 | 226,550 | 207,850 |
| 25-29 | 519,850 | 440,950 | 78,900 | 268,750 | 251,100 |
| 30-34 | 526,150 | 445,800 | 80,350 | 263,600 | 262,550 |
| 35-39 | 492,250 | 421,150 | 71,100 | 246,150 | 246,100 |
| 40-44 | 470,600 | 416,900 | 53,700 | 236,800 | 233,800 |
| 45-49 | 344,800 | 303,250 | 41,550 | 164,950 | 179,850 |
| 50-54 | 279,350 | 243,000 | 36,350 | 135,050 | 144,300 |
| 55-59 | 247,000 | 213,150 | 33,850 | 115,450 | 131,550 |
| 60-64 | 232,900 | 201,800 | 31,100 | 103,300 | 129,600 |
| 65-69 | 207,450 | 180,600 | 26,850 | 85,450 | 122,000 |
| 70-74 | 152,400 | 133,050 | 19,350 | 58,600 | 93,800 |
| 75-79 | 99,100 | 86,800 | 12,300 | 33,050 | 66,050 |
| 80-84 | 53,250 | 46,550 | 6,700 | 14,450 | 38,800 |
| 85+ | 33,900 | 27,150 | 6,750 | 10,400 | 23,500 |
| Total | 5,981,050 | 5,039,400 | 941,650 | 2,923,650 | 3,057,400 |

Table A6.2   (cont.)

---

1995 - I-B

| Age   | Total     | White     | Nonwhite | Male      | Female    |
|-------|-----------|-----------|----------|-----------|-----------|
| 0-4   | 479,400   | 386,750   | 92,650   | 244,200   | 235,200   |
| 5-9   | 481,850   | 390,150   | 91,700   | 245,150   | 236,700   |
| 10-14 | 487,700   | 395,400   | 92,300   | 248,100   | 239,600   |
| 15-19 | 482,400   | 392,400   | 90,000   | 246,100   | 236,300   |
| 20-24 | 485,650   | 405,400   | 80,250   | 253,400   | 232,250   |
| 25-29 | 447,250   | 382,650   | 64,600   | 230,900   | 216,350   |
| 30-34 | 518,050   | 444,650   | 73,400   | 259,650   | 258,400   |
| 35-39 | 539,600   | 463,300   | 76,300   | 269,700   | 269,900   |
| 40-44 | 498,500   | 431,400   | 67,100   | 248,400   | 250,100   |
| 45-49 | 467,100   | 416,950   | 50,150   | 233,150   | 233,950   |
| 50-54 | 334,750   | 296,600   | 38,150   | 157,600   | 177,150   |
| 55-59 | 264,800   | 232,050   | 32,750   | 124,750   | 140,050   |
| 60-64 | 226,250   | 197,450   | 28,800   | 101,050   | 125,200   |
| 65-69 | 204,200   | 178,800   | 25,400   | 84,500    | 119,700   |
| 70-74 | 169,950   | 150,050   | 19,900   | 63,050    | 106,900   |
| 75-79 | 110,950   | 98,350    | 12,600   | 36,450    | 74,500    |
| 80-84 | 59,700    | 52,450    | 7,250    | 15,950    | 43,750    |
| 85+   | 37,350    | 30,600    | 6,750    | 10,650    | 26,700    |
|       |           |           |          |           |           |
| Total | 6,295,450 | 5,345,400 | 950,050  | 3,072,750 | 3,222,700 |

Table A6.2   (cont.)

| 2000 - I-B | | | | | |
|---|---|---|---|---|---|
| Age | Total | White | Nonwhite | Male | Female |
| 0-4 | 488,900 | 396,350 | 92,550 | 249,050 | 239,850 |
| 5-9 | 479,450 | 389,500 | 89,950 | 244,050 | 235,400 |
| 10-14 | 490,100 | 401,150 | 88,950 | 249,350 | 240,750 |
| 15-19 | 497,450 | 408,800 | 88,650 | 253,800 | 243,650 |
| 20-24 | 517,850 | 434,700 | 83,150 | 270,200 | 247,650 |
| 25-29 | 500,100 | 428,700 | 71,400 | 258,250 | 241,850 |
| 30-34 | 446,000 | 385,900 | 60,100 | 223,200 | 222,800 |
| 35-39 | 531,850 | 462,150 | 69,700 | 266,000 | 265,850 |
| 40-44 | 546,600 | 474,550 | 72,050 | 272,250 | 274,350 |
| 45-49 | 494,100 | 431,450 | 62,650 | 244,100 | 250,000 |
| 50-54 | 453,900 | 407,900 | 46,000 | 223,250 | 230,650 |
| 55-59 | 317,450 | 283,450 | 34,000 | 145,250 | 172,200 |
| 60-64 | 242,550 | 214,950 | 27,600 | 109,050 | 133,500 |
| 65-69 | 198,400 | 174,850 | 23,550 | 82,750 | 115,650 |
| 70-74 | 167,250 | 148,400 | 18,850 | 62,350 | 104,900 |
| 75-79 | 124,250 | 111,250 | 13,000 | 39,250 | 85,000 |
| 80-84 | 66,950 | 59,500 | 7,450 | 17,600 | 49,350 |
| 85+ | 41,300 | 34,300 | 7,000 | 11,450 | 29,850 |
| | | | | | |
| Total | 6,604,450 | 5,647,850 | 956,600 | 3,221,200 | 3,383,250 |

Table A6.2  (cont.)

---

1975 - II-B

| Age | Total | White | Nonwhite | Male | Female |
|-----|-------|-------|----------|------|--------|
| 0-4 | 437,350 | 340,600 | 96,750 | 222,650 | 214,700 |
| 5-9 | 391,350 | 306,850 | 84,500 | 199,000 | 192,350 |
| 10-14 | 462,900 | 362,700 | 100,200 | 235,550 | 227,350 |
| 15-19 | 481,100 | 375,600 | 105,500 | 245,250 | 235,850 |
| 20-24 | 466,350 | 375,150 | 91,200 | 242,700 | 223,650 |
| 25-29 | 450,850 | 385,650 | 65,200 | 235,250 | 215,600 |
| 30-34 | 333,850 | 284,000 | 49,850 | 162,400 | 171,450 |
| 35-39 | 285,950 | 241,050 | 44,900 | 141,850 | 144,100 |
| 40-44 | 271,200 | 227,000 | 44,200 | 133,400 | 137,800 |
| 45-49 | 276,100 | 231,350 | 44,750 | 134,400 | 141,700 |
| 50-54 | 273,250 | 229,500 | 43,750 | 130,300 | 142,950 |
| 55-59 | 233,650 | 195,500 | 38,150 | 111,600 | 122,050 |
| 60-64 | 191,950 | 160,200 | 31,750 | 88,750 | 103,200 |
| 65-69 | 149,850 | 126,000 | 23,850 | 65,450 | 84,400 |
| 70-74 | 108,550 | 89,950 | 18,600 | 43,200 | 65,350 |
| 75-79 | 71,150 | 59,800 | 11,350 | 25,350 | 45,800 |
| 80-84 | 40,500 | 33,950 | 6,550 | 13,700 | 26,800 |
| 85+ | 27,350 | 21,600 | 5,750 | 10,000 | 17,350 |
| | | | | | |
| Total | 4,953,250 | 4,046,450 | 906,800 | 2,440,800 | 2,512,450 |

Table A6.2   (cont.)

### 1980 - II-B

| Age | Total | White | Nonwhite | Male | Female |
|---|---|---|---|---|---|
| 0-4 | 462,150 | 360,000 | 102,150 | 235,350 | 226,800 |
| 5-9 | 436,400 | 341,700 | 94,700 | 222,050 | 214,350 |
| 10-14 | 394,900 | 312,050 | 82,850 | 200,750 | 194,150 |
| 15-19 | 467,500 | 369,900 | 97,600 | 238,200 | 229,300 |
| 20-24 | 500,300 | 400,250 | 100,050 | 258,500 | 241,800 |
| 25-29 | 472,350 | 387,850 | 84,500 | 244,050 | 228,300 |
| 30-34 | 448,700 | 386,700 | 62,000 | 229,450 | 219,250 |
| 35-39 | 337,950 | 290,050 | 47,900 | 164,050 | 173,900 |
| 40-44 | 287,000 | 243,550 | 43,450 | 142,200 | 144,800 |
| 45-49 | 266,900 | 225,300 | 41,600 | 130,200 | 136,700 |
| 50-54 | 266,550 | 225,250 | 41,300 | 127,850 | 138,700 |
| 55-59 | 257,650 | 218,550 | 39,100 | 119,550 | 138,100 |
| 60-64 | 213,000 | 180,500 | 32,500 | 97,350 | 115,650 |
| 65-69 | 167,200 | 141,400 | 25,800 | 72,300 | 94,900 |
| 70-74 | 121,500 | 103,850 | 17,650 | 48,150 | 73,350 |
| 75-79 | 78,200 | 66,050 | 12,150 | 26,850 | 51,350 |
| 80-84 | 43,850 | 37,200 | 6,650 | 13,750 | 30,100 |
| 85+ | 28,550 | 22,350 | 6,200 | 10,200 | 18,350 |
| | | | | | |
| Total | 5,250,650 | 4,312,500 | 938,150 | 2,580,800 | 2,669,850 |

Table A6.2   (cont.)

**1985 - II-B**

| Age | Total | White | Nonwhite | Male | Female |
|-----|-------|-------|----------|------|--------|
| 0-4 | 469,800 | 366,150 | 103,650 | 239,250 | 230,550 |
| 5-9 | 460,900 | 360,700 | 100,200 | 234,500 | 226,400 |
| 10-14 | 440,100 | 346,850 | 93,250 | 223,550 | 216,550 |
| 15-19 | 397,900 | 316,850 | 81,050 | 202,450 | 195,450 |
| 20-24 | 482,250 | 388,900 | 93,350 | 248,300 | 233,950 |
| 25-29 | 504,500 | 410,600 | 93,900 | 259,000 | 245,500 |
| 30-34 | 469,100 | 388,250 | 80,850 | 238,350 | 230,750 |
| 35-39 | 452,400 | 392,650 | 59,750 | 230,850 | 221,550 |
| 40-44 | 337,550 | 291,800 | 45,750 | 163,250 | 174,300 |
| 45-49 | 280,550 | 239,600 | 40,950 | 138,600 | 141,950 |
| 50-54 | 257,450 | 219,000 | 38,450 | 123,800 | 133,650 |
| 55-59 | 251,250 | 214,200 | 37,050 | 117,350 | 133,900 |
| 60-64 | 235,300 | 201,850 | 33,450 | 104,400 | 130,900 |
| 65-69 | 185,750 | 159,250 | 26,500 | 79,450 | 106,300 |
| 70-74 | 135,600 | 116,450 | 19,150 | 53,250 | 82,350 |
| 75-79 | 87,750 | 76,200 | 11,550 | 30,000 | 57,750 |
| 80-84 | 47,750 | 40,600 | 7,150 | 14,050 | 33,700 |
| 85+ | 30,850 | 24,450 | 6,400 | 10,250 | 20,600 |
| Total | 5,526,750 | 4,554,350 | 972,400 | 2,710,650 | 2,816,100 |

Table A6.2 (cont.)

1990 - II-B

| Age | Total | White | Nonwhite | Male | Female |
|-----|-------|-------|----------|------|--------|
| 0-4 | 465,550 | 362,900 | 102,650 | 237,100 | 228,450 |
| 5-9 | 468,500 | 366,850 | 101,650 | 238,350 | 230,150 |
| 10-14 | 464,700 | 366,100 | 98,600 | 236,700 | 228,000 |
| 15-19 | 443,300 | 352,150 | 91,150 | 225,350 | 217,950 |
| 20-24 | 410,600 | 333,050 | 77,550 | 211,100 | 199,500 |
| 25-29 | 486,650 | 399,050 | 87,600 | 249,000 | 237,650 |
| 30-34 | 501,050 | 411,150 | 89,900 | 253,000 | 248,050 |
| 35-39 | 472,200 | 394,250 | 77,950 | 239,350 | 232,850 |
| 40-44 | 451,950 | 394,900 | 57,050 | 229,850 | 222,100 |
| 45-49 | 331,950 | 288,850 | 43,100 | 159,200 | 172,750 |
| 50-54 | 270,800 | 232,950 | 37,850 | 131,900 | 138,900 |
| 55-59 | 242,750 | 208,250 | 34,500 | 113,750 | 129,000 |
| 60-64 | 229,450 | 197,650 | 31,800 | 102,600 | 126,850 |
| 65-69 | 205,650 | 178,350 | 27,300 | 85,250 | 120,400 |
| 70-74 | 150,900 | 131,200 | 19,700 | 58,550 | 92,350 |
| 75-79 | 98,050 | 85,450 | 12,600 | 33,200 | 64,850 |
| 80-84 | 52,550 | 45,750 | 6,800 | 14,600 | 37,950 |
| 85+ | 33,450 | 26,600 | 6,850 | 10,450 | 23,000 |
| | | | | | |
| Total | 5,780,050 | 4,775,450 | 1,004,600 | 2,829,300 | 2,950,750 |

Table A6.2   (cont.)

**1995 - II-B**

| Age | Total | White | Nonwhite | Male | Female |
|-----|-------|-------|----------|------|--------|
| 0-4 | 458,900 | 356,500 | 102,400 | 233,700 | 225,200 |
| 5-9 | 464,300 | 363,650 | 100,650 | 236,250 | 228,050 |
| 10-14 | 471,800 | 371,700 | 100,100 | 240,000 | 231,800 |
| 15-19 | 468,150 | 371,700 | 96,450 | 238,600 | 229,550 |
| 20-24 | 457,500 | 370,250 | 87,250 | 235,000 | 222,500 |
| 25-29 | 414,600 | 341,800 | 72,800 | 211,750 | 202,850 |
| 30-34 | 483,400 | 399,550 | 83,850 | 243,200 | 240,200 |
| 35-39 | 504,100 | 417,450 | 86,650 | 253,900 | 250,200 |
| 40-44 | 470,900 | 396,500 | 74,400 | 237,750 | 233,150 |
| 45-49 | 444,500 | 390,800 | 53,700 | 224,300 | 220,200 |
| 50-54 | 320,700 | 280,900 | 39,800 | 151,500 | 169,200 |
| 55-59 | 255,300 | 221,400 | 33,900 | 121,200 | 134,100 |
| 60-64 | 221,750 | 192,150 | 29,600 | 99,500 | 122,250 |
| 65-69 | 200,550 | 174,500 | 26,050 | 83,900 | 116,650 |
| 70-74 | 167,600 | 147,200 | 20,400 | 62,900 | 104,700 |
| 75-79 | 109,300 | 96,350 | 12,950 | 36,500 | 72,800 |
| 80-84 | 58,700 | 51,300 | 7,400 | 16,100 | 42,600 |
| 85+ | 36,700 | 29,900 | 6,800 | 10,750 | 25,950 |
| Total | 6,008,750 | 4,973,600 | 1,035,150 | 2,936,800 | 3,071,950 |

Table A6.2   (cont.)

2000 - II-B

| Age | Total | White | Nonwhite | Male | Female |
|-----|-------|-------|----------|------|--------|
| 0-4 | 464,600 | 360,250 | 104,350 | 236,600 | 228,000 |
| 5-9 | 457,650 | 357,200 | 100,450 | 232,850 | 224,800 |
| 10-14 | 467,900 | 368,450 | 99,450 | 238,250 | 229,650 |
| 15-19 | 472,200 | 374,350 | 97,850 | 238,900 | 233,300 |
| 20-24 | 483,100 | 390,800 | 92,300 | 248,850 | 234,250 |
| 25-29 | 461,800 | 379,850 | 81,950 | 235,600 | 226,200 |
| 30-34 | 411,850 | 342,200 | 69,650 | 206,850 | 205,000 |
| 35-39 | 486,600 | 405,750 | 80,850 | 244,200 | 242,400 |
| 40-44 | 502,650 | 419,900 | 82,750 | 252,200 | 250,450 |
| 45-49 | 462,450 | 392,400 | 70,050 | 231,600 | 230,850 |
| 50-54 | 429,300 | 379,750 | 49,550 | 213,600 | 215,700 |
| 55-59 | 302,900 | 267,200 | 35,700 | 139,350 | 163,550 |
| 60-64 | 233,300 | 204,200 | 29,100 | 106,050 | 127,250 |
| 65-69 | 193,800 | 169,550 | 24,250 | 81,400 | 112,400 |
| 70-74 | 163,400 | 143,900 | 19,500 | 62,000 | 101,400 |
| 75-79 | 121,850 | 108,400 | 13,450 | 39,250 | 82,600 |
| 80-84 | 65,550 | 57,900 | 7,650 | 17,700 | 47,850 |
| 85+ | 40,550 | 33,400 | 7,150 | 11,600 | 28,950 |
| Total | 6,221,450 | 5,155,450 | 1,066,000 | 3,036,850 | 3,184,600 |

Table A6.2    (cont.)

1975 - III-B

| Age | Total | White | Nonwhite | Male | Female |
|-----|-------|-------|----------|------|--------|
| 0-4 | 436,600 | 339,350 | 97,250 | 222,300 | 214,300 |
| 5-9 | 391,250 | 306,450 | 84,800 | 198,950 | 192,300 |
| 10-14 | 461,900 | 361,350 | 100,550 | 235,000 | 226,900 |
| 15-19 | 479,900 | 373,950 | 105,950 | 244,500 | 235,400 |
| 20-24 | 462,350 | 370,300 | 92,050 | 239,900 | 222,450 |
| 25-29 | 448,850 | 382,800 | 66,050 | 234,400 | 214,450 |
| 30-34 | 333,650 | 283,450 | 50,200 | 162,900 | 170,750 |
| 35-39 | 284,750 | 239,650 | 45,100 | 141,250 | 143,500 |
| 40-44 | 270,300 | 226,000 | 44,300 | 132,950 | 137,350 |
| 45-49 | 276,600 | 231,700 | 44,900 | 134,200 | 142,400 |
| 50-54 | 272,900 | 229,100 | 43,800 | 130,150 | 142,750 |
| 55-59 | 233,550 | 195,350 | 38,200 | 111,700 | 121,850 |
| 60-64 | 191,850 | 160,000 | 31,850 | 88,750 | 103,100 |
| 65-69 | 149,750 | 125,900 | 23,850 | 65,450 | 84,300 |
| 70-74 | 108,500 | 89,800 | 18,700 | 43,250 | 65,250 |
| 75-79 | 71,100 | 59,700 | 11,400 | 25,400 | 45,700 |
| 80-84 | 40,450 | 33,900 | 6,550 | 13,700 | 26,750 |
| 85+ | 27,400 | 21,650 | 5,750 | 10,000 | 17,400 |
| Total | 4,941,650 | 4,030,400 | 911,250 | 2,434,750 | 2,506,900 |

Table A6.2   (cont.)

---

1980 - III-B

| Age | Total | White | Nonwhite | Male | Female |
|-----|-------|-------|----------|------|--------|
| 0-4 | 458,250 | 353,550 | 104,700 | 233,400 | 224,850 |
| 5-9 | 435,150 | 339,150 | 96,000 | 221,400 | 213,750 |
| 10-14 | 392,200 | 308,200 | 84,000 | 199,350 | 192,850 |
| 15-19 | 462,800 | 363,600 | 99,200 | 235,400 | 227,400 |
| 20-24 | 485,700 | 382,550 | 103,150 | 248,450 | 237,250 |
| 25-29 | 462,650 | 374,100 | 88,550 | 238,900 | 223,750 |
| 30-34 | 445,850 | 381,750 | 64,100 | 230,550 | 215,300 |
| 35-39 | 333,150 | 284,450 | 48,700 | 162,250 | 170,900 |
| 40-44 | 282,200 | 238,850 | 43,350 | 139,450 | 142,750 |
| 45-49 | 264,500 | 222,500 | 42,000 | 129,050 | 135,450 |
| 50-54 | 266,150 | 224,550 | 41,600 | 127,250 | 138,900 |
| 55-59 | 256,800 | 217,450 | 39,350 | 119,350 | 137,450 |
| 60-64 | 212,650 | 179,900 | 32,750 | 97,400 | 115,250 |
| 65-69 | 166,850 | 140,900 | 25,950 | 72,350 | 94,500 |
| 70-74 | 121,700 | 103,900 | 17,800 | 48,200 | 73,500 |
| 75-79 | 77,950 | 65,650 | 12,300 | 26,900 | 51,050 |
| 80-84 | 43,400 | 36,750 | 6,650 | 13,500 | 29,900 |
| 85+ | 28,400 | 22,200 | 6,200 | 10,200 | 18,200 |
| Total | 5,196,350 | 4,240,000 | 956,350 | 2,553,350 | 2,643,000 |

Table A6.2  (cont.)

1985 - III-B

| Age | Total | White | Nonwhite | Male | Female |
|------|-----------|-----------|-----------|-----------|-----------|
| 0-4 | 460,100 | 350,800 | 109,300 | 234,350 | 225,750 |
| 5-9 | 456,400 | 352,350 | 104,050 | 232,300 | 224,100 |
| 10-14 | 434,250 | 338,500 | 95,750 | 220,800 | 213,450 |
| 15-19 | 390,800 | 307,200 | 83,600 | 198,350 | 192,450 |
| 20-24 | 459,900 | 361,700 | 98,200 | 233,300 | 226,600 |
| 25-29 | 482,250 | 380,450 | 101,800 | 245,900 | 236,350 |
| 30-34 | 458,850 | 371,700 | 87,150 | 236,200 | 222,650 |
| 35-39 | 441,200 | 378,500 | 62,700 | 227,600 | 213,600 |
| 40-44 | 327,950 | 280,850 | 47,100 | 159,100 | 168,850 |
| 45-49 | 275,100 | 233,900 | 41,200 | 134,900 | 140,200 |
| 50-54 | 253,950 | 214,900 | 39,050 | 122,150 | 131,800 |
| 55-59 | 250,100 | 212,550 | 37,550 | 116,700 | 133,400 |
| 60-64 | 233,900 | 200,000 | 33,900 | 104,150 | 129,750 |
| 65-69 | 184,950 | 158,150 | 26,800 | 79,500 | 105,450 |
| 70-74 | 134,800 | 115,350 | 19,450 | 53,350 | 81,450 |
| 75-79 | 87,550 | 75,800 | 11,750 | 30,100 | 57,450 |
| 80-84 | 47,450 | 40,200 | 7,250 | 14,150 | 33,300 |
| 85+ | 30,550 | 24,150 | 6,400 | 10,300 | 20,250 |
| | | | | | |
| Total | 5,410,050 | 4,397,050 | 1,013,000 | 2,653,200 | 2,756,850 |

Table A6.2  (cont.)

1990 - III-B

| Age | Total | White | Nonwhite | Male | Female |
|------|-----------|-----------|-----------|-----------|-----------|
| 0-4 | 450,350 | 339,350 | 111,000 | 229,350 | 221,000 |
| 5-9 | 458,250 | 349,650 | 108,600 | 233,200 | 225,050 |
| 10-14 | 455,550 | 351,750 | 103,800 | 231,750 | 223,800 |
| 15-19 | 432,600 | 337,300 | 95,300 | 219,600 | 213,000 |
| 20-24 | 388,350 | 305,600 | 82,750 | 196,600 | 191,750 |
| 25-29 | 456,550 | 359,650 | 96,900 | 230,850 | 225,700 |
| 30-34 | 478,200 | 378,050 | 100,150 | 243,000 | 235,200 |
| 35-39 | 453,750 | 368,550 | 85,200 | 232,950 | 220,800 |
| 40-44 | 434,300 | 373,700 | 60,600 | 223,200 | 211,100 |
| 45-49 | 319,850 | 275,100 | 44,750 | 153,900 | 165,950 |
| 50-54 | 264,200 | 225,900 | 38,300 | 127,750 | 136,450 |
| 55-59 | 238,700 | 203,400 | 35,300 | 112,100 | 126,600 |
| 60-64 | 227,850 | 195,450 | 32,400 | 101,900 | 125,950 |
| 65-69 | 203,950 | 176,150 | 27,800 | 85,100 | 118,850 |
| 70-74 | 149,700 | 129,600 | 20,100 | 58,700 | 91,000 |
| 75-79 | 97,050 | 84,150 | 12,900 | 33,350 | 63,700 |
| 80-84 | 52,200 | 45,250 | 6,950 | 14,750 | 37,450 |
| 85+ | 33,050 | 26,150 | 6,900 | 10,500 | 22,550 |
| Total | 5,594,450 | 4,524,750 | 1,069,700 | 2,738,550 | 2,855,900 |

Table A6.2  (cont.)

## 1995 - III-B

| Age | Total | White | Nonwhite | Male | Female |
|-----|-------|-------|----------|------|--------|
| 0-4 | 439,850 | 326,950 | 112,900 | 224,200 | 215,650 |
| 5-9 | 448,600 | 338,300 | 110,300 | 228,250 | 220,350 |
| 10-14 | 457,350 | 349,000 | 108,350 | 232,650 | 224,700 |
| 15-19 | 453,900 | 350,600 | 103,300 | 230,550 | 223,350 |
| 20-24 | 430,050 | 335,700 | 94,350 | 217,750 | 212,300 |
| 25-29 | 385,650 | 303,900 | 81,750 | 194,600 | 191,050 |
| 30-34 | 452,800 | 357,450 | 95,350 | 228,200 | 224,600 |
| 35-39 | 472,800 | 374,900 | 97,900 | 239,600 | 233,200 |
| 40-44 | 446,200 | 363,900 | 82,300 | 228,150 | 218,050 |
| 45-49 | 423,350 | 365,850 | 57,500 | 215,900 | 207,450 |
| 50-54 | 307,400 | 265,800 | 41,600 | 145,800 | 161,600 |
| 55-59 | 248,400 | 213,800 | 34,600 | 117,250 | 131,150 |
| 60-64 | 217,400 | 186,900 | 30,500 | 97,950 | 119,450 |
| 65-69 | 198,600 | 171,950 | 26,650 | 83,350 | 115,250 |
| 70-74 | 165,450 | 144,500 | 20,950 | 62,850 | 102,600 |
| 75-79 | 107,850 | 94,450 | 13,400 | 36,700 | 71,150 |
| 80-84 | 57,800 | 50,200 | 7,600 | 16,300 | 41,500 |
| 85+ | 36,350 | 29,400 | 6,950 | 10,850 | 25,500 |
| Total | 5,749,800 | 4,623,550 | 1,126,250 | 2,810,900 | 2,938,900 |

Table A6.2  (cont.)

| 2000 - III-B | | | | |
|---|---|---|---|---|
| Age | Total | White | Nonwhite | Male | Female |
| 0-4 | 443,250 | 325,950 | 117,300 | 225,650 | 217,600 |
| 5-9 | 438,050 | 325,850 | 112,200 | 223,100 | 214,950 |
| 10-14 | 447,700 | 337,650 | 110,050 | 227,700 | 220,000 |
| 15-19 | 455,700 | 347,900 | 107,800 | 231,450 | 224,250 |
| 20-24 | 451,050 | 348,800 | 102,250 | 228,500 | 222,550 |
| 25-29 | 426,900 | 333,800 | 93,100 | 215,450 | 211,450 |
| 30-34 | 382,450 | 302,000 | 80,450 | 192,350 | 190,100 |
| 35-39 | 447,650 | 354,450 | 93,200 | 224,950 | 222,700 |
| 40-44 | 464,700 | 370,100 | 94,600 | 234,550 | 230,150 |
| 45-49 | 434,350 | 356,250 | 78,100 | 220,300 | 214,050 |
| 50-54 | 406,600 | 353,200 | 53,400 | 204,600 | 202,000 |
| 55-59 | 289,250 | 251,700 | 37,550 | 133,850 | 155,400 |
| 60-64 | 226,350 | 196,450 | 29,900 | 102,500 | 123,850 |
| 65-69 | 189,450 | 164,350 | 25,100 | 80,100 | 109,350 |
| 70-74 | 161,100 | 141,000 | 20,100 | 61,600 | 99,500 |
| 75-79 | 119,600 | 105,650 | 13,950 | 39,300 | 80,300 |
| 80-84 | 64,300 | 56,400 | 7,900 | 17,900 | 46,400 |
| 85+ | 39,750 | 32,450 | 7,300 | 11,700 | 28,050 |
| | | | | | |
| Total | 5,888,200 | 4,703,950 | 1,184,250 | 2,875,550 | 3,012,650 |

Table A-7.1.  Alternative labor force projections by age and sex, 1975-2000

| Series I-A Age | 1975 | 1980 | 1985 | 1990 | 1995 | 2000 |
|---|---|---|---|---|---|---|
| **Male** | | | | | | |
| 15-19 | 93,972 | 90,895 | 76,235 | 87,363 | 98,072 | 103,850 |
| 20-24 | 207,939 | 224,860 | 219,606 | 187,583 | 215,653 | 242,314 |
| 25-29 | 222,689 | 234,591 | 256,347 | 252,356 | 216,815 | 249,305 |
| 30-34 | 152,766 | 214,877 | 226,017 | 247,520 | 243,811 | 209,585 |
| | | | | | | |
| 35-39 | 134,567 | 156,065 | 219,867 | 230,643 | 252,709 | 249,242 |
| 40-44 | 126,354 | 135,316 | 157,283 | 221,882 | 232,751 | 255,098 |
| 45-59 | 122,666 | 119,094 | 127,735 | 148,785 | 210,301 | 220,178 |
| 50-54 | 118,794 | 116,376 | 113,407 | 121,815 | 142,155 | 201,372 |
| 55-59 | 93,270 | 99,273 | 97,433 | 94,900 | 102,545 | 119,396 |
| 60-64 | 61,114 | 65,584 | 69,559 | 68,178 | 66,693 | 71,973 |
| | | | | | | |
| 65-69 | 24,478 | 25,233 | 26,808 | 28,199 | 27,885 | 27,308 |
| 70-74 | 6,610 | 6,349 | 6,431 | 6,739 | 7,251 | 7,710 |
| 75-79 | 3,879 | 3,531 | 3,612 | 3,801 | 4,192 | 4,514 |
| 80-84 | 2,088 | 1,775 | 1,688 | 1,662 | 1,834 | 2,024 |
| 85+ | 1,530 | 1,340 | 1,246 | 1,196 | 1,225 | 1,317 |
| | | | | | | |
| Total | 1,372,716 | 1,495,159 | 1,603,274 | 1,702,622 | 1,823,892 | 1,964,646 |
| **Female** | | | | | | |
| 15-19 | 56,015 | 55,963 | 48,645 | 56,598 | 63,507 | 67,242 |
| 20-24 | 133,141 | 150,550 | 151,148 | 125,957 | 144,198 | 161,984 |
| 25-29 | 107,075 | 119,296 | 132,042 | 130,823 | 112,718 | 129,078 |
| 30-34 | 85,017 | 114,304 | 123,796 | 136,789 | 134,626 | 116,079 |
| | | | | | | |
| 35-39 | 75,244 | 93,757 | 124,525 | 135,109 | 148,175 | 145,952 |
| 40-44 | 71,942 | 77,831 | 97,479 | 128,356 | 137,140 | 150,618 |
| 45-49 | 74,880 | 73,803 | 80,071 | 99,277 | 129,140 | 138,000 |
| 50-54 | 74,984 | 75,168 | 74,065 | 79,654 | 97,787 | 127,319 |
| | | | | | | |
| 65-69 | 14,281 | 15,898 | 17,902 | 20,252 | 19,870 | 19,198 |
| 70-74 | 3,927 | 4,207 | 4,662 | 5,065 | 5,773 | 5,665 |
| 75-79 | 2,754 | 2,974 | 3,276 | 3,567 | 4,023 | 4,590 |
| 80-84 | 1,608 | 1,727 | 1,915 | 2,095 | 2,363 | 2,665 |
| 85+ | 1,038 | 1,052 | 1,170 | 1,269 | 1,442 | 1,612 |
| | | | | | | |
| Total | 797,839 | 898,163 | 979,503 | 1,041,789 | 1,120,349 | 1,209,067 |

Table A7.1 (cont.)

| Series II-A Age | 1975 | 1980 | 1985 | 1990 | 1995 | 2000 |
|---|---|---|---|---|---|---|
| **Male** | | | | | | |
| 15-19 | 93,686 | 89,801 | 74,704 | 88,982 | 98,808 | 102,893 |
| 20-24 | 205,657 | 216,365 | 206,586 | 174,791 | 208,946 | 232,006 |
| 25-29 | 221,841 | 229,651 | 243,201 | 233,811 | 198,833 | 237,802 |
| 30-34 | 153,143 | 215,912 | 223,811 | 237,567 | 228,365 | 194,232 |
| 35-39 | 133,906 | 154,371 | 216,768 | 224,271 | 237,904 | 228,815 |
| 40-44 | 125,930 | 133,810 | 153,292 | 215,369 | 222,772 | 236,311 |
| 45-49 | 1,224,438 | 117,961 | 125,294 | 143,598 | 202,319 | 208,903 |
| 50-54 | 118,703 | 115,832 | 111,915 | 118,974 | 136,653 | 192,667 |
| 55-59 | 93,186 | 99,107 | 96,814 | 93,503 | 99,626 | 114,546 |
| 60-64 | 61,149 | 65,517 | 65,426 | 69,716 | 65,670 | 69,993 |
| 65-69 | 24,478 | 25,233 | 26,775 | 28,133 | 27,687 | 26,862 |
| 70-74 | 6,610 | 6,356 | 6,443 | 6,733 | 7,234 | 7,130 |
| 75-79 | 3,879 | 3,544 | 3,630 | 3,818 | 4,198 | 4,514 |
| 80-84 | 2,096 | 1,815 | 1,700 | 1,679 | 1,852 | 2,036 |
| 85+ | 1,530 | 1,346 | 1,240 | 1,202 | 1,236 | 1,334 |
| Total | 1,368,142 | 1,476,621 | 1,561,599 | 1,640,147 | 1,742,103 | 1,860,044 |
| **Female** | | | | | | |
| 15-19 | 55,896 | 55,491 | 47,885 | 55,602 | 61,677 | 64,379 |
| 20-34 | 132,401 | 147,740 | 146,453 | 120,897 | 138,138 | 153,197 |
| 25-29 | 106,506 | 116,890 | 126,924 | 123,816 | 105,685 | 120,690 |
| 30-34 | 84,696 | 112,256 | 119,298 | 129,208 | 125,144 | 106,805 |
| 35-39 | 74,932 | 92,167 | 120,080 | 127,835 | 137,360 | 133,078 |
| 40-44 | 71,656 | 76,744 | 94,471 | 121,933 | 127,999 | 137,497 |
| 45-49 | 74,251 | 73,108 | 77,505 | 95,358 | 121,550 | 127,429 |
| 50-54 | 74,906 | 74,205 | 72,973 | 76,673 | 93,398 | 119,066 |
| 55-59 | 58,096 | 67,669 | 66,950 | 65,274 | 67,855 | 82,756 |
| 60-64 | 37,771 | 43,484 | 50,266 | 49,345 | 47,555 | 49,500 |
| 65-69 | 14,264 | 15,848 | 17,752 | 19,986 | 19,364 | 18,658 |
| 70-74 | 3,921 | 4,181 | 4,612 | 4,987 | 5,654 | 5,476 |
| 75-79 | 2,748 | 2,927 | 3,234 | 3,502 | 3,931 | 4,460 |
| 80-84 | 1,608 | 1,716 | 1,887 | 2,049 | 2,300 | 2,584 |
| 85+ | 1,041 | 1,046 | 1,154 | 1,242 | 1,401 | 1,563 |
| Total | 794,693 | 885,472 | 951,444 | 997,011 | 1,059,011 | 1,127,138 |

Table A7.1 (cont.)

| Series III-A Age | 1975 | 1980 | 1985 | 1990 | 1995 | 2000 |
|---|---|---|---|---|---|---|
| **Male** | | | | | | |
| 15-19 | 93,399 | 88,746 | 73,191 | 83,094 | 91,871 | 94,705 |
| 20-24 | 203,195 | 207,953 | 194,106 | 162,785 | 185,306 | 204,847 |
| 25-29 | 221,039 | 224,805 | 230,900 | 216,768 | 182,729 | 207,989 |
| 30-34 | 153,615 | 216,948 | 221,792 | 228,177 | 214,280 | 180,617 |
| 35-39 | 133,340 | 152,677 | 213,716 | 218,274 | 224,505 | 210,778 |
| 40-44 | 125,505 | 131,222 | 149,395 | 209,138 | 213,777 | 219,773 |
| 45-49 | 122,256 | 116,919 | 121,950 | 138,818 | 194,742 | 198,711 |
| 50-54 | 118,567 | 115,289 | 110,424 | 115,231 | 131,512 | 184,549 |
| 55-59 | 93,270 | 98,941 | 96,278 | 92,146 | 96,380 | 110,025 |
| 60-64 | 61,149 | 65,550 | 69,260 | 67,254 | 64,647 | 67,650 |
| 65-69 | 24,478 | 25,250 | 26,792 | 28,083 | 27,506 | 26,433 |
| 70-74 | 6,617 | 6,362 | 6,455 | 6,751 | 7,228 | 7,084 |
| 75-79 | 3,886 | 3,551 | 3,642 | 3,835 | 4,221 | 4,520 |
| 80-84 | 2,096 | 1,782 | 1,712 | 1,696 | 1,875 | 2,059 |
| 85+ | 1,530 | 1,346 | 1,246 | 1,208 | 1,248 | 1,346 |
| Total | 1,363,942 | 1,457,341 | 1,520,859 | 1,573,258 | 1,641,827 | 1,721,086 |
| **Female** | | | | | | |
| 15-19 | 55,790 | 55,031 | 47,150 | 54,344 | 60,046 | 61,899 |
| 20-24 | 131,690 | 144,960 | 141,852 | 116,201 | 131,805 | 145,622 |
| 25-29 | 105,938 | 114,560 | 122,193 | 117,590 | 99,537 | 112,901 |
| 30-34 | 84,351 | 110,234 | 115,110 | 122,539 | 117,017 | 99,042 |
| 35-39 | 74,620 | 90,577 | 115,771 | 121,219 | 128,027 | 122,262 |
| 40-44 | 71,422 | 75,658 | 91,517 | 115,894 | 119,709 | 126,352 |
| 45-49 | 74,618 | 72,466 | 76,549 | 91,604 | 114,512 | 118,156 |
| 50-54 | 74,801 | 74,312 | 71,963 | 75,320 | 89,231 | 111,504 |
| 55-59 | 58,001 | 67,351 | 66,700 | 64,060 | 66,362 | 78,632 |
| 60-64 | 37,735 | 43,334 | 49,824 | 48,975 | 46,466 | 48,178 |
| 65-69 | 14,247 | 15,782 | 17,610 | 19,729 | 19,132 | 18,152 |
| 70-74 | 3,915 | 4,190 | 4,561 | 4,914 | 5,540 | 5,373 |
| 75-79 | 2,742 | 2,910 | 3,217 | 3,440 | 3,842 | 4,336 |
| 80-84 | 1,605 | 1,704 | 1,865 | 2,022 | 2,241 | 2,506 |
| 85+ | 1,044 | 1,037 | 1,134 | 1,218 | 1,377 | 1,520 |
| Total | 792,519 | 874,106 | 927,016 | 959,069 | 1,004,844 | 1,056,425 |

Table A7.1 (cont.)

| Series I-B Age | 1975 | 1980 | 1985 | 1990 | 1995 | 2000 |
|---|---|---|---|---|---|---|
| **Male** | | | | | | |
| 15-19 | 93,972 | 90,895 | 76,235 | 84,990 | 90,565 | 93,398 |
| 20-24 | 207,939 | 224,860 | 219,606 | 187,583 | 209,815 | 228,726 |
| 25-29 | 222,689 | 234,591 | 256,347 | 252,356 | 216,815 | 242,497 |
| 30-34 | 152,766 | 214,877 | 226,017 | 247,520 | 243,811 | 209,585 |
| 35-39 | 134,567 | 156,065 | 219,867 | 230,643 | 252,709 | 249,242 |
| 40-44 | 126,354 | 135,316 | 157,283 | 221,882 | 232,751 | 255,098 |
| 45-49 | 122,666 | 119,094 | 127,735 | 148,785 | 210,301 | 220,178 |
| 50-54 | 118,794 | 116,376 | 113,407 | 121,815 | 142,155 | 201,372 |
| 55-59 | 93,270 | 99,273 | 97,433 | 94,900 | 102,545 | 119,396 |
| 60-64 | 61,114 | 65,584 | 69,559 | 68,178 | 66,693 | 71,973 |
| 65-69 | 24,478 | 25,233 | 26,808 | 28,199 | 27,885 | 27,308 |
| 70-74 | 6,609 | 6,349 | 6,431 | 6,739 | 7,251 | 7,170 |
| 75-79 | 3,878 | 3,531 | 3,612 | 3,801 | 4,192 | 4,514 |
| 80-84 | 2,088 | 1,775 | 1,688 | 1,317 | 1,834 | 2,024 |
| 85+ | 1,530 | 1,340 | 1,246 | 1,196 | 1,225 | 1,317 |
| Total | 1,372,714 | 1,495,159 | 1,603,274 | 1,699,904 | 1,810,547 | 1,928,798 |
| **Female** | | | | | | |
| 15-19 | 56,251 | 56,194 | 49,042 | 55,684 | 59,311 | 61,156 |
| 20-24 | 133,141 | 155,725 | 156,348 | 137,181 | 153,285 | 163,449 |
| 25-29 | 109,459 | 124,422 | 138,427 | 137,603 | 118,560 | 132,534 |
| 30-34 | 86,911 | 119,216 | 129,782 | 143,877 | 141,603 | 122,094 |
| 35-39 | 74,533 | 94,465 | 125,444 | 136,339 | 149,525 | 147,281 |
| 40-44 | 72,219 | 78,418 | 98,198 | 129,525 | 138,555 | 151,990 |
| 45-49 | 74,880 | 73,803 | 80,071 | 99,001 | 129,140 | 138,000 |
| 50-54 | 74,984 | 75,168 | 74,065 | 79,654 | 97,787 | 127,319 |
| 55-59 | 58,143 | 67,988 | 68,100 | 66,564 | 70,865 | 87,133 |
| 60-64 | 37,790 | 43,672 | 50,707 | 50,414 | 48,703 | 51,132 |
| 65-69 | 14,281 | 15,898 | 17,902 | 20,252 | 19,870 | 19,198 |
| 70-74 | 3,927 | 4,207 | 4,662 | 5,065 | 5,773 | 5,665 |
| 75-79 | 2,754 | 2,947 | 3,276 | 3,567 | 4,023 | 4,590 |
| 80-84 | 1,608 | 1,727 | 1,915 | 2,095 | 2,363 | 2,665 |
| 85+ | 1,038 | 1,052 | 1,170 | 1,269 | 1,442 | 1,612 |
| Total | 802,919 | 914,902 | 999,109 | 1,068,090 | 1,140,805 | 1,216,618 |

Table A7.1 (cont.)

| Series II-B<br>Age | 1975 | 1980 | 1985 | 1990 | 1995 | 2000 |
|---|---|---|---|---|---|---|
| **Male** | | | | | | |
| 15-19 | 93,686 | 89,801 | 74,704 | 82,929 | 87,805 | 87,915 |
| 20-24 | 205,567 | 216,365 | 206,586 | 174,791 | 194,580 | 206,048 |
| 25-29 | 221,841 | 229,651 | 243,201 | 233,811 | 198,833 | 221,228 |
| 30-34 | 153,143 | 215,912 | 223,811 | 237,567 | 228,365 | 194,232 |
| | | | | | | |
| 35-39 | 133,906 | 154,371 | 216,768 | 224,271 | 237,904 | 228,815 |
| 40-44 | 125,930 | 133,910 | 153,292 | 215,360 | 222,772 | 236,311 |
| 45-49 | 122,438 | 117,961 | 125,294 | 143,598 | 202,319 | 208,903 |
| 50-54 | 118,703 | 115,832 | 111,915 | 118,974 | 136,653 | 192,667 |
| 55-59 | 93,186 | 99,107 | 96,814 | 93,503 | 99,626 | 114,546 |
| 60-64 | 61,149 | 65,517 | 69,426 | 67,716 | 65,670 | 69,993 |
| | | | | | | |
| 65-69 | 24,478 | 25,233 | 26,775 | 28,133 | 27,687 | 26,862 |
| 70-74 | 6,610 | 6,356 | 6,443 | 6,733 | 7,234 | 7,130 |
| 75-79 | 3,879 | 3,544 | 3,630 | 3,818 | 4,198 | 4,514 |
| 80-84 | 2,096 | 1,815 | 1,700 | 1,679 | 1,852 | 2,036 |
| 85+ | 1,530 | 1,346 | 1,240 | 1,202 | 1,236 | 1,334 |
| | | | | | | |
| Total | 1,368,142 | 1,476,621 | 1,561,599 | 1,634,094 | 1,716,734 | 1,802,534 |
| **Female** | | | | | | |
| 15-19 | 56,132 | 55,720 | 48,276 | 54,705 | 57,617 | 58,558 |
| 20-24 | 134,637 | 152,818 | 151,366 | 131,670 | 146,850 | 154,605 |
| 25-29 | 108,878 | 121,912 | 133,061 | 130,232 | 111,162 | 123,958 |
| 30-34 | 86,582 | 117,080 | 125,067 | 135,931 | 131,630 | 112,340 |
| | | | | | | |
| 35-39 | 75,220 | 92,863 | 120,966 | 128,999 | 138,611 | 134,290 |
| 40-44 | 71,932 | 77,323 | 95,168 | 123,043 | 129,165 | 138,749 |
| 45-49 | 74,251 | 73,135 | 77,505 | 95,358 | 121,550 | 127,429 |
| 50-54 | 74,906 | 74,205 | 72,973 | 76,673 | 93,398 | 119,066 |
| 55-59 | 58,096 | 67,669 | 66,950 | 65,274 | 67,855 | 82,756 |
| 60-64 | 37,771 | 43,484 | 50,266 | 49,345 | 47,555 | 49,500 |
| | | | | | | |
| 65-69 | 14,264 | 15,848 | 17,752 | 19,986 | 19,364 | 18,658 |
| 70-74 | 3,921 | 4,181 | 4,612 | 4,987 | 5,654 | 5,476 |
| 75-79 | 2,748 | 2,927 | 3,234 | 3,502 | 3,931 | 4,460 |
| 80-84 | 1,608 | 1,716 | 1,887 | 2,125 | 2,300 | 2,584 |
| 85+ | 1,041 | 1,046 | 1,154 | 1,288 | 1,401 | 1,563 |
| | | | | | | |
| Total | 801,987 | 901,927 | 970,237 | 1,023,118 | 1,078,043 | 1,133,992 |

Table A7.1   (cont.)

| Series III-B Age | 1975 | 1980 | 1985 | 1990 | 1995 | 2000 |
|---|---|---|---|---|---|---|
| **Male** | | | | | | |
| 15-19 | 93,399 | 88,746 | 73,191 | 80,813 | 84,842 | 85,174 |
| 20-24 | 203,195 | 207,953 | 194,106 | 162,785 | 180,297 | 189,198 |
| 25-29 | 221,039 | 224,805 | 230,900 | 216,768 | 182,729 | 202,308 |
| 30-34 | 153,615 | 216,948 | 221,792 | 228,177 | 214,280 | 180,617 |
| 35-39 | 133,340 | 152,677 | 213,716 | 218,274 | 224,505 | 210,778 |
| 40-44 | 125,505 | 131,222 | 149,395 | 209,138 | 213,777 | 219,773 |
| 45-49 | 122,256 | 116,919 | 121,950 | 138,818 | 194,742 | 198,711 |
| 50-54 | 118,567 | 115,289 | 110,424 | 115,231 | 131,512 | 184,549 |
| 55-59 | 93,270 | 98,941 | 96,278 | 92,146 | 96,380 | 110,025 |
| 60-64 | 61,149 | 65,550 | 69,260 | 67,254 | 64,647 | 67,650 |
| 65-69 | 24,478 | 25,250 | 26,792 | 28,083 | 27,506 | 26,433 |
| 70-74 | 6,617 | 6,362 | 6,455 | 6,751 | 7,228 | 7,084 |
| 75-79 | 3,886 | 3,551 | 3,642 | 3,835 | 4,221 | 4,520 |
| 80-84 | 2,096 | 1,782 | 1,712 | 1,696 | 1,875 | 2,059 |
| 85+ | 1,530 | 1,346 | 1,246 | 1,208 | 1,248 | 1,346 |
| Total | 1,363,942 | 1,457,341 | 1,520,859 | 1,570,977 | 1,629,789 | 1,690,225 |
| **Female** | | | | | | |
| 15-19 | 56,025 | 55,258 | 47,535 | 53,463 | 56,061 | 56,287 |
| 20-24 | 133,915 | 149,942 | 146,610 | 126,555 | 140,118 | 146,883 |
| 25-29 | 108,297 | 119,483 | 129,520 | 123,684 | 104,695 | 115,875 |
| 30-34 | 86,229 | 114,970 | 122,012 | 128,890 | 123,081 | 104,175 |
| 35-39 | 74,907 | 91,261 | 118,334 | 122,323 | 129,193 | 123,376 |
| 40-44 | 71,697 | 76,229 | 93,543 | 116,949 | 120,800 | 127,503 |
| 45-49 | 74,618 | 72,466 | 77,390 | 91,604 | 114,512 | 118,156 |
| 50-54 | 74,801 | 74,312 | 71,963 | 75,320 | 89,203 | 111,504 |
| 55-59 | 58,001 | 67,351 | 66,700 | 64,060 | 66,362 | 78,632 |
| 60-64 | 37,735 | 43,334 | 49,824 | 48,995 | 46,466 | 48,178 |
| 65-69 | 14,247 | 15,782 | 17,610 | 19,729 | 19,132 | 18,152 |
| 70-74 | 3,915 | 4,190 | 4,561 | 4,914 | 5,540 | 5,373 |
| 75-79 | 2,742 | 2,910 | 3,217 | 3,440 | 3,842 | 4,336 |
| 80-84 | 1,605 | 1,704 | 1,865 | 2,022 | 2,241 | 2,506 |
| 85+ | 1,044 | 1,037 | 1,134 | 1,218 | 1,377 | 1,515 |
| Total | 799,778 | 890,229 | 951,818 | 983,166 | 1,022,623 | 1,062,451 |

Table A7.2. Projected number of families, primary individuals, and households, by age and sex of head, Virginia, 1970-2000

| Age | Male | | | Female | | | Total | | |
|---|---|---|---|---|---|---|---|---|---|
| | Families | Primary Individuals | Total | Families | Primary Individuals | Total | Families | Primary Individuals | Total |
| 1970* | | | | | | | | | |
| 15-19 | 6,387 | 1,084 | 7,471 | 960 | 1,671 | 2,631 | 7,347 | 2,755 | 10,102 |
| 20-29 | 196,105 | 21,569 | 217,674 | 17,914 | 19,701 | 37,615 | 214,019 | 41,270 | 255,289 |
| 30-39 | 226,295 | 11,800 | 238,095 | 24,832 | 6,989 | 31,821 | 251,127 | 18,789 | 269,916 |
| 40-49 | 237,177 | 12,481 | 249,658 | 27,585 | 12,936 | 40,521 | 264,762 | 25,417 | 290,179 |
| 50-59 | 191,064 | 13,643 | 204,707 | 22,322 | 25,611 | 47,933 | 213,386 | 392,254 | 252,640 |
| 60-64 | 66,952 | 6,509 | 73,461 | 9,450 | 18,464 | 27,914 | 76,402 | 24,973 | 101,375 |
| 65-74 | 77,745 | 11,471 | 89,216 | 15,598 | 38,556 | 54,154 | 93,343 | 50,027 | 143,370 |
| 71+ | 30,864 | 7,557 | 38,421 | 10,465 | 23,045 | 33,510 | 41,329 | 30,602 | 71,931 |
| Total | 1,032,589 | 86,114 | 1,118,703 | 129,126 | 146,973 | 276,099 | 1,161,715 | 233,087 | 1,394,802 |

*Excludes 599 households with head aged 14 or under.

Table A7.2  (cont.)

| Series I-A | Male | | | Female | | | Total | | |
|---|---|---|---|---|---|---|---|---|---|
| Age | Families | Primary Individuals | Total | Families | Primary Individuals | Total | Families | Primary Individuals | Total |
| **1980** | | | | | | | | | |
| 15-19 | 6,847 | 1,157 | 8,004 | 1,041 | 1,781 | 2,822 | 7,888 | 2,938 | 10,826 |
| 20-29 | 266,483 | 28,567 | 295,050 | 23,415 | 24,893 | 48,308 | 289,898 | 53,460 | 343,358 |
| 30-39 | 326,517 | 17,231 | 343,748 | 35,617 | 10,136 | 45,753 | 362,134 | 27,367 | 389,501 |
| 40-49 | 238,033 | 12,512 | 250,545 | 27,201 | 12,642 | 39,843 | 265,234 | 25,154 | 290,388 |
| 50-59 | 213,201 | 15,262 | 228,463 | 26,346 | 31,148 | 57,494 | 239,547 | 46,410 | 285,957 |
| 60-64 | 81,186 | 7,893 | 89,079 | 11,975 | 23,393 | 35,368 | 93,161 | 31,286 | 124,447 |
| 65-74 | 93,769 | 13,799 | 107,568 | 19,782 | 48,888 | 68,670 | 113,551 | 62,687 | 176,238 |
| 75+ | 31,403 | 7,704 | 39,107 | 12,609 | 28,046 | 40,657 | 44,012 | 35,750 | 79,762 |
| Total | 1,257,439 | 104,125 | 1,361,564 | 157,988 | 180,924 | 338,912 | 1,415,427 | 285,049 | 1,700,476 |
| **1990** | | | | | | | | | |
| 15-19 | 6,742 | 1,140 | 7,882 | 1,023 | 1,750 | 2,773 | 7,765 | 2,890 | 10,655 |
| 20-29 | 266,293 | 27,882 | 294,175 | 23,232 | 23,480 | 46,712 | 289,525 | 51,362 | 340,887 |
| 30-39 | 423,485 | 22,117 | 445,602 | 45,491 | 12,818 | 58,309 | 468,976 | 34,935 | 503,911 |
| 40-49 | 347,114 | 18,215 | 365,329 | 38,031 | 17,956 | 55,987 | 385,145 | 36,171 | 421,316 |
| 50-59 | 215,281 | 15,309 | 240,590 | 26,013 | 30,490 | 56,503 | 241,294 | 45,799 | 287,093 |
| 60-64 | 86,059 | 8,367 | 94,426 | 13,362 | 26,101 | 39,463 | 99,421 | 34,468 | 133,889 |
| 65-74 | 112,166 | 16,535 | 138,761 | 25,256 | 62,405 | 87,461 | 137,422 | 78,940 | 216,362 |
| 75+ | 36,544 | 8,833 | 45,377 | 16,113 | 35,842 | 51,955 | 52,657 | 44,675 | 97,332 |
| Total | 1,493,684 | 118,398 | 1,612,082 | 188,521 | 210,843 | 399,363 | 1,682,205 | 329,241 | 2,011,446 |
| **2000** | | | | | | | | | |
| 15-19 | 8,014 | 1,355 | 9,369 | 1,215 | 2,079 | 3,294 | 9,229 | 3,434 | 12,663 |
| 20-29 | 285,976 | 30,724 | 316,700 | 25,081 | 26,777 | 51,858 | 311,157 | 57,501 | 368,658 |
| 30-39 | 407,595 | 21,071 | 428,666 | 44,033 | 12,223 | 56,226 | 451,598 | 33,294 | 484,892 |
| 40-49 | 446,504 | 23,468 | 469,972 | 50,097 | 23,197 | 73,294 | 496,601 | 56,665 | 553,266 |
| 50-59 | 317,165 | 22,087 | 339,252 | 37,948 | 43,519 | 81,467 | 355,113 | 65,606 | 420,719 |
| 60-64 | 90,850 | 8,833 | 99,683 | 13,764 | 26,887 | 40,651 | 104,614 | 35,720 | 140,334 |
| 65-74 | 112,915 | 16,736 | 129,651 | 25,883 | 64,209 | 90,092 | 138,798 | 80,945 | 219,743 |
| 75+ | 43,281 | 10,430 | 53,711 | 20,617 | 45,893 | 66,510 | 63,898 | 56,323 | 120,221 |
| Total | 1,712,300 | 134,706 | 1,847,006 | 218,606 | 244,785 | 463,391 | 1,930,906 | 379,491 | 2,310,397 |

Table A7.2 (cont.)

Series II-A

| | Male | | | Female | | | Total | | |
|---|---|---|---|---|---|---|---|---|---|
| Age | Families | Primary Individuals | Total | Families | Primary Individuals | Total | Families | Primary Individuals | Total |
| **1980** | | | | | | | | | |
| 15-19 | 6,764 | 1,143 | 7,907 | 1,032 | 1,766 | 2,796 | 2,909 | 2,909 | 10,705 |
| 20-29 | 259,376 | 27,757 | 287,133 | 22,956 | 24,412 | 47,368 | 282,332 | 52,169 | 334,501 |
| 30-39 | 325,878 | 17,209 | 343,087 | 34,995 | 9,958 | 44,953 | 360,873 | 27,167 | 388,040 |
| 40-49 | 235,569 | 12,383 | 247,952 | 26,881 | 12,500 | 39,381 | 262,450 | 24,883 | 287,333 |
| 50-59 | 212,510 | 15,216 | 217,726 | 26,116 | 30,904 | 57,020 | 238,626 | 46,120 | 284,746 |
| 60-64 | 81,102 | 7,885 | 88,987 | 11,924 | 23,292 | 35,216 | 93,026 | 31,177 | 124,203 |
| 65-74 | 93,807 | 13,805 | 107,612 | 19,693 | 48,664 | 68,357 | 113,500 | 62,469 | 175,969 |
| 75+ | 31,678 | 7,778 | 39,456 | 12,527 | 27,863 | 40,390 | 44,205 | 35,641 | 79,846 |
| Total | 1,246,684 | 103,176 | 1,349,860 | 156,124 | 179,359 | 335,483 | 1,402,808 | 282,535 | 1,685,343 |
| **1990** | | | | | | | | | |
| 15-19 | 6,867 | 1,161 | 8,028 | 1,005 | 1,719 | 2,724 | 7,872 | 2,880 | 10,752 |
| 20-29 | 247,123 | 25,888 | 273,011 | 22,085 | 22,384 | 44,469 | 269,208 | 48,272 | 317,480 |
| 30-39 | 409,094 | 21,355 | 430,449 | 43,007 | 12,117 | 55,124 | 452,101 | 33,472 | 486,203 |
| 40-49 | 336,134 | 17,638 | 353,772 | 37,785 | 17,161 | 54,946 | 373,919 | 34,799 | 408,718 |
| 50-59 | 211,103 | 15,022 | 226,125 | 25,266 | 29,674 | 54,940 | 236,369 | 44,696 | 281,065 |
| 60-64 | 85,476 | 8,311 | 93,787 | 13,078 | 25,548 | 38,626 | 98,554 | 33,859 | 132,413 |
| 65-74 | 111,971 | 16,508 | 128,479 | 24,898 | 61,516 | 86,414 | 136,869 | 78,024 | 214,893 |
| 75+ | 36,763 | 8,888 | 45,651 | 15,793 | 35,138 | 50,931 | 52,556 | 44,026 | 96,582 |
| Total | 1,444,531 | 114,771 | 1,559,302 | 182,919 | 205,257 | 388,176 | 1,627,450 | 320,028 | 1,947,478 |
| **2000** | | | | | | | | | |
| 15-19 | 7,941 | 1,342 | 9,283 | 1,163 | 1,991 | 3,154 | 9,104 | 3,333 | 12,437 |
| 20-29 | 273,132 | 29,356 | 302,488 | 23,551 | 25,202 | 48,753 | 296,683 | 54,558 | 351,241 |
| 30-39 | 375,766 | 19,433 | 395,199 | 40,278 | 11,195 | 51,473 | 416,044 | 30,628 | 446,672 |
| 40-49 | 418,390 | 21,994 | 440,384 | 45,978 | 21,320 | 67,298 | 464,368 | 43,314 | 507,682 |
| 50-59 | 303,777 | 21,159 | 324,936 | 35,728 | 41,042 | 76,770 | 339,505 | 62,201 | 401,706 |
| 60-64 | 88,350 | 8,590 | 96,940 | 13,119 | 25,628 | 38,747 | 101,469 | 34,218 | 135,687 |
| 65-74 | 111,585 | 16,549 | 128,134 | 25,089 | 62,231 | 87,320 | 136,674 | 78,780 | 215,454 |
| 75+ | 43,407 | 10,469 | 53,876 | 20,013 | 44,558 | 64,571 | 63,420 | 55,027 | 118,447 |
| Total | 1,622,348 | 128,892 | 1,751,240 | 204,919 | 233,167 | 438,086 | 1,827,267 | 362,059 | 2,189,326 |

Table A7.2  (cont.)

Series III-A

| Age | Male | | | Female | | | Total | | |
|---|---|---|---|---|---|---|---|---|---|
| | Families | Primary Individuals | Total | Families | Primary Individuals | Total | Families | Primary Individuals | Total |
| **1980** | | | | | | | | | |
| 15-19 | 6,685 | 1,130 | 7,815 | 1,023 | 1,751 | 2,774 | 7,708 | 2,881 | 10,589 |
| 20-29 | 252,374 | 26,959 | 279,333 | 22,508 | 23,942 | 46,450 | 274,882 | 50,901 | 325,783 |
| 30-39 | 325,237 | 17,186 | 342,423 | 34,377 | 9,782 | 44,159 | 359,614 | 26,968 | 386,582 |
| 40-49 | 232,205 | 12,207 | 244,412 | 26,569 | 12,364 | 38,933 | 258,774 | 24,571 | 283,345 |
| 50-59 | 211,819 | 15,170 | 226,989 | 26,072 | 30,832 | 56,910 | 237,891 | 46,002 | 283,893 |
| 60-64 | 81,144 | 7,889 | 89,033 | 11,882 | 23,211 | 35,093 | 93,026 | 31,100 | 124,126 |
| 64-74 | 93,884 | 13,817 | 107,701 | 19,665 | 48,605 | 68,270 | 113,549 | 62,422 | 175,971 |
| 75+ | 31,559 | 7,742 | 39,301 | 12,446 | 27,686 | 40,132 | 44,005 | 35,428 | 79,433 |
| Total | 1,234,907 | 102,100 | 1,337,007 | 154,542 | 178,173 | 332,715 | 1,389,449 | 280,273 | 1,669,722 |
| **1990** | | | | | | | | | |
| 15-19 | 6,413 | 1,084 | 7,497 | 982 | 1,681 | 2,395 | 7,395 | 2,765 | 10,160 |
| 20-29 | 229,405 | 24,042 | 253,447 | 21,054 | 21,391 | 42,445 | 250,459 | 45,433 | 295,892 |
| 30-39 | 395,529 | 20,995 | 416,524 | 40,784 | 11,491 | 52,275 | 436,313 | 32,486 | 468,799 |
| 40-49 | 325,805 | 17,096 | 342,901 | 36,077 | 16,407 | 52,484 | 361,882 | 33,503 | 395,385 |
| 50-59 | 206,098 | 14,685 | 220,783 | 24,809 | 29,133 | 53,942 | 230,907 | 43,818 | 274,725 |
| 60-64 | 84,893 | 8,254 | 93,147 | 12,980 | 25,356 | 38,336 | 97,873 | 33,610 | 131,483 |
| 65-74 | 111,968 | 16,511 | 128,479 | 24,558 | 60,673 | 85,231 | 136,526 | 77,184 | 213,710 |
| 75+ | 36,981 | 8,942 | 45,923 | 15,530 | 34,554 | 50,084 | 52,511 | 43,496 | 96,007 |
| Total | 1,397,092 | 111,609 | 1,508,701 | 176,774 | 200,686 | 377,460 | 1,573,866 | 312,295 | 1,886,161 |
| **2000** | | | | | | | | | |
| 15-19 | 7,309 | 1,235 | 8,544 | 1,118 | 1,914 | 3,032 | 8,427 | 3,149 | 11,576 |
| 20-29 | 239,664 | 25,783 | 265,447 | 22,163 | 23,797 | 45,960 | 261,827 | 49,580 | 311,407 |
| 30-39 | 347,611 | 17,984 | 365,595 | 37,153 | 10,332 | 47,485 | 384,764 | 28,316 | 413,080 |
| 40-49 | 393,384 | 20,683 | 414,067 | 42,431 | 19,696 | 62,127 | 435,815 | 40,379 | 476,194 |
| 50-59 | 291,293 | 20,294 | 311,587 | 33,672 | 38,743 | 72,415 | 324,965 | 59,037 | 384,002 |
| 60-64 | 85,393 | 8,303 | 93,696 | 12,769 | 24,943 | 37,712 | 98,162 | 33,246 | 131,408 |
| 65-74 | 110,255 | 16,361 | 126,616 | 25,511 | 60,812 | 85,323 | 134,766 | 77,173 | 211,939 |
| 75+ | 43,609 | 10,527 | 54,136 | 19,441 | 43,286 | 62,729 | 63,050 | 53,813 | 116,863 |
| Total | 1,518,518 | 121,170 | 1,639,688 | 193,258 | 223,523 | 416,781 | 1,711,766 | 344,693 | 2,056,469 |

Table A7.2  (cont.)

Series I-B

| Age | Male Families | Male Primary Individuals | Male Total | Female Families | Female Primary Individuals | Female Total | Total Families | Total Primary Individuals | Total Total |
|---|---|---|---|---|---|---|---|---|---|
| **1980** | | | | | | | | | |
| 15-19 | 6,847 | 1,157 | 8,004 | 1,041 | 1,781 | 2,822 | 7,888 | 2,938 | 10,826 |
| 20-29 | 266,483 | 28,567 | 295,050 | 23,415 | 24,893 | 48,308 | 289,898 | 53,460 | 343,358 |
| 30-39 | 326,517 | 17,231 | 343,748 | 35,617 | 10,136 | 45,753 | 362,134 | 27,367 | 389,501 |
| 40-49 | 238,033 | 12,512 | 250,545 | 27,201 | 12,642 | 39,843 | 265,234 | 25,154 | 290,388 |
| 50-59 | 213,201 | 15,262 | 228,463 | 26,346 | 31,148 | 57,494 | 239,547 | 46,410 | 285,957 |
| 60-64 | 81,186 | 7,893 | 89,079 | 11,075 | 23,393 | 35,368 | 93,161 | 31,286 | 124,447 |
| 65-74 | 93,769 | 13,799 | 107,568 | 19,782 | 48,888 | 68,670 | 113,551 | 62,687 | 176,238 |
| 75+ | 31,403 | 7,704 | 39,107 | 12,609 | 28,046 | 40,657 | 44,012 | 35,750 | 79,762 |
| Total | 1,257,439 | 104,125 | 1,361,654 | 157,988 | 180,924 | 338,912 | 1,415,427 | 285,049 | 1,700,476 |
| **1990** | | | | | | | | | |
| 15-19 | 6,559 | 1,109 | 7,668 | 998 | 1,708 | 2,706 | 7,557 | 2,817 | 10,374 |
| 20-29 | 266,293 | 27,882 | 294,175 | 23,232 | 23,480 | 46,712 | 289,525 | 51,362 | 340,887 |
| 30-39 | 423,485 | 22,117 | 445,602 | 45,491 | 12,818 | 58,309 | 468,976 | 34,935 | 503,911 |
| 40-49 | 347,114 | 18,215 | 365,329 | 38,031 | 17,956 | 55,987 | 385,145 | 36,171 | 421,316 |
| 50-59 | 215,281 | 15,309 | 240,590 | 26,013 | 30,490 | 56,503 | 241,294 | 45,799 | 287,093 |
| 60-64 | 86,059 | 8,367 | 94,426 | 13,362 | 26,101 | 39,463 | 99,421 | 34,468 | 133,889 |
| 65-74 | 112,166 | 16,535 | 128,701 | 25,256 | 62,405 | 87,461 | 137,422 | 78,940 | 216,362 |
| 75+ | 36,544 | 8,833 | 45,377 | 16,113 | 35,842 | 51,955 | 52,657 | 44,675 | 97,332 |
| Total | 1,493,501 | 118,367 | 1,611,868 | 188,496 | 210,801 | 399,296 | 1,681,197 | 329,168 | 2,011,165 |
| **2000** | | | | | | | | | |
| 15-19 | 7,208 | 1,218 | 8,426 | 1,096 | 1,876 | 2,972 | 8,304 | 3,094 | 11,398 |
| 20-29 | 273,357 | 29,218 | 302,575 | 24,034 | 25,368 | 49,391 | 297,380 | 54,586 | 351,966 |
| 30-39 | 407,595 | 21,071 | 428,666 | 44,003 | 12,223 | 56,226 | 451,598 | 33,294 | 484,892 |
| 40-49 | 446,504 | 23,468 | 469,972 | 50,097 | 23,197 | 73,294 | 496,601 | 56,665 | 553,266 |
| 50-59 | 317,165 | 22,087 | 339,252 | 37,948 | 43,519 | 81,467 | 355,113 | 65,606 | 420,719 |
| 60-64 | 90,850 | 8,833 | 99,683 | 13,764 | 26,887 | 40,651 | 104,614 | 35,720 | 146,334 |
| 65-74 | 112,915 | 16,736 | 129,651 | 25,883 | 64,209 | 90,092 | 138,798 | 80,945 | 219,743 |
| 75+ | 43,281 | 10,430 | 53,711 | 20,617 | 45,893 | 66,510 | 66,898 | 56,323 | 120,221 |
| Total | 1,698,875 | 133,063 | 1,831,938 | 217,429 | 243,173 | 460,602 | 1,916,304 | 376,236 | 2,292,540 |

Table A7.2 (cont.)

| | Male | | | Female | | | Total | | |
|---|---|---|---|---|---|---|---|---|---|
| Series II-B | Families | Primary Individuals | Total | Families | Primary Individuals | Total | Families | Primary Individuals | Total |
| Age 1980 | | | | | | | | | |
| 15-19 | 6,764 | 1,143 | 7,907 | 1,032 | 1,766 | 2,798 | 7,796 | 2,909 | 10,705 |
| 20-29 | 259,376 | 27,757 | 287,133 | 22,956 | 24,412 | 47,368 | 282,332 | 52,169 | 334,501 |
| 30-39 | 325,878 | 17,209 | 343,087 | 34,995 | 9,958 | 44,953 | 360,873 | 27,167 | 388,040 |
| 40-49 | 235,569 | 12,383 | 247,952 | 26,881 | 12,500 | 39,381 | 262,450 | 24,883 | 287,333 |
| 50-59 | 212,510 | 15,216 | 217,726 | 26,116 | 30,904 | 57,020 | 238,626 | 46,120 | 284,746 |
| 60-64 | 81,102 | 7,885 | 88,987 | 11,924 | 23,292 | 35,216 | 93,026 | 31,177 | 124,203 |
| 65-74 | 93,807 | 13,805 | 107,612 | 19,693 | 48,664 | 68,357 | 113,500 | 62,469 | 175,969 |
| 75+ | 31,678 | 7,778 | 39,456 | 12,527 | 27,863 | 40,390 | 44,205 | 35,641 | 79,846 |
| Total | 1,246,684 | 103,176 | 1,349,860 | 156,124 | 179,359 | 335,483 | 1,403,808 | 282,535 | 1,685,343 |
| 1990 | | | | | | | | | |
| 15-19 | 6,400 | 1,082 | 7,482 | 981 | 1,678 | 2,659 | 7,381 | 2,760 | 10,141 |
| 20-29 | 247,123 | 25,888 | 273,011 | 22,085 | 22,384 | 44,469 | 269,208 | 48,272 | 317,480 |
| 30-39 | 409,094 | 21,355 | 430,449 | 43,007 | 12,117 | 55,124 | 452,101 | 33,472 | 486,203 |
| 40-49 | 336,134 | 17,638 | 353,772 | 37,785 | 17,161 | 54,946 | 373,919 | 34,799 | 408,718 |
| 50-59 | 211,103 | 15,022 | 226,125 | 25,266 | 29,674 | 54,940 | 236,369 | 44,696 | 281,065 |
| 60-64 | 85,476 | 8,311 | 93,787 | 13,078 | 25,548 | 38,626 | 98,554 | 33,859 | 132,413 |
| 65-74 | 111,971 | 16,508 | 128,479 | 24,898 | 61,516 | 86,414 | 136,869 | 78,024 | 214,893 |
| 75+ | 36,763 | 8,888 | 45,651 | 15,793 | 35,138 | 50,931 | 52,556 | 44,026 | 96,582 |
| Total | 1,444,064 | 114,632 | 1,558,696 | 182,895 | 205,217 | 388,112 | 1,626,959 | 319,849 | 1,946,808 |
| 2000 | | | | | | | | | |
| 15-19 | 6,785 | 1,147 | 7,932 | 1,050 | 1,796 | 2,846 | 7,835 | 2,943 | 10,778 |
| 20-29 | 250,162 | 26,764 | 276,926 | 22,560 | 23,879 | 46,439 | 272,722 | 50,643 | 323,365 |
| 30-39 | 375,766 | 19,433 | 395,199 | 40,278 | 11,195 | 51,473 | 416,044 | 30,628 | 446,672 |
| 40-49 | 418,390 | 21,994 | 440,384 | 45,978 | 21,320 | 67,298 | 464,368 | 43,314 | 507,682 |
| 50-59 | 303,777 | 21,159 | 324,936 | 35,728 | 41,042 | 76,770 | 339,505 | 62,201 | 401,706 |
| 60-64 | 88,350 | 8,590 | 96,940 | 13,119 | 25,628 | 38,747 | 101,469 | 34,218 | 135,687 |
| 65-74 | 111,585 | 16,549 | 128,134 | 25,089 | 62,231 | 87,320 | 136,674 | 78,780 | 215,454 |
| 75+ | 43,407 | 10,469 | 53,876 | 20,013 | 44,558 | 64,571 | 63,420 | 55,027 | 118,447 |
| Total | 1,598,222 | 126,105 | 1,724,327 | 203,815 | 231,649 | 435,464 | 1,802,037 | 357,754 | 2,159,791 |

Table A7.2 (cont.)

Series III-B

| | Male | | | Female | | | Total | | |
|---|---|---|---|---|---|---|---|---|---|
| Age | Families | Primary Individual | Total | Families | Primary Individual | Total | Families | Primary Individuals | Total |
| **1980** | | | | | | | | | |
| 15-19 | 6,685 | 1,130 | 7,815 | 1,023 | 1,751 | 2,774 | 7,708 | 2,881 | 10,589 |
| 20-29 | 252,374 | 26,959 | 279,333 | 22,508 | 23,942 | 46,450 | 274,882 | 50,901 | 325,783 |
| 30-39 | 325,237 | 17,186 | 342,423 | 34,377 | 9,782 | 44,159 | 359,614 | 26,968 | 386,582 |
| 40-49 | 232,205 | 12,207 | 244,412 | 26,569 | 12,364 | 38,933 | 258,774 | 24,571 | 283,345 |
| 50-59 | 211,819 | 15,170 | 226,989 | 26,072 | 30,832 | 56,910 | 237,891 | 46,002 | 283,893 |
| 60-64 | 81,144 | 7,889 | 89,033 | 11,882 | 23,211 | 35,093 | 93,026 | 31,100 | 124,126 |
| 65-74 | 93,884 | 13,817 | 107,701 | 19,665 | 48,605 | 68,270 | 113,549 | 62,422 | 175,971 |
| 75+ | 31,559 | 7,742 | 39,301 | 13,446 | 27,686 | 40,132 | 44,005 | 35,428 | 79,433 |
| Total | 1,234,907 | 102,100 | 1,337,007 | 154,542 | 178,173 | 332,715 | 1,389,449 | 280,273 | 1,669,722 |
| **1990** | | | | | | | | | |
| 15-19 | 6,236 | 1,054 | 7,290 | 959 | 1,640 | 2,599 | 7,195 | 2,694 | 9,889 |
| 20-29 | 229,405 | 24,042 | 253,447 | 21,054 | 21,391 | 42,445 | 250,459 | 45,433 | 295,892 |
| 30-39 | 395,529 | 20,995 | 416,524 | 40,784 | 11,491 | 52,275 | 436,313 | 32,486 | 468,799 |
| 40-49 | 325,805 | 17,096 | 242,901 | 36,077 | 16,407 | 52,484 | 361,882 | 33,503 | 395,385 |
| 50-59 | 206,098 | 14,685 | 220,783 | 24,809 | 29,133 | 53,942 | 230,907 | 43,818 | 274,725 |
| 60-64 | 84,893 | 8,254 | 93,147 | 12,980 | 25,356 | 38,336 | 97,873 | 33,610 | 131,483 |
| 65-74 | 111,968 | 16,511 | 128,479 | 24,558 | 60,673 | 85,231 | 136,526 | 77,184 | 213,710 |
| 75+ | 36,981 | 8,942 | 45,923 | 15,530 | 34,554 | 50,084 | 52,511 | 43,496 | 96,007 |
| Total | 1,396,915 | 111,579 | 1,508,494 | 176,751 | 200,645 | 3,773,396 | 1,573,666 | 312,224 | 1,885,890 |
| **2000** | | | | | | | | | |
| 15-19 | 6,573 | 1,111 | 7,684 | 1,009 | 1,727 | 2,736 | 7,582 | 2,838 | 10,420 |
| 20-29 | 229,078 | 24,518 | 253,596 | 21,213 | 22,529 | 43,742 | 250,291 | 47,047 | 297,338 |
| 30-39 | 347,611 | 17,984 | 365,595 | 37,153 | 10,332 | 47,485 | 384,764 | 28,316 | 413,080 |
| 40-49 | 393,384 | 20,683 | 414,067 | 42,431 | 19,696 | 62,127 | 435,815 | 40,379 | 476,194 |
| 50-59 | 291,293 | 20,294 | 311,587 | 33,672 | 38,743 | 72,415 | 324,965 | 59,037 | 384,002 |
| 60-64 | 85,393 | 8,303 | 93,696 | 12,769 | 24,943 | 37,712 | 98,162 | 33,246 | 131,408 |
| 64-74 | 110,255 | 16,361 | 126,616 | 24,511 | 60,812 | 85,323 | 134,766 | 77,173 | 211,939 |
| 75+ | 43,609 | 10,527 | 54,136 | 19,441 | 43,286 | 62,729 | 63,050 | 53,813 | 116,863 |
| Total | 1,507,196 | 119,781 | 1,626,977 | 192,199 | 222,068 | 414,267 | 1,699,395 | 341,849 | 2,041,244 |

# Index